AMERICAN MUSLIMS:
A COMMUNITY UNDER SIEGE

Dr. Ahmed Yousef

Since 1989

UASR PUBLISHING GROUP

Springfield, Virginia – U.S.A.

We are a nation of many nationalities, many races, many religions—bound together by a single unity, the unity of freedom and equality. Whoever seeks to set one nationality against another seeks to degrade all nationalities. Whoever seeks to set one race against another seeks to enslave all races. Whoever seeks to set one religion against another seeks to destroy all religion.

—Franklin D. Roosevelt, November 1, 1940.

Americans have faced an intensified assault on their civil liberties as a result of the U.S. "war on terror" —at home and abroad. But the crackdown on therights of these vulnerable populations alsothreatens numerous immigrants, activists, tradeunionists, academics, and writers—or anyonewho the government wishes to define s a "threat"to national security.

—Elaine Hagopian, *Civil Rights in Peril: The Targeting of Arabs and Muslims*, 2004.

AMERICAN MUSLIMS: A COMMUNITY UNDER SIEGE

Library of Congress Cataloging-in-Publication Data
     Yousef, Ahmed, 1950-
     American Muslims: A Community Under Siege / by Ahmed
Yousef.—1st ed.
     p. cm.
     ISBN 1-882669-42-8
     1. Islam—United States 2. Muslims—United States Terrorism—
Government policy—United States 4. Civil Rights—United States I. Title.

Published by:
United Association for Studies and Research (UASR)
P.O. Box 1210, Annandale, VA 22003-1210
Tel: (703) 750-9011
Fax: (703) 750-9010
E-mail: uasr@aol.com
www.uasr.org

Photo credits:
IAP Photo Library; Dar Al Hijra; UASR Photo Library;
Gamal Abdul Motti; Al-Anwar Designs.

Dedication

*T*his work is dedicated to the wives of America's political prisoners, who have had to endure a life of hardship and struggle with little recognition as their husbands are persecuted behind bars. For years, these women have been at the forefront of the struggle for justice and freedom for American Muslim leaders and civil rights advocates. The following pages are dedicated to Asmaa Al-Ashqar, wife of Abdulhaleem, who stood by her husband as he faced death by hunger strike rather than betray his principles. It is dedicated to Karima Al-Amin, wife of Imam Jamil, a lifelong voice for equality and freedom. It is dedicated to Shifaa Alamoudi, Abdurahman's wife, forced to raise their children without their loving father. The El-Ashi family has suffered from the tremendous loss of four brothers. This book is dedicated to their wives, Majida, Fairuz, Lima, and Wafaa, and the ordeal they have faced for nearly two years. It is also dedicated to Nahla Al-Arian, wife of Sami and sister of Mazen Al-Najjar, forced to endure a doubly grueling struggle, with Mazen's three and a half year incarceration, followed by Sami's current internationally publicized predicament as he struggles to fight for truth. Through it all, she has been the rock of support and the beacon of light for her family. The dedication to truth expressed in this book is embodied in the lives of Priscilla Dhafir, Sima Somaira, Maha Al-Hussayen, Salma Al-Rusheid, Mirsada Royer, Mina Hammad, and Ola Chapman.

Finally, I dedicate this work to my wife Mahdia, who, like these women, has taught me the meaning of courage and dedication, patience and perseverance. I pray that God one day reunites all of His devoted servants under the most blissful of circumstances. ■

Acknowledgements

$\mathcal{T}$hough I have written many books in the past, *American Muslims: A Community Under Siege* was not an easy book to write. As a massive volume that has set out to chronicle the Muslim experience in the United States in light of (or perhaps more aptly, under the shadow of) present circumstances, it required a tremendous degree of resolve in the face of a situation so delicate that it experienced massive changes on a daily basis. Since I began writing this book in the summer of 2003, a number of the case studies I highlight experienced extraordinary changes, sometimes for better, but very often, as with the "Virginia 11" convictions, for worse.

In most instances, the victims and their families are people that I have come to know over the course of the last two decades. Maintaining a resolute demeanor in the face of such a highly charged, extremely volatile, and emotionally draining period in American Muslim history was one of the biggest challenges as I researched the historical roots of today's most important civil rights cases, while also staying abreast of the constantly evolving events. A special thanks is in order for Abdullah al-Arian for aiding me throughout this process. His meticulous research in the overwhelming amount of information made available daily saw to it that readers would have a painstaking viewpoint of the civil rights cases as they were experienced on the frontlines of the community's leadership. Throughout this journey, Abdullah has been diligent and dedicated in his pursuit of the hard facts behind every saga.

I must also thank the many individuals who contributed their time and energy into ensuring the accuracy and fluidity of the chapters in this book, many of whom had firsthand experiences with the events recounted throughout the chapters. Anisa Abd el Fattah and Robert D. Crane had a helpful hand in editing. Attorneys Ashraf Nubani, Asim Ghafoor and Betty Molchany lent their expertise in some of the most highly publicized civil liberties cases in the pages of this book, including the cases of Abdurahman Alamoudi and Rafil Dhafir. Noted activist Mauri Saalakhan edited and provided material for various chapters, including that on the Virginia Paintball 11 case and the Jamil Al-Amin case. Also special thanks to Manal Harrisi, who helped in highlighting the Sabri Somaira Case. Altaf Hussein and Ismail Kamal from MSA-National, Imam Muhammad Asi, Iman Potter, Lorie Jaghlit, Aisha Sobh, Ahmed Rashad, Waseem Nasrallah, and Ali Ramadan have similarly contributed their knowledge and expertise in the specific areas covered in these chapters. I am indebted to all of them for their continued help and support.

Finally, as with many things in life, this experience has been dual-sided. I am deeply saddened that such a book as this even had to be written, with so much suffering experienced by these men, their families, and their communities. On the other hand, I am proud to have had the honor of chronicling the extraordinary sacrifices made by America's Muslim civil rights leaders to ensure that Islam can thrive under the American tradition of tolerance and pluralism and to ensure that no future generations will have to endure the xenophobic targeting that Muslims have faced in America based solely on their ethnic, religious, and national origin and their political beliefs.

I pray that through this historic civil rights struggle, under the dark cloud of suspicion and enmity, a brighter day can emerge. ■

TABLE OF CONTENTS

Part One
THE AMERICAN MUSLIM DREAM

Part Two
THE AGENTS OF ISLAMOPHOBIA

Part Three
THE AMERICAN MUSLIM NIGHTMARE

Part Four
MUSLIM LEADERSHIP UNDER SIEGE

Part Five
BANKRUPTING MUSLIM INSTITUTIONS

Foreword

Improving our understanding of the faith of our fellow citizens and neighbors will require that we look at Muslims with new eyes, and judge Islam by the totality and teachings of the faith, not just the beliefs and actions of a few radicals.

> John L. Esposito, *Unholy War: Terror in the Name of Islam*, 2002.

The history of minorities in America is dark. Everyone, even the Europeans who immigrated to the United States as indentured servants, the first minority, met upon hard times. Yet, the indigenous Native Americans have suffered more and longer than any other Americans, with the possible exception of the African slaves. The United States, unlike perhaps any other nation, seems eternally trapped in cycles of immigration and integration, with each decade of U.S. history colored by the migration experience of one group or another.

Those migrating to America are often disappointed,

perhaps even heart-broken, at discovering the difference between their idealized image of a land laden with milk and honey and the stark reality of a nation consistently struggling to include more and different people.

Catholics, for example, tell their story of migration and assimilation through Irish and Italian history - groups that escaped natural disaster, famine, and poverty by coming to America, only to experience prejudice and discrimination in a new world where the teeming masses of new and old émigrés clash over jobs, territory, and political clout.

Dr. Ahmed Yousef makes the point in this book that Muslims are being mistreated in America, and that this mistreatment represents a threat not only to the development of healthy Muslim community life, but also to our Constitution and national traditions.

He also emphasizes a major theme throughout this book, namely, the poor preparedness of the Muslim community's leadership. Their intentions are not called into question. Their optimistic hopes are rather laid out in splendid form in the book's opening chapters, which illustrate the vision with which Muslim migration to America took place, and the roots of American Muslim activism, which rose to its heights in the late 1990s, capped by major successes in the 2000 elections.

The community's failings can be viewed as two sides of a coin, one representing the internal weaknesses, such as a lack of a unified and coherent agenda, and an unusually slow process of "Americanization," which was all the more compounded by the other side of the coin in the form of external pressures from influential forces in society determined to marginalize the American Muslim community and deny its right to a seat at the table. More often than not, this was represented by Israel's lobby in America and by actors in government and the media to whom a powerful Muslim voice signaled a threat to the overarching geopolitical agenda. Faced with such difficulties from all sides, progress was modest but nonetheless effectual in some regards, such as the struggle against a single civil rights crisis in the mid-1990s.

Indeed, Yousef gives ample attention to that second side of the coin, as the concerted campaign against Islam is revealed in a series of chapters devoted to the phenomenon of Islamophobia in America. The effect of this development on the American stage is of earth-shattering importance. Since the end of the Cold War, in effect this phenomenon has pitted the emergent Western liberal democratic system, exemplified by unrivaled American power, against the world's 1.2 billion-strong Islamic civilization stretching from West Africa to East Asia. The impending clash, most infamously proclaimed by scholar Samuel Huntington, became a self-fulfilling prophecy once particular actors in the American public sphere laid the tar and concrete for the collision course with Islam.

Caught on the frontline of this path toward unholy conflict were America's seven million Muslims and their rising stars. These included a number of longtime activists, many of them immigrants and outspoken on global issues of human rights, not the least of which is the Israeli-Palestinian conflict. The proponents of Islamophobia, classified in this work as extending from the academy to the media and from powerful lobbies and policy advocates to high political office, have in effect positioned America on the opposing side of every major conflict involving Muslims across the globe, beginning with the Middle East, with

America's ever-increasing support for Israel, and extending into South Asia's Kashmir conflict and beyond. It is no coincidence, Yousef points out again and again, that Islam's biggest opponents in America also happen to be, almost invariably, Israel's most vocal advocates. These personalities and institutions are explored and scrutinized in a way that few observers have bothered to do in the past, and in some ways, as Yousef tacitly points out, this has been partly responsible for the community's failed response. It has not studied the hefty opposition.

As the American Muslim community awakened to throw its hat into the American political ring, the community's leaders could not have been prepared for the struggle that followed. Visionary leaders, such as Abdurahman Alamoudi, who together with Isa Smith founded the American Muslim Council, the first organization of its kind to demand a seat at America's political table, found themselves being viciously opposed by a well-entrenched anti-Muslim presence. This struggle continued for over a decade, culminating in the dark cloud currently hanging over the heads of America's Muslims, agonizingly detailed in the later chapters.

The very same men spearheading the effort to build a bridge between Islam and the West by opening the lines of communication and calling for balance in America's foreign policy have been marginalized by the extremist core of Islamophobes and currently face trials in American courts for their activities. Sami al-Arian, a respected professor who became a leading civil rights advocate in America during the 1990s, now finds himself the target of an unprecedented campaign by certain government agencies and the most virulent Muslim-bashers. He was also a vocal advocate for Palestinian rights, with successful outreach to all segments of American society. He thus posed a threat to Israel's proponents and had to be neutralized. This and many other tragic tales serve both as lessons to all Americans and a source of inspiration toward change, with many of their fates still hanging in the balance. The struggle, as Yousef continuously reminds readers, is ongoing.

Ahmed Yousef is optimistic in asking whether the suffering of Muslim America can herald the advance of American freedom beyond the paradigm of civil rights, and open the door to a discussion of civil morality that has been missing from the modern American discourse.

Unfortunately Muslim activists for the most part have examined their experience in the United States in comparison to other racial groups, forgetting that the social psyche has been rent by constitutional interpretations that dictate radical separation between the heart and soul of man. This has resulted in a type of national psychosis that prevents human beings from viewing religion as a system of belief, and promotes it rather as a panacea allowed by the state to assuage the fears and weaknesses of the uneducated and lower classes. Since the great secularization of the United States that took place in the 50s and 60s, religion has been positioned as the realm of superstition and absurdity, whereas secular logic is sited as the true springboard of progress.

Muslims cannot become equal by the law of the land until they have contributed a body of law to the Constitution or an interpretation that speaks to their unique identity as a group of people who profess to be a modern and recent rendition of monotheism, possessing its own Book, while also introducing a new prophet. Until this is successfully accomplished Muslims will not likely enjoy political influence or economic prosperity as a community.

The overt power of religion in America was purposely sequestered to allow space for other and all types of religious and non-religious practices to find equal space and accommodation in private and public domains. That one will enter the arena and espouse claims to a special morality or doctrinal supremacy to others, especially to Judaism and Christianity, is a non-starter. Muslims will learn that they are not being challenged because Americans hate differences, the Prophet Muhammad, or the headscarf. They are being targeted because they achieved a level of influence that can be enjoyed only by groups that have either conformed to the secular dictate, renouncing religion as other than a hobby or therapy, or because they have reached agreement with the Christian and Jewish hierarchy to co-exist by not threatening or challenging, and, beyond this, to cooperate proactively in fulfilling the spiritual and moral destiny of America.

Sometimes it is the immigrants themselves who make the process more difficult than it should be. And sometimes leaders of new communities resist too strongly the realities of their new environs and attempt to create new spaces and norms without first taking up the challenge to create new law.

The Muslim American community in the United States is a talented and vibrant community that is as diverse as the nation itself. And, as it matures, it will become a more integral part of the American fabric. As John Esposito articulately notes: "Looking to the future, as we become more familiar with Islam as a major world religion and the soon-to-be second largest faith in America, the idea of a Judeo-Christian-Islamic religious tradition will become more internalized. We will recognize that each faith represents shared beliefs and values as well as distinctive differences."

We have yet to understand what covenant Muslims will offer, yet, if the Qur'an is an indication, it will be a covenant of peace and cooperation and joint effort with every other American's effort to make this union of states and different peoples a more perfect union. This could be the meaning of the verse in the Qur'an that says, "And when Abraham had rejected the things that his father worshipped other than the One God, God guided him to the land that had been promised to the righteous." ■

Caroline F. Keeble
May 2004

Introduction

In the name of fighting terrorism, our government has targeted Muslims and Arabs using secret evidence, secret arrests, and detentions without due process of law. These departures from our constitutional norms are sending shock waves through Arab and Muslim communities in the United States and abroad, and they are placing all Americans at risk.

—Nancy Chang, senior litigation attorney,
Center for Constitutional Rights.

Future historians may regard this monumental account of Islam and Muslims at the beginning of the twenty-first century as the best primary source material to understand the rise and fall of freedom and human rights in America. This 700-page running account of history in the making gives both an analytical summary of the political dynamics after 9/11 and an encyclopedic account of the persons and institutions who made history through their battle to preserve America as an open society in the face of the pressures to protect Americans from terrorism by curtailing their freedoms.

This is the story of countless thousands of Muslims from all over the world who left their countries to find civil liberty, economic opportunity, and intellectual challenges in America as the universally admired and most beloved country on earth. This is also the story of shattered dreams, as the homeland security apparatus of government singled out the community leaders as an inherent threat to everything they valued most. It is also the story of how the neo-conservative supporters of secular and apocalyptic Zionism tried to intimidate an entire community into passive submission.

The story of individual persons and institutions is developed in detail to expose the entire process of disinformation designed, first, to demonize Islam as inherently favorable to violence and oppression, and then to neutralize an entire community of ten million people before they could gain the political clout needed to promote an even-handed American foreign policy of justice in the Middle East. A major thesis running through the entire book is that the tragedy of 9/11 provided the opportunity for the extremists among the Jews successfully to brand as extremists all Muslims who supported American independence from entangling foreign alliances.

In chapter five, entitled "Political Agendas under the Guise of Academia," the writings of Bernard Lewis and other scholars are analyzed to expose their contention that America's policy of unilateral preemption against the peoples of the Middle East is justified by its "continuous struggle to 'civilize' Muslim society and essentially 'free' them from themselves."

Although this book does not discuss the challenges to American foreign policy in Iraq, the success of a vocal minority of academics in demonizing both Islam and Muslims is dramatically shown by President George W. Bush's assertion on April 7, 2004, at South Arkansas Community College in response to the beginning of an Iraqi intifada against American occupation: "We've got tough work there because, you see, there are terrorists there who would rather kill innocent people than allow for the advance of freedom. That's what you're seeing going on: These people hate freedom and we love freedom, and that's where the clash occurs."

The extent to which a concerted policy of disinformation had blinded even the military commanders on the ground in Iraq was best shown, according to the April 23rd issue of *USA Today* by General Eaton, who explained why the 2nd Battalion of the new Iraq army refused to fight in Falluja. He declared, "What I had was a battalion that just didn't understand why they were engaged by their own people." They did not understand that the resistance fighters were willing to die by the hundreds because they hated freedom.

This bizarre mindset is introduced in chapter 7 of this book, entitled "The Pro-Israeli Lobbies and Think-Tanks," which discusses the 1992 Soref Symposium of the Washington Institute for Near East Policy (WINEP), entitled "Islam and the U.S.: Challenges for the Nineties." At this symposium, the former Assistant Secretary of State and Ambassador to Israel, Martin Indyk, argued that the United States should not encourage democracy in countries that were friendly to Washington because their peoples are not friendly to Israel. As Ahmed Yousef argues in this book, "This recommendation seemed like a formula for ensuring that Islamist forces would forsake legal political action and engage in armed struggle—precisely what happened."

This assessment of Muslim activism and ways to combat it is discussed a few pages later in an account of the declaration of war in 2003 by the neo-conservative, Frank Gaffney, one of the original members of the Project for the New American Century, against the paleo-conservative, Grover Norquist, President of Americans for Tax Reform, for daring to serve as a "fifth column" by facilitating the access of American Muslim leaders to President Bush. This phrase is part of a mimetic or psywar campaign to brand both Muslim and non-Muslim opponents of neo-con strategies as fascists and Nazis. The neo-conservative strategy appears to be designed to prevent any understanding of the Muslims' search for justice as a cause for political opposition to America's Middle East policies. The preferred neo-conservative strategy is to exploit every possible excuse to neutralize the leadership of the Muslim community by deporting them or arresting and imprisoning them indefinitely in a state of limbo.

When no proof can be brought to link them with Al Qa'ida or other radical militants, as has been the case with virtually all of the victims of post-9/11 hysteria, they are eliminated by resort to visa technicalities. As Ahmed Yousef notes in the next chapter, entitled "Targeting Islam in America," concerning the thousands of people arrested after 9/11, "Not a single one of them was ever charged in connection with the September 11th attacks. This raised serious questions, as there are nearly five million people in violation of U.S. immigration laws, but only those of Arab or Muslim backgrounds have been prosecuted." In chapter 11, "Improbable Targets: Indigenous Muslims," the author notes that, "Unfortunately, few critics of the Muslim immigrant community would even attempt to reconcile their bias with the fact that these people had left their homelands, which implied a respect and admiration for the United States and its opportunities and what it offered in terms of freedom and quality of life."

The demonization of Arabs is relatively easy, because they are considered to be foreigners, even though they might have lived in America most of their lives and raised their children here. The demonization of indigenous Muslims did not take place until after 9/11, because by birth and culture they are prima facie loyal Americans. The African-American Muslims, who constitute as much as half of all Muslims in America, have never integrated with the Muslims from abroad because of what Ahmed Yousef refers to as a "benign racism" among many immigrant Muslims. Furthermore, it is difficult to demonize them because they know the ropes in Congress and how to operate in American society.

The Euro-American Muslims are even more difficult to brand as potential terrorists, because they tend to be concerned not with the Muslim community as such, either at home or abroad, but rather with the problems and opportunities that face all Americans in addressing universal issues of conscience. Nevertheless, as Ahmed Yousef details the story in chapter 17, entitled "Virginia Jihad Network," the latest trend in the saga of Muslims in America is precisely to focus on blue-eyed Americans who emphasize interfaith cooperation, because they can more effectively address the issues of justice that the political Zionists might like to keep off the American public policy agenda.

Perhaps the most powerful chapters are on the

emasculation of Muslim charitable organizations, especially those that gave charity to help the Palestinians survive as human beings and maintain their dignity; on the demonization of the Muslim community in Chicago because it traditionally has been the center of Palestinian immigration; and on the Palestinian activists, Sami al Arian, Mazen al-Najjar, and Abdelhaleem Ashqar, whose served as ground zero in the battle to disenfranchise Muslim leaders committed to justice and humanitarian help for the Palestinians under siege in the Holy Land.

As stated in chapter 9 on "The Holy Land Foundation and the Saga of HAMAS in America": "The American campaign to demonize and criminalize Muslim and Palestinian activism in support of their brethren in Palestine has its roots squarely in Israel's desire to extinguish the source of any aid and comfort whatsoever to the subjects of its occupation. This desire is part of a strategy to ultimately achieve the surrender of the Palestinians through demoralization and humiliation. As American Islamic activism grew in scale and sophistication, and as attention turned toward supporting the Palestinians, Israel and its U.S. supporters grew increasingly worried that support from American Muslims would undermine their campaign of military subjugation. It also disapproved of successful efforts to feed, house, and clothe its Palestinian subjects, since this alleviated the despair that Israel hoped would lead to surrender. Consequently, the pro-Israel lobby made the unraveling of American Muslim activism in support of Palestinians a top priority."

The perversion of justice involved in the persecution of the above three Muslim leaders lay in the government's decision "to take a political debate and give it a legal face."

This is profoundly unconstitutional because by definition it is the very opposite of the rule of law.

The hopes and prayers of Muslims in America are that they will eventually be free to integrate into American society by bringing the wisdom of their tradition to enrich America as other minorities have done in the past. More than that, however, they hope that their travails in the post-9/11 era of American vulnerability to the problems of the world will highlight the dangers that blind reaction to the new era of insecurity may pose to the survival of America as a freedom loving country. They may serve as the canary in the coal mine, so that when the canary sickens or dies the miners know that the poisons in the air have become lethal.

Perhaps the most useful chapter in this entire 700-page book is chapter 15, "The Raid on the IIIT: Assault on Muslim American Intellectualization," which is a core chapter in Part Five on "Bankrupting Muslim Institutions." The International Institute of Islamic Thought (IIIT) was founded a quarter century ago as a means to institutionalize the movement among Muslim intellectuals to overcome the backward and confrontational culture of "Mullah Islam" by introducing fundamental reforms rooted in enlightened understanding not only of Islam but of all the world religions. When a task force of 150 FBI and other agents stormed its offices in March, 2002, confiscated its computers, invaded the homes of its officials, and even handcuffed one executive's wife and children, the entire Muslim community was dumbfounded. This was even more oxymoranic than implying that the Iraqi freedom fighters hate freedom.

The Institute's entire reason for being is to develop the message that the fundamental reform involved in civilizational renewal requires a paradigm shift, which, in turn, requires a foundation and a diagnostic method to interpret reality. This is cast in the terms of Islamizing thought, but it calls for reviving the best of classical Islamic thought and the best of classical American thought, because they are the same.

The purpose and consistent teachings of the IIIT are best expressed by its founding director, Dr. Jamal Barzinji: "In its rational and methodical approach, the Institute stands for the reformist trend in Islam that holds human reasoning in high esteem and is very critical of literalist or dogmatic interpretations. The Institute is opposed to mental reclusiveness. It very much encourages *ijtihad* [reasoning], pragmatism, and pluralism. It respects all Scriptural religions. It also is an advocate of closer inter-faith relations and ties. The Institute's 'school of thought' envisions the consolidation of all the common values among the three Abrahamic religions so that humanity can better solve its problems and employ its potentials in the service of humankind. It teaches that in the normal course of life the relationships between Muslims and others are based on and produce peace, dialogue, healing, forgiveness, and cooperation in common concerns on a moral basis that respects differing points of view. ... The reformist school of thought believes in the application of Islamic law in the cosmopolitan and universal sense that serves the interests of all people and their needs. It follows that divine laws, beliefs, and religions are meant to help humans construct a better world through cooperation and solidarity."

All Americans should welcome Islam as an enlightened religion so that its enlightened followers can better counter those self-proclaimed Muslims who would hijack Islam as a religion for evil ends. If Christians and Jews succeed in making common cause with the enlightened Muslims who make up the vast majority of all Muslims in America, they can better succeed in rescuing their own religions from extremists who are exploiting 9/11 as a means to hijack Christianity and Judaism. If the current crusade against Islam succeeds, however, as waged by those who through ignorance or design have made a career in demonizing it, Americans will have lost their most powerful ally in restoring America to its role as a moral leader in the world.

The entire world may be approaching the end times in the sense that awareness of the transcendent and the resulting responsibility to translate knowledge into justice will disappear. But the very process of approaching a nadir or "end" in global civilization can serve as shock therapy for the revival of civilization in a new world. This may be the lesson that one should learn from this monumental book by Dr. Ahmed Yousef on *American Muslims: A Community Under Siege.* ■

Dr. Robert Dickson Crane
Center for Policy Research,
Santa Fe, New Mexico
May 2004

Part One

THE AMERICAN MUSLIM DREAM

Give me your tired, your poor, your huddled masses yearning to be free.

Emma Lazarus, *Statue of Liberty*

PROFILE: THE FOUNDING FATHERS OF THE AFRICAN AMERICAN MUSLIM COMMUNITY

• Noble Drew Ali

• Elijah Muhammad

• Malcolm X

• Warith D. Muhammad

• Imam Warith speaks at Saviours' Day 2000 in Chicago

• Louis Farrakhan

• Million-Man March, Washington, D.C., 1995

Chapter 1

A GLIMPSE AT MUSLIM IMMIGRATION TO THE UNITED STATES THROUGH THE 1960s

Against extreme odds, Islam has discreetly survived in the fiber of American society. In the New World, some of the African slaves suffered a doubly tragic fate. Initially, they were enslaved because they were African, but when it was discovered that they were also Muslims., their suffering was compounded. They were tortured, burned alive, hung, and shot unless they renounced their religions and their names.

—Amir N. Ali, *Muslims in America: Seven Centuries of History* (1312-2000), Amana Publications, Beltsville, Maryland, 2001.

The new world and the new continent of the Americas became the old world's land of milk and honey. People from all around the world were keen to leave their homelands and start a new life on the American continent. The United States of America was the prime jewel among all of the American territories, which stretched from Canada to Argentina. Many local and regional reasons motivated the European emigrants to set sail for the new world. Muslims shared some of these same reasons to leave their ancestral lands and look beyond the horizons for a land of freedom and opportunity. What follows is an attempt to recapture the dynamics of those early years that persuaded immigrant Muslims to seek a permanent home in America for themselves and future generations.

Among the many reasons behind the early waves of immigration, as alluded to by Yvonne Haddad, Professor of History of Islam and Christian Muslim Relations, Georgetown University, one of the often overlooked catalysts was economic. During the late nineteenth and early twentieth centuries, economic opportunities in the Muslim world were limited. Production and revenue generating sectors of life were down to a minimum, so people began to look elsewhere for their livelihood. Word was circulating that economic and commercial opportunities were endless in the United States. In financially depressed areas of the Muslim world, this became an important incentive for people to leave their homeland and resettle in a land of economic prosperity and unlimited possibilities.[1]

This economic factor motivated early communities of Muslims to resettle from various corners of the extremely weakened Ottoman Empire just prior to World War I.[2] The first wave of Muslim immigrants to the United States also included people from the Indian subcontinent and from the West Indies along with another influx of Muslims from the Punjab in 1906. These Punjabis are said to have left their country to avoid the pressures of British Colonialism and the devastating effects of famine. Heavy immigration restrictions and economic depression halted this outpouring of laborers during the interwar period, but small communities had already settled, mostly in the Midwest, where they worked in manufacturing plants. Small mosques and Islamic centers were built in the 1930s and 1940s in cities such as Chicago, Illinois, Dearborn, Michigan, and Cedar Rapids, Iowa.[3] These communities were very small in number, however, and did not expand the size and the scope of their activities until the next wave of immigration, which began following the Second World War.

Though the economic situation throughout the Muslim world caused opportunities to be limited, the following period of immigration featured those fleeing primarily in response to political instability, especially following the end of European rule and the beginning of oppressive autocratic regimes, such as came to power in much of the Arab world. Others were escaping a radically new political environment following the partition of the Indian subcontinent, in which millions of Muslims were left to live under a Hindu government in India. Partition led to the migration of thousands of Muslims to the United States. Also, people living under Communist dictatorships wanted to escape the restrictions, oppression, and state interference in their lives. This included Muslims living under the Communist yoke in the Soviet Union, China, and Eastern Europe who were anxious to find a life of liberty and freedom in the United States. Some Muslims lived under occupation in Muslim countries that were occupied by expansionist regimes. These Muslims wanted freedom from the treatment they were receiving by their colonial oppressors, for example, the Palestinians, the Kashmiris, and the Afghans after the Soviet invasion and occupation.

Clearly, during this era the tumultuous political situation throughout the heavily weakened and increasingly dependent

Muslim world had presented little alternative for thousands of Muslims except to seek better opportunities in the West, but specifically America, because it offered a unique society that was open to pluralism and welcomed other faiths and cultures. Muslims who lived as minorities and were officially second and third class citizens wanted to gain civic equality by leaving the apartheid governments in their countries in order to acquire a sense of equality with their fellow citizens. Examples of these types of countries are India, the Philippines, and Sri Lanka. Many of the people of this period were relatively poor and uneducated, and, while some came to seek educational opportunities, most sought to start their own businesses.

In later years, the makeup of Muslim immigrants would change dramatically. A younger generation of students who finished their educational programs in their respective countries had their sights fixed on a higher level of education that was not available to them in their homelands. Post-graduate studies were especially important for highly specialized fields, such as medicine, engineering, and the sciences. Because of the special relationship emerging between the United States and many countries in the Muslim world, opportunities were offered to students to continue their higher education at American colleges and universities. Kuwait, whose oil reserves were important to meet the growing American need for such resources, sent thousands of its sons and daughters to continue their studies in America. Many more poured in from Pakistan, Egypt, and Syria. These immigrants dominated the final major wave of migration, beginning in the early 1960s, which is covered in the next chapter.

Throughout the history of these waves of migration, the United States of America offered these Muslims most of what they were looking for, at least in theory and in relative terms. For these immigrants, the United States was an economically prosperous country with opportunities galore. Civil liberties were a hallmark of American life, and the opportunities for a better life were unlimited. Muslims could pursue their potential without the prejudices and limitations of the old country. During the course of the first half of the twentieth century, economic incentives drove immigration to America, whereas in the latter half of that century, the quest for education was the main driving force that brought waves of immigrants. During the 1970s, nearly half a million students are estimated to have left their countries of origin to acquire academic degrees and to conduct advanced research in the United States. Many of them would later decide to reside permanently in America and to begin building "Islamic bridges" in the United States between Muslims and non-Muslims.

There is no Muslim country that does not have emigrants in the United States. Significant among these immigrant-contributing regions are the Arab countries, some of which had generated harsh conditions that forced some inhabitants to flee westward to greener pastures. Many of these emigrants were searching for their freedom as well as their livelihood. One of the Arab areas notorious for driving out its inhabitants was the Levant (Syria, Lebanon, and Palestine), particularly through steep taxation and monetary burdens placed on the population by the Turkish Ottoman state. Contrasted with this is the wave of immigrants who came to the United States in the latter half of the twentieth century. Between 1967 and 1976 around 23,000 immigrants came from Iraq alone. From Jordan and Palestine there were more than 25,000 immigrants. Syria had around 10,000, while Egypt had more than 26,000.[4]

Demographics

After a slow period of growth at the onset of the twentieth century, Muslims began to increase exponentially in later decades. The increase in the number of Muslims in America can be attributed to three reasons.[5] First was the natural increase by way of birthrate, which was higher than the average national birthrate in the United States. The immigrant Muslim community maintained its traditional cultural norms, which generally included lower age of marriage, higher per capita births, and little reliance on family planning methods such as birth control. Second was the continuing influx of immigrants, which sociologists refer to as an unnatural increase controlled by government regulations, the most notable of which allowed much higher rates of immigration following the passage of a 1965 law that greatly expanded the acceptance of immigrants from non-white countries.

Finally, non-Muslims' conversion to Islam, which is also an abnormal way of increasing the Muslim population, was a huge factor not to be discounted. In recent years, Islam has attained the title of "the fastest growing religion," in large part due to its popularity among segments of American society, most notably the African-American community, but with some significant conversions of white Euro-Americans and Latinos. One phenomenon responsible for conversion has been incarceration. More than 160,000 individuals have embraced Islam through the prison system, most of them African-Americans.[6] Muslims account for more than ten percent of arriving immigrants. As a combined result of all the above reasons, Islam is the fastest growing religion in America.

Initial Organizations

The early immigrants arriving in small groups at the beginning of the twentieth century continued intermittently until half way through the century. These early immigrants are best described as adventurers who came to the new world to make money. Unlike many Europeans, Muslims did not initially come to the United States to reside here permanently. They wanted to make as much money as they could in the shortest possible time and then return to their countries of origin. But in the process of making money, many of them settled down and formed businesses and families, all of which undermined their initial intention to return to their land of birth. When small business ventures drew in other family members, affiliations to the homeland and even cultural ties begin to wane.

Their entrepreneurial and business successes caused these earlier immigrants to call more of their family members to join them in this new life of luxury. Success stories were enough to entice other family members across the ocean to join their booming and flourishing relatives in America. The new reality in a secular and materialistic United States was at odds with the homegrown and deeply religious and conservative character that was central to the lives of these Muslim immigrants. Social and cultural pressures increased so dramatically in the lives of these conventional and traditionalist Muslims that they felt they had to try to preserve their morals and ethical standards or they would eventually be overtaken by crass materialistic forces. Some of these immigrant families took it upon themselves to build mosques. They also founded social, cultural, and entertainment organizations. These cultural and religious hallmarks of Islamic identity developed at all levels, local, national, and North American.

The Federation of Islamic Associations of the United States and Canada (FIA)

Muslims in the United States were numerically insignificant in the first half of the last century. During those "slow times" one of the attempts to organize Muslims was the International Muslim Society, whose first chairman was 'Abdullah 'Ajram of Cedar Rapids, Iowa. Its second convention was held in Toledo, Ohio, in 1953. The third convention was in Chicago. At that convention, an idea was adopted to form a general association that would bind all other local groups together. Thus, the Federation of Islamic Associations of the U.S. and Canada was created. It served as the barebones association of Muslims throughout the country, providing basic services and holding cultural events. On the scale of American Muslim organizations, it ranked at the most primitive level, but it was vital as a pioneer for things to come. As such, the FIA was dissolved a decade later, and a new organization was established that better reflected the changing demographics of America's Muslim community: the Muslim Students Association.

Pre-Immigration Muslims in the United States

While all of the discussion thus far has centered on the waves of Muslim migration, primarily from the Middle East and South Asia, an entirely separate but equally important discussion of America's native Muslim population is essential. Predominantly African in origin, this segment of the American Muslim community is much older and more ingrained into American culture and life. This era begins with the slave trade of four centuries ago. Unfortunately, there is no accurate record of Muslims who came to America in the early years of its colonization. We do know that the slave trade, which was very active on the shores of western Africa, definitely had Muslim slaves as a main component of the millions of slaves that were forced onto the high seas to be sold to plantations in America. Noted author Alex Haley, in his book *Roots*, managed to track his genealogical family of the slave trade to a Muslim part of West Africa. It only stands to reason that a high ratio of African Muslims were dislocated from their African countries of origin into the labor, agricultural, plantation, and exploitative markets of America. The harsh conditions of slavery resulted in many of the subsequent generations of those initial African Muslims losing their religious affiliation and identity. Slavery was not only physically brutal, but was socially vicious and culturally cruel.

Nevertheless, at the beginning of the twentieth century, stemming from the post slavery movement, local African American communities developed an interest in African origins and some various aspects of Islam. The results were new religions that incorporated some Islamic symbols or words in their sermons or public addresses. This was often done without knowledge of normative Islam. One such example was Noble Drew Ali, who established the Moorish Science Temple of America. On a larger and more profound level, Elijah Muhammad managed to present an organized albeit distorted image of Islam to a much larger audience of African Americans. This explanation of Islam was cast in a racially reactive mode to counter the prevailing racism that was part and parcel of social, official, and religious America. Before we go into other details about this most significant influence on African American Muslims we should also note other less acknowledged and less obvious expressions of a misunderstood Islam in America. Some called themselves *Ansaru Allah*, and others *The Nubian Islamic Hebrews*. Among the African Americans some had a more or less accurate and wholesome understanding of Islam but could never reach a wider audience. Included in this category were *The Hanafis* and The Islamic Party of North America, both of which were located in Washington, D.C.

The most important of all these is what was originally referred to as the Nation of Islam. Its most notable leaders were Elijah Muhammad, Malcolm X, Louis Farrakhan, and Warith Deen Muhammad. Regardless of the original theological deviations in the origins of this African American Muslim movement, it was the largest and the most prevalent in the African American community prior to the civil rights movement. Warith Deen Muhammad guided this community by merging into the world community of Muslims.

The early community of African American Muslims had limited contact with the Muslim immigrants who came to this country, perhaps because both groups in the first half of the twentieth century were preoccupied with self preservation. Within their own cultural "shells" they were trying to preserve their cultural identities as best they could. African Americans who endured hundreds of years of oppression and discrimination were not readily accessible to "exotic looking" Muslims in the same cities where the Nation of Islam was concentrated, namely, Detroit, Chicago, New York, and Philadelphia.[7]

To the credit of the Nation of Islam, one of its sons known as Malcolm X or El-Hajj Malik al-Shabazz went through a lifelong struggle against racism to then have an eye-opening experience in Makkah when he went to perform the pilgrimage ritual. There he saw white, black, brown, red, and yellow people all coming together without race consciousness. This triggered a fundamental change in his psychology that he brought back with him and which caused the first seeds of change in the Nation of Islam. It should be noted that Malik al-Shabazz also was acquainted with immigrant Muslims in the United States who may have helped him overcome his previously racist views concerning Islam.

As the African American Muslim evolution continued, there were more contacts between them and their immigrant Muslim brethren. After the death of Elijah Muhammad in the mid 1970s, his son Wallace Muhammad (Warith Deen Muhammad) assumed the leadership of the Nation of Islam and eventually brought the great majority of its adherents into substantial theological harmony with the rest of the Muslims. In the course of this evolution of Islamic consciousness among African Americans, the Nation of Islam had established elementary and secondary schools known as "Sister Clara Muhammad" schools in the major cities. Eventually, the name Nation of Islam was replaced by "The World Community of Islam in the West." Its institutionalized activities besides the Clara Muhammad schools included the *Bilalian News* which subsequently became *World Muslim News*. Its circulation in 2003 stood at 50,000. Among its many accomplishments, in May 1981, the American Muslim Mission (AMM) (previously the Nation of Islam) announced that the Illinois State Board of

Education had approved a teacher training college to be launched by AMM.[8]

The Nation of Islam (NOI)

Louis Farrakhan became prominent within the Nation of Islam (NOI) under the leadership of Elijah Muhammad during the 1960's and 70's. After Elijah's death in 1975, he left the movement led by Elijah's son, Wallace Muhammad, whom he considered out of touch with his father's teachings and doctrines. Farrakhan continues to concentrate on the Nation of Islam, which is noted for its counseling programs for drug addicts, alcoholics, and street gangs. He is said to have more than 80 mosques under his control, and became famous worldwide through his Million-Man March of black men in Washington, D.C., on October 16, 1995. The purpose of the march was to inspire a moral and spiritual rebirth among African-American men.

During the last decade, the level of coordination between native American Muslims and immigrant American Muslims has been increasing. In 1989, AMM adopted a resolution recognizing fourteen centuries of Islam and pledged to improve the understanding of Islam in America. Warith Deen Muhammad received the Walter Reuther Humanities Award and the Four Freedoms Award. He has been recognized by some as the *de facto* leader of Muslims in America, and was even called upon to offer the opening prayer for the U.S. Senate in 1992.

Islam is multiplying all over the continent, and its adherents are making themselves known in all walks of life. Mosques and cultural centers have become part of the

American landscape. Islam and Muslims are at a delicate juncture in their involvement in American participatory politics. Democracy, pluralism, and newly gained freedoms are a challenge to immigrant Muslims who fled oppressive governments and to American Muslims who are still emerging from institutionalized racism. Muslims are challenged today to address the American people in the language of the U.S. Constitution and the American Bill of Rights. Muslims are treading on new territory not only geographically, but politically and socially. They have an opportunity to prove to themselves and to others that they are able and willing to contribute to a better tomorrow and a brighter future for all Americans, regardless of religion, race, country of origin, or gender.

The work is cut out for these multi-cultural and multi-racial Muslims. They need to do much work among themselves in order to put together a consolidated Islamic program and prove their ability to work with others on issues that are morally mutual and socially feasible. Muslims, both American-born and immigrant, have a rich background and centuries of experience to offer. ■

• Black Muslim women on their way by bus to hear their supreme leader, Elijah Muhammad.

Imams and Activists of the African-American Muslim Community

• Captain Abdul Rasheed

• African-American leaders participate in rally against genocide in Bosnia, 1995.

• Mujahid Ramadan

• Minister Farrakhan meets with American Muslim leaders after September 11, Washington, D.C.

• Imam Johari Abdul Malik

• Imam Abdelaleem Mousa

• Mauri Saalakhan

Islam among African Americans

Muslims may have entered the Americas as early as 1717. Scholars have noted records of Arabic-speaking slaves who refrained from eating pork. Perhaps a fifth of all slaves brought to the Americas from Africa in the eighteenth and eighteenth centuries were Muslims, but most of these converted to Christianity.

Historical Moments in the 1900s

1913   Noble Drew Ali founded the Moorish Science Temple of America in Newark, New Jersey. Ali was born Timothy Drew in January 1886, in Sampson, North Carolina. The Sultan of Morocco commissioned Drew Ali to teach Islam to African Americans in the United States. He blended together elements of Islam, Black Nationalism, and freemasonry. Noble Drew Ali died in Chicago in 1929.

1921   Ahmadiya Movement in Islam

1925   Moorish Temple of Science with Noble True Ali

1926   Duse Muhammad Ali, mentor of Marcus Garvey helped establish an organization in Detroit known as the Universal Islamic Society. Its motto was "One God, One Aim, One Destiny." He was also known to be frequently in the company of Muhammad Pickthall, the English Muslim scholar who translated the Holy *Qur'an* into English. Duse had considerable influence upon Garvey's movement.

1933   W.D. Fard's Temple of Islam in Detroit.
Chief follower is Elijah Muhammad—Fard disappears.

1935-1975	Nation of Islam (NOI) with Elijah Muhammad headquarters in Chicago.
1956	Malcolm X became an active preacher for the Nation of Islam. He started working with the Nation of Islam in 1952 when he was released from jail.
1958	Khalifa Hamas Abdul breaks with Nation of Islam and establishes Hanafi Center.
1960	The first African American Muslim newspaper *Muhammad Speaks* was launched. It became the largest minority weekly paper in the country. At its peak it reached more than 800,000 readers. Since its conception it has undergone various name changes. It became the Bilalian News and then the *American Muslim Journal*. Currently its name is *Muslim Journal*.
1960	The largest Sunni Muslim community of African Americans was centered in Brooklyn, New York. Shaykh Daoud and Malcolm X had their mosques in Brooklyn NY.
1964	Clarence 13X expelled from Nation of Islam, establishes Five Percent Nation of Islam.
1964	Malcolm X and Wallace D. Muhammad expelled from Nation of Islam, and Louis Farrakhan replaces Malcolm X as national spokesman.
1964	Malcolm X establishes Muslim Mosque, Inc.
1965	Malcolm X is assassinated, and Muslim Mosque Inc. disintegrates.

1969	Wallace Muhammad reinstated by his father Elijah.
1970	Nubian Islamic Hebrews established by Muhammad Ahmed Abdullah
1975	Elijah Muhammad dies.
1975	Wallace D. Muhammad assumes leadership of Nation of Islam. Wallace changes name to Warith.
1975	Bilalian Community replaces Nation of Islam under Warith D. Muhammad.
1976	Silas Muhammad breaks with Warith D. Muhammad; Silas begins "Lost, Found Nation of Islam."
1977	Louis Farrakhan breaks with Warith D. Muhammad; re-establishes original Nation of Islam (Elijah Muhammad).
1978	John Muhammad breaks with Warith D. Muhammad; forms Nation of Islam under his name.
1978	Warith D. Muhammad was named consultant and trustee by the Gulf States to distribute funds and Islamic missionary activities in the United States.
1980	American Muslim Mission replaces World Community of Islam in the West; Warith D. Muhammad leads in direction of Sunni Islam.
1985	American Muslim Mission decentralized; Warith D. Muhammad presides over South Side Temple in Chicago.

1991	Imam Siraj Wahhaj became the first Muslim in U.S. history to recite the invocation (opening prayer) in the U.S. House of Representatives.
1992	Imam Warith D. Muhammad became the second Muslim in U.S. history to offer invocation in U.S. House of Representatives.
1993	Captain Abdul Rasheed became the first Muslim Army Chaplain in the U.S. Army.
1996	LTJG Monje Malak Noel became the first Muslim Naval Chaplain in the U.S. Navy.
1999	The U.S. Post office published a stamp to honor the Muslim leader el-Hajj Malik el-Shabazz (Malcolm X).

Historical Moments in the 2000s

2000	Hassan el-Amin was appointed as a District Judge in Prince George County Maryland.
2001	Muslim Alliance of North America (MANA) is inaugurated.
2003	Muslim Alliance of North America publishes first issue of *Grassroots* Newspaper.
2003	W. D. Muhammad resigns from the leadership of the American Society of Muslims (ASM).

*Sources: George W. Braswell, *ISLAM: Its Prophet, People, Politics and Power*, Broadman & Holman Publishers, 1996, and Amir N. Ali, *Muslims in America (1312-2000)*, Amana Publications, 1998.

PROFILE: MUSLIM STUDENTS ASSOCIATION:
FOUR DECADES OF ACTIVISM

The positive hands-on approach undertaken by Muslim students to promote Islamic activities confirms the notion that as "the first organized Islamic work and strong Islamic foundation in this country, MSA established the basis for the institutionalization of Islamic work in North America and different parts of the world. Whether it was in Asia, Europe, or Africa, Muslims looked up to MSA as a role model.

—Ahmad Totonji, *AMSS Bulletin*, Summer 2001

When Muslim student leaders formed the Muslim Students Association of the U.S. and Canada in 1963, they were responding to a deeply felt need: to have a united voice that would facilitate the development of Islam and the Muslim community in North America. This sentiment was reflected by their motto: *"And hold fast, all together, by the rope which Allah (stretches out for you), and be not divided among yourselves. Remember with gratitude Allah's favor upon you, for you were enemies and He joined your hearts in love, so that, by His Grace, you became brothers. You were on the brink of the pit of Fire, and He saved you from it. Thus does*

Dr. Mahmoud Rashdan

Dr. Ahmed Sakr

Dr. Cherif Bassiouni

Dr. Sayyid M. Syeed

Allah make His Signs clear to you, that you may be guided." (Qur'an 3:103)

The early years of the MSA were spent in establishing strong relationships and building the bonds of brotherhood through a shared Islamic identity. Services were offered to allow Muslim students to practice their faith openly and adhere to their strongly held beliefs. In this era, regular on-campus prayers were established, along with rigorous Islamic programming, publications, and national conferences.

By the 1970s and 1980s, the MSA experienced a period of transition, with the infusion of younger immigrants from the Muslim world who took the leadership reigns and steered the organization into greater arenas, including political and social activism, especially in response to the dire state of affairs for their fellow Muslims across the world, in Palestine, Kashmir, Iran, and Afghanistan. The numbers of MSA members were growing by the day, and MSA National began to take a lead role in affairs of the growing Muslim community, especially on college campuses. There were also early signs of an organization wanting to break out of its shell and integrate

Imam Abolfazl Nahidian

El-Tijani Abugedeiri

Dr. Jamal Badawi

Dr. Muhammad Jaghlit

into mainstream campus life, with the beginnings of interfaith dialogues, *da'wa* activities, campus lecture series, and increased volunteerism.

The 1990s was the beginning of a new era of Muslim students, those who were primarily American by birth and upbringing, but nonetheless conscientious of their religious identity. The MSA of this period began to integrate steadily, and was finally accepted as part of the diverse tradition of religions in America. The organization had gained in prominence on many campuses, and had grown in numbers, reaching tens of thousands of college students at more than 340 universities in North America. Muslim students increased their outreach, becoming part of the social fabric of America, and participated in the public sphere, integrating into the political process at a pace that outdid the generation of their parents. Volunteerism and activism on behalf of Islamic causes worldwide was also reaching its pinnacle.

At the dawn of the new millennium, the Muslim Students Association was one of the most widely respected national organizations on many college campuses, and

Altaf Hussein

Dr. Ahmed Elkadi

Dr. Mohamed Omeish

had gained a tremendous following. Its leadership was instrumental in informing Americans of all stripes about the virtues of Islam and bridging the divide between Islam and the West. On September 11, 2001, MSA members everywhere were the first to respond in mourning for their nation, and in defense of their religion against those who would see it denigrated and maligned. They eloquently condemned the attacks, and continued to preach for peace, justice, and understanding for all people everywhere. Throughout its history, the MSA has been the leading voice of activism in the American Muslim community, a tradition that has lasted through many generations, and one that, God willing, will continue for generations to come.

MSA Link, a publication of Muslim Students Association (MSA)

Chapter 2

MUSLIM STUDENTS ASSOCIATION: PIONEERING ACTIVISM IN AMERICA

The events of 9/11 sent shockwaves throughout the world, whose ripples are still being felt. It woke up our Muslim campus communities like never before. Throughout North America, MSA chapters became the flag bearers of Islam within their local communities. As local chapters geared up to deal with their share of goodwill and hate, MSA National prepared itself to provide direction and guidance in dealing with the many daily onslaughts.

—MSA U.S./Canada,
2001 Annual Report as submitted to ISNA.

Humble Beginnings

The drive toward Islamic activism in America began with one segment of the community's early population: students. As is the case with most modern social movements, college students provide the core body of the drive toward political and social activism, and the Muslim community was no exception. The immigration from the Islamic world had a number of key features. First, the immigrants emerged out of a climate of political and civil unrest, in which Islam as a religion was the driving force toward change. Many people of this generation, which grew up in the 1950s and 1960s were reared in Islamic youth movements and beyond that in political movements such as the Muslim Brotherhood in most of the Arab world, Jama'ti Islami in South Asia, and other similar traditions. These organizations bridged the way toward the second feature of this immigrant generation, namely, education. While education in the traditional Islamic sciences was certainly a vital tool toward building the model citizen of the Muslim world, modern education in the arts and especially the sciences was viewed as an essential aspect of community life and important for it to thrive. Therefore, while most of these young men and women steeped themselves in knowledge of Islamic sciences, they often pursued collegiate studies in areas such as medical science, natural science, and engineering even while in their own countries.

In effect, however, the opportunities for a young Egyptian, Palestinian, or Pakistani in their respective lands were severely limited, forcing many to leave for a more superior offering from Western nations, especially the United States. Moreover, not only did the United States offer a better educational system and the most advanced study of the sciences, but even the environment for Islamic activism was far less confining than under the staunchly secular governments in the Muslim world, in which social repression against this idealistic generation was a common feature. In essence, as more young Muslims began to come to the United States, an immediate acculturation process was to take place, in which they would learn the norms and values of the American liberal democratic system, above all, individual freedoms, liberties, and equality.

By the early 1960s, more Muslim students had integrated into the American educational system, enrolling in degree programs at colleges and universities across the country. In states ranging from New York, Ohio, and Indiana, to California, Michigan, and Illinois, thousands of young Muslims (primarily males) had settled comfortably into their academic environment. Moreover, members of this group became committed to practicing their faith openly, and with each other. As the notion of community is important in Islam, these students did not settle for individual practice, but yearned for a more organized structure developed to serve their needs as a small but significant group. The basic needs involved were simple, setting up a time and place for religious worship, which included daily prayers and weekly services, communal gatherings to commemorate special religious holidays as well as the daily breaking of fast during the month of Ramadan, and a forum to discuss religious issues and build a sense of camaraderie with fellow Muslim immigrants.

In most places, these needs were met by loosely organized groups led by the most active Muslims who took on leadership roles. Within a few years, however, it became clear that the "program" of the Muslim students, as it had been defined years earlier in their native countries, could not proceed without a number of conditions being met. First and foremost, with small pockets of Muslim students spread throughout the country, there was little opportunity for communication or organization. And so this was a need that had to be fulfilled. Second, no central structure existed as a backbone to serve them. And finally, very few Muslim students had attempted to branch out beyond their own cocoons, whether to mainstream America or to the minority of indigenous Muslims within it. Many of the Muslim students at the time believed that all three would be necessary to embark on their activist program.

The movement began with local student groups that organized around giving Muslims an opportunity to practice their faith and live an Islamic way of life even while in a foreign society that did not follow their traditional norms. These organizations, with names such as "Muslim Cultural and Educational Society," and "Islamic International Organizations," were relatively modest in size and budget. But according to former leaders, these groups, "although small, became recognized for their intellectual activities, including lectures by renowned professors, symposia, panel discussions, radio/television debates, and mini-conferences, as well as for holding regular and weekly prayers."[1] The transition from local, individual groups to a national structure was highly significant, given the potential it gave for activism. "Individual Muslim student organizations appeared and existed like islands, isolated without any contact with one another."[2] Finally, in late 1962, efforts were made among student leaders at various college campuses, to establish a unified entity of Muslims across the country. And so on January 1, 1963, the Muslim Students Association was born.

MSA: The Early Years

The first meeting of the Muslim Students Association's national body was held at the University of Illinois at Urbana-Champaign on the first day of January 1963. That cold winter day, as many students recall, featured a few dozen students representing thirteen different universities.[3] The group elected Mehdi Bahadouri, an Iranian graduate student, as its first national president. The first budget was a paltry $200, which increased to $2,000 the following year, and $20,000 in 1965. Most of the money was raised from donations by families and friends, with some coming from student activities funding at different schools.

The early ideology of MSA was fairly simple. It wished "to nurture true Islamic kinship," which would set the stage for unity in action toward the many causes on which all Muslims agreed.[4] Much of this vision was based on the tenets put forth by global Islamic political movements in the Arab world as well as South Asia and North Africa. It was a strong desire to bring out the best of Islamic knowledge and principles into civil society and the public sphere. Intellectual discourse, long stifled under colonial rule and subsequent oppressive regimes, was rekindled again in the hearts and minds of America's Muslim students. Jamal Barzinji, a pioneer during this era, best describes the mentality that kindled its spirit and the experiences behind it:

> The Islamic movement discovered that immense losses and sacrifices had been made in various parts of the Muslim world, whether in the Arab world, the Indian subcontinent, or Southeast Asia, and that the gap between the ideals of establishing Islamic societies and the reality in the Muslim world was rapidly widening. This led to an honest, open, and serious internal self-critique to discover the cause of this failure. The Islamic movement had undoubtedly made the most sacrifices of any movement and the proportion of dedicated people was higher than in any other

movement on earth. But, in spite of that we found that the successes were very limited, which was a source of concern for many people. After many meetings and discussions during the 1960s and early 1970s, it appeared to us that the breakdown of Islamic movements lay in their failure to follow the values of the Qur'an and the Prophetic traditions as texts to apply in real-world situations by taking practical steps to steer the Muslim Ummah toward the realization of its goals. This led us to develop what we referred to as "the crisis in dealing with the Holy Qur'an and the Prophetic tradition." This crisis of the Muslim mind and Islamic thought had led to the abandonment of these values and the adoption of a nonfunctional strategy, inadequate to accomplish the movement's goals.[5]

In essence, a new type of ideology, one capable of embracing the traditions on which Islam was based, while incorporating the best of what the modern world, including Western society, had to offer, was necessary in order to accomplish the movement's goals. Moreover, many of the movement's directions reflected the developments in the Arab and Muslim world. Specifically, the humiliating defeat of the Arab countries by Israel in 1967 was a monumental turning point in the eyes of many young people. A new strategy had to be formulated to bring "the Ummah" or the Muslim nation across the world, out of its abysmal state of affairs.

A Time for Reflection and Change

The early Muslim leaders came from a diverse array of backgrounds, including members of various races, ethnicities, nationalities, and Islamic sects. Ahmad Totonji, an Iraqi, had already helped set up the Muslim Students Society of the United Kingdom and Ireland, and followed up that effort with the United Muslim Student Organization of Europe (USMO) in 1961, the largest Islamic student group in all of Europe, as well as the Federation of Student Islamic Societies of the UK (FOSIS) in 1963, which embraced all ethnic and thought groups. Totonji brought this experience of institution building to the United States the following year, as he arrived to begin his graduate studies. Also heavily involved was Ahmed Husein Sakr, who served a number of terms as MSA president and was instrumental in orchestrating its activities during the early years. Mahmoud Rashdan, another former president, understood from the outset the mission of the Muslim community in America, and the qualities of life therein: "The students saw in America an open and tolerant society that would allow them to grow professionally, permit free expression, and accept the practice of their faith."[6]

The newly formed student movement was marked by its modest means of operation and the devotion and dedication of its members. Sakr recalls, "everyone was a volunteer and contributed whatever they could afford."[7] They had the determination, though not the means. The following months and early years were spent trying to garner as much support from various pockets of Muslim students across the country. Many workers paid for their own bus fare to travel far and wide to organize college campuses into developing their own chapters of the MSA.

By late 1963, only months following the initial creation of the Muslim Students Association, the organization doubled its membership to twenty chapters. This momentum allowed it to hold its first national conference in which various committees were assigned to lead the way in the planning of events, projects, and activities for the coming years. The MSA's main work focused on several fronts. The first dealt with establishing Islam on individual campuses, by providing students with prayer space, and offering services to Muslim students, while also developing the intellectual program to include weekly discussion groups and sponsoring lectures by Muslim scholars. Secondly, these latter events were expanded to the regional and national level, so that larger, more comprehensive conferences could take place, drawing hundreds of young Muslims to discuss relevant issues, exchange ideas, and learn from scholarly and intellectual figures. Other events included weekend retreats and religious camps, all designed to strengthen the camaraderie and unity among the Muslim students. Programs such as these could never have thrived in the Muslim world, partly because of lack of religious freedom, and also because the motivation was simply absent. The feeling of being in a minority in a new land was often a driving force behind strengthening the bonds of brotherhood among Muslims in America, as is often the case with most immigrant communities that derive a sense of strength from coming together.

In fact, during these early years the efforts were so focused on the MSA forging its identity and figuring out its internal structure that there was very minimal interaction with mainstream American society. Sakr recalls that there were "sympathetic foreign student advisers [who] allowed their office staff to help with typing and duplication," as well as other needs such as finding facilities to use for MSA events.[8] In addition, one outcome of some MSA events was the need for *da'wa* activities to educate Americans about Islam. These efforts were modest, but significant in that they were the first official display of organized and formal interaction between the Muslim student community and their American hosts.

To better accomplish these many ambitions, the Muslim Students Association needed, among other things, a way to print and publish written materials. In 1965, Muhammad Abdul Mateen Chida and two others at the University of Minnesota initiated the Islamic Book Service (IBS) with only $65 in capital. The students imported books on Islam and sold them to fellow students, while publications developed by the MSA were published out of State College, Pennsylvania, where Totonji lived. In late 1968, Mohammad Fazil Khan launched the MSA printing press under the title International Graphics Press, which slowly developed into a successful company. Totonji developed *Al-Ittihad* as MSA's primary journal. By 1967, the fifth annual MSA conference held in Columbus, Ohio, boasted membership from 36 college campuses and a mailing list for its newsletter of more than 3,000 addresses. That year, Cherif Bassiouni, a young Chicago lawyer, helped the MSA obtain recognition from the federal government and the U.S. postal service.[9] The following year, campus affiliations reached 52 universities, while the mailing list featured 6,000 addresses. Another regular publication by the MSA was its newsletter, *Muslim Link*, which gained in prominence in subsequent years.

Indeed, the need for the MSA became increasingly apparent as hundreds of students were joining its ranks each year, becoming a part of something special. Meanwhile, the leadership was encouraged by its reception in various places and strove toward even greater progress in the coming decade.

The 1970s: Refining Ideals

By the end of the 1960s, the Muslim Students Association of the U.S. and Canada had formed chapters on 68 college campuses, with hundreds of students representing 49 countries holding MSA membership.[10] The divide that so plagued their brethren in the Muslim world was wiped away in the United States. Local chapters as well as national committees featured Arabs and non-Arabs, Sunnis and Shi'as, blacks and whites, representing all Islamic schools of thought, united in a common endeavor. The period of the 1970s was an era of refining ideals, a period of incredible growth and expansion. Muslim immigrant students were pouring into the country in much greater numbers than before and settling in colleges throughout the United States. In fact, many of the current leaders of the American Muslim community are of this subsequent generation that arrived in the mid-1970s. These young men (and increasingly, women) provided a much-needed boost to the existing structure of the MSA, bringing with them the energy and enthusiasm as well as the reality of the current situation in the Muslim world. They clearly benefited from the experiences of the earlier pioneers and the institutional structures that they found ready and waiting for their rise into positions of leadership. This period found the activities of the MSA in full swing. Regional and national conferences became regular events that attracted hundreds of students, scholars, and activists, and even attained international recognition, with the likes of the esteemed Sudanese intellectual Dr. Hassan Al-Turabi coming to speak at conferences. Islamic publications were also reaching unprecedented heights, as the intellectual debate surrounding the Islamic movement in America became a heated topic among the leadership of the old guard and the new institutions.

In 1975, the MSA officially moved its headquarters from the simple premises of Masjid al-Ameen in Gary, Indiana, to a building of its own. MSA leaders hoped this would signal the beginning of a new era of organizational expansion.[11] As more of the original Muslim students were settling in the United States following the completion of their studies, a push was made to develop a more community-oriented organization to address the needs of America's growing Muslim population outside of the college and university system. Many MSA leaders resisted this call. Mahmoud Rashdan, MSA President in 1974, would ask rhetorically, "What is the most important word in the Muslim Students Association? Why have another organization when MSA can do the job?"[12] But by the late 1970s, this debate had already been settled, as the move toward a larger social organization dedicated to Muslim families and professions was established, with the MSA taking a backseat to focus more intently on the needs of the ever-growing population of students. In 1979, the national election held at the MSA convention in Ohio featured an executive committee made up entirely of non-students, with the exception of the president. A proposal was put forth for the creation of a new organization. Out of this decision came the Islamic Society of North America (ISNA), an organization devoted to the social concerns of American Muslims. Aside from holding annual conferences and providing a network of services to Muslim families, ISNA had a number of groups develop under its tutelage, including the Islamic Medical Association (IMA), the Association of Muslim Scientists and Engineers (AMSE), Association of Muslim Social Scientists (AMSS), and many other groups that came along to fill a void within the newly created segment of Muslim society.

In addition to such challenges from within an older generation wanting to move on, MSA also faced internal debates regarding the direction of its activity, which was both inclusive and far-reaching, but without specific attention given to certain important concerns for much of its constituency. This era saw the creation of other groups by those who wished to pay specific attention to various political issues and concerns. The Muslim Arab Youth Association (MAYA) was developed to attune itself to the concerns of the Arab world, giving the issue of Palestine a certain importance not afforded to it under the wide-ranging Muslim Students Association. The leadership of groups such as MAYA were, however, rooted in the MSA, and continued to cooperate hand in hand on major issues and conferences, while branching out into their own activities. Dr. Sami al-Arian and Dr. Tariq al-Suwaidan, two of the more important figures in this movement, emerged from this divide. In the years to follow, MSA's activities, while remaining in the forefront of America's Muslim students' activity, were nonetheless marginalized in certain respects by groups with more limited focus and more expressly political. In addition, MSA was no longer at the heart of the intellectual developments in American Muslim

First 18 MSA Presidents

No.	Year	Place	President
1	April 1963	Urbana, IL	Mehdi Bahadouri
2	August 1964	Urbana, IL	Mehdi Bahadouri
3	August 1965	Carbondale, IL	Ahmad Totonji
4	August 1966	Ann Arbor, MI	Ahmad Sakr
5	August 1967	Columbus, OH	Hussein Al-Shahrestani
6	August 1968	Green Lake, WI	Yunus Mukhtarzadeh*
7	August 1969	Alma, MI	Osman Ahmad
8	August 1970	Green Lake, WI	Ibrahim Kellizy**
9	August 1971	Green Lake, WI	Ahmad Sakr
10	August 1972	St. Charles, MO	Jamal Barzinji
11	August 1973	Lansing, MI	El-Tijani Abugedeiri
12	August 1974	Toledo, OH	Mahmoud Rashdan
13	August 1975	Toledo, OH	Iqbal Unus
14	May 1976	Bloomington, IN	Ezzat Jaradat***
15	May 1977	Bloomington, IN	Yaqub Mirza
16	May 1978	Bloomington, IN	Rabi Ahmad
17	May 1979	Oxford, OH	M. Naziruddin Ali†
18	May 1980-82	Oxford, OH	Sayyid M. Syeed

*   Resigned after being injured in a car accident. Succeeded by Ilyas Ba Yunus.
** Succeeded by Mozaffar Partowmah.
*** Succeeded by Yaqub Mirza.
†   President's term raised to 2 years.

society. Rather, new institutions by MSA alumni were established to continue those debates and take them to greater heights. The International Institute of Islamic Thought (IIIT) was established in 1977 by the pioneers of the American Muslim student movement, including Dr. Barzinji, Dr. Totonji, and a number of other noted figures, becoming the premier institution for intellectual and academic research and debate, not only within the American Muslim context, but as a contributor to the world of Islam.

The 1980s: Solidifying the Message

In 1980, Sayyid Mohammad Syeed, a graduate student at Indiana University in Bloomington, was elected to a two-year term as the last President of the old Muslim Students Association. During his tenure, the constitution and bylaws of ISNA were passed, and ISNA's first elections were held in 1982. In May of that same year, MSA marked its twentieth anniversary, which fittingly featured the end of one era and the beginning of another. The event brought together eleven past presidents of the MSA toward the election of ISNA officials and an advisory board known as Majlis Ashura.[13]

The development of ISNA and the persistence of other outer organizations unaffiliated with MSA left the organization desperate to forge a new identity for itself and establish a unique place within the American Muslim community and the society at large. The first president of the post-ISNA MSA, which came to be known simply as MSA National, was Ghulam Nabi Fai, then a graduate student at Temple University. Fai recalls a sprouting up of many national organizations following ISNA's model. He contends, "None of these organizations, however, catered to the needs of the students. What they needed was an organization formed by them, for them and the many others who would come after. The MSA was established to provide and make sure that there was an identity for Muslim students in America. There was a need to preserve a lot of what the first migrating students brought with them. We also needed a dialogue among faiths because most college students are open-minded."[14]

Following from ISNA's expansion as a formidable organization of North American Muslims, another group was established soon thereafter. In 1985, a group of Muslim teenagers at an ISNA and MSA conference determined that, rather than be relegated to the limited "youth" programming of those conferences, they would like to create their own institution to address the needs of the nation's growing population of Muslim adolescents and teenagers. Out of this was born Muslim Youth of North America (MYNA). This organization began as a resource for education and activities, providing literature, organizing leadership training, recreation camps, and support groups, and ultimately providing an environment for developing the new American Muslim youth identity.[15] The Muslim youth who emerged out of MYNA were also better prepared to lead an Islamic lifestyle once they went off to colleges and universities, often taking the leadership reigns of their local MSA chapter, and further adapting them to changing realities. As such, both ISNA and MYNA were viewed as complimentary to the Muslim Students Association, though they detracted from its previously expansive mission.

The subsequent years were spent solidifying the mission

of the Muslim Students Association and pursuing its ultimate goal of providing a thriving environment of Islamic practice for their constituency, while also exposing the entire academic community to that environment. As Mahmoud Harmoush, former MSA National president explains, "There were three main things that the MSA did to serve college students. It recruited members to serve the MSA and its chapters. Members were required to distribute Islamic material and get involved in training programs, and provide leadership to the campus and campus activities. They were also responsible for securing financial resources."[16]   As such, the MSA's revitalized mission centered around a number of narrowly focused activities, such as establishing Islamic life on campus, promoting interfaith dialogue, and doing additional da'wa work to inform American students at large about Islam, an activity that reached its height up to that point during this era. Not to be neglected is MSA's political activism, which was generally in response to events in the Muslim world, from Afghanistan's struggle against Soviet invasion, the Palestinian resistance to Israeli occupation, which during these years had come to include south Lebanon, and the deepening crisis in Kashmir as events around the world unfolded. Activities included the regular conferences, but with the important addition of issue-oriented lectures, teach-ins, and debates, which often engaged professors and Islamic scholars along with students, as well as protest rallies, marches, and publication of leaflets and booklets explaining the issues from a Muslim perspective. Islamic charities were also a rather important aspect of this era. Though still students, MSA members devoted much of their efforts to collecting contributions from fellow students and alumni to identify and alleviate the causes of Muslim suffering around the world, as was the case with the Afghanistan Relief Fund, stemming from the crisis there, the Syrian relief fund following the Ba'athist atrocities against Islamists, and the Somalia Relief Fund to end the starvation of people there. In the case of Afghanistan, in the year 1980, more than 250,000 pounds of clothing, shoes, and blankets were sent, along with 1000 tents, and 12,000 pounds of medical supplies. In all, tens of thousands of dollars were collected each year toward these causes.[17]

By the close of the decade, though the MSA had established itself as the preeminent organization for Muslim students, with a couple of hundred chapters across North America and over a thousand members, the MSA's activities began to lag behind the events of other groups, especially those responding to current events around the world, such as the outbreak of the Palestinian *Intifada* in 1987, or the fall of the Soviet Union and the subsequent creation of Muslim republics across Central Asia in 1989. Indeed, while the MSA never lagged in providing services and programs to Muslim students, it did begin to face a new crisis of identity at the dawn of the 1990s and once again had to undergo a transformation, though, as opposed to the last one, this was purely on an informal level. The message of the MSA remained the same, but its essence and many features would differ entirely with the beginning of a new era, that of the second generation American Muslim.

The 1990s: The American Muslim Student

This period signaled a new lag in the Muslim student movement, with an especially pointed decline in MSA activity. Though the membership of the MSA was nonetheless experiencing a steady rise, reaching thousands of Muslim students in hundreds of chapters across the country, the overall intensity of the movement was in a state of stagnation. The passion which had fueled the struggle to find a place for Islam had been cooled by the availability of prayer space, meeting halls, halal food programs, and an annual Islamic Awareness Week full of *da'wa* events. The determination to extend their activism toward important causes in the Middle East was suppressed by current events as well as demographic developments within the community. The Gulf War, led by American forces fighting to end Iraq's occupation of Kuwait, completely changed the dynamic of Muslim activism in America. In addition, the U.S.-brokered peace agreement between Palestinian and Israeli leaders in 1993 served to silence the protests against Israeli occupation, despite the implausibility and the unfairness of the deal. These and other events, such as the crisis unfolding in Bosnia-Herzegovina, were the backdrop against which a changing world was marked by a changing community.

At home, the Muslim community in America was experiencing important changes. The makeup of the Muslim Students Association was changing rapidly. No longer was it led by members and presidents coming from foreign lands. Immigration to the United States from Muslim countries had been in steady decline since its peak decades earlier, and the main rise in the population was happening from within. The 1990s was the period for second-generation American Muslims to assert their newfound identity while rising to leadership positions within the MSA structure. The previous generation of immigrants that settled in America and established families were now seeing their children, who had grown up in America, leave for college and take on the responsibility of running the Muslim student movement as their parents once did. This new identity was devoid of many of the old traditions that Muslim immigrants brought with them, and was better able to assimilate to the cultural norms and values of American society. Rather than trying to live an Islamic way of life as foreign students, these young men and women were trying to nurture their Islamic values within an overall American identity. The MSA of this era was not viewed with the same suspicion and derision by mainstream Americans as were previous incarnations. It was not a foreign organization, but simply an extension of America's rich religious tapestry. As such, these young leaders sought to entrench themselves within the American cultural fabric and could do so based on their inherently American upbringing. In addition to the sons and daughters of immigrants, the MSA was increasingly becoming a home to students from America's indigenous Muslim population, led by the nearly two million African-American Muslims.

This transition occurred during the overall transformation of the Muslim community in America toward further integration and political empowerment, led by new organizations such as the American Muslim Council (AMC) and the Council on American-Islamic Relations (CAIR). Changes in the MSA were required to reflect this evolution. On the activities level, there was a relative rise in outreach programs devoted to informing the mainstream campus community on Islam and Muslims, while also stressing the need from within the Muslim students to develop a strong American Muslim identity based on good citizenship, social and political efficacy, and maintaining a strong system of values compatible with American society. The changes were also structural, according to Fatima Mirza, head of MSA National's Restructuring Committee and Secretary of the Washington D.C. Council of MSAs. "In the early 1990s, the MSA began to realize that its structure needed to be reformed in order to keep up with the maturing community. This gave rise to discussions of organizational restructuring so that it could reconnect with individual student members, facilitate student work, advocate for student needs, and engage with domestic and international issues."[18] These efforts crystallized into a reformed constitution and bylaws. The changes also refined the relationship between the national leadership of the MSA and local chapters, in order to maintain certain minimum standards and adhere to the central mission, but with enough freedom to act according to local leaders' judgment.

One major development in this era was the establishment of the Muslim Student Network (MSN) program. Developed by Marghoob and Iffat Qureishi, a couple in Palo Alto, California, the Muslim Student Network was a program designed to bring Muslim students into the public sphere, by offering an annual summer internship program in Washington, D.C. Interns would receive free housing and a stipend while working in government, media, non-profit organizations, or private companies in the nation's capital. Each year, roughly two-dozen young men and women would be selected from the nation's top universities to gain this valuable experience. The living arrangement was also conducive to building strong relationships and the pursuit of extracurricular activities involving Islamic training sessions as well as talks from past MSN alums who have since gone on to accomplish a great deal in the area of public service. The Muslim Student Network's former interns now work as congressional staffers, attorneys with the Department of Justice and in private law firms, and as economic and political consultants, as well as in the media and other such fields that until recently were scarcely populated by American Muslims.

As far as student activism is concerned, the 1990s was a period in which it reached an all-time low. Traditional issue areas such as Palestine and Kashmir had taken a backseat to domestic concerns, partly because MSA members were more distant from the causes, but also because of developments in the Muslim world and the United States. With the ushering in of a new era of relations between East and West, the United States seemed to be at odds with the Muslim world, leading to heightened tensions globally, but also to tensions on America's campuses, where thousands of Muslim students were residing. Following the beginning of the anti-Muslim campaign led by Islamophobes, such as Daniel Pipes and Steven Emerson, activism by Muslim students was put on the defensive and forced to cope with those who feared its potential and wished to destroy the many years of hard work. The MSA responded with greater enthusiasm to pursue its efforts on a national level by launching the movement to help American Muslims engage politically. The fierce debate which took place across mosques and community centers throughout the nation about the plausibility and permissibility of political participation was also a feature of the mid-1990s MSA, but with one distinction. The second-generation American Muslims were much less resistant than their immigrant parents to the notion of engaging themselves politically, and would often differ only in matters of strategy. Voting drives were set up in MSA chapters, and Muslim students were among the first within their community as a whole to meet with their representatives in Congress and other government officials. The Muslim Students Association also took to the forefront of the Muslim civil rights crisis in the mid-1990s, which was dominated by the "secret evidence" trials following the passage of the Anti-Terrorism Act in 1996.

American university campuses have historically been the site of major civil rights struggles, and the Muslim community's fight for its rights would be no exception. Events were held, often sponsored by local MSA chapters, in colleges across the country, especially those located near a secret evidence case. Notable was the University of South Florida and the struggle to end the unjust incarceration of one of its former instructors, Dr. Mazen al-Najjar. These events, organized by the USF MSA's mentor, Professor Sami al-Arian, were used to mobilize the student population in defense of true American values, and as a vehicle to increase the awareness and education of the society at large about issues involving civil rights. Speakers were often invited, including scholars, experts, activists, and members of Congress, to address packed auditoriums at USF and energize them into action. The most successful event took place on a national level, in February, 2000, as Muslim activists from across the United States gathered in the Rayburn Building in Congress for a forum against secret evidence, organized largely by Dr. Al-Arian, featuring dozens of speakers, including many members of Congress. The audience was made up of, among others, hundreds of Muslim students who traveled from far and wide to attend this monumental event signaling the shift in America against secret evidence. The MSA proved to be instrumental in mobilizing grassroots support of young, educated, and active Muslims in the emerging struggle for American Muslim survival.

Leaders and members in the MSA during this period focused much of their activity on combating the racism and anti-Muslim propaganda that was spreading in many academic and social circles. Editorial pages in newspapers and student government meetings became avenues for change, as was discovered by popular columnists Laila el-Haddad and Abdullah al-Arian at Duke University's *The Chronicle* and others, like Ameer Shaikh and Adnan Zulfiqar, former president and vice-president of their local MSA chapter, respectively, who contributed to Emory University's student newspaper. Muslims had begun to branch out from the MSA, becoming elected by their fellow students to offices such as student body president, as occurred at USF in 2003, or becoming appointed as editors-in-chief of their student newspapers, as with Sameer Ahmed, who headed the *Stanford Daily* in 2002. Muslims had achieved such a prominent status as hard-working, socially conscientious, and intellectually bright students that their accomplishments were being noticed in spite of the prevailing anti-Muslim prejudice. In May, 2000, Khurram Baig, then Emory University MSA's president, delivered the oratory speech at the graduation ceremony, in which he addressed the thousands of graduating students on the universal moral principles espoused not only by Islam, but by all the major world religions.

Despite some modest struggles as it searched for a new identity, by the end of the 1990s, the Muslim student movement had reached unprecedented heights. The Muslim Students Association had reached more than 350 colleges and universities in the United States and Canada, attracting thousands of members, operating on a relatively sizeable budget, and making a name for itself both on campus and off within the Muslim community and the American community at large. Even high school students were joining in, with dozens of high schools in many major cities establishing their own chapters of the Muslim Students Association, in which they were trained from an even younger age to live an Islamic lifestyle in a non-Muslim academic environment, so that they could better face the rigors of college life. The future appeared bright for a movement with such humble beginnings nearly four decades earlier.

Activism Revisited

By the beginning of the new millennium, the American Muslim student movement was at its greatest moment. It had a number of important accomplishments to its name. Its appeal was reaching both Muslims and non-Muslims alike, making it the leading outlet for *da'wa* among all Muslim groups. Its activities were finally beginning to reflect an active interest in the affairs of Muslims across the world, while also maintaining a decidedly American identity and mobilizing the grassroots toward political empowerment. Altaf Hussein was serving his term as the President of MSA National during this era. Among the many activities he acknowledged:

> Our many chapters are involved in numerous
> activities, including the establishment of prayer

halls in various campuses, of which we have over one hundred. We are heavily engaged in *da'wa* activity through the publishing and distributing of materials informing about Islam. We also take part in important causes important to all Muslims, such as Palestine, Kashmir, Chechnya, and others, while trying to bring awareness of these issues to all Americans by bringing notable speakers to campuses and holding lectures and forums, including at least four regional conferences in the United States each year, and two in Canada. All of this occurs in an effort to develop a strong Islamic identity capable of serving Muslims and non-Muslims alike.[19]

Hussein acknowledges a more recent trend toward uniting the movement on a more national level, with extra care given to local branches. "The new generation of students has appreciated the need for great unity in action, especially following the weakness suffered in recent years. Following the lack of unity and central purpose, all agreed that unifying the effort was of vital importance."[20] In 2000, the Muslim student movement did just that, as it became heavily engaged in the political process, especially the onset of the presidential elections that fall. Young Muslims, most of them first-time voters, took to the polls to voice their concern about the status of Muslim civil rights and hoping for a more solidified and certain future in which they can live and thrive in freedom. Indeed, thousands of Muslim students participated in the first-ever Muslim voting bloc, signaling the beginning of a new era of American Muslim political involvement. Many even abandoned their traditional party affiliation to vote for a Republican candidate, just to maintain the unity of the community during this uneasy period.

Middle East Peace through Justice

The new millennium also marked the return of one of the MSA's traditional issue areas to the forefront. As the Peace Process slowly proved to be a failure to bring justice to the people in the region, the humanitarian crisis unfolding in the Holy Land became a major concern of the American Muslim student movement. According to Hussein, this began with one major event, which signaled the Al-Aqsa Intifada.

> Following [Ariel] Sharon's attempted desecration of the blessed Al-Aqsa Mosque, we immediately established a special committee called the Jerusalem Committee, which serves to inform students of the importance of Jerusalem in Islam and the necessity to defend it. This was followed by actual development of strategies to educate non-Muslims on the issue and how to produce effective responses to media attacks and anti-Palestinian propaganda. This is what drew the ire and concern of pro-Israel groups, as Jewish students did not initially know how to respond, and their reactions were often rooted in emotion and reflected a real ignorance of the issue.[21]

Also important during this period was the convergence of the Muslim student activist movement with the agenda of other activist and human rights circles, often involving leftist progressive groups. This alliance generated much buzz and activity surrounding issues of civil rights, minority rights, racial, religious and economic inequality, and the plight of Iraqis under sanctions and Palestinians under occupation. With regard to the issue of Palestine, a new movement was developed, not under the traditional rubric of Islamic activism, as it had come to be known in the United States and elsewhere, but under the umbrella of the general progressive movement, with a long history of activism in America. Modeled on the protest movement against the Apartheid regime in South Africa during the early 1980s, the new campaign was geared toward economic divestment from Israel in opposition to its continued occupation and gross human rights violations, the latest of which involved the construction of an apartheid wall.

The divestment campaign, as it came to be called, began as purely a student movement, led by both Muslim and non-Muslim students at most major colleges and universities, but led by particularly powerful efforts at a few universities, including the University of California at Berkeley, with its rich history of political and social advocacy, the University of Michigan at Ann Arbor, with a higher than average Arab and Muslim population, and other schools such as Ohio State University and Rutgers University in New Jersey. The divestment campaign had a simple message and clearly defined goals that were well within its reach. It sought an economic boycott by their universities of major multinational corporations as well as small companies that do business with the Israeli government, especially ones as blatantly complicit in the destruction of Palestinian lives as Catapillar, which manufactures the bulldozers responsible for the demolition of hundreds of Palestinian homes in the West Bank and Gaza on a regular basis. The divestment campaign was successful in uniting numerous student groups, including the MSA, under a common theme. Petitions circulated at numerous campuses, generating tens of thousands of signatures from students, faculty, and staff. The debate, which until recently had focused on vilifying Palestinians as terrorists and opposed to any peace settlement, was finally beginning to take into account Israel's culpability in creating Palestinian suffering. Lectures, seminars, and teach-ins discussed the issue at length. The pages of campus newspapers were filled with coverage of these events and opinion pieces discussing the movement's merits and shortcomings. An annual national conference was devoted entirely to the divestment campaign, meeting for the first time at Berkeley in 2001.

The divestment campaign picked up much steam in its early months, which inevitably meant that it would face a rise in opposition from pro-Israel groups, many of which were beginning finally to tap into their campus population, primarily of Jewish, Evangelical Christian, and radical conservative students. Wealthy donors and noted political figures pressured many universities to restrain the divestment campaign and ban it outright. But while university officials could not do that, they did release strong statements denouncing the movement and its goals, while anti-divestment groups circulated their own petitions repudiating the campaign and declaring solidarity with Israel. Lawrence Summers, the Jewish president of Harvard University, began issuing warnings about a rise in anti-

Semitism, condemning the divestment campaign as people "advocating actions anti-Semitic in effect if not in intent."[22]

Powerful lobby groups led by the American Israeli Public Affairs Committee (AIPAC) began active recruitment of university students to counter the message being delivered by the grassroots activist movement about the truth in the Middle East conflict. Oftentimes, AIPAC will even sponsor trips to Israel to indoctrinate students with the militant Zionism they observe there and build a strong personal and emotional connection with young American Jews that has been severely lacking in recent years. The response has clearly been one of worried anxiety about the ground being made up by groups advocating justice for Palestinians. According to one report, "In response to this, Jewish organizations that work with students have retooled their Israel-advocacy programs and allocated more resources for them. Hillel, for example, is sending Israel advocacy interns to 40 campuses to help the existing staff, while also holding intensive leadership training programs over the summer, sending some students to Israel for seminars."[23] The same report goes on to mention the creation of the Israel on Campus Coalition, "a group which is bringing together some 20 national Jewish organizations (including Hillel) to coordinate their Israel propaganda and education efforts."[24] The reactionary nature of this movement is best summed up by the words of Lynn Schusterman, president of the Oklahoma-based Charles and Lynn Schusterman Family Foundation. "Given the grave crisis in Israel and the resurgence of anti-Israel activity on college campuses, it is vitally important that the community join forces to develop a unified approach to educating and training students to support and defend Israel."[25] Schusterman also happened to be funding this initiative with a $250,000 contribution for 2003. In contrast to the pro-Palestinian activism which operates on nominal funds, the pro-Israel sponsorship is a bottomless well.

In the aftermath of 9/11, the attacks on Muslim and progressive activism would increase dramatically. Campus Watch, a website that blacklists and intimidates students, professors, and university departments, was established by notorious Islamophobes Daniel Pipes and Martin Kramer. Pipes and his cohorts continuously attacked the MSA as one of the leading organizations taking a strong stance on the Palestinian issue. He has described the group as "a fifth column," as extremist, and as a supporter of terror with "Wahhabi" ties and even alleged direct ties with the Saudi government. Under the cloud of false allegations, the MSA has struggled to maintain its stance and its prominent position on Palestine, among many other issues.

In spite of these challenges to their efforts, the leaders of the movement would not be deterred. The divestment campaign proceeded to produce more published material and organize many additional events, including an annual national conference in each of the next two years. Through it all, the Muslim Students Association and the collective body of Muslims at universities and colleges across America have played an instrumental role in bringing this vital issue to the fore of public attention.

9/11: Shattered Idealism

In spite of all of the many achievements, accomplishments, and advancements in status that the Muslim Students Association had made in the years leading up to 9/11,

• Demonstrators at U.C. Berkeley, California, 2003

• Muslim students participate in the massive demonstration by International ANSWER.

nothing in the world could have prepared it for the events of September 11, 2001. On that morning, college students across the nation, Muslim and non-Muslim, saw their world shattered forever. In the case of American Muslims, however, they suffered a dual blow, not only having to watch the devastating attacks on their country, but also fearing the reprisals by their overzealous compatriots seeking vengeance.

The university environment immediately following the 9/11 attacks had two faces. On the one hand, America's academic community was viewed as a safe haven from the ignorance plaguing most Americans about the events in general and Muslims in particular. University administrators in every college took care to speak out against hate crimes and enter immediately into a phase of collective healing, using interfaith prayer vigils and so forth. Muslim students could count on their non-Muslim friends for consolation and support, while professors were often understanding and happy to lend a hand of support to the new targets of discrimination. On the other hand, living in such close quarters among non-Muslims, and in such a young environment, Muslim students, especially those from other countries, were quite often the most at risk to be subjected to verbal insults, physical abuse, and other hate crimes. Leaders of the MSA, Altaf Hussein recalls, turned to political advocacy groups such as CAIR and the American Civil Liberties Union (ACLU) for help and guidance during this difficult time. "As the MSA, however, we took it upon ourselves to educate Muslim students on how to respond to the events, how to handle media requests for interviews, how to deal with an overreaching law enforcement official, and generally on their rights as citizens of this country."[26]

There was also a fear, according to Hussein, that more Muslims among the student population would forego their Islamic identity following 9/11, for fear of being singled out and targeted. Now more than ever, it appeared that unity in the face of adversity was necessary to keep these young men, and especially women, given their particular vulnerability, strong and unified.

In the aftermath of September 11, there were certainly many assaults on Muslim students, both verbal and physical. At the University of South Florida, Muslim girls reported being harassed, spit on, and having their scarves tugged by rowdy groups of men. At one New Jersey school, a prayer room was vandalized. Anti-Muslim graffiti was commonplace, especially on signs and fliers posted by local MSA members. At the same time, it is the community of Muslim students that truly rose to the occasion to defend Islam and the unending assaults on their religion and their people that became commonplace across the airwaves. At Georgetown University, students Nada Unus, Laila al-Arian, an editor of the campus newspaper, and Uwais Balti, that MSA chapter's president, were interviewed for a positive feature on the ABC program "Nightline." Muslim students from Occidental College in Los Angeles appeared on another ABC program, "Politically Incorrect with Bill Moyer," to discuss current events and defend Islam against attacks from all directions, including from the host of the show himself. At New York University, only minutes from the site of the World Trade Center, MSA president Haroon Moghul was beleaguered with requests for interviews and responses to attacks from anti-Muslim bigots who truly capitalized on the moment to demand the elimination of any Muslim presence in America. Moghul responded admirably, leading his MSA to a strong showing both in the press and among New Yorkers.

Ultimately, the attacks of September 11 inevitably proved devastating to the entire Muslim community in the United States, but the population of Muslim students, given its more tolerant and limited environment, was arguably the most able to respond and proceed on the road to steady recovery in image and public standing. In September, 2002, one year following the attacks, the annual MSA national conference was held in Washington, D.C., where several thousand MSA students attended in order to regroup and develop a single message. Moreover, when the antiwar movement emerged as a response to the Pentagon's determination to attack a defenseless Middle Eastern nation, MSA-National was among the first to join the Steering Committee of the International ANSWER Coalition that led the major antiwar demonstrations. Also, MSA was a member of the National Youth and Student Peace Coalition (NYSPC). Roughly forty years following the initial establishment of the Muslim Students Association, it was clear that the organization, built on such humble beginnings, had accomplished more than anyone could ever have envisioned. The mood at this conference, however, was somber, given the increased civil rights crisis in the community and such new policies as registration of Muslim immigrants and the interviewing of thousands of Arab men. Most of the men in these instances were students. Still though, in spite of the difficult times, there was also a sense that the MSA, led by a renewed optimism in its mission and its members, would once again resume its leadership position in the Muslim community and build a place for Muslims in America. ■

PROFILE: MUSLIMS FROM THE MARGINS
TO THE MAINSTREAM

• Interfaith Roundtable at UASR

• Abdul Rahman Alamoudi,
American Muslim Foundation

• Demonstration for Bosnia

• Professor Ali Mazrui
Binghamton University

• AMJ Rallies for Palestine

• Laila al-Marayati, M.D.
Muslim Women's League

Chapter 3

INSTITUTIONALIZING MUSLIM ACTIVISM

History will record that as the second millennium drew to a close, Muslims in North America were coming of age—their numbers had grown enough to allow them to establish a local presence in every major city and town, and they had shown all the signs of determination to carve a space for themselves in the continent's pluralistic mosaic.

—Mohamed Nimer, *The North American Muslim Resource Guide: Muslim Community Life in the United States and Canada.*

American society has had a longstanding tradition of community organization and activism to institute political change. Each segment of society has looked after its own interests by becoming organized and getting involved in civic and political affairs. Muslims have become targets of vicious bigotry, prejudice, harassment, and discrimination, which have posed a difficult challenge. Negative and hostile experiences compelled American Muslims to establish

---

This chapter was inspired by a paper written by Professor Ghulam Hanif and published in the *Middle East Affairs Journal*, vol. 9, no. 1-2, Winter/Spring 2003.

organizations to safeguard their rights, to combat bigotry and Islamophobia and, ultimately, to change public perceptions and attitudes regarding their religion.

American Muslim Council

The first organization to surface in the public arena at the national level was the American Muslim Council (AMC). Established in 1990, the AMC became an advocate for the community, lobbying on its behalf at the centers of power. It provided the opportunity for its director of legal affairs, Dr. Robert D. Crane, in 1992 to form the Muslim American Bar Association, now very active as the National Association of Muslim Lawyers, designed to organize free legal services and to join with the American Bar Association in shaping the civil rights movement in America and both articulating and promoting a full spectrum of human rights in America.

During a decade of dedicated efforts, the AMC become known within the political circles of Washington. In conjunction with other bodies, the AMC was instrumental in having the Muslim community of America recognized and its representatives invited regularly to important meetings in the White House.[1] Led by its first executive director, Abdurahman Alamoudi, the AMC set out to establish itself as a link between the American Muslim community and their political leaders. "From the beginning," Alamoudi declared, "the primary mandate of the AMC has been political advocacy on behalf of American Muslims before the three branches of the federal government: executive, legislative, and judicial. These activities included intense lobbying campaigns that garnered the attention of a number of political leaders. While the AMC

• Chairman Alamoudi addresses audience at AMC National Conference, Washington, D.C., April 1997.

• AMC members from across the nation participate in AMC's national conference.

• AMC National Leadership Conference for Imams, Directors and Board Members of Islamic Centers, Washington, D.C., April 26-29, 2002.

could not boast much legislative success in its early years, many policy-makers in Washington took notice of the Muslim community's emerging involvement in the decision-making process. This led to a number of meetings with high-ranking officials, including members of Congress and the President. For the first time in history, politicians expressed their verbal support for modest policy initiatives brought forward by Muslim leaders. Realizing that a new political constituency was taking root, the two major parties would eventually compete for its support."[2]

Muslim Public Affairs Council

The idea of involvement in the political process was initially explored by another organization, the Muslim Public Affairs Council (MPAC). It was launched in 1988 as a regional operation confined to Southern California, but it expanded a decade later when it set up an office in the nation's capital. The MPAC is oriented toward grassroots politics and has supported friendly candidates for election at all levels of government. Its foremost objective is to encourage Muslims to become activists and get involved in the political process.[3] It has billed itself as the "progressive voice for American Muslims." "It has established this reputation, in part, because of its success in creating alliances with groups outside of the Muslim community, a feat all of the political organizations have attempted, but with mixed results. The MPAC has also had success in media outreach, gaining access to the American public to inform them about Islam and promote its policy positions. Membership in MPAC is still largely regional, with limited reach outside of the West Coast."[4] Its founder, Maher Hathout, established it as an innovation from the norm of Muslim organizations by being more outward looking and action-oriented. Aside from publishing frequent position papers, MPAC undertakes some lobbying efforts with regard to specific issue areas, among them protecting civil liberties, combating hate crimes and anti-Muslim bias, and U.S. policy toward Palestine and Kashmir.

The Muslim American Society (MAS)

According to its brochure, the MAS was established in 1962 under the name "The Culture Society." It remained until 1998 as an informal movement headquarters aimed at carrying the correct and comprehensive message of Islam and its beliefs to Muslims and non-Muslims in North America. The members of the Society established several Islamic organizations and institutions that have been contributing to the advancement of Islam in the North American continent. The best examples of such organizations are the Muslim Students Association of the United States and Canada, the Muslim Arab Youth Association, and the Islamic Society of North America, known as ISNA.[5]

The MAS is dedicated to building Muslim religious centers in a Western society, and therefore has embarked on a mission aimed at a coherent reconciliation of the Muslim and Western worlds. According to its brochure, following the model of Hassan al Banna, "The society has about three hundred small study circles spread over seventy-eight cities in the form of chapters. MAS chapters serve as a catalyst to initiate, coordinate, and supervise the local Islamic fieldwork carried out by the Islamic centers and Islamic schools."[6]

Because the group works with the grassroots, the leaders believe their mission must be seen as a long-term project of a global nature. MAS has concluded that the goal of instilling an Islamic character in persons and communities does not necessarily imply any set of political convictions. Thus the group encourages its members to participate fully in American society and advocates accommodation with all that is best in America in order to preserve their local culture for converts to Islam.[7]

This body represents in the United States the American version of the ideals of *Ikhwan al Muslimeen*, the Muslim Brotherhood. The aim of MAS clearly is to encourage the revival of Islam in its pristine form and to garner support among Muslims in the United States for the Islamic movements around the world.

Like some of the preceding organizations discussed above, MAS since 1999 has put out a glossy publication *The American Muslim*. This should be distinguished from the highly intellectual and somewhat Sufi-oriented journal, *The American Muslim*, which was put out by American-born, primarily Euro-American converts from 1989 to 1995 in paper and from 2001 until the present on the internet at www.theamericanmuslim.org.

In the year 2000, the MAS Youth Center was launched in Brooklyn, New York, in order to cater to the growing Muslim teen population. At the same time, MAS sponsored the establishment of the Islamic American University, a distance-learning program of classical Islamic studies over the internet with administrative offices in Southfield, Michigan, and Kansas City, Missouri.[8]

MAS and ICNA have grown closer together as they recognize that they share the mission of promoting a strong

• MAS Annual Convention, Chicago, Illinois, 2002.

• MAS secretary-General Shakir El-Sayyed and Shura Member Jamal Badawi.

• MAS hosts the First National Council of Imams and Islamic Centers on March 27, 2004, Alexandria, Virginia.

sense of Muslim identity. Since survival as Muslims seems to be an overriding priority, the largely Arab MAS and the largely south-Asian ICNA acknowledge that their ethnic and homeland differences are bound to become less important than their common destiny as Muslims in North America. Now members of ICNA and MAS undergo the same training, which is designed to develop a model Muslim who is health-conscious, devoted to one's faith and community, well-versed in the Islamic sciences of knowledge, and well-acquainted with the contemporary conditions of the Muslim world, especially in North America.[9]

Council on American-Islamic Relations

The notion of protecting rights and fighting harassment, discrimination, stereotyping, and defamation became the specialty of the Council on American-Islamic Relations

• CAIR's staff at the capital headquarters in Washington, D.C.

(CAIR). Founded in 1994 by Nihad Awad, a former activist in the Islamic Association for Palestine (IAP), CAIR is widely supported by Muslims since it has confronted media bias head-on and doggedly fought against bigotry and prejudice. There is some indication to suggest that, as a result of CAIR's activities, a degree of change has been introduced into the world of media journalism. In addition, CAIR continuously intercedes on behalf of victims of discrimination and has obtained favorable settlements in many cases. The organization champions the rights of Muslims from the local to the national level, and attempts to find relief for the victims of hate crimes. It has also worked on behalf of Jewish and Christian adherents to secure their rights to religious freedom in the public sphere.[10] Its development really emerged following the realization that:

> With increased participation and involvement in the larger society came incidents of backlash and discrimination. While most of the organizations were intent on advancing the Muslim agenda, CAIR was more interested in protecting the community's rights by responding to specific incidents across the country. ... CAIR functions primarily as a watchdog group by having a coordinated response to incidents of hate crime, discrimination in the workplace, and anti-Muslim rhetoric in the media or from political leaders. With a prominent national office in Washington, D.C., and twenty operationally independent chapters across

the country, CAIR prides itself on giving
voice to a voiceless minority in American
society and defending the rights of those who
cannot defend themselves. The community
becomes effectively empowered with
organized action alerts and mobilizing efforts
coming from the CAIR leadership in order
to address crises from a grassroots level.
Moreover, CAIR has been extremely
effective especially in addressing specific
cases reported by its large constituency.
Founders Omar Ahmad, Ibrahim Hooper,
and Nihad Awad pride themselves on
building immense credibility with the
Muslim community at large. Additionally,
CAIR publishes annual reports of its
activities, along with documentation on the
status of Muslim civil rights that chronicles
abuses and recommends reforms.[11]

American Muslim Alliance

Two years after the AMC was established, a charismatic and
energetic political science professor in California founded
the American Muslim Alliance. Agha Saeed had been a
long-time activist and a visionary of widespread Muslim
political participation that went beyond voting and
lobbying. "Our main goal is to organize Muslims in the
mainstream of public affairs, civic discourse, and political
party activity in all fifty states. We believe that political
power is not a function of numbers alone but is a combined

product of initiative, innovation, and determination. We need to transform our pent-up frustration, anger, and pain into creative and meaningful steps for self-empowerment."[12] With Saeed as its chairman, the AMA quickly spread across the country with chapters forming in all major Muslim population centers. To date, the AMA claims 98 chapters in 31 states. This emphasis on grassroots mobilization is particular to AMA as it seeks not only to encourage members to vote in elections, but even to become candidates themselves in local, state, and national government. This effort to promote the involvement of Muslims in electoral politics at the grassroots has occurred only under the indefatigable leadership of Professor Agha Saeed. He has worked relentlessly, mostly in cooperation with the AMC and other organizations, to get Muslims elected to various political offices.[13]

American Muslim Political Coordination Council

These four organizations, working under an umbrella coordinating body, developed the American Muslim Political Coordination Council (AMPCC). In the midst of the struggle for their civil rights, American Muslims learned a number of hard lessons. The first was the realization that any community that is not politically represented is vulnerable to the government's abuses. A former Executive Director of the AMC, Aly Abuzaakouk, explains, "The more we participate, the more people will listen to us. We want our community to play politics, starting from the Parent-Teacher Associations and continuing to Pennsylvania Avenue in the nation's capital. We tell them, if you are voteless, you are weightless in this society." From their experience in combating secret evidence and other civil liberties abuses, Muslim leaders would learn how to advance a political platform. Politicians in Washington, they discovered, responded to two things: money and votes. The result was a push to establish American Muslims in both of these areas. As a wealthy community known for its generosity, an effort was made to redirect much of the resources from traditional causes to more urgent political campaigns.[14]

By the fall of 2000, under Agha Saeed as chairman, the AMPCC decided to throw its weight behind a candidate in the upcoming presidential election. Following a heightened debate within the community culminating in a powerful statement against secret evidence by George W. Bush in the second of three presidential debates, the AMPCC decided to endorse the Republican candidate for the presidency in the elections of 2000. The AMPCC endorsement had a widespread impact on the Muslim community, encouraging many to register to vote and then participate in the elections. According to CAIR exit polling, overwhelming numbers of Muslim voters in the area of suburban mosques, 72 percent to be exact, cast their ballot for George Bush. The AMPCC endorsement was listed as the major reason why Florida Muslims voted for the Republican candidate. In Florida, the state that ultimately decided the election, the role of Muslims was not to be underestimated. Following concerted efforts by a leading activist professor, Sami al-Arian, Florida's Muslim community delivered the presidency to George W. Bush handily. A study in that state demonstrated that of the roughly 24,000 Muslims who voted in the general election, 78 percent voted for Bush. More telling, however, is that 69 percent reported that they voted as part of the Muslim voting bloc. In fact, only 30 percent of Florida Muslims are registered as Republicans, yet two and a half times that figure supported the Republican candidate. Although 43 percent are registered as Democrats, only 16 percent voted for Al Gore.[15]

Ultimately, while they cooperate in pursuing a common goal, each of the four constituent organizations of AMPCC has its own particular niche and separate agenda.[16] The founders of AMC, MPAC, CAIR and AMA were already in contact with one another even before their organizations began to address concerns together. As activists in the American Muslim community they have maintained personal relationships with one another and have cooperated in lobbying efforts and political involvement at the highest levels.

Other Organizations

As the Muslim understanding of the political process has deepened, additional groups have appeared on the scene. The recently established American Muslims for Jerusalem (AMJ) is one of them. Others include the Islamic Institute (II), which is an arm of the Republican Party, led by Muslim Republican insider Khalid Saffuri, and Muslim Americans for Global Peace and Justice (MAGPJ), founded to lobby for social justice by building interfaith coalitions. In several communities social and political action groups have sprung up in response to local conditions. These motivate Muslims to become activists at the grassroots level.

Another local organization of particular note is the United Muslim American Association (UMAA), founded in 1999 to encourage Muslims at the grassroots to become active in politics. Based in the greater Chicago area, it has endorsed a number of candidates for political offices at the local, state, and national levels. In the 2000 elections, 38 of the 42 candidates endorsed by UMAA won, even as some controversy flared due to its endorsements. Having learned from experience, two years later it was even more active in the elections of 2002 by educating Muslims and providing them with voter guides. It claims to have mobilized 50,000 voters in and around the city of Chicago and entered into a coalition with other organizations in support of several candidates. When the final results were in, 43 of the 57 candidates it endorsed won in the general election. Located in a pivotal city with a large Muslim population, UMAA seems to be emerging as an important civic action organization.

In response to a growing need and desire among indigenous Muslims to craft an organizational structure and initiate a movement that would speak from the unique perspectives of the indigenous community, while addressing grass roots communal needs, the Muslim Alliance of North America (MANA) was established in 2001. The Alliance is headed by Imam Siraj Wahhaj, and is based in New York. In 2003 MANA published its first issue of the newspaper *Grassroots*.

In February, 2004, The American Muslim Task Force was formed. The Task Force is an umbrella group for the American Muslim Alliance, the Council on American Islamic Relations, the Islamic Circle of North America, and the Muslim Alliance of North America. Other groups under this umbrella include the Islamic Circle of North America, Muslim American Society, Muslim Public Affairs Council, Muslim Student Association, and Project Islamic Hope. The groups' objective is to organize Muslim American political activism in the year 2004 presidential election.

Intra-Faith Organizations

The growth of outreach efforts to non-Muslims after 9/11 was accompanied by in-reach among Muslims from the external periphery of divergent practice to the central care of universal understanding. This new ecumenical movement spawned the founding of what was widely recognized as the first ever global summit of Shia Muslims, primarily from Pakistan, Iran, and Iraq. The Universal Muslim Association of America held the first annual UMAA Convention on May 23-25, 2003, in Washington, D.C. The Under Secretary of Defense, Paul Wolfowitz, in his banquet speech urged the nearly 3,000 Muslims present to overcome the parochial forces that threatened to divide Muslims in both Iraq and America. The second UMAA convention on May 28-30th, 2004, highlighted the common threads of justice in Shia, Sunni, Jewish and Christian tradition.

The twelve objectives of UMAA are similar to those of other national Muslim organizations and serve UMAA's official mission, which is: "To provide a forum to foster unity among Muslims, to encourage Muslims to participate in civic and political responsibilities, to dispel misgivings about Islam and the Muslims and help fellow Americans better understand Islam in the light of the Qur'an and the teachings and practice of the Prophet Muhammad (ﷺ) and his Ahlul Bayt (a), and take all necessary measures to help implement the UMAA Objectives that, among other things, include social, religious, economic and political advancement of Muslims in America.

Muslim Think-Tanks

During the 1990s several attempts were made to establish Muslim centers for public policy research, designed to influence policy making indirectly by shaping paradigms of thought, but the intellectual gap between potential donors and the policy analysts caused every one to fail for lack of funds. The sole exception is the first of these policy research centers, the United Association for Studies and Research (UASR), which was initiated by several Palestinian intellectuals in 1989 to serve as an association of independent research centers to coordinate outreach of the general Muslim community with American academia and public policymakers.[17] Beginning with the first Gulf War in the early 1990s, the UASR maintained a sophisticated media monitoring program, but shifted then to personal outreach through forums and publications. Over the years the UASR has organized roundtable discussions with U.S. officials, academics, policy advisors, Muslim activists, and scholars serving as panelists. Since 1992, the UASR has produced an internationally acclaimed quarterly publication, the *Middle East Affairs Journal*, and has published more than 100 occasional and policy papers by Muslim and non-Muslim academics.

From its founding in 1989 in Chicago and its move in

• UASR Interfaith Roundtable with Ed Miller

• Joint Conference with Georgetown University's Center for Muslim Christian Understanding (CMCU), April 2000.

• Anisa Abdulfattah, UASR Media Director speaks at a symposium, Washington, D.C.

1991 to its own building in Annandale, Virginia, outside the nation's capital, the UASR has kept its focus narrowed to the relations between Western countries and Islamic movements, including those involved in the Israeli-Palestinian conflict. This intellectual journal also presents perspectives on country-specific and regional dynamics, as well as on global strategic issues, including the role of Muslim intellectuals in shaping the premises of thought that shape the American foreign policy agenda and the role of this agenda in managing global policies.[18]

In treating the dynamics of life in the Holy Land, its conferences of Muslim leaders, academics, and other think-tank professionals, including such non-Muslims as Daniel Pipes, focus on the religious dimension. It has given special attention to the rise of Hamas within Palestinian society, but declines to take a position on its future or on any specific recommendation for bringing peace through justice.

Perhaps its greatest contribution to mutual understanding has been the UASR's success in facilitating a dialogue between Islamic leaders and Western analysts and policy advisors through its seminars and writings. Although it covers the role of NGOs in working with grass-roots social and civic associations, as well as the effectiveness of education policies promoted by Islamic revivalist groups, it restricts its focus to the broad political implications that face American long-range forecasters and policy planners, especially from the point of view of what is best for America. For this reason, its outreach and products have been in much demand by specialists in Middle Eastern studies.

Short-lived think-tanks like the Center for Public Policy Research and the Islamic Institute for Strategic Studies, both started by former White House official, Dr. Robert D.

Crane, as well as other outreach organizations who rented office space in UASR's building during the late 1990s, failed to survive.

Three other think-tanks were organized in the mid-1990s, but never succeeded in obtaining even initial funding. The first one, organized in Chicago, published a book and then went into eclipse. The two others, both in California, survive on an on-again-off-again basis. One is Syed Rifaat Mahmud's American Institute of International Studies, based in Union City, California. The other currently more active one is Marghoub Quraishi's Strategic Research Foundation in Palo Alto, which started a 15-page publication in 2001, entitled *Geopolitics Review*.

Muslim Research Centers

As indicated above, despite the rapid growth of the Muslim community in America, or perhaps because of it, the area of research and scholarship is still in a state of underdevelopment. Survey findings indicate that the general level of educational achievement among Muslims is very high, although it is lopsidedly heavy in technical and scientific fields, to the neglect of scholarship in social sciences and humanities. Social science professionals are still in short supply, although this is beginning to change with second-generation American Muslims.

Nevertheless, the first Muslim research center, the International Institute of Islamic Thought (IIIT), was established by former members of the MSA in 1981 to research and promote the "Islamization of knowledge." To date it has published a wealth of material on the topics of its concern and has continued to make contributions to the revival of Islamic learning through a variety of means. Closely related, yet different, is the Council on Islamic Education (CIE), which provides academic information about Islam, Muslims, and world history to educational professionals and policymakers. Founded in 1990, it has become an important center housing information, services, and resources on Islam for K-12 textbook publishers, state education officials, curriculum developers, and teachers. Owing to the existence of CIE, the textbook publishing industry for primary and secondary schools is undergoing a revolutionary change through the inclusion of material on Islam in a balanced and sensitive manner.

The Muslim concern with liberty and the free market economy, both here and abroad, inspired the founding in the mid-nineties of the Minaret of Freedom Institute (MFI). During the past few years, the MFI has published a number of research studies authored mostly by its founder, Imad-ad-Dean Ahmad. Seminars and academic meetings are held each year to explore the ideas of liberty for Muslim societies in the contemporary world.

The concern with the lack of democracy in the Muslim world has led to the founding of the Center for the Study of Islam and Democracy (CSID). As a think tank established in the earlier part of the nineties, just when Muslims were beginning to become involved in civic and political affairs, the CSID concentrates on research and the study of democracy in the context of Islam. Each year this academic institute organizes several scholarly meetings where research papers are presented. In its short history it has attracted considerable interest among academics. For the first time in 2003 the CSID organized several workshops in the Muslim countries where this type of experience is sorely needed. It publishes a quarterly journal, *The Muslim Democrat*.

Seeking to encourage Muslim youth to become active in community affairs, a well-known Islamic personality, Marghoub Quraishi, founded the American Muslims Intent on Learning and Activism (AMILA) on the West coast in 1992. This body is dedicated to the spiritual enrichment of the younger generation through involvement in community service. Seminars and discussions are organized and research projects undertaken as a means of fostering intellectual freedom among the young people.

The Center for Understanding Islam (CUI) was founded by Drs. Ali Chaudry and Robert D. Crane as a grass-roots organization to help imams and Muslims generally in northern New Jersey present Islam effectively both to Muslims and the general public. Its speakers address mosques all over New Jersey, make presentations to colleges, boards of education, and police academies, and participate in various interfaith activities. Its president, Ali Chaudry, retired in 2000 as CFO (Chief Financial Officer) of AT&T after thirty years, and in 2004 was elected mayor of Bernardsville, New Jersey, perhaps the only Muslim mayor elected after 9/11 in America. The objective behind the work of the CUI is both in-reach (to Muslims) and outreach (to non-Muslims) in order to help correct distortions in the understanding of Islam and to erase biases against it.

Glimpses of Progress

Mainstream media attention paid to Muslim communities, besides appearing sporadically in localized media reports, first emerged in 1991 when a Muslim religious personality,

Imam Siraj Wahhaj, opened a session of the U.S. House of Representatives with a prayer. The following year, Warith Deen Muhammad gave the invocation at the opening of a Senate session. Since then, this practice has been repeated in the Congress and adopted by a number of state legislatures. During the last year of his administration, President George Bush used the phrase "churches, synagogues, and mosques" for the first time ever by a public official. In 1992, he also issued a message to the Muslim community on the occasion of Ramadan.

These practices have subsequently become routine, and later even the President began to reach out to the Muslim community. During the administration of President Bill Clinton, several Islamic occasions were celebrated at the White House, including the annual holiday marking the end of Ramadan. These have been observed under the presidency of George W. Bush, with additional Ramadan dinners being organized by cabinet secretaries, as was done

• American Muslim leaders unveil the first American postal stamp to commemorate the Islamic holiday of Eid.

in 2002 by Secretary of State Colin Powell and Secretary of Treasury Paul O'Neil.

The Muslim community is now accepted as a part of the American landscape, though prejudice and bigotry continue to hamper the lives of individual followers of Islam. The tragic events of 9/11 have become an albatross around the neck of the Muslim community, drawing sad and unfortunate comments by numerous commentators. The tragedy has also made the community known throughout the world. It is as though Americans have suddenly become aware of Islam in the United States. In an oblique way, the fallout from the tragedy has also galvanized the Muslims to become activists and seek accommodation in mainstream American society, even though the local Muslims as financial supporters of their work have had to struggle against their own fears of retaliation for their courage.

Conclusion

The narrative presented in this chapter indicates the emergence of a vibrant Muslim community in America during the last decade. Today, Muslims are visible on the national scene, increasingly present in the public square, and active in building their communities under the media spotlight. They numbered less than ten thousand at the end of the Second World War, in contrast to approximately seven million today.[19] At the mid-century mark, outside of the inner cities, Islamic institutions were virtually non-existent except for three or four mosques that functioned intermittently at best. Fifty years later, institutions of Muslims have proliferated, with numerous organizations, schools, charitable bodies, and mosques thriving across the nation. Much credit for laying the groundwork for a Muslim presence in America rightfully goes to the students who, fired by zeal and enthusiasm for an Islamic revival, launched the Muslim Students Association (MSA). This organization has actually proved to be the progenitor of most political activism in North America. The pursuit of Islamic goals would not have been possible had it not been for the freedom that exists in America. The following section, however, will explore the hurdles that have since emerged and the exploitation of that freedom by some in society wishing to bring an end to these mild and major successes in the hopes of advancing a racist agenda harmful to the America that the world has come to know. ■

• Dr. Anwar Hajjaj, MAS Da'wa Committee, leads interfaith dialogue.

Part Two

THE AGENTS
OF ISLAMOPHOBIA

What matters to 'experts' like Miller, Samuel Huntington, Martin Kramer, Bernard Lewis, Daniel Pipes, Steven Emerson, and Barry Rubin, plus a whole battery of Israeli academics, is to make sure that the 'threat' is kept before our eyes, the better to excoriate Islam for terror, despotism, and violence, while assuring themselves profitable consultancies, frequent TV appearances, and book contracts. The Islamic threat is made to seem disproportionately fearsome, lending support to the thesis (which is an interesting parallel to anti-Semitic paranoia) that there is a worldwide conspiracy behind every explosion.

—Edward W. Said, "A Devil Theory of Islam,"
The Nation, August 12, 1996.

THE AGENTS OF ISLAMOPHOBIA

Since last summer, apologists for Israel's "right" to be a racist state (and to use whatever violence it can muster in defence of that "right") have begun a campaign of defamation against anyone in the U.S. academy who dares to question any Israeli action or practice. This campaign is part of a larger effort to discredit U.S. universities as arenas for independent scholarship and thought. It also aims to delegitimise universities who refuse to serve the interests of either the national security state or the Israeli government. The fact that those spearheading this campaign are almost exclusively part of a large conglomerate known as the pro-Israel lobby in the U.S. is hardly surprising. Since 11 September, the campaign has expanded to include any academic who believes that Islam is not a terroristic evil religion bent on murdering the "civilised," and that Muslims and Arabs are humans who are entitled to civil, political, and human rights in their own countries as well as in the United States.

—Professor Joseph Massad, Columbia University,
Al Ahram Weekly, April 10-16, 2003.

All evidence suggests that the anti-Muslim campaign in America is the product of a complex, dynamic relationship among a set of political interest groups who believe their diverse goals are furthered by the denigration of Islam or Muslims. These interest groups are quite frequently at odds with each other on core issues, but cooperate with one another on the common strategy of attempting to frame Islam and Muslims as entities that inherently pose a danger to the United States and its citizens.

The most important of these interest groups is the pro-Israel lobby. Israel's primary interest in smearing Islam is derived from its overwhelming need to eliminate domestic American opposition to pro-Israeli policies, both by weakening American Muslim political activism and by eroding support for Palestinians among politicians and their constituencies. Whether through direct sponsorship or by playing an enabling or facilitating role, Israel's proxies form the backbone for most of the activism of the individuals and organizations that make up the anti-Islam campaign.

Among Israel's allies are elements of America's domestic security authorities and military leaders, which have looked to Islam as the answer to the threat to their livelihood posed by the collapse of the Soviet Union. They eagerly embrace and magnify the "terrorist threat" and view it as the savior of their budgets and essentially a new *raison d'etré*. For this group, Islam has become a reason to go to war abroad, and an excuse to strip Americans of their civil liberties at home.

Politically, the Christian Right is one of the strongest sources of anti-Islamic agitation in the United States. Fundamentalist Christians have long been gunning for Islam; they fear the religion's rapid spread in America and in overseas theaters of missionary activity. Their doctrine centers around the millenarian notion that support for the state of Israel will facilitate the return of Jesus Christ, so that Israel's cause becomes their own.

Another component of the anti-Islam campaign is a collection of expatriate organizations representing ethnic and religious minorities from the Muslim world, such as Coptic Christians from Egypt, Maronite Christians from Lebanon, and animists and Christians from the south of Sudan. Most of these groups perform a covert or outright supporting role to the pro-Israeli lobby, either for reasons related to political conditions in their home countries, as with the Lebanese, or because they perceive a political benefit in cooperating on a mutually beneficial strategy with one of the most powerful lobbies in U.S. politics. In addition, the Hindu lobby, representing India's interests, has recently colluded with the Israeli lobby in unity against the supposed "Muslim threat" facing both nations. The recent Indo-Israeli alliance has been viewed by most Muslims across the world, but especially those from the Indian Subcontinent, as an increasingly hostile force that threatens regional stability, both in the Middle East and in South Asia. Moreover, these tensions have continued to play out within the American political scene with both lobbies uniting in a common front against Islam.

Finally, extremist secular interests constitute a subtle but active intellectual force that often cooperates or is used by the other groups in their anti-Islam activities. Their goal is to undermine religion in general, but they focus much of their effort on Islam because of its popularity and powerful role in fomenting consciousness of God in public and private life.

The dynamic cooperation among these various interest groups produces fascinating examples of how the American political process and public sentiment can be manipulated for the goals of a political fringe contrary to the national interest. Sometimes their activities fail to do much more than sustain a constant anti-Islam drumbeat in political discourse; often, however, their lobbying has resulted in significant policy shifts that have had a severe long-term impact on America's domestic and foreign policy interests.

The disconnect between the goals of these groups and the national interest is glaring in the aftermath of the terrorist attacks of September 11. The groups constituting the anti-Muslim campaign have always used national tragedy as a vehicle for their goals, but never before has their exploitation of tragedy been as gaudy or destructive to long-term U.S. national interests or global stability. The past decade has seen the emergence of a number of key figures central to this campaign. These individuals and their precarious contributions to the escalation of anti-Muslim sentiment, both on the popular level and in elite politics, will be explored in detail in the pages to follow. From the extremists masquerading as academics, such as Martin Kramer, to those who advance their ideas through the media, such as Judith Miller, this concerted effort has not gone unnoticed by all, and will inevitably be shown in its true form.

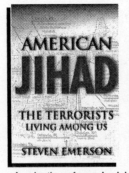 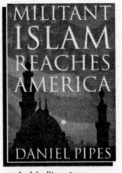 

• A selection of popular Islamophobic literature

PROFILE: THE ZIONIST MASTERS
OF DECEPTION

• **Joseph Bodansky**

– Author of *Target America: Terror in the U.S.*

• **Judith Miller**

– Author of *God Has Ninety Nine Names: Reporting from a Militant Middle East.*

• **Steven Emerson**

– Author of *Jihad in America: The Terrorists Living Among Us.*

• **Rita Katz**

– Author of *Terrorist Hunter.*

Chapter 4

GUNS FOR HIRE

With the absence of moral values and principles in the rapacious world of money and politics, many journalists, scholars, think tanks, and policy makers have become guns for hire, at times advancing the political agendas of foreign entities.

—Ahmed Yousef, *The American Muslim*, April 2004.

While the campaign to denigrate Islam and Muslims across the American political and cultural landscape has been led by individuals in all walks of life, ranging from journalists to academics, and politicians to lobbyists, it is seldom that one finds an individual whose whole life has been devoted to fighting this crusade in every medium possible. These callous chameleons shift their trade in any given moment depending on which way the winds are blowing. Whenever expert testimony is needed before a government body, or an article must be written about an ensuing investigation or pending legislation, or government authorities have found no wrongdoing by an organization or an individual, these guns for hire rise to the occasion and distort reality to support their agenda.

Of the host of individuals engaged in this endeavor over the course of their careers, this chapter will highlight four of the most important figures in this relentless campaign. Their records are plain to see by anyone with an eye for the bigotry and intolerance they convey in a variety of forums. Each of their resumes, whether as authors, journalists, political lobbyists, terrorism "experts," or intelligence agents, is rife with a history of promoting the pro-Israeli rightwing platform through the defilement of its opposition, namely the Islamic faith, culture, and people. Invariably, just about every American has at one time or another been exposed, whether directly or by proxy, to the work of Joseph Bodansky, Judith Miller, Steven Emerson, or Rita Katz. These self-promoting agents have had undue influence in corrupting the hearts and minds of Americans and their leaders at the expense of a voiceless minority.

• Joseph Bodansky

Considered by many to be one of the original Islamophobes, Joseph Bodansky or Yossef Bodansky, as he is also known, emerged on the scene in the 1980s after arriving in the United States from Israel. Little is known of Bodansky during his time in Israel, but he immediately became prominent in U.S. policy-making circles—though he was a noncitizen. He acted as a senior consultant to the State Department and Defense Department during the Reagan and first Bush administrations. By 1990, he was appointed Director of the Congressional Task Force on Terrorism and Unconventional Warfare in the House of Representatives. While heading this task force, Bodansky published a number of reports on terrorism. Rather than undertake an objective study of the topic, Bodansky instead released a number of ideological attacks on Islam.

From start to finish, every report issued by the task force was laced with verbal assaults on Islam and Muslims across a wide array of countries and movements. "A Question of Trust" is a fierce critique of American support for the Afghan mujahideen that relies on fabrications and half-truths. "Iran's European Springboard" attempts to show that Islamist radicals want to invade Europe by way of the crisis in Bosnia. The report was so extremist that it condoned the Serbian genocide against Bosnian Muslims and at times even suggested that the massacres were committed by Bosnians themselves in a "propaganda ploy." It also attempted to build a nonexistent bridge between the "fundamentalist" Iranian government and Bosnia's Muslim leaders in an effort to portray a wider Islamist conspiracy creeping into the West. By far the most outrageous of Bodansky's treatises, however, was entitled "The New Islamist International."[1] This shocking report, submitted to an entire congressional committee, unabashedly set out to invent a global Muslim terrorist network, motivated by a conspiratorial urge to destroy the detested West. Throughout this 93-page document Bodansky employs the most loaded terminology, which has since become standard vocabulary by government officials and the media. Words such as "radical," "extremist," "militant," "fundamentalist," and "conspiratorial" are littered throughout the pages. The word "terrorist" appears 288 times.[2] In all, Bodansky's report provides no factual data, no truthful evidence, and no realistic basis to justify his claims. Unfortunately, however, its sensationalistic and frivolous content was heralded by most policy circles in Washington, D.C. In addition, no one dared question the loyalties of a man who was not even a naturalized U.S. citizen until 1993 and who continued to journey to Israel at least four times a year during this period.

From that point on, Bodansky operated from within diminutive self-serving organizations such as the unheard of International Strategic Studies Association and the Freeman Center for Strategic Studies. In the mid-1990s, Bodansky continued to publish many articles that built upon the emerging anti-Muslim hysteria within policy circles and the media. Such articles included "Pakistan's Islamic Bomb" and "Islamic Anti-Semitism as a Political Instrument." He also expanded upon his vindictive and intolerant views in a number of books, the most notable of which are *TARGET AMERICA: Terror in the U.S.* (1993) and *Terror: The Inside Story of the Terrorist Conspiracy in America* (1994), both published by Shapolsky Publishers. Both books attempt to lay out an international conspiracy of nations and individuals coordinating an all-out terrorist war against the West, led by an "unholy alliance" among Iran, Sudan, and Pakistan. While citing no evidence of anything he claims, Bodansky set out to poison the minds of Americans and continues to spew his agenda-driven hyperbole to anyone who would listen. Most recently, Bodansky wrote a biography of Osama bin Laden in 2001, just prior to the September 11 attacks, which has since become a favorite of mainstream audiences. The book, *Bin Laden: The Man Who Declared War on America*, simply rehashes all of Bodansky's previous claims of an international web of terrorism across the entire Middle East. Much of the information he gives seems to exceed that of all U.S. intelligence agencies. More likely, it is simply baseless propaganda.

Nonetheless, in the aftermath of 9/11, Joseph Bodansky, along with countless other anti-Muslim xenophobes driven by their Zionist agenda, was anointed with the title of "terrorism expert," simply for his ability to make outrageous claims about the looming "Islamic terrorist threat." Unfortunately for Bodansky, his concoctions were not well received in Sweden, after he claimed that Stockholm was home to one of the biggest Al-Qaida cells in the world. Such was the statement made to a local newspaper in Stockholm in early 2002, which prompted strong responses from the Swedish government.[3] The Swedish chief of security, along with the head of intelligence and the top counter-terrorism official, all dismissed Bodansky's claims as completely unfounded. Moreover, when prompted for evidence, Bodansky refused to back his allegations with any facts, instead assuring the newspaper that such was his information. The strong response from Swedish officials, however, was enough to thoroughly discredit Bodansky, at least within the scope of that country, as he attempted to target a number of legitimate Muslim organizations, which had operated within Sweden openly for years.

Ultimately, the sum of Joseph Bodansky's career clearly demonstrates that he is simply another foot soldier for Israel's propaganda war in America. As one of the first such agents and one with such a direct link to the Jewish state, it is incredible that even the slightest air of legitimacy could be given to him, but such has been the state of American politics, especially in the past two decades.

• Judith Miller

Along with figures that engage in the political spheres of America to promote anti-Islamic policies are mainstream media outlets. In a career that spans three decades, Judith Miller is a testament to the notion that media objectivity is an elusive myth, consistently abused by ideologically motivated reporters. Miller joined *The New York Times'* Washington D.C. bureau in 1977, where she immediately began covering Congress, politics, and even the Middle East, though she had no specific expertise on the region. By 1983, she was appointed chief of the *Times'* Middle East Bureau based in Cairo, Egypt. From there, she covered all affairs in the Arab world, providing Americans with a narrow view of the region's events, before returning to Washington in 1989. From the onset of her reporting career, Miller's articles discreetly reflected an inherent bias in her views on Arab and Muslim societies, as well as events in the Middle East. Her writing was consistently soft on the oppressive and destructive policies of Arab regimes, and especially toward Israel's occupation of Palestinian and Lebanese lands. Moreover, her obsession with "Islamic militants" provides an even more stark example of her bias, as she frequently attempted to "unveil" Islamist movements throughout the Arab world in the most sinister and violent tone.

During the 1990s, in addition to her continued reporting, Miller would become better known for authoring a number of books. Her first book, *One, By One, By One* (1990), is described as a "highly praised account of how people in six nations have distorted the memory of the Holocaust." In fact, this book is in some ways guilty of exactly the type of offense it supposedly denounces. As Norman Finkelstein, author of

The Holocaust Industry argues, the Holocaust itself has become exploited to advance the Zionist agenda, and, in this case, Judith Miller is no exception. Her true colors would only further be revealed in the years to follow, as she became a leading voice of anti-Muslim rhetoric within the mainstream press as well as in her books.

Perhaps her seminal work in this regard is *God Has Ninety-Nine Names: Reporting From a Militant Middle East*, published in 1996. While the book received critical acclaim from some circles (primarily pro-Israeli), it was severely criticized in many others as a completely one-sided and skewed firsthand account of Miller's travels throughout the Middle East. Without fail, she paints the plethora of Islamic movements in the Middle East with the brush of extremism and militancy, and argues that this behavior is inherent to the religion itself and that Islam is ultimately interested only in seizing power. The bias is especially evident in the many hypocritical statements she makes. While condemning the violent reaction by Algeria's Islamists after their election victory was overturned, she is nonetheless "relieved" that the government refused to allow them entry into parliament. She also supports "Egypt's suppression of violent Islamist militants" while denouncing the Islamic Republic of Iran's suppression of its own domestic insurgents. Her many shallow observations reflect a pervasive ignorance of the realities within the Muslim world, and a conscious effort to conceal the legitimate grievances of Islamist movements and the complex and multi-faceted structure of the movements themselves, of which violent action, when it exists, is but a miniscule factor. Ultimately, her writing has worked only to further the demonization of Muslim society within the American mainstream, while promoting the Zionist agenda, a feat that did not go unnoticed. Miller instantly became the darling of the Zionist lobby, becoming a featured guest at functions for the American Jewish Committee and a favorite source of quotes for the American-Israel Public Affairs Committee (AIPAC).[4]

As she gained in status and prominence, Miller continued along the same path of assaulting Islam under the guise of exposing its militant side, ultimately culminating in her domestic attacks against noted Muslim leaders and institutions in the United States. Her articles frequently featured unassuming Muslim figures in a grossly negative light, twisting their words and mischaracterizing their statements in an attempt to generate hostility against Islamic work in America. Efforts to spread hysteria among Americans were redoubled following the September 11 attacks, when she published *Germs: Biological Weapons, and America's Secret War.* An alleged anthrax scare at Miller's *New York Times* desk in October, 2001, furthered the book's popularity, propelling it to number one on the *New York Times* bestseller list only two weeks later. Miller, who has absolutely no background knowledge or expertise in the field of biological warfare sought to add to the post-9/11 hysteria that had spread across the country with ridiculous posturing and false alarmist writings.[5]

It was also during this period that Miller began her latest feat, leading the war cry against Iraq. Her supposed exposés on Iraq's weapons of mass destruction were a staple of the Bush administration's rally to war against the impoverished nation. From late 2001 through June, 2003, Miller authored dozens of sensationalistic pieces with the obvious agenda to spread fear of an imminent Iraqi attack in order to shift public opinion in favor of a preemptive attack with or without international approval. As writer Alexander Cockburn points out, all of Miller's articles "promoted disingenuous lies. There were no secret biolabs under Saddam's palaces; no nuclear factories across Iraq working secretly at full tilt. A huge percentage of what Miller wrote was garbage, garbage that powered the Bush administration's propaganda drive towards invasion."[6] Miller's secret sources for many of her stories were later revealed to be Ahmad Chalabi, the leading Iraqi exile, who most aggressively pushed for the war, and Khidir Hamza, an Iraqi defector claiming to be Saddam Hussein's bombmaker, who was exposed as a complete and utter fraud.

None of that mattered to Judith Miller. The damage had been done and the fraudulent war was successfully sold to the American public by March 2003. As the subsequent search for WMDs proved fruitless for the U.S. military, Miller's work came under intense scrutiny, and before long, her agenda was obvious to anyone who read the writing on the wall. In sum, Miller's contributions to the rising Islamophobia and increasingly hostile shift in both domestic and foreign U.S. policy toward Islam and Muslims have been vast. Particularly, her access to the American public as well as policy-makers under the cover of a mainstream media outlet have made her successful at promoting her underlying agenda.

• Steven Emerson

On the list of infamous figures responsible for the most destructive damage to the face of Islam in America, Steven Emerson ranks on a level all his own. For nearly two decades, he has been the head of the xenophobic snake that has sunk its venomous fangs into all areas of American society. From his grotesquely inaccurate books and films, to his malicious testimonies before congressional committees, Emerson's affronts are too numerous to mention.

Little is known of Steven Emerson before his emergence onto the scene in the mid-1980s. He has directly refused to answer any questions about his past, but records indicate that Steven Abram Emerson was born to a Jewish family in New York. The son of a salesman and a teacher, he lived in Lawrence, New York, before attending college at Brown University, and received a degree in "urban studies" in 1977.[7] Emerson emerged as a staff member of the Senate Foreign Relations Committee in Congress soon thereafter, and also worked in the office of the late Frank Church, a Senator from Idaho who also happened to be on the Select Committee for Government Intelligence Activities. By 1985, Emerson quit to write his first book, *The American House of Saud: The Secret Petrodollar Connection*, a scathing attack against Saudi Arabia and its economic partnership with the United States. A year later, he joined *U.S. News & World Report*, Mortimer Zuckerman's rabidly pro-Zionist magazine. While at the magazine, Emerson wrote two more books: one "investigating" Pan Am Flight 103 and another detailing covert U.S. operations. The former received a damning reception from the *Columbia Journalism Review*, as it suggested that some of its content was plagiarized from a Syracuse, New York newspaper.[8] Emerson was subsequently forced to apologize to the reporters whose work he had passed off as his own. In 1990, however, he was ready to pass himself off as a legitimate journalist, landing a reporting position with CNN.

For three years, Emerson's reports generated countless complaints from American Arab and Muslim groups for their inherent pro-Israel bias and sensationalistic assaults on Islam.

Though in his most recent book, *American Jihad*, Emerson claims that he was only "by chance" led to his fixation on Islamic militants in 1992, his record prior to that—which he zealously attempts to conceal—dates back to at least 1985 and completely belies the notion that he coincidentally came upon the topic years later. In fact, his 1991 book, *Terrorist*, received a scathing review from the *New York Times*, which stated that the book was "marred by factual errors ... and by a pervasive anti-Arab and anti-Palestinian bias."[9] Despite his lifelong record of attacks on the Muslim faith and its institutions, Emerson's agenda would become painfully obvious following his seminal project.

In 1993, Emerson quit CNN to pursue his agenda on a fulltime basis in the form of a television documentary entitled *Jihad in America*. The main purpose of the film was to capitalize on the recent World Trade Center bombing to advance the notion that the United States had become a hotbed for Muslim extremism. The video, which aired on PBS in 1994, was routinely condemned by American Muslim groups as inciting Islamophobia and supporting the assault on their civil liberties. As most observers noted, the entire video left one with the image that every Muslim in America was a suspected terrorist and that every mosque was a terrorist cell and at the center of a grand conspiracy. Respected news reporter Robert Friedman accused Emerson thereafter of "creating mass hysteria against American Arabs."[10] The malevolent film persisted to point fingers at mainstream Muslim organizations as "fronts" for terrorist groups and respected community leaders as undercover extremists plotting attacks on their adopted country.

Barely six months after the film's release, Emerson would take to the airwaves and capitalize on one of America's most vulnerable moments, as he would continue to do in later years, to disseminate his groundless accusations. Only minutes following the Oklahoma City bombing, Emerson was on network television asserting that Muslim terrorists were responsible. His "expertise" gave him insight into the bombing. He claimed that it "was done to inflict as many casualties as possible," which is "a Middle Eastern trait."[11] He also claimed Oklahoma City to be one of the biggest hotbeds of Muslim extremism outside of the Middle East. The accusations were quickly proven false, as responsible law enforcement authorities pursued more promising leads and ultimately captured the culprits, two homegrown Americans. Nonetheless, his baseless assertions incited a wave of attacks against American Muslims across the country that resulted in at least one death. Emerson was quickly cast out from the mainstream media, but continued to rise from the ashes of every tragic event.

While the Oklahoma City incident is one for which he is most notorious, outrageous accusations were nothing new to Steve Emerson. In 1993, he claimed that Yugoslavians perpetrated the World Trade Center bombing. Then, in 1996, he reappeared on television to claim that, "I have no doubt whatsoever, at this point, that it was a bomb that brought down TWA Flight 800 - not a missile, but a bomb."[12] As always, each allegation proved completely fabricated by the dubious reporter, and any credibility he could have hoped to maintain to advance his agenda was destroyed. But as destructive as Emerson has been in his limited capacity as a self-styled journalist in the public eye, his most damaging work has undoubtedly been done behind the scenes.

Following the release of his documentary, Emerson established The Investigative Project, a platform of his own from which he could continue to launch his attacks. Hiding behind this organization, Emerson attempted to pervade the mainstream media with his hidden agenda. Investigative journalist and former editor of a Tampa, Florida newspaper, John Sugg has written extensively on Emerson's secret projects and questionable connections. In 1997, the Associated Press was researching for a feature on terrorism and Emerson came calling. As Sugg reports, AP journalists were fed documents by Emerson, which he claimed was an official FBI dossier. One of the reporters, Richard Cole, "uncovered an earlier, almost identical document authored by Emerson. The purported FBI dossier 'was really his'," according to Cole. "He had edited out all phrases, taken out anything that made it look like his." Emerson "could never back up what he said. We couldn't believe that document was from the FBI files," according to Fred Bayles, another AP journalist.[13] In the aftermath of this debacle, Emerson attempted to sue Sugg, his newspaper, and the AP journalist for their revelations, but that suit was ultimately dismissed by a court in the summer of 2003, a decision Emerson did not contest.

Among Emerson's countless offenses, another glaring one from June, 1998, particularly stands out. That month, an article appeared in a British newspaper claiming that, "Pakistan is planning a nuclear first strike on India." The report was based on a supposed "senior Pakistani weapons scientist who has defected." The following days were marked by an extreme level of tension in the Indian subcontinent, as the possibility for nuclear war seemed more likely than ever. In reality, the scientist was revealed to be a fraud passed off by Emerson to the media. The man, Iftekhar Khan, was actually an accountant at a small company in Pakistan who desired political asylum in the United States and worked in collusion with Emerson to concoct the phony claims against his native country. Emerson worked behind the scenes to advance the story throughout the media. As Sugg points out, "A top network news producer in New York told me his congressional sources and news contacts were tipped to the story by Emerson. 'He called two people (associated with the network) within an hour,' said the producer. 'He was definitely pushing the story'."[14]   Although Khan was revealed as a complete fraud upon being interviewed by American nuclear scientists, the damage had already been done. As the two South Asian nations had recently acquired nuclear weapons capabilities, Emerson succeeded in promoting the notion that Pakistan was the more hostile, unstable, and aggressive of the two. The threat of the "Islamic bomb" was real and dangerous to all civilized nations. This was the sole message that came across from that bizarre episode.

Emerson's most vicious assaults, however, have been against the American Muslim community. His most glaring attack occurred in the aftermath of the debut of *Jihad in America*. Among its wild allegations was that Islamic and Palestinian intellectual activism in Florida was actually secretly supporting terrorism. The attacks continued in 1995 and beyond as part of a series of newspaper articles by the *Tampa Tribune*, and specifically by its overzealous reporter, Michael Fechter. This journalist held a close relationship with Emerson, who inspired many of the stories and was often the primary source. In fact, Fechter's relationship with Emerson goes even further back. As a writer with absolutely no experience in covering the Middle East or terrorism, he echoed Emerson's assertions that the Oklahoma City bombing was committed by Muslim terrorists in a front-page article the day following the attacks. Fechter's attacks against the University of South Florida and a number of professors there prompted widespread attention and the launching of a federal investigation. As a result of the disruption caused by the unfounded assertions in the articles, the organizations under scrutiny were shut down, and one of the local leaders, Dr. Mazen al-Najjar, was detained for more than three years on the basis of secret evidence. Another professor, Dr. Sami al-Arian, who was at the center of the attacks, was denied his citizenship application though he had been in the country for more than two decades. When the INS revealed their reasons, it turned out to be nothing but a collection of Emerson-inspired *Tampa Tribune* articles by Michael Fechter. Emerson even at one time announced that Tampa Muslim leaders were directly involved in plotting the first World Trade Center attack in 1993, an allegation so outrageous that he did not dare repeat it.[15]

In the historic civil rights battle against the use of secret evidence, Emerson predictably sided with the bigoted special interest groups, led mainly by the pro-Israeli lobby, to halt efforts in Congress to outlaw the unconstitutional practice. In the spring of 2000, he submitted his testimony to Congress rehashing the same slanderous lies he had made for years.[16] Nonetheless, the bill to outlaw secret evidence passed through the Judiciary Committee in spite of his protestations. In fact, by 2001, Emerson had been virtually cast out of mainstream political and media circles. Appearances on television had come to a halt, as did the publication of his articles in mainstream national newspapers. He was not even being used as a source by any major media outlets. As one ranking Associated Press editor in Washington, D.C., said, "I would be very, very, very, very leery of using Steve Emerson."[17] For all purposes, the pseudo-journalist had lost all credibility and was reduced to publishing his drivel in small-time, self-serving magazines and journals, some of which were of his own creation.

And then disaster struck. On September 11, 2001, Steven Emerson was again resurrected to the fore as he had been in the aftermath of previous attacks. Due to the magnitude of 9/11, he came back stronger than ever. Within hours of the attack, Emerson was on every major network, from NBC and Fox to CNN and CBS. He would eventually come to be hired as NBC's "terrorism expert," though he certainly has no professional qualifications in the area, aside from his own anti-Muslim posturing. Within only a few months, he had written a new book, which capitalized on the post-9/11 hysteria and widespread obsession with "Muslim terrorists." His book, however, had little to do with the September 11 attacks themselves, which were purely foreign in origin. Rather, he once again attacked the domestic Muslim community. This book, *American Jihad: The Terrorists Living Among Us*, was not given the cold and skeptical reception usually given to Emerson's hateful words. Rather, the national mood was quick to receive the flawed work, despite the fact that it continued to spread lies, fabrications, misconceptions, and simply groundless attacks on many of America's most respected Muslim leaders. These attacks were especially meant to heighten the fear and suspicion of the community at large and to undermine recent efforts by mainstream Muslim groups to engage in the political process.

One did not have to look far to discover Emerson's views on Islam. In one article for a Jewish magazine in 1995, he rebuked mainstream Americans for not being more forceful against Islam. He blamed this weakness on political correctness, because, as he put it, to be honest about Islam would be to acknowledge that Islam "sanctions genocide, planned genocide, as part of its religious doctrine."[18]

Indeed, if one were to follow it from the beginning to the present, Emerson's career has been nothing more than Islam-bashing, from his early days attacking Saudi Arabia, to his allegations that Muslim Yugoslavians committed terrorism on U.S. soil, to his demonization of the entire country of Pakistan, and of course his constant obsession with Palestinians, a whole population which he has cast into the "terrorist" category.

From the pattern of his entire career, it is not terribly difficult to deduce whom Emerson has been serving continually throughout his relentless crusade. Every one of his malicious attacks has worked directly for the benefit of Israel. His only allies have been Israeli or pro-Zionist zealots. This has included Yigal Carmon, according to Sugg, "a right-wing Israeli intelligence commander who endorses the use of torture, and who has stayed at Emerson's Washington apartment on trips to lobby Congress against the Middle East peace initiatives"[19] in the mid-1990s. Vince Cannistraro, an ABC consultant and retired CIA counterterrorism official, told Sugg, "They're Israeli-funded. How do I know? Because they tried to recruit me."[20] Indeed, Emerson has refused in the past to reveal the source of funding for his work, but it is likely pro-Israeli groups, if not the Jewish state itself. The right-wing Israeli newspaper, the *Jerusalem Post*, has said that Emerson has "close ties to Israeli intelligence."[21] Meanwhile former Mossad agent Victor Ostrovsky refers to Emerson as "the horn" for trumpeting Israeli intelligence, and further supports the notion of Emerson's underlying loyalty to Israel.

In recent years, Emerson has been increasingly self-obsessed, frequently harping about potential attempts on his life and having to check under his car for explosives before each trip. In testimony before a Senate subcommittee in 1998, he claimed that a federal agent told him "radical Islamic fundamentalists had been assigned to carry out an assassination of me. An actual hit team had been dispatched."[22] He then proceeded to state that authorities told him he could get permission to enter the Witness Security Program. Law enforcement officials later denied that claim and stated that no such consideration ever existed, and there was no truth to the assassination plot whatsoever. It seems Steven Emerson has made his entire career on such bold fabrications. Such a long history of lies would be enough to bury anyone.

• Rita Katz

One of Steven Emerson's main disciples, lurking behind the scenes for years, has been Rita Katz. An Iraqi Jew who fled Saddam Hussein's regime at a young age after her father was executed for being an Israeli spy, Katz moved to Israel where she lived for many years before coming to the United States as an adult. Unlike all the other agents of anti-Islamic hysteria, Katz's very existence was not known on the scene until early 2003, though she had been working secretly for many years to harm the community. In May of that year an anonymous book emerged entitled *Terrorist Hunter* that was later revealed to be the work of Katz. The book proceeds to chronicle the experiences of an undercover agent infiltrating virtually every major Muslim institution operating within the United States. It tempts to weave a web of deceit, duplicity, and malice. If one were to believe Katz's very personal and emotionally charged account, Americans should have cause for concern because American Muslim institutions consist of a large and widespread terror network, with their terrorist leaders plotting international terrorist mayhem using the limitless funds from terrorism sponsors across the United States and the world. Until they parted ways in 2002, Katz was employed as Emerson's "research director" and her book reveals the extent of her spying, as she dressed in disguises to infiltrate America's mosques and Islamic centers. She claims to have spent most of her time documenting support for terrorists, yet expresses outbursts of frustration that federal officials were not pursuing the leads she had supposedly found. In one instance, Katz vividly describes crawling around in a garbage dumpster belonging to a Muslim institution in Northern Virginia, looking for damaging documents to prove her bizarre suspicions, but finds nothing but ordinary documents and a mess of chicken bones.[23]   In another instance, among her laundry list of allegations, she accuses Muslim intellectual institutes of smuggling tens of thousands of chickens from a chicken farm in Georgia and funneling the profits to terrorists.

As journalist John Sugg notes, "The book appears to have two purposes—to broadly link outspoken domestic Muslim and Arab groups with Osama bin Laden, and to undermine the FBI."[24] Indeed, Katz is highly contemptuous of the FBI, which she perceives as being too soft on terrorists and not going after them with nearly enough force. In actuality, Katz's consistent nagging in this regard may be in part responsible for the massive raids that took place in March, 2002, on dozens of Islamic centers, institutions, and homes of their employees in the Northern Virginia area. Although Katz gained much prominence following her book's release, she has also been subjected to much scrutiny as well. An appearance on the CBS program "60 Minutes," in which she detailed in dramatic tone the "terrorist chickens" affair, generated an immediate response from those she targeted. While asserting her suspicions, she says, "Chicken is one of the things that no one can really track down. If you say in one year that you lost 10 million chickens, no one can prove it. They just died. You can't trace money with chickens."[25] The groups she mentioned by name responded with an $80 million lawsuit against CBS and Katz for the "malicious lies" they helped perpetuate.

Katz founded a cover organization called Search for International Terrorist Entities (SITE), and has refused to reveal the funding for her group. She has written a number of commentaries in various newspapers promoting her book and her dubious work. A former high-level CIA counter-terrorism official considered *Terrorist Hunter* "a joke."[26] Ultimately, however, the devastating effects Katz has caused with her pandering as a self-styled spy has been no laughing matter. ∎

PROFILE: ACADEMICIAN WITH A
HIDDEN AGENDA

• Martin Kramer

— Author of *Ivory Towers on Sand.*

• Daniel Pipes

— Author of *Militant Islam Reaches America.*

• Reuven Paz

— Author of *Tangled Web: The Culture of Global Jihad.*

• Bernard Lewis

— Author of *What Went Wrong? Western Impact and Middle Eastern Response.*

Chapter 5

POLITICAL AGENDAS UNDER THE GUISE OF ACADEMIA

In America witches were not only burnt at the stake in Salem Massachusetts; but "Witch hunts" like the one inspired by Senator Joseph McCarthy still flare up here, now and then.

Murad Hoffman, *Religion on the Rise: Islam in the Third Milllennium*, Amana Publications, p.198.

Many of the values upon which the United States of America was built form the foundations of American academia. The notions of academic freedom, and higher education institutions steeped in objectivity and motivated by a pure passion for the pursuit of knowledge, lie in stark contrast to the academic establishment in many other countries that features underlying motives, hidden agendas, and the attempt to shape popular opinion and advance government policy through the guise of scholarly research. It is in this vein that a number of individuals operating within the secure confines of American academia have exploited the good standing and strong place of higher learning in American public life to advance the interests of Israel and its allies in America. These individuals have disgraced the sanctity of intellectual debate and scholarly research by proving themselves to be agents of a cause altogether incompatible with the search for truth and the dissemination of knowledge. Rather, they have used the cloak of advanced academic degrees to provide an air of legitimacy to the intolerant and deceptive information they disperse to an unassuming audience of Americans.

These so-called academics are marked by a superficial concern for their standing in scholarly circles (which is usually very low) that is usually surpassed by their desire to gain the limelight by passing themselves off as experts in front of the cameras, in newspaper opinion pages, and especially among policy-makers in Washington and federal law enforcement agencies. Quite often, there is enough in their past and present affiliations, let alone in their public and private statements, to show that these individuals have shielded themselves with an academic standing only to legitimate what would otherwise be considered the rabid and unyielding support of a political interest group. While they may often be observed promoting a distortedly positive image of Israel, its policies, and American support for them, they also consistently define Islam in their own way, often in inflammatory language, to reap benefits for their agenda which includes dramatic repercussions against the Muslim world. This chapter examines four such individuals who have operated for years under the guise of academia. Two of them are Israelis who have since taken advantage of America's open arms to poison the minds of its citizens and create enmity among them, while spreading hysteria, insecurity, and xenophobia. One can only hope that America's academic establishment will call to task those who exploit its ideals and virtues to promote what is in fact inimical to it in every way.

• Martin Kramer

Of the many ideologically oriented agents of anti-Islamic hysteria, Martin Kramer has been operating from under a different backdrop. Similar to Judith Miller, he has adopted a position within the mainstream from which to wage his relentless battle. Kramer has built his reputation as a supposed academic and scholar of the Middle East, though he does not hold any position at a U.S. university. In fact, his only academic position is with the Moshe Dayan Center for Middle Eastern and African Studies at Tel Aviv University in Israel. Despite the obvious conflict of interest, Kramer, who came to the United States from Israel in the early 1970s before returning there to teach and direct the Dayan Center, has been given multiple grants from pro-Israel groups to conduct research into Islamic movements and the Arab-Israeli conflict.[1] Without fail, his supposedly scholarly publications have been nothing more than anti-Muslim rhetoric cloaked in the language of academia.

With his doctorate in Near Eastern Studies from Princeton University, Kramer has gained a platform in recent years from which to propagate his message, primarily hoping to influence American foreign policy toward the Middle East. Kramer's supposedly academic articles read more like position papers that take an unabashedly pro-Israeli stance, while effectively attempting to make Israel's enemies America's enemies as well. His undying obsession with Islamic movements has attempted to shift the terms of the debate within academic circles over the years. Rather than engage in an objective discussion and research on Islamic movements across the Middle East with an unbiased attitude, Kramer has sought to push American academia toward an outright rejection and condemnation of Islam, and to view all such movements with suspicion and indignation. Like the previously discussed figures, Kramer has attempted to build in the American mindset a perception of an Islamic threat, the appropriate response to which is not unlike that advanced by the extremist Israeli right. Through a number of various temporary teaching positions in American universities, Kramer was better able to advance his intolerant ideas within a mainstream academic setting.

Although he has published a number of propaganda pieces, such as *The Jewish Discovery of Islam*, and *Arab Awakening and Islamic Revival*, Kramer achieved infamy with his exploitation of the September 11 tragedy. Only weeks following the attacks, he published *Ivory Towers on Sand: The Failure of Middle Eastern Studies in America*, a derisive assault on the decades old academic establishment. Interestingly enough, Kramer's criticisms are so shallow as to not merit any response from most distinguished academics. He did not engage in any thorough scholarly discussion, but simply lobbed insults at the most respected professors and researchers in the field of Middle Eastern Studies. Once again, however, in the period immediately following 9/11, with emotions running high, people were willing to give Kramer's position a platform. More specifically, his assault was meant to stop the flow of public funds into various Middle Eastern studies departments and centers nationwide, if those departments did not endorse Kramer's extremist views. Additionally, Kramer's thesis was advanced by certain news outlets and some members of government. Across the country, professors found themselves under attack as being "terrorist sympathizers," or "soft on Islamic extremism," all because of Kramer's own twisted views. His book especially expressed disdain for the late Edward Said, the noted Palestinian-American scholar who created a whole new field of study with his seminal work, *Orientalism*. According to Kramer's thinly veiled worldview, Middle East scholars were all divided along the lines of those who fall under Said's "terrorist-loving" scholarship, or the likes of pro-Israeli critic of Islam Bernard Lewis. Kramer's obscured black and white picture offended a number of distinguished professors, including Richard Bulliet of Columbia University, John Esposito of Georgetown University, and Roger Owen of Harvard University's Center for Middle Eastern Studies, among many others. While most of them initially ignored Kramer's crude manifesto, the increased attention it received prompted many of them to respond. Many professors dismissed his arguments as completely illegitimate, and went to great lengths to provide evidence that the scenario he describes was certainly not the case. In addition, his ad hominem attacks on individuals were inappropriate in any civilized discussion among academics. Some also addressed his proposal to cut government funding to Middle Eastern studies programs by arguing that following 9/11 it was actually more urgent that this particular part of the world be studied in more depth.

Harvard's Roger Owen questioned Kramer's background as a supposed scholar. In an article he said, "Martin Kramer is an Israeli/American with a number of indifferent books on political Islam to his name, none of which I've seen on any British or American academic reading lists. He is probably better known as a former director of the Dayan Center at Tel Aviv University, with its strong connections to Israeli military intelligence."[2] Indeed, Kramer's political allegiances were rarely, if ever, mentioned while his tirade was receiving widespread attention. No one questioned how an Israeli with obvious rightwing leanings could have the audacity to disparage American scholarship on the Middle East.

Kramer's nefarious crusade continued in a variety of ways. As a fellow at the radically pro-Israel Washington Institute for Near East Policy (which incidentally published *Ivory Towers on Sand*), he advanced his Zionist agenda into policy-making circles especially after September 11. Kramer also edits the Institute's publication, *Middle East Quarterly*, also an unabashedly anti-Muslim journal that receives very limited reception from true scholarly institutes and academics. Perhaps Kramer's greatest claim to infamy in recent times has been the web site he helped launch with noted Islamophobe Daniel Pipes, titled campuswatch.org. This site reeks of a McCarthyite stench, in that it attempts to track any and all academics that present any views on the Middle East, Israel, or the United States, with which its creators do not agree. This attempted blacklist has aimed to intimidate and silence dissent, free speech, or any criticism of Israel or U.S. policy. It is yet another example of Kramer's despicable resumé of actions that completely betrays his supposedly scholarly background in favor of promoting his ongoing crusade for Israel.

• Daniel Pipes

In the war against Islam during the past decades, Daniel Pipes has been a leading general. The documented Muslim-basher has gained prominence as a so-called "expert" on Islam, the Middle East, and terrorism. Since the early 1980s, Pipes has led the charge against Islam. Through a number of positions within the federal government, he has poisoned the minds of policymakers in Washington. He has also been responsible for the dissemination of an inherently pro-Israeli, anti-Arab agenda through various think tanks and research institutes, some of which were of his own creation. The Middle East Forum is a rabidly rightwing pro-Israeli institute founded by Pipes with an egregiously misleading motto, "promoting American interests." In fact, the Middle East Forum has never given a second thought to America's interests in the region, instead promoting the Israeli agenda at the expense of American security, prosperity, and popularity within the Arab and Muslim worlds. Pipes has even had undue public exposure with the publication of his many columns in newspapers across the country, though mainly in conservative newspapers such as the *New York Post* and the *Wall Street Journal*.

What is perhaps most disturbing, however, is that Pipes' rabidly anti-Muslim bigotry has not been a secret. A *Washington Post* review in 1983 of one of his earlier books stated that Pipes displayed "a disturbing hostility to contemporary Muslims. ...He professes respect for Muslims but is frequently contemptuous of them. [He] is swayed by the writings of anti-Muslim writers ... [The book] is marred by exaggerations, inconsistencies, and evidence of hostility to the subject."[3] Pipes has made countless derogatory and racist statements against Muslims, consistently defaming their faith and their culture. He once wrote that "Western European societies are unprepared for the massive immigration of brown-skinned peoples cooking strange foods and maintaining different standards of hygiene. ... All immigrants bring exotic customs and attitudes, but Muslim customs are more troublesome than most."[4] He has also frequently trumpeted the cry of anti-Semitism whenever anyone critical of Israel speaks out. At one point, he even stated that the rise of anti-Semitism in the United States was directly linked to the rising population of Muslims in America, despite the lengthy history of good relations between Muslims and Jews in the Middle East prior to 1948.[5]

The supposed "expert" on Islam has also denied that Jerusalem holds any importance to the world's 1.3 billion Muslims.[6] In fact, Pipes' worldview has openly pitted Islam as the rising threat to Western civilization, once writing, "Following Marxism, Leninism, and Fascism, comes Islamism. ...Islamism is a phenomenon that has the power to do mischief."[7] This one statement is the crux of Pipes' lifelong mission to demonize Islam and present it as the ultimate enemy to the West, thereby promoting the Israeli agenda and legitimizing its policies. Pipes further castigates all American Muslim organizations by arguing that they are bent on taking over the American government and turning the United States into an Islamic state. The sheer absurdity of such allegations unfortunately has not been enough to compromise any credibility Pipes holds within mainstream media and policymaking circles. At one point, he came out in support of racial profiling, after an incident in which two Arab students were wrongly pulled off of a flight and detained. He said, "It seems well worth it in order to keep would-be terrorists off-guard."[8] In a more recent book, he wrote, "All Muslims, unfortunately, are suspect." Like Steve Emerson, Pipes too initially claimed that the Oklahoma City bombing in 1995 was the work of Muslims. He told *USA Today*, "People need to understand that this is just the beginning. The fundamentalists are on the upsurge, and they make it very clear that they are targeting us. They are absolutely obsessed with us."[9] It seems Pipes is the one with the obsession. In fact, he has had a longstanding relationship with the notorious Emerson. They have co-authored many articles, including the most aggressive attacks on American Muslim leaders. Emerson's Investigative Project is also funded by Pipes' Middle East Forum and each of the two is frequently seen applauding the other. "I am proud to work with him,"[10] Pipes said of Emerson.

With regard to his views on the Middle East conflict, Pipes is more militant than those he often criticizes. According to *Mother Jones* magazine, "Pipes sees no room for negotiation, no hope for compromise, and no use for diplomacy." He once declared, "What war had achieved for Israel, diplomacy has undone." According to the same article, "His solution is simple: The Israeli military must force what Pipes describes as a 'change of heart' by the Palestinians in the West Bank and Gaza—a sapping of the Palestinian will to fight which can lead to a complete surrender. Pipes continued, 'How is a change of heart achieved? It is achieved by an Israeli victory and a Palestinian defeat. The Palestinians need to be defeated even more than Israel needs to defeat them'."[11] Such views are to the right of the Israeli Likudists and reflect Pipes' fanaticism, of which he has accused every Muslim in some fashion.

Criticism of Pipes has come from all sides, not only the Muslim leadership. Even academics, journalists, and Christian and Jewish leaders have held highly unfavorable opinions of Pipes and his resumé. Noted scholar Edward Said viewed Pipes as part of a growing but exclusive group of Islamophobes who seek to "make sure that 'the [Islamic] threat' is kept before our eyes, the better to excoriate Islam for terror, despotism and violence, while assuring themselves profitable consultancies, frequent TV appearances, and book contracts."[12] One of Pipes' own professors and former director of Harvard's Center for Middle Eastern Studies, William A. Graham, was highly critical of his former student. "To speak for myself, I have been appalled frequently by his polemical stance on almost everything having to do with Islam, Muslims, or the Palestinian/Israeli issue. ...The irony [in an article by Pipes] is of course that Dr. Pipes and other radically and blindly pro-Zionist American Jews are much farther along the chauvinist and ultimately anti-American spectrum than are even radical American Muslims. Yet Dr. Pipes, despite his own apparently strong, even blind, support for the Israeli state and its policies—even those policies that are attacked by thoughtful Israelis themselves as racist and oppressive—sees no incongruity in his condemnation of many Muslim Americans as a threat to the American state and democracy."[13]

Dr. Pipes came under more fire after President Bush nominated him to the board of the U.S. Institute of Peace in the summer of 2003. The irony, of course, is that, in everything he has said or done, Daniel Pipes is the furthest person away from a position intended to promote harmony. What Pipes represents is intolerance, division, and violence. His writings are and have been consistently against the cause of peace. The *Washington Post* and *Chicago Tribune* both condemned the President's decision as wrong and divisive. Senator Edward Kennedy (D-MA), who sits on the committee that would have to approve Pipes' nomination, expressed serious misgivings about the choice and his intent to oppose it. Susannah Heschel, co-chair of Tikkun, a Jewish group, said simply, "Daniel Pipes is not a peacemaker."[14] His nomination also received resounding condemnation by American Muslim groups, to which Pipes responded with characteristic acrimony: "My nomination is merely a stepping stone in their assertion of power to achieve a militant Islamic state. To put it more graphically: the substitution of the Constitution by the Koran."[15] Many of Pipes' most controversial views came to light during the battle over his nomination. One specific opinion he issued in 1990, called for the forcible expulsion of all Palestinians into Jordan with Israel annexing the West Bank, Gaza, and Jerusalem. "These are views that are not particularly mainstream or tolerant of the other," Judith Kipper, a Middle East fellow at the Center for Strategic and International Studies, told *Mother Jones*. "A number of people have raised a question of having someone on the board with extreme views because democracy thrives in the center."[16] In fact, Pipes' only supporters seem to have come from the rabidly pro-Zionist groups, such as the American Israel Public Affairs Committee, the Zionist Organization of America, and the American Jewish Congress.

• Daniel Pipes was a guest speaker at a UASR roundtable in 1999.

The controversy was inflamed further as President Bush appointed Pipes during the Congressional recess in September, 2003, bypassing the normal channels of confirmation through a Senate committee hearing. While it ultimately laid to rest efforts to have the nomination withdrawn, it only stood as additional proof of the Bush administration's contempt for the Muslim community, in spite of all its verbal promises to the contrary. Throughout his career, Pipes has proven himself a tactless bigot and a premier agent of anti-Muslim sentiment within American policy. His new appointment to the Institute of Peace has given him a new platform from which to espouse those intolerant views and advance the interests of the Zionist lobby that has propped him up.

• Reuven Paz

Similar to Martin Kramer, Paz is an Israeli professor at Haifa University, whose "expertise" is claimed to be in "Palestinian society and politics, Islam, Islamic movements in the Muslim world, Islamic fundamentalism, and Islamist international terrorist networks."[17] In the late 1980s, Paz was a visiting fellow at the Dayan Center in Tel Aviv University, where Kramer was the director. The Dayan Center is known for its close ties to Israeli intelligence services and Paz is living proof of that, having worked as an officer of the Shin Bet, Israel's internal intelligence agency, for twenty-five years. In spite of this fact, his credibility as an academic was never called to account by those critiquing his work. While in Israel, Paz published a number of articles and several books concerning Palestinian Islamic movements with a particularly subjective view of the matter, condemning them and manipulating facts to support his conclusions. He first emerged in the United States as a Senior Visiting Fellow at the Washington Institute for Near East Policy, a notoriously pro-Israeli think tank with heavy lobbying power in Washington. Through the Washington Institute, Paz was given a position from which to advance the anti-Islamic agenda, frequently speaking and writing against Islamic movements. He also testified as an expert witness in a number of court cases against supposed international terrorist sponsors. His main claim to fame, however, was his assertion of a global terrorist network that connects movements in countries ranging from Iraq to Chechnya, and Morocco to the Palestinian territories. He effectively coined the concept of

"Islamist terrorist internationale" which essentially removes specific Muslim grievances within each set of circumstances (Israel's occupation of Palestine, for instance) and instead lumps all Islamic movements together as one sinister endeavor bent on death and destruction across the world.[18] This is precisely the notion advanced by his book, *Tangled Web: The Culture of Global Jihad*, published by the Washington Institute itself. In 2002, Paz founded the Project for the Research of Islamist Movements (PRISM), "in order to combine academic and field research of new developments of radical Islam and Islamist movements."[19] In effect, this new front group seeks to advance the same malicious agenda characteristic of Israel's propaganda machine. In a blatant example of historical revisionism, Paz authored an article in December, 2003, arguing that the rabid "anti-American" terrorism by Muslims has its roots in Islamic revival movements of the early 20th century (pre-dating Israel's creation), rather than it being simply a consequence of recent American policies and blind support of Israel.[20] While he may be performing his duty as an Israeli intelligence officer, Paz is simply not the academic he pretends to be.

• Bernard Lewis

Through the years, British academic Bernard Lewis has billed himself as a temperate, mainstream scholar of Islam and the Middle East. Of all the listed individuals in this section, he has attained the most prominence and has become a staple of Middle Eastern studies. His work has served as an inspiration to many colleagues, students, policymakers, foreign leaders, and the media. In his 65 years as a professor, Lewis has had a permanent effect on the study of Islam and the Middle East, but, as many would contend, this has not been for the improvement of its understanding, but rather to deliberately distort reality.

Bernard Lewis received his education at the University of London in the 1930s, receiving his doctorate in Middle Eastern history in 1938. That year he was admitted to the faculty of the School of Oriental and African Studies in London. His earliest academic interest was of small strands within Islam, such as the Assassins and the Ismailis, of which he wrote his early works. Lewis has been vague on his activities between 1940 and 1945, except to say that he was "otherwise engaged." Records show, however, that he was a wartime British Military Intelligence officer, later promoted to the British Foreign Office. He remained a lecturer in England until his arrival at Princeton University's History Department in 1974.

As early as 1960, however, Lewis appeared to take on a radical approach to issues in the Middle East. That year, he authored *The Emergence of Modern Turkey*, in which he advocates the exploitation of the political events in the Middle East to develop a Western buffer against the Soviet Union. This was a telltale sign of Lewis' contempt for Middle Eastern and Muslim peoples (which he did not differentiate) and his view of them solely through the lens of advancing the interests of Western civilization, which he consistently viewed as the standard by which all others should be judged. In his 1978 treatise, Edward Said developed an entire study of this phenomenon, entitled *Orientalism*. In fact, *Orientalism* specifically cites Lewis as one of the most prominent individuals guilty of abuses against the region of the world on which he is a purported expert. Years later, Professor M. Shahid Alam would comment, "It would appear that Lewis is still the reigning monarch of Orientalism, as he was some twenty-five years back when Edward Said, in his *Orientalism*, dissected and exposed the intentions, modalities, deceptions, and imperialist connections of this ideological enterprise." Said writes of Lewis:

> [His] work purports to be liberal objective scholarship but is in reality very close to being propaganda *against* his subject material... [Lewis's work] is aggressively ideological.
> The core of Lewis's ideology about Islam is that it never changes, and his whole mission is to inform conservative segments of the Jewish reading public, and anyone else who cares to listen, that any political, historical, and scholarly account of Muslims must begin and end with the fact that Muslims are Muslims.

Many observers, led by Said, agree that Lewis' primary objective has always been "to debunk, to whittle down, and to discredit the Arabs and Islam." This becomes even more evident in that the bulk of his work since the 1970s has been openly hostile and ill-mannered in its analysis of Islam and the Middle East. From the administration of Jimmy Carter, Lewis began infusing American policymakers with his skewed perceptions of the Middle East, leading to a number of the antagonistic policies that emerged from that era, most notably his obsession with Iran as an extremist, unstable, rogue state following the Islamic Revolution. The contempt he shows for his subject matter becomes even more evident when one notes the sharp contrast in his treatment of Israel. As Alam notes:

> Once [Lewis] is seated on his high Orientalist perch, he goes about cleverly insinuating how Islam is deficient in and opposed to universal values, which, of course, always originate in the West. It is because of this deficiency in values that Arabs have trouble accepting a democratic Israel—it is always "democratic" Israel. Lewis can write "objectively" about the Arab's "ingrained" opposition to Israel without ever telling his readers that Israel is an imperialist creation, and an expansionist, colonial-settler state that was founded on terror, wars, and ethnic cleansing.[21]

Over the years, Lewis' agenda would become crystal clear to any who followed his work. Specifically, a September 1990 article in the *Atlantic Monthly*, entitled "The Roots of Muslim Rage," showed his true colors. Only months following the fall of the Berlin Wall, effectively ending the Cold War, Lewis was already busy pitting Islam as the new enemy against Western democracy. In fact, it is Bernard Lewis who coined the term "clash of civilizations" in this article, three years before Samuel Huntington would author the book espousing the theory. His book, *The Roots of Muslim Rage*, expounded upon his diatribe, attempting to condense fourteen centuries of Islamic civilization into a few broad and grossly inaccurate generalizations. These ideas, often parroted by mainstream pundits such as Thomas Friedman, simply state that the open hostility from Muslims toward the West is as a direct result of its internal collapse as a civilization and the inherent jealousy, envy, and resentment toward the scientific, technological, ideological, and social advancements made by the enlightened Western societies. Modern Islamic movements are dismissed as pathetic and misguided attempts to reclaim the preeminence enjoyed by the Ottoman Empire centuries ago over its Christian neighbors. Islam is always presented as being in constant struggle against its favorite historic enemy, Christianity. In fact, the modern skirmishes between Muslim groups and Western (primarily American or Israeli) targets are portrayed simply as a continuation of the ideologically motivated crusades of the thirteenth century without any explanation of current political realities and foreign policy objectives of the United States. Though he frequently masks them in the language of objective academia, Lewis' opinions are clear: Islam is inherently antagonistic to all notions of freedom, democracy, and the enlightened values of Western civilization.

Additionally, the tendency toward violence is explained as inherent to Middle Eastern cultures and the Muslim faith. In 1998, Lewis argued that the edict issued by Osama bin Laden against the West was emblematic of mainstream Islamic ideology and sentiment toward outside cultures. His glaringly inaccurate oversimplification depicts Islam's worldview as divided into two halves, the world of Islam, where the religion reigns supreme, and the world of warfare, where it is in a state of constant enmity with those who have yet to accept the faith or submit to its rule. Here, as in many other places, Lewis clearly misrepresents hundreds of years of Islamic history and tradition with the intention of presenting it as a threat to the West.

Bernard Lewis has had tremendous influence on pro-Israeli zealots in Western academia, as well as in the halls of power in Washington and Tel Aviv. He is hailed as "the doyen of Middle Eastern studies," the "father" of Islamic studies, "[a]rguably the West's most distinguished scholar on the Middle East," and "[a] Sage for the Age." He is frequently welcomed in Israel and in pro-Israel circles in the United States. In fact, his son, Michael Lewis, is the head of the "opposition research" department at the American Israel Public Affairs Committee (AIPAC), Israel's chief lobby in the United States. While portraying himself as an objective academic, Bernard Lewis has wandered into the area of lobbying on numerous occasions. Following the 1998 embassy bombings in Kenya and Tanzania, Lewis signed a widely circulated letter to President Clinton calling for him to begin a major military campaign in Iraq, supported by the corrupt Iraqi National Congress, to overthrow Saddam Hussein. Along with Lewis, the letter's endorsers consisted of a who's who of Washington's pro-Israel zealots, including Paul Wolfowitz, Richard Perle, Frank Gaffney, AIPAC's David Wurmser, Eliot Abrams, and Steven Bryen, friend of convicted Israeli spy Jonathan Pollard.

In all, Lewis' activities reached a new level of notoriety following the attacks of September 11. As with other Islamophobes during this period of widespread hysteria and obsession with Islamic fanaticism, Lewis took to the airwaves, where he flaunted his rancorous assertions regarding Islam, Muslims, and the Middle East. Of his many colorful statements, one particularly stands out for its brashness. In an April 16, 2002 interview by Charlie Rose, Lewis casually stated, "Asking Arafat to give up terrorism would be like asking Tiger to give up golf." As Alam contends, "That is a statement whose malicious intent and vindictive meanness might have been excusable if it came from an official Israeli spokesman."[22]

Perhaps his most important recent accomplishment, however, has been his book following 9/11. As seemingly every Islamophobe seems to have cashed in on the tragedy by authoring a piece of exploitative propaganda, Bernard Lewis would be no exception. In mid-2002, he published *What Went Wrong? Western Impact and Middle Eastern Response*, a book aiming to explore the roots of Islam's civilizational collapse. As before, Lewis engages in a futile exercise in broad generalizations and manipulation of history to advance his ideologically directed views on the subject. He paints a vivid picture of an arrogant and stubborn civilization that refuses to look within itself for the answer to its steady decline toward the end of the Ottoman era, but rather continuously placed the blame on the West, ultimately pitting a return to a puritanical Islam as the only solution, further driving it into a new dark age and an eternal "holy" conflict with an enlightened Western civilization. Alim further explains Lewis' line of reasoning as follows:

> Clearly, Lewis's presentation of his narrative of
> Middle Eastern decline without any context is
> a ploy. His objective is to whittle down world
> history, to reduce it to a primordial contest

between two historical adversaries, the West and Islam. This is historiography in the crusading mode, one that purports to resume the Crusades and carry them to their unfinished conclusion, the triumph of the West or, conversely, the humiliation and defeat of Middle Eastern Islam. Once this framework has been established, with its exclusive focus on a failing Islamic civilization, it is quite easy to cast the narrative of this decay as a uniquely Islamic phenomenon, which must then be explained in terms of specifically Islamic failures. Thus Lewis's agenda in *What Went Wrong?* is to discover all that was and is "wrong" with Islamic societies and to explain their decline and present troubles in terms of these "wrongs."[23]

The aims of Bernard Lewis were widely successful, as the book was hailed as a much-needed honest look at the dilemma in the Middle East and its historical underpinnings, all of which led to the era of "bin Ladenism" and open war between East and West. This ostensible academic analysis served as the backbone for the radical neo-conservative shift in American policy toward the Middle East post-9/11. This deliberately faulty reasoning has left the American people and their leaders feeling completely blameless for the state of affairs both in the Middle East and at home, but rather justified in their continuous struggle to "civilize" Muslim society and essentially "free" them from themselves, as was the thunderous rhetoric in the months that followed September 11, 2001. ■

PROFILE: THE WARMONGERS OF
PAX AMERICANA

• William Kristol

• Paul Wolfowitz

• Richard Perle

While Bush had taken office as a traditional conservative skeptical of "nation-building" and calling for a more "humble" foreign policy, after 9-11, he was captured by the neocons and converted to an agenda they had worked up years before. Suddenly, he sounded just like them, threatening wars on "axis-of-evil" nations that had nothing to do with 9-11.

—Patrick J. Buchanan, http://antiwar.com, February 16, 2004.

• Douglas Feith

• Elliott Abrams

• David Wurmser

Neocons believe it is better for the government to control teaching and research rather than to allow established policy to be questioned. But we are more likely to understand "why they hate us," and what we can do about it when old ideas can be challenged without fear. Freedom, including academic freedom, is the best way to make Americans safe.

—Joel Beinin, professor of history, Stanford University,
Media Monitors Network, April 2004.

Chapter 6

NEO-CONS AND ANTI-MUSLIM FOREIGN POLICY*

The attacks of 9/11 provided a heaven-sent opportunity to a cabal of neo-conservatives and Zionist extremists close to Israel's Likud to capture American foreign policy ... The alliance of American supremacists, right-wing Jews, and fundamentalist Christians has produced ... the doctrine of global hegemony.

—Patrick Seale, British specialist on the Middle East,
March 11, 2003.

Amerian foreign policy shifted dramatically after the 9/11 attacks on America's symbols of economic and military power. Before 9/11, the establishment figures, led for almost half a century by Henry Kissinger, followed a policy basically of containment. The goal was stability without

---

The discussion of neo-conservatism in this chapter was taken from an article by Dr. Robert Dickson Crane, entitled "The Neo-Conservative Alliance: Its Overt and Covert Roots," which appeared in the Summer/Fall 2003 volume of the Middle East Affairs Journal and is expanded in his latest book, Shaping a Common Vision for America: Challenge and Response.

concern for any higher values. During the last decade of the twentieth century, Samuel Huntington's paradigm of civilizational clash dominated, but the option of containment was preferred to the alternative of rollback. In effect, the foreign policy was to buy time in the hope that problems would go away. This view was shared by all of America's allies. Though the gears were in motion for many years prior to it, September 11 would change everything. It opened the way for a closely knit group, known as the neo-conservatives, to emerge from the shadows, where for more than a decade they had been building competence in the expectation that eventually they would be needed to implement a new foreign policy of roll-back designed to destroy the "Islamic threat to civilization."

Normally foreign policy in America is formed by intellectual leaders who migrate regularly within the troika of academia, think-tanks, and government. Unlike the shapers of domestic policy, these intellectual leaders influence policy primarily by shaping ideological paradigms of thought and are little influenced by domestic special interests. Multinational oil and construction giants as well as lobbyists for Israeli interests operate within the framework, constraints, and guidance of these competing paradigms.

The traumatic event of 9/11 made it possible and mandatory for the leaders of three such paradigms for the first time to ally in support of a single foreign policy. These three are: the permanent bi-partisan foreign policy establishment, typified by the scion of the status quo, Henry Kissinger, and the annual Bilderberg conferences; the Christian evangelical movement, as represented by the millenarian Pat Robertson, which had become enamored of Christian Zionism; and the neo-conservative revolutionaries, proto-typified by the father and son duo, Irving and William

Kristol. The single foreign policy on which all agreed as an ultimate goal was the institution of a Pax America through bold policies of unilateral, military pre-emption.

A primary paradigm, influential for the first time in the White House, is the millenarian mission of the 30 million or so radical Protestants in the United States who support Israel as a means to accelerate the return of the Messiah. George W. Bush was already familiar with the Evangelical movement and its pro-Zionist policies long before he became a student of foreign policy, and, in fact, reportedly gave talks on more than one occasion to its supporters. This movement originated more than 130 years ago in the form of Christian Zionism, but did not affect foreign policy until the so-called religious right decided to go into politics as an organized movement in the early 1970s.

Perhaps more important as a paradigmatic movement after 9/11 is, neo-conservatism. The modern history of the neo-conservative movement has become the subject of hundreds of scholarly articles and dozens of books, including analysis of its penetration into Washington's foreign policy think-tanks and among the boards and program officers of their supporting charitable foundations. A wealth of details emerged about individual personalities and policy manifestos that led directly to the attack on Iraq in March, 2003, and to a promise of possibly more such attacks to come.

The origin of the neo-conservative paradigm of thought is still little known except by those who have been fighting it all their lives. It originated in a commendable desire to bring freedom and democracy to the entire world and in the conviction that only America could bring this about. This background put it at loggerheads with the establishment paradigm of stability as the only legitimate purpose of foreign policy.

Neo-conservatism originated during the late 1960s in the rise within foreign policy circles of what might be termed a fundamentalist version of the older movement known as secular humanism. There is no reason to believe that President Bush favored or even knew anything about neo-conservatism until the election campaign of 2000. The principal leader of neo-conservatism at the time was William Kristol, who edited the openly imperialist journal, the *Weekly Standard*. Kristol's journal supported Bush's principal rival in the 2000 primaries, Senator John McCain. As a result, until 9/11, the President's chief advisor, Karl Rove, consigned the neo-conservatives to an outer limbo in Washington. Although they had some "sleepers" in the Pentagon, the neo-cons had virtually no access to the White House.

The appellation "neo-conservative" was invented by liberal leftists to attack two of their own, the neo-conservative god-fathers, Irving Kristol and Norman Podhoretz, who are founders of the movement's principal publications. They committed treason against the liberal establishment by attacking both Lyndon Johnson's welfare economics as ineffective in his "war against poverty" and the strategy of compromise rather than victory as self-defeating in Vietnam. They were refugees from the McGovern Revolution. Irving Kristol once joked that a neo-conservative is a liberal mugged by reality.

Although their congressional heroes were the two Democratic senators, Pat Moynihan in domestic policy and Henry "Scoop" Jackson in military strategy, the founding neo-cons openly shifted party alliances by joining the Republicans, despite their total opposition to the philosophical bases of what became the Reagan Revolution. They were welcomed by the three principal conservative think-tanks at the time. These in chronological order of founding were: the domestic-oriented American Enterprise Institute for Public Policy Research, founded in 1943; the Center for Strategic and International Studies founded in 1962; and the Heritage Foundation, founded in 1973.

Under the neo-cons' dynamic influence, these once paleo-conservative centers soon transmuted into bastions of neo-conservative thought and action in Washington, as did eventually the supporting conservative foundations. The last foreign policy think-tank to come under the sway of the neo-conservatives, and the first one in date of founding (1955), was Robert Strausz Hupe's Foreign Policy Research Institute. In 1987, Daniel Pipes became the FPRI's sole Director. The last conservative foundation to hold out on behalf of paleo-conservatism was the Earhart Foundation, which went the way of all the others when its long-serving Program Director, Tony Sullivan, quit in the year 2001.

The neo-conservatives were the very opposite of traditional conservatism, which builds on respect for the past wisdom of America's founders. The founders' paleo-conservative paradigm emphasized a reinforcing balance of order, justice, and freedom, based on recognition of the flaws in human nature and the dangers of utopian ventures in either domestic or foreign policy. The neo-cons, on the other hand, are virulently anti-establishment, and hence basically hostile both to the paleo-conservative paradigm of traditionalism and to the Kissingerian pursuit of a permanent status quo. Neo-conservatism was conceived in reaction against the moral relativism of the 1960s, represented by the "new age" openness to all cultures, and against Kissinger's pursuit of a value-free alliance of "moral equivalence" in a condominium of Soviet and American power to stabilize the world. The neo-cons preferred moral clarity, though not religious dogma, in opposition to diplomatic finesse.

They were skeptical of old alliances and multilateral institutions, and preferred the unhindered pursuit of America's destiny to shape a new world of its own making.

The Mentors of Neo-Conservatism

The two widely known mentors of all modern neo-conservatives are Albert Wohlstetter in military strategy, originally from the U.S. Air Force's captive think-tank, The RAND Corporation, and Leo Strauss in paradigmatic philosophy, who brought a European version of conservatism to the University of Chicago from Germany. Wohlstetter opposed detente with the Soviet Union, even the very thought of disarmament, and pioneered, together with Herman Kahn, a fellow RANDian who founded the Hudson Institute in 1961, a sophisticated nuclear doctrine of escalation dominance to legitimate the use of nuclear weapons, especially preemptively in tactical warfare against the enemies of America. Instead of the paralyzing strategy of arms control through Mutual Assured Destruction (MAD) among equals, Wohlstetter favored preparation for limited wars, both locally and globally, based on building unrivaled technological superiority and new generations of "smart" high-precision weapons capable of disrupting the enemy's tactical command and control. This strategy, which Wohlstetter and Kahn promoted perhaps ahead of its time in the 1960s, was the inspiration for President Reagan's Star Wars initiative in the 1980's and is precisely what their disciples under Donald Rumsfeld, who started his political career in 1962 at the age of 29 in the House Science and Astronautics Committee, are trying to apply in the Pentagon today.

The neo-conservatives' principal political mentor was Scoop Jackson. Senator Jackson was a student of Wohlstetter, as was the principal neo-conservative policy-maker in Washington today, Deputy Secretary of Defense Paul Wolfowitz, whom Wohlstetter mentored during Wolfowitz' doctoral studies at the University of California in the late 1960s and early 1970s. Fully half of the leading neo-conservatives in Washington today, Wolfowitz, Richard Perle, Doug Feith, and Elliott Abrams, worked on the Hill for Scoop Jackson. The depth and breadth of the neo-con old-boy's network is shown by the fact that in 1985 Wohlstetter introduced to Perle the "man with the inside track" in the Pentagon for support in governing Iraq, Ahmed Chalabi.

The grand old man of the neo-conservative grand strategy, for whom Wohlstetter was relatively only a tactician, was the social philosopher, Leo Strauss. Born in 1899 in Germany, he was deeply influenced by the Nazi takeover of Germany in 1933 from the Weimar Republic, which Strauss asserted "presented the spectacle of justice without power, or of a justice incapable of resorting to power." The Straussians, based in his Committee on Social Thought at the University of Chicago, laid the foundation for the neo-conservatives' near paranoia about the threat of universal chaos and for their conviction that peace is possible only by proactive projection of force to preempt the very possibility of attacks on America's vital interests.

Strauss's influence on neo-conservatism and its effect today is perhaps best shown by the impact on President Bush in March, 2001, before 9/11, by the former Israeli military man, Robert D. Kaplan, who briefed President Bush on his book, *The Coming Anarchy: Shattering the Dreams of the Post Cold War*. Kaplan presented his thesis that the world faces a meltdown, that America's dominance is tenuous, and that "the most important moral commitment for America is to preserve its power." The only realistic grand strategy for America after 9/11 is to follow the "enduring relevance of ancient principles" represented by the great empires of antiquity. The new element in the world after 9/11, according to Kaplan, is that barbarians have exploited a global ideology, Islam, to recruit "holy warriors" and allies in a global war that has now struck at the heart of the empire. The only adequate counter-strategy is to remake the map of the Middle East, and indeed of the world, not geographically but through regime change in order to eliminate the ideological infrastructure of terrorism.

This is right out of Leo Strauss's playbook, though Strauss was a master of the classical philosophy of the ancients and not a military strategist. Strauss saw an inherent tension between liberalism, which can lead to relativism, and the active defense of democracy by bold measures against forces that do not share American values. Although he was an atheist Jew, Strauss emphasized the necessity of superiority in principles, even if this required the ministrations of religion to maintain the solidarity of the populace. He taught that the key to pro-active democracy against its enemies is the "superiority of the regime," by which the younger or second-generation Straussians understand a quasi-religious exaltation of American values worldwide against the threat of both state and sub-state tyrannies of thought and action.

This new interpretation of Strauss's basic concepts can embody utopian messianism on a par with that of modern Evangelicals. Both the first and second-generation followers of Leo Strauss call for the rule of law in the world but only after a new world order has been established by astute orchestration of

America's overwhelming military and economic power. True to their philosophical godfather, the present-day neo-cons had no qualms about exploiting the crisis of 9/11 to construct a working alliance among establishmentarians, religious devotees, and their own revolutionary vision. This vision calls for global acceptance of their own universal paradigm under the auspices of their own planetary regime.

Another primary figure, Robert Strausz-Hupe, brought long-range global vision from Austria to America's first foreign policy think tank, the Foreign Policy Research Institute. Of the three main figures, he was perhaps the most profound. A former investment banker, Robert Strausz-Hupe fled Germany during the depression. He considered himself to be a principled conservative but was a progenitor of neo-conservatism in the sense that he first presented coherently the concept of unilateral American leadership in the world. In his seminal article, "The Balance of Tomorrow," published at the beginning of 1957 in the first issue of his journal, *Orbis: A Quarterly Journal of World Affairs*, he introduced the founding paradigm of America's first foreign policy think-tank, the Foreign Policy Research Institute. More than a third of a century before the demise of Communism and Francis Fukuyama's paradigm of "the end of history," Strausz-Hupe formulated what we might call the mother of all imperialist paradigms. He forecast not only that Communism was doomed to failure and extinction but that democracy would succeed it as the world-ordering principle if the United States were prepared to seize the opportunity. Strausz-Hupe's paradigm was known as a forward strategy to win the protracted conflict against the forces of chaos. The following are quotes from his seminal articulation of this paradigm in his founding think-piece, "The Balance of Tomorrow," published in 1957, almost half a century before its progeny in the neo-conservatives came before the public spotlight:

> The issue before the United States is the unification of the globe under its leadership within this generation. How effectively and rapidly the United States will accomplish this task will determine the survival of the United States as a leading power, probably the survival of Western culture, and conceivably the survival of mankind.

> This task must be accomplished within the near future because of two overriding considerations: 1) the political emergence of the Asian peoples, together with their tremendous population growth, is altering profoundly the international and regional balance of power and presages regional and international conflicts and war; and 2) within the foreseeable future, a number of nations, other than the United States, the Soviet Union, and Britain, will acquire nuclear weapons and other means of mass destruction.

This almost forgotten formulation of the mother of all imperialist paradigms became part of the neo-conservative movement when Daniel Pipes revived it in the Winter 1991-1992 issue of *Orbis*. Many others co-opted the works of the founders of neo-conservatism in the early 1990s. Joining Pipes on the Board of Advisers of *Orbis* were Martin Indyk, a well-known Zionist stalwart who later became

Assistant Secretary of State, Samuel P. Huntington, who at that time postulated that Islam is the arch enemy of Western civilization, and Bernard Lewis, who had become famous as the scholar who attributed the dynamics of Islam to "rage" and prepared the way psychologically in May, 1990, for the confrontation between Iraq and the United States three months later in the build-up to the Gulf War.

The editorial in the Winter 1991-1992 issue of Orbis, entitled "Foreign Policy Research Institute: Seeking a New World," states that most issues of Orbis do not represent the institutional views of its governing body, the FPRI, but that this special issue is to serve in the nature of a "house organ" "in order to give our readers a flavor of the research being done at our sponsoring institution." The editorial adds, "Robert Strausz-Hupe wrote in this introductory essay that Americans were just then assuming the leadership of a new universal empire. The research done at the FPRI and elsewhere continues to testify to the perceptiveness of Strausz-Hupe's vision, and the soundness of his policies." Furthermore, rather ominously, the editorial lauds the "forward strategy" of Strausz-Hupe in what he called the "protracted conflict" against the USSR and, referring to another article in the same issue of the journal, states that, "the USSR is not the last of America's totalitarian enemies; he [the author] recommends that the same forward strategy used successfully against Moscow now be used elsewhere."

The meaning of this veiled threat was detailed three years later by House Speaker, Newt Gingrich, who in the year 2003 showed his true stripes by emerging as a leading neo-conservative extremist. On February 8, 1995, at a conference of military and intelligence officers on developing global strategy, Speaker Gingrich announced, "I have yet to see a coherent strategy for fighting Islamic totalitarianism." This neo-conservative attack on Islam as a religion reverses the normal distinction between Islam as a peaceful religion and Muslims as a diverse people. To attack the religion, as distinct from its followers, is a technique of mimetic warfare to control the terminology of public debate by introducing mimes or words as symbolic shorthand for entire visions, paradigms, and accompanying strategies.

The purpose of such disinformation is to revive the concept of protracted conflict between the old forces of the "totalitarian" Evil Empire or Axis of Evil and the white knights of the "free world" fighting for "freedom and democracy." The emotive word "totalitarian" becomes an instrument of thought control designed to escalate the battle against terrorism to the ideological level of grand strategy, because totalitarianism was the major global threat to Western civilization for most of the twentieth century.

By the mere turn of a phrase, Islam becomes not merely a religion that occasionally has been distorted by some to produce both private and state-sponsored terrorism, but a generic monster that must be fought wherever it raises its ugly head, because "Islamic totalitarianism" by definition threatens the survival of the free world. This simple turn of terminology serves to short-circuit thought so that operational doctrine and specific military plans no longer have to be based on knowledge. The thinking has already been done and encapsulated in the new language, where symbolism becomes an unchallengable reality. And by a process of self-fulfilling prophecy, the potential danger becomes real and thereby triggers a spiraling confrontation of action and reaction with the zero-sum result of universal chaos.

The persons involved in this campaign are too numerous to discuss in full depth. Generally, they are involved in the campaign to publicly denigrate Islam and Muslims, as well as the mission to implement policies for the benefit of Israel rather than the United States and the underlying motive of pax Americana. This chapter will briefly touch upon certain figures central to this phenomenon, whose ideology stems from the philosophy of neo-conservatism. As will become clearer, the web has continued to grow ever larger, with consistent links to the many Zionist Islamophobes within it.

• William Kristol

As the son of Irving Kristol, one of the founders of neo-conservatism, William Kristol has been an important figure, especially in recent years, in the direction of American foreign policy. As a Harvard student, Kristol was heavily influenced by the works of Leo Strauss. In the mid-1980s, he rose to become chief of staff at the Department of Education during the Reagan administration. With the election of George Bush in 1988, Kristol was appointed to work directly under Vice President Dan Quayle as his chief of staff. Following Bush's reelection defeat in 1992, Kristol left politics to become a television commentator on ABC's "This Week." Three years later, he was fired from ABC and began his own conservative magazine, *The Weekly Standard.* Since its inception, the magazine has promoted vastly rightwing neo-conservative views associated mainly with the Israeli Likud Party. Although the magazine floundered with low subscription rates and huge losses, it has been consistently financed by right-wing media mogul Rupert Murdoch. *The Weekly Standard* has also been one of the leading voices in attacking American Muslim leaders and their institutions. In his various media appearances, Kristol has trumpeted the imminent danger of "radical Islam," while promoting the American-Israel alliance as necessary to fend off terrorism. He has also been a leading voice in the denigration of Muslim political organizations that have tried to voice themselves politically in recent years. He grew especially uncomfortable at the prospect of an American Muslim bloc vote supporting a presidential candidate in 2000 and a Republican at that.

Moreover, one of Kristol's more infamous feats was his chairmanship of the Project for the New American Century, a neo-conservative ad hoc think tank established in 1997 that sought to push foreign policy proposals on behalf of Israel's Likud Party. PNAC's ultimate aim is to establish what it refers to as "Pax Americana" across the globe. Essentially, the goal is to transform America, the sole remaining superpower, into a planetary empire by force of arms. A report released by PNAC in September of 2000 entitled "Rebuilding America's Defenses" codifies this plan, which requires a massive increase in defense spending and the conduct of multiple major theater wars in order to establish American dominance. One of George W. Bush's first budget plans called for the exact dollar amount to be spent on defense that was requested by PNAC in 2000. Among its initiatives was a strategy to "reshape the Middle East," which essentially entailed military campaigns in "hostile" countries, beginning with Iraq, then moving onto Iran, Syria, Saudi Arabia, and a final and complete defeat of the Palestinians. What is more alarming is that this document, first published in 1998, suggested that such an endeavor could only be justified politically if America were to suffer an attack similar to that of Pearl Harbor. The 9/11 attacks have since been used to justify an all-out war on terrorism, with campaigns in Afghanistan, Iraq, and a more hard-line policy against Iran, Syria, Saudi Arabia, and the American government's unconditional and blind support of Ariel Sharon's policies toward the Palestinians. Moreover, many of Kristol's colleagues in this policy initiative have since become high-ranking members of the Bush administration, including the Deputy Secretary of Defense, Paul Wolfowitz. Kristol, who also sat on the board of Enron and received at least $100,000 in two years, has been a chief architect of the Bush administration's post-9/11 policy, and has been seen widely on TV selling these initiatives as serving the best interest of all Americans, though they have clearly advantaged only Israel.

• Paul Wolfowitz

Of all the agents of Islamophobia operating within the past few decades, Paul Wolfowitz has probably risen to the highest rank. As a veteran of both the Reagan and first Bush administrations, Wolfowitz served in various capacities in the Pentagon, and then as ambassador to Indonesia, the largest Muslim country in the world. Unfortunately, Wolfwitz's views on Islam have been very inhospitable. He is seen all around as being the most "hawkish" member of government in every administration he has served. What has recently been termed the "Bush doctrine" is actually a Wolfowitz concoction from as early as the first Bush administration. During both, the Bush I and Clinton administrations, Wolfowitz advocated the policy of preemption, as opposed to containment. He frequently proposed military action to eliminate threats posed by "rogue regimes" or "terrorist states," emphasizing the Arab and

Muslim world. Moreover, despite his many positions within government, Wolfowitz had no qualms about associating with clearly partisan organizations that espouse extremist views. He holds a position on the board of the Washington Institute for Near East Policy, and was a crucial member of the Project for the New American Century. He was one of the earliest signatories of a 1998 PNAC letter to President Clinton urging a preemptive military campaign against Iraq. By 2001, everything was going in Wolfowitz's favor. He was appointed second-in-command at the Pentagon, under Defense Secretary and fellow hawk, Donald Rumsfeld. Following the 9/11 attacks later that year, Wolfowitz and his ideological extremist clique had finally caught the ear of an American president. Within months, Bush Jr. had adopted the Wolfowitz doctrine as his own, and the path to preemptive war against Iraq was wide open.

• Richard Perle

Often referred to as the "architect" of the U.S. war on Iraq, or the "ideological father" of the American war on terror, Richard Perle has a particularly immense reputation for shady dealings. In Washington, D.C., he earned himself the nickname, "Prince of Darkness" for his questionable methods in achieving his goals. He has been an insider on the national political scene for four decades, since first working at the office of Senator Scoop Jackson—a name one might recall from reading about William Kristol and Frank Gaffney, who also served there during this time. Perle then worked at a military consulting firm before being appointed Assistant

Secretary of Defense under Ronald Reagan. Perle's hawkish ideology has never been a secret, as he is frequently seen rabidly supporting Israel while being highly critical of even moderate Arab states like Jordan and Egypt. In fact, Perle has often been accused of being an Israeli agent. A report stated that while he worked for Jackson, "an FBI summary of a 1970 wiretap recorded Perle discussing classified information with someone in the Israeli embassy." Even after he was in the Pentagon, Perle was known to have taken a $50,000 payment from an Israeli arms manufacturer. No stranger to controversy, Perle also hired Stephen Bryen as a Pentagon aide, amid objections from prominent senators, because Bryen, who had also worked for AIPAC, was dismissed from his job in the Senate Foreign Relations Committee for trying to gain intelligence information for the Israeli government.

Perle relentlessly pursued his neo-conservative objectives, becoming a policy advisor to the Likud party in 1996, and affiliating with dozens of questionable organizations. Like nearly all the others profiled in this chapter, Perle is a member of the Washington Institute for Near East Policy. But, he has also been listed on the roster of the Israeli Institute, the Jewish Institute for National Security Affairs, the staunchly conservative American Enterprise Institute, and of course, the Project for the New American Century. Perle also became a member of the important Defense Policy Board, a panel appointed by the Pentagon to provide it with "independent, informed advice and opinion concerning major matters of defense policy."

Under President George W. Bush, Perle became the chairman of the Defense Policy Board, which is credited with forming the strategy for the invasion of Iraq. Nearly all of the thirty members of this board, however, have strong business and corporate ties, and therefore reap tremendous financial benefits from the policies they advocate. Not the least of these is Richard Perle, who was forced to resign from his position as chairman after some of these business ties surfaced in the spring of 2003—though not until after the first bombs had already fallen on Baghdad. Indeed, Perle's corporate ties run very deep, as he is on the board of Hollinger Digital, and through that company, many others. His corporate ties have even allotted him publicity, such as through his close business associate Conrad Black and the over 400 newspapers he owns worldwide. Many of Perle's writings, such as the rant against Iraq published in *Israel Insider*, have actually surfaced in speeches by President Bush. Perle has also been involved in the highly controversial Total Information Awareness project, which would allow complete surveillance or "data mining" of all electronic communications among Americans, a most gross violation of privacy.

It should be deeply disturbing to all concerned citizens that such a disreputable individual has been able to attain the amount of power and influence that Richard Perle has had.

• Douglas Feith

Another of the close-knit neo-conservative bunch, Feith has also played an instrumental role in shaping American policy, especially with regard to the Middle East. He is another remnant of the Reagan-era Pentagon, serving as Deputy Assistant Secretary of Defense for Negotiations from 1984-1986.

His current position is Undersecretary of Defense for Policy, the third-ranking civilian position at the Pentagon—directly under Paul Wolfowitz. Feith also has very strong ties to Richard Perle. In 1989, he registered a company, International Advisors, Inc., as a foreign agent to represent the Turkish government to "promote the objective of U.S.-Turkey defense industrial cooperation." According to one article, "The IAI was described in both the United States and Turkey as the brainchild of Richard N. Perle. ... One report states that official documents filed with the U.S. Department of Justice Criminal Division show Douglas Feith as not only the CEO of IAI but also its only stockholder."[1] Perle was also the single highest-paid consultant of IAI, while Feith's law firm received hundreds of thousands of dollars from the company. In 1992, Feith and Perle joined together with other neo-cons in staunch opposition to President Bush Sr.'s peace initiatives for the Middle East. They formed the Committee on U.S. Interests in the Middle East, a militantly pro-Israeli group. Feith has continued to play a strong role in current policy initiatives, especially the U.S. campaign in Iraq.

• Elliott Abrams

Labeled by the *New York Times* as "a passionate advocate for Israel," having worked tirelessly in support of the most rightwing policies of the Jewish state, it was yet another disappointment when Abrams was appointed by President George W. Bush to the National Security Council in June 2001. Moreover, by December, he became Special

Assistant to the President and Senior Director for Near East and North African Affairs, including Arab/Israel relations. So with the man whom the *Washington Report on Middle East Affairs* has dubbed a "militant Zionist" at the helm, it is little wonder that President Bush has taken such a hard-line policy in support of Israel's atrocities.[2] As a zealous opponent of the Oslo Peace Process since its inception, Abrams successfully halted that process by promoting the Bush administration's position to cut off ties with the Palestinian Authority while providing unlimited support to Ariel Sharon in all his actions, including military strikes against Syria in October 2003. Moreover, Abrams has a more spotty record than any of his cohorts, stemming from the Iran-Contra scandal of the 1980s, in which he played a major role. As Assistant Secretary of State for Inter-American Affairs under Reagan, Abrams was personally responsible for the scheme of pushing Israel to sell American weapons to Iran in its war against Iraq (which the U.S. was also supporting militarily) and in turn selling weapons to Nicaraguan rebels, against an explicit ban by Congress. In 1991, Abrams pleaded guilty to lying to Congress about the affair during his testimonies before congressional committees. President Bush Sr. ultimately pardoned him in 1992. As the son-in-law of one of the founders of neo-conservatism, N. P. Podhoretz, Abrams is a vocal proponent of its extremist philosophy. He authored a book in 1997 entitled *Faith or Fear: How Jews Can Survive in Christian America*, arguing for the importance of racial purity, while nonetheless trumpeting the call to evangelical Christians to step up their support of Israel. Abrams is closely tied to many of the previously mentioned Zionist stalwarts. He is one of the original signatories of the Project for the New American Century, chaired by William Kristol. He is affiliated with Frank Gaffney's Center for Security Policy, and the American Enterprise Institute, where Richard Perle was one of his early mentors. He also was associated with the Committee on U.S. Interests in the Middle East, founded by Perle and Douglas Feith. As has now been made more apparent, these various policy-makers and government bureaucrats are all inextricably linked by their various front organizations, shady business dealings, and a binding philosophy of extremism.

• David Wurmser

As a former special assistant to the Undersecretary of State John Bolton, who was promoted in September 2003 to the office of Vice President Dick Cheney, David Wurmser rounds out the usual suspects of neo-cons occupying high political appointments. Wurmser is married to an Israeli and served as advisor to Israeli Prime Minister Benjamin Netanyahu in 1996. A paper submitted to Netanyahu by Wurmser, written primarily by Richard Perle and Douglas Feith, was entitled "A Clean Break: A New Strategy for Securing the Realm" and laid out plans to eliminate the Iraqi regime in favor of a pro-American monarchy, while isolating Syria with an alliance of Israel, Turkey, Jordan, and a new Iraq. The plan then calls for a military assault on Syria, ending its influence in Lebanon, and bringing down the ruling Ba'ath Party of President Assad. Ultimately, the goal of the policy was to end Israel's short-lived "land for peace" strategy in dealing with Palestinians by shifting the balance of power in the entire region. These ideas ultimately translated into actual American policy under the Bush administration, by successful lobbying for the invasion of Iraq. Moreover, Wurmser and his former boss Bolton are viewed as personally responsible for the administration's designation in early 2003 of Syria, Libya, and Cuba as a secondary "axis of evil." Wurmser does not try to hide his ideological leanings, as he is affiliated with the AIPAC-funded Washington Institute for Near East Policy, the American Enterprise Institute, and an Israeli-based think tank, the Institute for Advanced Strategic and Political Studies. He wrote a book several years before September 11, calling for war with Iraq. The introduction to Wurmser's 1999 book, *Tyranny's Ally: America's Failure to Defeat Saddam Hussein*, was written by Perle. ∎

Chapter 7

THE PRO-ISRAELI
LOBBIES AND
THINK-TANKS

One day, God willing, the American people will wake up and
realize what a painful price has been exacted for allowing their
politicians to sell their souls to the Israeli lobby. I have to give the
Israeli lobby credit. They recognized the souls weren't worth
much and bought them on the cheap.

Charley Reese, King Features Syndicate, Inc.,
April 24, 2002.

Thus far, the focus of the discussion surrounding the
anti-Muslim policy and propaganda war has been
individuals, whether operating in the mainstream media,
academia, policy-making circles, or high public office. In
reality, American politics is based heavily on the role that
institutions play in shaping public opinion and affecting
policy. Very rarely do individuals have any real effect without
financial and logistical support, along with the eminent
platform provided by institutions. The pro-Israeli forces in

America are no exception. Virtually every person previously outlined is in some way, shape, or form affiliated with the countless organizations that exist to promote Israel's interests while simultaneously undermining Islam and the Muslim community and thereby creating the tensions and enmity that have plagued recent history. Groups have emerged to address the various needs of this campaign. Some, such as the Middle East Media Research Institute (MEMRI) focus their efforts on distorting the flow of information to the media and effectively misinforming the American public. Others, such as the Washington Institute for Near East Policy (WINEP), masquerade as academic think tanks while promoting its members into positions of influence within the government, or flouting them as scholars on the Middle East or "terrorism experts" on television. So-called "watchdog" groups, such as the Anti-Defamation League (ADL), are devoted to protecting the image of Israel by lobbing accusations of anti-Semitism against any critics. They also spend considerable energy and resources defaming Muslim institutions in America.

Some groups prefer to remain small and below the radar, operating behind the scenes to manipulate law enforcement authorities by collecting so-called "intelligence" through questionably legal methods. Such are the groups founded by Steven Emerson and Rita Katz.

And finally, there is the outright Israeli lobby in the United States, led by the American Israel Public Affairs Committee (AIPAC), a group well-known for making members of Congress cow to its demands in fear of incurring its wrath. This group which holds such an infamously tight grip on the discussion of Middle East politics in Washington, is consistently ranked as one of the most powerful lobbies in

America. While previous chapters have made passing mention of the many institutions that have given the Islamophobes a foothold in American politics, this chapter will address these groups head-on, detailing their roles in the ongoing campaign of at least the past decade, but in some cases, many decades.

American Israel Public Affairs Committee (AIPAC)

The pro-Israel lobby's principal American Jewish component is the American Israel Public Affairs Committee. AIPAC became a significant force in shaping public opinion and U.S. Middle East policy after the 1967 Arab-Israeli war. Its power was simultaneously enabled and enhanced by Israel's emergence as a regional surrogate for U.S. military power in the Middle East in the terms outlined by the 1969 Nixon Doctrine. In the 1970s and 1980s, the lobby was able to unseat representatives and senators who could not be counted on to support Israel without qualification, such as Sen. Charles Percy (R-IL), Rep. Paul Findley (R-IL) and Rep. Pete McCloskey (R-CA). In 2002, the pro-Israel lobby successfully targeted African-American representatives Earl Hilliard (D-AL) and Cynthia McKinney (D-GA) for defeat in Democratic primaries. Their defeat enhanced the impression that the pro-Israel lobby wields great power in electoral politics.

An April 2002 feature article in *Prospect* magazine analyzes the influence of the Israeli lobby on American foreign policy. The article identifies AIPAC as the most prominent of the pro-Israel groups in America. It further describes its highly detrimental effects on American politics:

Today the Israel lobby distorts U.S. foreign
policy in a number of ways. Israel's
occupation of the West Bank and Gaza,
enabled by U.S. weapons and money, inflames
anti-American attitudes in Arab and Muslim
countries. The expansion of Israeli settlements
on Palestinian land makes a mockery of the
U.S. commitment to self-determination for
Kosovo, East Timor, and Tibet. The U.S.
strategy of dual containment of Iraq and Iran,
pleases Israel—which is most threatened by
them—but violates the logic of real politik
and alienates most of America's other allies.[1]

The power displayed by groups such as AIPAC is
concentrated in major areas. According to *Prospect*, "The
first is massive U.S. funding for Israel. As Stephen Walt
writes in *International Security*, 'In 1967, Israel's defense
spending was less than half the combined defense
expenditures of Egypt, Iraq, Jordan, and Syria; today,
Israel's defense expenditure is 30 percent larger than the
combined defense spending of these four Arab states'."[2] As
all advocates of Palestinian rights continue to emphasize,
the United States is responsible for Israel's military might by
providing it with nearly $5 billion in annual aid, much of
which is strictly military aid to a country with a nuclear,
chemical, and biological weapons program, as well as the
latest and most advanced conventional weapons technology.
All of this prowess comes courtesy of American taxpayer
dollars. In fact, groups such as SUSTAIN (Stop U.S. Taxpayer Aid to Israel Now) have emerged solely to combat this
egregious sin of American foreign policy. More American

aid goes to Israel than any other country in the world, and the $5 billion even surpasses the amount given to the entire continent of Africa each year, home to the most poverty-stricken populations on earth.

Prospect's report continues, "Along with aid, the Israel lobby demands unconditional U.S. diplomatic protection of Israel in the United Nations and other forums."[3] Historically, the United States has been the only country to consistently support Israel's defiance of international law, exemplified by frequent resolutions in the U.N. General Assembly in which the only two votes against them, out of a body of over 180 countries, come from Israel and the United States of America. In addition, the United States has incurred bad relations with the Arab and Muslim world, and even allies in Europe, Asia, and Latin America, simply because of its flagrant double standard with regard to the Arab-Israeli conflict, which has become the focal point of U.S.-Arab relations. In one instance, during a stopover in Kuwait on his way to a state visit in South Asia, former President Clinton devoted the entire two-hour meeting with Kuwaiti leaders to the issue of Israel's security and prosperity.

The pro-Israeli lobby's tactics have been less about churning out voters and more about elevating donors. While heavily pro-Israel districts are certainly prominent in parts of Florida, New York, and California, AIPAC has taken on a nationwide strategy of supporting a candidate in virtually every congressional district. This support has been overwhelmingly financial in nature. As the *St. Petersburg Times* reported, "pro-Israel groups have contributed $41.3 million to federal candidates and political party committees since 1989. In the same period, pro-Arab and pro-Muslim interests have given $297,000."[4] With tens of thousands of dollars given on a regular basis to a large majority of Congress, it is little wonder that America's legislative body has been completely beholden to Israel's interests. Some of the most outrageous resolutions passed in recent years include overwhelming support to move the American embassy in Israel from Tel Aviv to Jerusalem, thereby officially recognizing Israel's occupation of Palestinian lands. "Clearly, the giving by the pro-Israel interests has an impact in Congress," said Larry Noble, executive director of the Center for Responsive Politics.[5] This is the center that came up with the figures for the Israeli lobby's massive donations.

Another resolution passed in May, 2002, expressed unequivocal support for Israel and castigated the Palestinians by a margin of 352 to 82 votes in the House of Representatives. Following its passage, Representative Peter Deutsch (D-FL) hand-delivered the resolution to Israeli Prime Minister Ariel Sharon along with a delegation of other members of Congress. In fact, AIPAC sponsors frequent trips to the region for a number of policymakers. These one-sided journeys include meetings with high-level Israeli officials, military leaders, and victims of Palestinian terrorism, with virtually no meetings with the victims of Israeli terrorism and their leaders and no exposure to the apartheid and countless abuses taking place in the Palestinian territories.

Former Congressman Paul Findley (R-IL) wrote of the Israeli pressure on members of Congress as well as other government leaders in his book, *They Dare to Speak Out*, which chronicles the many instances in which the lives and reputations of those who opposed Israel's massively powerful lobby were ruined. He explains how this unchecked influence has continued to keep all members of Congress in line, many of whom are unwilling to speak their mind for fear of being driven out of office by Israel's influential supporters, led by AIPAC. Findley personally experienced the influence of this sector of American interest groups, leading to his defeat after he spoke out in favor of a more balanced American policy toward Israel. More recent victims include Congresswoman Cynthia McKinney (D-GA) and Congressman Earl Hilliard (D-AL).

Groups like AIPAC even proceed to indoctrinate their targets with their own skewed vision for policy toward the Middle East. According to *Detroit Jewish News*, AIPAC is "a veritable training camp for Capitol Hill staffers." The media is also a frequent target, disseminating AIPAC's version of events as fact for the American public to consume as the truth, leading to widespread misinformation and a false sense of America's relationship with Israel, of which the policy imbalance is a direct consequence.

Washington Institute for Near East Policy (WINEP)

The establishment of the Washington Institute for Near East Policy (WINEP) in 1985 greatly expanded the pro-Israel lobby's influence over policy. WINEP's founding director, Martin Indyk, had previously been research director of AIPAC, which then, as now, focuses much of its efforts on Congress. The Israeli-American Indyk "developed WINEP into a highly effective think tank devoted to maintaining and strengthening the U.S.-Israel alliance through advocacy in the media and lobbying the executive branch."[6]

On the eve of the 1988 presidential elections, with the first Palestinian intifada underway, WINEP made its bid to become a major player in U.S. Middle East policy discussions by issuing a report entitled "Building for Peace: An American Strategy for the Middle East." The report urged the incoming administration to "resist pressures for a procedural breakthrough (on Palestinian-Israeli peace issues) until conditions have ripened." Six members of the study group responsible for the report joined the first Bush administration, which adopted this stalemate recipe not to change until change was unavoidable. Hence, the United States acceded to Israel's refusal to negotiate with the Palestine Liberation Organization despite the PLO's recognition of Israel at the November 1988 session of the Palestine National Council.

When some Israeli leaders became serious about attempting to reach an agreement with the Palestinians, they circumvented the U.S.-sponsored negotiations in Washington (and the pro-Israel lobby) and spoke directly to representatives of the PLO in Oslo. The result was the 1993 Oslo Declaration of Principles. Thus, the adoption of WINEP's policy recommendation to "resist pressures for a procedural breakthrough" by both the Bush and Clinton administrations delayed the start of meaningful Israeli-Palestinian negotiations, contributed to the demonization of the PLO, and multiplied the casualty rate of the first Palestinian intifada.

WINEP's advocacy extended to matters far beyond the Israeli-Palestinian conflict. Well before most Americans took note of radical Islam as a potential threat to their security, for instance, WINEP and its associates were promoting the notion that Israel is a reliable U.S. ally against the spread of Islamism. After Israel expelled more than 400 alleged Palestinian Islamist activists from the West Bank and the Gaza Strip in December, 1992, Israeli television Middle East analyst and WINEP associate Ehud Yaari wrote an op-ed in the *New York Times* summarizing his Hebrew television report on a vast U.S.-based conspiracy to fund Hamas. WINEP's 1992 annual Soref Symposium *"Islam and the US: Challenges for the Nineties"* focused on whether or not Islam was a danger to the United States. At that event, Martin Indyk argued that the United States ought not to encourage democracy in countries that were friendly to Washington, like Jordan and Egypt, and that political participation should be limited to secular parties. This recommendation seemed like a formula for ensuring that Islamist forces would forsake legal political action and engage in armed struggle—precisely what happened in Egypt from 1992 to 1997.

As director for policy and planning at the Washington Institute for Near East Policy, Robert Satloff has been a central figure in the Zionist campaign to promote the Israeli agenda through preaching hatred of Islam. Although claiming to be objective, WINEP is so radically right wing, it frequently opposes "concessions" made by Israeli Prime Minister Ariel Sharon. Satloff himself came out in strong opposition to the U.S. "road map for peace," claiming it was too lenient on the Palestinians. In his capacity as director, Satloff is responsible for providing a whole host of so-called "Middle East experts" to take to the airwaves on television shows and radio programs, while publishing articles in newspapers and magazines nationwide. While feigning impartiality, these figures proceed to tow the Israeli line and ultimately influence the national sentiment and specifically the policy direction in Washington. These ultra-Zionist opinions frequently prevail in magazines such as *The New Republic* and *U.S.*

News and World Report, both of whose editors, Martin Peretz and Mortimer Zuckerman, respectively, also happen to sit on WINEP's board of advisors.

According to Stanford history professor Joel Beinin, "During the 1990s it seemed that the end of the Cold War might diminish the strategic value of the U.S.-Israel alliance. WINEP and its associates strove to maintain the U.S.-Israel relationship as the principle factor in U.S. Middle East policy by promoting Israeli prime minister Yitzhak Rabin's view that Israel was a reliable U.S. ally against radical Islam, which was a new enemy in the post-cold war world order."[7] And aside from simply lobbying successive administrations on Israel's behalf, WINEP has been equally successful in having its affiliates placed within the halls of power. More than ten such individuals were appointed to the highest of ranks under the Clinton administration. Under George W. Bush, the figure more than doubled, including some of the top Pentagon officials.

The Clinton administration was more thoroughly colonized by WINEP associates than its predecessor. Eleven signatories of the final report of WINEP's 1992 commission on U.S.-Israeli relations, "Enduring Partnership," joined the Clinton administration. Among them were National Security Advisor Anthony Lake, U.N. Ambassador and later Secretary of State Madeleine Albright, Undersecretary of Commerce Stuart Eisenstat, and the late Les Aspin, Clinton's first secretary of defense. Shortly after assuming office in 1993, the Clinton administration announced a policy of "dual containment" aimed at isolating Iran and Iraq. The principal formulator and spokesperson for that policy was Martin Indyk, in his new role as Special Assistant to the President and Senior

Director for Near East and South Asian Affairs at the National Security Council. "Dual containment" was the forerunner of George W. Bush's "axis of evil" policy.

In the Bush administration, however, WINEP's influence was outflanked on the right by individuals linked to more monolithically neo-conservative and hawkish think tanks like the Jewish Institute for National Security Affairs (JINSA) and the Project for the New American Century (PNAC). As the London-based Arabic newspaper *Al-Hayat* observed from its onset, "once again, a Washington-based institute was created with Jewish-American money to serve Israel's interests. ... The Washington Institute represents a laboratory for the development of anti-Arab sentiments."[8]

Jewish Institute for National Security Affairs (JINSA)

Founded in 1976, JINSA began as the only U.S. think tank that put "the US-Israel strategic relationship first," citing a concern that U.S. leaders were mistakenly neglecting the relationship between the United States and the only democracy in the Middle East. In the late 1980s, JINSA underwent a profound repurposing of mission which, although retaining the interest in maintaining and strengthening the U.S.-Israeli defense relationship, widened its focus to U.S. defense and foreign policy in general by hosting missions and meetings with national leaders and military officials from countries as diverse as Ethiopia, Belgium, South Korea, India, Bulgaria, Italy, Taiwan, Uzbekistan, Costa Rica, Spain, Eritrea, Jordan, China, and Germany, to name a few. JINSA's aim is three-fold: to ensure a strong and effective U.S. national security policy; to educate American leadership figures on the vital strategic relationship between the United States and Israel; and to strengthen U.S. cooperation with democratic allies, including Taiwan, Jordan, Hungary, Turkey, India, and NATO member nations, among others.[9]

JINSA's policy recommendations for the U.S. government include: national ballistic missile defense systems, curbing of regional ballistic missile development and production worldwide, increased counter-terrorism training and funding even prior to September 11, substantially improved quality-of-life for U.S. service personnel and their families, support for joint U.S.-Israeli training and weapons development programs, and a rejection of any peace process with the Palestinians that is not prefaced by a full renunciation of terrorism and a full and effective Palestinian effort to combat terrorism in Palestinian Authority-controlled areas. Further, JINSA supports regime change in nation-states known to provide support or knowingly harbor terrorist groups, including Iraq, Iran, Syria, Lebanon, and Libya.

One of JINSA's most important programs is to invite, with the assistance of the Pentagon and the U.S. Department of State, retired U.S. senior military officers to Israel and Jordan. The General and Flag Officer's program, as it is known, allows participants to see with their own eyes, the problems facing the Middle East, in meetings with Israeli and Jordanian political and military leaders. More than 200 retired admirals and generals, including Shock and Awe author Adm. Leon "Bud" Edney, USN, Lt. Gen. Jay Garner, USA, Maj. Gen. David Grange, USA, Maj. Gen. Jarvis Lynch, USMC, Maj. Gen. Sidney Shachnow, USA, Adm. Leighton "Snuffy" Smith, USN, Adm. Carl Trost,

USN, and Brig. Gen. Thomas White, USA, have participated in the trips over the last 21 years. Participation in the program makes no requirements of the invitees to make statements, form opinions, or maintain any further relationship with JINSA, yet many trip alums have participated more than once, and 50 past participants co-authored a statement on violence in the Palestinian-controlled territories that appeared in the *New York Times* in October 2000.

JINSA also acts as a liaison among the U.S. military, concerned U.S. citizens, and America's leaders in Washington, by facilitating base visits, symposia, and publications that highlight future trends, growing threats, and areas of concern within the realm of U.S. national security.

Center for Security Policy (CSP)

The Center for Security Policy was founded in 1988 and states that it operates as a non-profit, non-partisan organization "committed to the time-tested philosophy of promoting international peace through American strength."

A very influential organization within the Center for Security Policy is the Center's National Security Advisory Council, whose members hold senior positions in the Bush administration. The CSP has strong ties with the Republican Party. Many members have held senior posts in the Reagan and Bush Jr administrations. Donald Rumsfeld, Secretary of Defense under Bush, is a recipient of the the Center's Keeper of the Flame Award. The Center is not shy in touting its strong ties with the U.S. government.

At least twenty-two CSP advisers—including additional

Reagan-era remnants like Elliott Abrams, Ken deGraffenreid, Paula Dobriansky, Sven Kraemer, Robert Joseph, Robert Andrews, and J.D. Crouch—have reoccupied key positions in the national security establishment, as have other true believers of more recent vintage. While the CSP boasts an impressive advisory list of hawkish luminaries, its star is Frank Gaffney, its founder, president, and CEO. Gaffney and CSP's prescriptions for national security have been fairly simple: Gut all arms control treaties, push ahead with weapons systems virtually everyone agrees should be killed, give no quarter to the Palestinians, and, most important, go full steam ahead on just about every national missile defense program.

Frank Gaffney, Jr. is another of the anti-Muslim bigots operating in Washington, D.C. In the late 1970s, Gaffney was a staff member on the Senate Armed Services Committee. He also worked briefly with Senator Scoop Jackson in the areas of defense and foreign policy. William Kristol, already mentioned, also worked briefly in this Senator's attempt to run for the presidency. In the 1980s, Gaffney found his way within Reagan's Defense Department, being appointed Deputy Assistant Secretary of Defense for Nuclear Forces and Arms Control Policy under none other than the neo-conservative Richard Perle. Throughout his career, Gaffney has pushed the Zionist agenda under the guise of promoting American interests. He founded the CSP in 1988. Gaffney, whose writings appear frequently in such conservative publications as the *New Republic* and the *Washington Times*, and on Internet sites such as the *National Review Online* and *Jewish World Review*, is simply another mouthpiece for intolerant views, frequently bashing Islam and Muslims and taking a narrow approach to the Middle East conflict. In one column, Gaffney castigated Secretary of State Colin Powell for simply hearing the concerns of Palestinians during a visit to the region. He was also one of the original members of the Project for the New American Century, the neo-conservative group that ultimately looks to advance the Zionist cause through American policy.

More so than others, one of Gaffney's more infamous offenses is his constant attempt to invoke patriotism, while lashing out against American Muslims, especially those attempting to participate politically. He has frequently written excessively slanderous and libelous articles against some of the top leaders of the American Muslim community, accusing them of terrorism. His incongruous statements seem to cast these relationships with top elected officials, including the President, in the most sinister light, as if any supporters of terrorism would actually go through mainstream political channels to achieve their secret hidden agenda. Gaffney has even gone so far as to attack the Muslim community's supporters, such as distinguished lobbyist and conservative activist Grover Norquist, president of Americans for Tax Reform. In doing so, Gaffney has shown nothing but contempt for the democratic process, attempting to deter any legitimate political activity by effectively scaring into silent submission any opponents of his extremist views.

Middle East Forum (MEF)

As was previously stated in the section devoted to Daniel Pipes, the Middle East Forum is a think tank of his creation that advances the Zionist agenda under the token motto of "promoting American interests." Pipes founded the Forum in 1990, but it was not an independent organization until 1994. Operating out of Philadelphia, the Middle East Forum is devoted to a number of activities on behalf of Israel. Its publications are numerous, including a plethora of Pipes' rants against Islam, Muslims, and any individual daring to speak out against Israeli aggression and American complicity in it. In January, 2004, the Forum spent time, energy, and plenty of ink slandering prominent Christian theologian, Biblical archeologist, and well-traveled author William W. Baker, branding him a "neo-Nazi."[10] Baker, whose books have been translated into at least five languages, has spoken about building a bridge of understanding between Christians and Muslims, especially during times of heightened tensions. His book, *More in Common Than You Think*, was widely received, but it is his speaking on behalf of Palestinian rights that made him a target for the extremists at the Middle East Forum.

The Forum expanded its attacks on such figures with the launch of Campus Watch following the September 11 attacks. The web site, developed as a watchdog group, is an attempt to stifle free and open debate, curtail free speech, and manipulate the public discussion on the Middle East by creating a blacklist of professors, scholars, and intellectuals who are critical of U.S. and Israeli policies. While the list on Campus Watch continued to grow steadily over the course of the months after it was introduced, its organizers were careful not to saturate it, for fear of creating a critical mass, thereby demonstrating that in fact a significant percentage of the academic community does not espouse the Middle East Forum's extremist views. Moreover, the strategy was meant to isolate the group of professors listed, so as to enhance the pressure on their institutions by inciting ignorant rabble-rousers to send a deluge of threatening and vulgar letters and phone calls. Campus Watch's actions against free speech and academic freedom have never been equaled since the height of the Cold War decades ago.

Also as part of the Middle East Forum's many activities is its primary publication, *Middle East Quarterly*. The journal was founded in 1994 and is edited by notorious Israeli right-winger Martin Kramer. The Forum refers to *MEQ* as "America's most authoritative journal of Middle Eastern affairs," a claim so preposterous it does not merit a response.[11] Needless to say, the journal flouted by Pipes, Kramer, and company is considered by much of the academic community as extremist. It demonstrates excessive bias and a clear cut agenda, while being regarded as "authoritative" only by the same extremists who put it out and their cohorts. The main effect of this journal is to disseminate a regular collection of long-winded propaganda pieces disguised as academic articles, though their sole purpose is to demonize Islam, mischaracterize realities of the Middle East, and thereby formulate a policy hostile to the Muslim world and the Muslim community in America.

The quarterly journal is only one feature of the Middle East Forum's publicity and propaganda machine. Part of the Forum's mission is devoted to self-promotion, by actively seeking as many television, radio, and print interviews as possible to advance its agenda among as wide an audience as possible. It is because of this well-oiled and heavily funded machine that lazy media outlets often resort to obvious bigots, such as Daniel Pipes and the rest of his staff, as experts on anything from terrorism and Middle East politics to

American military strategy. This campaign of misinformation was at a relative low point at the time of the September 11 attacks, after which no network could get enough of their services to spread hysteria, panic, and xenophobia, while beating the drums of war. And though the Middle East Forum is much smaller than true lobbying think tanks such as the Washington Institute, it nonetheless endeavors to reinforce the efforts of Washington-based pro-Israel lobbies with its own drumbeat on the ears of members of Congress, the Department of Defense, and the White House.

Middle East Media Research Institute (Memri)

In their effort to shape popular and official perceptions of the Middle East within the United States, a pro-Israeli group calling itself the Middle East Media Research Institute, or Memri, emerged in February 1998.[12] The group bills itself as simply wanting "to inform the debate over U.S. policy in the Middle East," and characterizes itself as being "an independent, nonpartisan, nonprofit, 501(c)3 organization."[13] Those groups, of course, enjoy tax-exempt status from the government, and thus Memri's activities are subsidized by American taxpayers. While this is not wholly unusual, what is thoroughly disturbing is that Memri is not the objective, well-intentioned organization it purports to be. As with other groups listed in this chapter, it feigns impartiality and detachment while simultaneously promoting a vicious agenda. This becomes immediately clear if one considers who, in fact, founded this institute.

As was reported in a British newspaper that exposed Memri, the group was founded by Colonel Yigal Carmon, who served as an Israeli military intelligence officer for 22 years, before becoming counter-terrorism advisor to two Israeli Prime Ministers.[14] That resumé alone is enough to discredit an organization whose purpose is supposedly to translate Middle Eastern media into Western languages. In fact, its mission is to exploit the lack of reliably translated media sources in the West by monopolizing the limited access that Western media and political leaders have to Middle Eastern resources. And while Carmon is the founder, president, and registered owner of Memri's web site, he is not the only culprit behind its underhanded mission. Co-founding the institute is the Israeli Meyrav Wurmser, wife of David Wurmser, the neo-conservative appointed to work under Cheney. Meyrav Wurmser "is the author of an academic paper entitled 'Can Israel Survive Post-Zionism?' in which she argues that leftwing Israeli intellectuals pose 'more than a passing threat' to the state of Israel, undermining its soul and reducing its will for self-defense."[15] In fact, "Of the six people named [as staff members], three ... are described as having worked for Israeli intelligence."[16] Its web site has listed "the continuing relevance of Zionism to the Jewish people and to the state of Israel" as one of its founding principles.[17]

All of this information on the character of Memri's founders and staffers certainly does not bode well for the legitimacy of the organization. This notion is only confirmed once Memri's work is brought to light. As a group whose supposed sole purpose is to translate important articles, speeches, and interviews from the

Middle East for the purpose of informing Western audiences, it is quite interesting to note the selection process that goes on in this endeavor. To any objective observer familiar with Memri's biweekly submissions, it becomes increasingly clear that the chosen articles point to a distinct message and an underlying agenda. The institute's undeclared objective has been to disseminate far and wide a negative portrait of the Arab world as violent, extremist, fundamentalist, anti-Semitic, anti-American, and backwards. All of this is done by highlighting a carefully selected assortment of articles from within the Arab press (although it is part of the region it supposedly covers, the extremism in the Hebrew press is never brought to light). Carmon and company have had a number of recent successes that stand out, particularly because of the widespread national attention that these Memri stories received throughout the United States.

One such story was a column in a Saudi newspaper that claimed that Jews used the blood of Christians and Muslims in celebration of one of their festivals. The article caused an outrage in America and became the topic of talk shows and political debates surrounding Arab culture and American relations with Saudi Arabia, an area that neo-conservatives and pro-Israeli zealots desperately wanted to reconfigure. In fact, the article, which relied on an ancient myth, was unrepresentative of the general population, and the writer was subsequently fired by the publisher who failed to notice the error originally. None of this was ever reported by Memri, let alone the American press. In fact, Memri described the newspaper as Saudi owned, suggesting that these views had official approval by the government, whereas the newspaper is privately owned and no one, whether government official or staff within the newspaper itself, subscribes to the views expressed by that one column.[18]

Critics of Memri have been very diverse, ranging from American Muslim leaders to former top government officials. Ibrahim Hooper, spokesman for the Council on American-Islamic Relations said, "Memri's intent is to find the worst possible quotes from the Muslim world and disseminate them as widely as possible." Indeed, this has been the picture given by Memri's choice of articles, which often include out-of-context statements by various officials or figures in the Arab world, or badly misinterpreted accounts, as happened with the poem by the Saudi ambassador to the United Kingdom published in an Arabic newspaper, in which he discusses a female suicide bomber. The poem was promoted by Memri to provoke outrage in the West that a high-ranking Saudi official would condone such acts. Though this was not the case, the plan worked to perfection, and Saudi Arabia was pressured into recalling its ambassador. According to Vince Cannistraro, former head of CIA counterintelligence, "They are selective and act as propagandists for their political point of view, which is the extreme right of Likud. They simply don't present the whole picture."[19] In fact, the politics of Memri's Israeli agents has never been secret. In 1992, Carmon and others lobbied the U.S. government against the Oslo Peace Process, calling it "a historic disaster."[20] With its $1.2 million annual budget, Memri has since opened branch offices in London, Berlin, and Jerusalem. Carmon refuses to reveal his funding sources, but the agenda of Memri's campaign of disinformation is clear for all to see. ■

Part Three

THE AMERICAN MUSLIM NIGHTMARE

The community is confused, scared, not certain of the directions.

—Professor Akbar Ahmed,
Christian Science Monitor, January 10, 2002.

Chapter 8

TARGETING ISLAM
IN AMERICA

From his very first speeches following the horrifying events of September 11, President Bush has maintained that the terrorists attacked us because they hate our freedoms. Hence the war on terrorism's official title—'Operation Enduring Freedom.' But one year later, it appears that the greatest threat to our freedoms is posed not by the terrorists themselves but by our own government's response.

—David Cole, J.D., "Enemy aliens and American freedoms,"
The Nation, September 2003.

Since the attacks of September 11, 2001, the Arab and Muslim communities in America have suffered from a hostile campaign to malign them in the American media and incite fear and hatred. This relentless campaign has resulted in thousands of interrogations, arrests, and imprisonments, including often-lengthy solitary confinement without charges of terrorism or wrongdoing. In their meetings and gatherings, American Muslims today are concerned about who among them is going to be the next victim. Since September 11, the Justice Department has specifically targeted Islamic humanitarian and charitable organizations and institutions and their supporters and donors. Legal expert David Cole observed a real problem in the recent policy: "Ashcroft's dragnet approach has targeted tens of thousands of Arabs and Muslims for registration, interviews, mass arrests, deportation, and automatic detention, effectively treating an entire, overwhelmingly law-abiding community as suspect. Such broad measures deeply alienate the targeted communities, making them far less likely to assist law enforcement efforts to identify the actual perpetrators."[1]

The cause of the fear and anxiety in the Muslim community is that the charges are groundless allegations based on American pro-Israeli opinion articles and foreign (usually Israeli) intelligence. In a March 2003 article, the Jewish publication *Forward* stated that the Israeli government had provided the U.S. government with all the evidence that the FBI used in its case against Dr. Sami al-Arian, the professor and Palestinian rights activist, and three others of Palestinian origin. The allegations targeted other noted personalities, including the author and scholar Dr. Basheer Nafi, currently residing in Great Britain.

This campaign started in the early 1990s, following an official Israeli policy after 1993 to shut down all Islamic networks, institutions, and other efforts undertaken in support of the Palestinian people against the occupation. This strategy came to be known as "drying up the wells"; it proceeded to target and close a number of successful organizations such as the Holy Land Foundation, which was the source of support for thousands of Palestinians in the West Bank and Gaza as well as for those in refugee camps in Lebanon, Jordan, and other Muslim countries.

A Calculated Campaign

What kind of trumped-up "evidence" has been unearthed by the campaigns of defamation and provocation and spread by the U.S. mass media? And to what extent has this resulted in the judicial prosecution of persons in a way that contravenes basic civil rights standards?

And what is the goal behind these campaigns? Have the American Muslim institutions themselves taken any measures to confront these campaigns? And what is the political backdrop to these cases that flout the constitution and denigrate those Americans expressing opposition to the removal of civil liberties?

Many observers note a radical change in behavior across the American landscape. Writer Anayat Durrani states, "An unfortunate but predictable outcome of the September 11 attacks has been the ongoing massive Islamophobic smear campaign launched against the Muslim and Arab communities and their leaders due to their increasing visibility and influence in the American political process. Actions have been taken to bar Arabs and Muslims from political participation and influence by those uncomfortable with what they perceive as growing Muslim prominence and greater accessibility to the White House."[2] Indeed, the attacks on Islam, Muslims, and their most respectable institutions and individuals by the U.S. media and government following September 11 appear to be a continuation of the Zionist campaign begun in 1948 to prevent sympathy for Arabs, especially the dispossessed Palestinians. It has escalated in the aftermath of the first World Trade Center bombing in 1993. These attacks against Muslims in America have intensified concurrently with the war in the Middle East, especially since the beginning of the Al-Aqsa (second) Intifada. The most common approach of pro-Israeli forces is to claim that certain Muslim institutions and individuals, especially those that provide humanitarian aid to Palestinians or support the Palestinian resistance organizations, specifically Hamas and the Islamic Jihad, are "terrorist fronts."

During the late 1990s, this campaign then proceeded to exploit Al-Qa'eda's attack on American interests, especially the African embassy bombings in 1998 and the USS Cole bombing in October 2000, with the aim of merging these two enemies into one.

All of these fortuitous events coincided to allow the strategy to succeed in making its war America's own by branding "Islamic fundamentalism" as an imminent threat and the new enemy of the Western world, succeeding Communist totalitarianism. The Zionists use ideological terms like "Islamic fundamentalism" and "Islamic extremism" in America in order to turn the entire Muslim world against America by demonstrating to Muslims that America is in fact targeting Islam as a whole. Fundamentalists, extremists, or terrorists of other faiths are not described or identified by their religion.

The initial Israeli task was to find a way to maintain its prominent role in the strategic security planning of the West, especially in the United States, once the United States had emerged victorious from the Cold War. That victory is credited to the combination of America's colossal military might and its democratic system of governance, as noted by Francis Fukuyama in his book, *The End of History*, which became the subject of much debate during the early 1990s. As American military and defense strategists were in need of a new threat, Israel promoted the notion that fundamentalist Islam, as a rejecter of Western values and modernity, was the natural choice. Israel's new agenda gained so much media attention that the "Islamic threat" soon became the top defense concern for the American government, much to the detriment of the Arab and Muslim world. As we have witnessed in the past three years, the Zionist fingerprints have been found throughout the media campaigns against Iraq, Iran, Syria, Saudi Arabia, Egypt, and the Palestinian resistance.

To defeat Hamas and the Islamic Jihad and other such movements whose militancy arose solely in self-defense against Israeli ethnic cleansing of Palestinians and against efforts to appropriate more land, Israel intensified its military actions and enacted new legislation to support its policies of confiscating land and starving and killing Palestinians. To do this, Israel felt it had to take on the entire Muslim world because it recognizes that there is no concern of Muslims so pervasive as the crisis of the Palestinians and the loss of their homeland. While Israel feels it is capable of destroying the entire Middle East, even all of Europe, it needs the sympathy and wants the additional monetary and political support of the United States. Arabs and Muslims interpret U.S. military action completely differently than does the average American. Muslims of all countries believe that the wars and threats of the United States are directed against Arab countries, such as Iraq, Syria, and Saudi Arabia, and other Muslim countries such as Iran and Afghanistan in order to consolidate Israel's control over the Middle East while providing the United States with profits from the natural resources of these countries. As noted by scholar Yvonne Haddad, "Muslims are aware of this historical relationship, and many believe that the West wants their resources, wants to keep them oppressed. President Bush's recent comment about mounting a 'crusade' and Secretary Powell's comments about 'we, the civilized world,' reinforced that notion. We don't know if the President's remark about a crusade was a slip of the tongue or a Freudian slip. But Muslims heard: 'Here they come again. They hate us; they want to destroy us'."[3]

Especially since 9/11, Israel has enhanced its propaganda war against Islam throughout the American media and halls of power, thus completely altering the previous terms of the debate between East and West and redefining this debate under the new banner of security threats and ideological warfare. In doing so, Israel has assiduously exploited the occasional event anywhere in the world that could help it to advance its hatred of Islam and Muslims. The Islamophobic campaign was successful in its early years in turning attention to the threat it termed "Islamic fundamentalism."

This movement was personified by the pseudo-journalist, Steven Emerson, who began his tirade with a 1994 PBS documentary entitled "Jihad in America." In that program, Emerson attempted to show that the military operations carried out against Israel by groups such as Hamas were receiving much of their financial and logistical support from within the United States. The Zionist attacks continued without fail, increasing from year to year in the dramatic nature of their scope and the outrageousness of their claims.

Before long, every humanitarian, charitable, political, and intellectual institution and every politically active Muslim came under constant surveillance. In time, many found themselves under official investigation. Accusations and suspicion provided by the Zionist press incited these attacks from every direction. The stakes gradually became higher, as U.S. authorities began actively targeting such individuals for criminal prosecution. People were arrested not because of any objectively criminal behavior, but rather because their constitutionally protected activities on behalf of the Palestinian and other causes had now been unjustly criminalized as being inconsistent with U.S. plans for the Arab-Muslim region. In short, these are America's new political prisoners, its dissidents, its prisoners of conscience, and they are being persecuted shamelessly and unabashedly for acting in accordance with their beliefs. The first of these individuals, such as Dr. Abdulhaleem al-Ashqar and Ismael al-Barasi, found themselves behind bars for the support work they had done during the previous Palestinian intifada in the late 1980s and early 1990s. Many more would later follow them.

The Phenomenon of Secret Evidence

As cruel and vindictive as was the campaign against American Muslims in the early 1990s, the five-year period prior to September 11 represented a momentous period in the history of the Arab and Muslim communities. During this period, beginning in 1996, the government first accepted "secret evidence" to send active members of the community to prison indefinitely. Such was the case of Dr. Mazen al-Najjar, the editor of the popular Arabic journal

Political Readings at the World and Islam Studies Enterprise in Florida, as well as the former member of the Algerian parliament, Anwar Haddam, and at least 20 others who suffered a similar fate during this period. These acts of persecution, however, were scattered and calculated, targeting only specific individuals and institutions and not the entire Muslim community, as would occur in the period following September 11.

The September 11 attacks presented a golden opportunity for the forces behind this campaign to step up their efforts exponentially, as they saw in those events a new justification for doing so. The American cable news networks were swamped with past and present Israeli leaders, such as Benjamin Netanyahu and Shimon Peres, issuing their own assessments of the current situation, in addition to several Zionist so-called "terrorism experts" such as Yousef Bodansky, and, of course, Steven Emerson. Their message could be summed up in the following sentence: The enemies that the United States and Israel face are one and the same, and they are called "Islamic fundamentalists." These and other propagandists justified such preposterous statements through a twisted logic that attempted to associate the entire Palestinian resistance against Israel with the Al-Qa'eda attacks on New York and Washington as all part of the same Islamic doctrine.

During those early moments following September 11, American public opinion was ready and willing to accept such loaded rhetoric, due not only to the emotionally charged moment but also to the ignorance prevalent in America about the Middle East and the nature of Islam and Islamic movements. The new and improved Zionist tactics were further advanced by the rise of a neo-conservative group within the Bush administration dedicated to promoting Israel's interests, coupled with the growing Christian Zionist movement. All these forces combined to persuade Muslims that they must abandon once and for all any hope that they could ever develop a balanced political presence in the United States or succeed in effecting changes in U.S. Middle East policy.

It was at this point that conditions changed dramatically and the pressure and scrutiny on the community intensified, placing it in a position in which it was unable to defend itself. Thus began the new phase of the campaign to destroy its presence and activities domestically. The Arab and Muslim communities in the United States, together with Arabs and Muslims under siege overseas, have paid a heavy price, as a number of humanitarian organizations, such as the Holy Land Foundation, Global Relief, Kinder International, and even Help the Needy, were declared illegal and shut down. Nor did this campaign end with the outlawing of important aid and relief organizations. Indeed, hundreds of Arab and Muslim youth were hauled away to prisons across the country without charges. In fact, a civil rights report from the Department of Justice indicated that most of those targeted had committed nothing more than minor immigration infractions. Not a single one of them was ever charged in connection with the September 11 attacks.

This raised serious questions, as there are nearly five million people in violation of U.S. immigration laws, but only those of Arab or Muslim backgrounds have been prosecuted. And what of the severe harassment of reputable academic institutions such as the International Institute of Islamic Thought (IIIT) or the Graduate School of Islamic and Social Sciences? Haddad refers to these incidents, in the aftermath of the unconstitutional provisions passed in the hysteria following 9/11. "With the USA Patriot Act, Arab Americans and Muslims are being specifically targeted as threatening elements in society. The March 2002 raids in Northern Virginia targeted people the U.S. government recognized as Muslim leaders, including the school that produced the Muslim chaplains for the U.S. military and the school's Director, Dr. Taha Jabir al-Alwani, who issued a *fatwa* to Muslims to go fight in the war against terrorism. His home was ransacked by federal agencies in March 2002."[4]

Indeed, attacks on Islam and Muslims have become commonplace in the American news media. The equating of Islam with terrorism has occurred regularly and openly, with Islam and Muslims suffering the brunt of the worst-ever defamation campaign against them in their history in the United States. These vicious public and political assaults on the Muslim community have resulted in the torpedoing of basic rights and liberties that were supposed to be ensured under the constitution. The Justice Department, led by its rabid right-wing attorney general, John Ashcroft, has sought to intimidate the Muslim community, placing it in a state of fear and under constant watch, reminiscent of a police state. These tactics have left the entire community powerless and in fear, too afraid to commit to a single legitimate cause, while at the same time forcing the dedicated element within the community to utilize all its efforts and resources to help free its many targeted individuals.

Pro-Israel forces have successfully exploited the wave of hysteria, which they created, to advance their agenda against the Muslim community, but especially with regard to its activities on behalf of the Palestinian cause. Their efforts led to the arrest of various members of the Islamic Association for Palestine. In Dallas, for instance, Ghassan Dahdouli and Hassan Sabri, were ultimately deported to Jordan. There is also the case of Dr. Sabri Samirah, head of the United Muslim Americans Association (UMAA), who was not even allowed to board his flight to the United States from Northern Ireland. He was instead forced into exile, also to Jordan. Prior to that, there was the closure of the Holy Land Foundation and the harassment of its staff members. Two of the most egregious instances were the arrest and imprisonment of Dr. Sami al-Arian, a Palestinian professor at the University of South Florida in Tampa, accused of supporting the Palestinian Islamic Jihad, and Abdurrahman Alamoudi, founder of the mainstream American Muslim Council (AMC) in Washington, D.C., who was charged with engaging in financial relations with Libya. These arrests of two of the most sincere and highly respected members of the community have served to further tighten the noose around the collective neck of the Muslim community in America. The noted organization Human Rights Watch released its annual report following the 2001 attacks in which it chronicled incidents as well as highlighted some important points:

> While acknowledging the importance of official condemnation of hate crimes and messages supporting tolerance, Arab and Muslim community leaders have expressed concern about federal government "mixed messages." Official statements exhorting the

public not to view Muslims or Arabs differently than anyone else were countered by measures taken as part of the anti-terrorist campaign that cast a cloud of suspicion over all Arabs and Muslims in the United States. Those measures have included, for example, the detention of some 1,200 persons of almost exclusively Arab, Muslim, or South Asian heritage because of "possible" links to terrorism; the FBI requests to interview over eight thousand men of Arab or Muslim heritage; and the decision that visitors to the United States from certain Middle Eastern countries would be fingerprinted. Activists believe these actions reinforce an image of Arabs and Muslims as potential terrorists or terrorist sympathizers. Referring to the effect of these policies on the perception of Muslims and Arabs in the general public, Joshua Salaam of CAIR, said: "Most people are probably asking, `If the government doesn't trust these people, why should I?'" People have come to expect more arrests in the future, as the situation deteriorates day by day.[5]

The Role of American Muslim Organizations

The advancements made by the American Muslim community in prior years, especially its role in the 2000 presidential elections, have turned it into a target for those who wish to keep the community permanently disenfranchised. The pro-Israel lobby had such an opportunity in the aftermath of September 11, when it accelerated its efforts to destroy what few political gains the community had made. While they had always maintained a strong degree of influence within the U.S. media and policymaking circles, these groups now had the full attention of the Bush administration and lawmakers on Capitol Hill, as well as access to the mass media outlets and thus public opinion. They combined their attacks with fervent support of Israel, especially as the devastation caused by Ariel Sharon's violent acts—such as that wrought by his army during its incursions into Jenin and other towns, cities, and refugee camps in the West Bank and Gaza—came into the full view of the American public.

Indeed, the September 11 attacks were as much of a shock to the American Muslim community as to all other Americans, if not more so. In fact, on that exact day, an afternoon meeting had been scheduled for Muslim leaders to meet with President Bush. He was expected to thank them for their financial support for his campaign and for the Republican Party, as well as for their turnout at the polls in the 2000 elections. In addition, he was expected to finally issue his long-awaited vow to support legislation banning the use of secret evidence, from which the community had suffered terribly for years. The community had pledged its support for Bush following his statements on that subject during the campaign. Of course that meeting never took place, nor was it ever re-scheduled.

Muslim leaders reacted swiftly following the devastation on September 11. They immediately asked the president to issue a strong statement calling for tolerance and unity in this time of crisis, especially with regard to the nation's Muslim minority, which was now in danger of attack. This, of course, did not deter the pro-Israel lobby from subjecting the community to a ferocious onslaught. The Muslim organizations, however, lacked the funds, political clout, and internal coherence needed to withstand such an assault on their basic rights. All of this, coupled with internal bickering within and among the various groups, shattered their unity, while also ending the shared American Muslim vision of America as a moral leader in the world. American Muslim Council interim director Nedzib Sacirbey was distraught at the unjustified attacks against Islam, Muslims, and their institutions, saying, "There is no Muslim organization in this country that did not condemn the al Qaeda terrorist attack, and many have given contributions to the fight against al Qaeda. Al Qaeda is an ulcer on the body of Muslims, and we want it to disappear as soon as possible because it gives a face to Muslims that is not our face."[6]

Weathering the Storm

The indulgence in the luxury of personal rivalries by some groups within the community and their inability to act in the face of danger ultimately proved their weakness in a very noticeable way. This crisis has been disastrous for the majority of American Muslims, who are tormented by the current situation but find their organizations unwilling to respond in any meaningful way. Many of the community's youth have become increasingly disenchanted with their leadership. They wonder, as do we: Why is it that when a catastrophe befalls the community, its organizations refuse to wake up and deal with it? Why are some of them still tripping over each other to beg for the approval of the very government officials and law enforcement authorities that are persecuting their community in the first place?

Any community of people in this situation demonstrates its exact character by how it deals with those among its number who have been unjustly imprisoned or otherwise persecuted by authorities, of which the Palestinians are a prime example: their prisoners are their heroes. Not so for most of the leading figures in the Muslim community in America today, who prefer to ignore and distance themselves from their own imprisoned members when they should be embracing and defending them. Is that not what leaders are for, to act in the people's defense during times of crisis? Are leaders not supposed to have courage and fortitude? Is that not what actually makes them leaders?

Were they leaders, then they would now be using whatever little access they had managed to acquire toward an effort to free Sami al-Arian, Abdulhaleem Ashqar, Abdurrahman Alamoudi, and others like them. Instead, they are teaching American Muslims that it is better to worry about their own personal reputations and ambitions and assimilate into America than to be concerned about the life and liberty of other Muslims, whether in the United States or overseas. This leads us to ask: Is it not for the defense of Muslims that the community sought to obtain access to the U.S. political system in the first place?

Certainly it was not to further the trivial political ambitions of a few individuals who happen to be both American and Muslim. If maintaining that access has today become more important to these leaders than the larger purpose it was supposed to serve, then there has been a quiet substitution of means for ends in the order of priorities for reasons of personal gain. That is corruption, pure and simple. It is also a betrayal of the position of leadership.

The Muslim community in America has reached a point of deep crisis. Events in the months following September 11 clearly illustrate this. As just a cross-section of some of these events:

> November 5, 2001: The U.S. Department of Justice announced that 1,147 people had been detained, but refused to provide any information on them, even to their families. The overwhelming majority of them were Muslim and/or Arabs.

> November 9, 2001: Ashcroft announced a plan to interview 5,000 foreign men ages 18 to 33, who had entered the United States from specified countries (namely all Arab or Muslim) after January 1, 2000. The Justice Department directed state and local law enforcement to conduct the interviews, in which the men were questioned about their activities, studies, and travel, and were asked to provide telephone numbers of their friends and relatives. While calling on the men to come forward for the "voluntary" interviews, the government also said that those questioned might be held without bond if investigators developed an interest in them or be deported if they had violated immigration laws.

November 13, 2001: President Bush issued a
military order allowing the government to try
non-citizens accused of terrorism-related
charges in military tribunals, which lack
many constitutional protections, rather than
civilian courts.[7]

These are only a few of the horrific policies to emerge
from this new era of policing by the state. And yet some of
the American Muslim leaders are still, even now,
notwithstanding all that Bush has done to Arabs and
Muslims everywhere, playing footsies with the Republican
Party. There are those who, even now, still call themselves
Republicans, as if the events of the past three years had
never happened, as if frozen in some kind of time warp.
They continue to work hard to ingratiate themselves to the
Republican Party apparatus by convincing Muslims to
contribute financially to its candidates and by registering
Muslims to vote for them in elections. In return, it is a sure
bet that they are not asking their new political party
functionary friends, to whom they now have access, for help
in freeing the community's political prisoners or ending the
occupation of Iraq or stopping Ariel Sharon from building
his apartheid wall in the West Bank. Are they pandering in
order to get American Muslims elected to office, so that
once they are elected, they also can ignore these momentous
problems so vital in the eyes of the community? Have they
forgotten that they were supposed to represent a community
of Muslim believers, committed to truth, integrity, strength
of will, courage, and faith in God?

A somewhat lesser absurdity in which the Muslim
organizations are presently indulging themselves and their

time and effort is the fomenting of petty rivalries among themselves, as if the outcomes of such infantile disputes even matter in the larger scheme of things. An example was the noble effort of the Muslim American Society, one of the larger Muslim organizations, in attempting to reach a consensus with other Muslim groups in response to the impending U.S. invasion of Iraq in early 2003. Following meetings on March 15, which took place just five days before the war began, the different groups could not agree even on what their position should be, which should have been obvious to anyone, given that a major Arab-Muslim country was about to be invaded and occupied by the United States. As if this were not enough, they allowed their own insignificant internal organizational political disputes, which have absolutely no bearing or impact on history or on the supposed larger objective of these organizations, to get in the way of quickly reaching what should have been an obvious consensus to oppose the U.S. action unequivocally and loudly. The refusal of these leaders to respond to such a serious turn in history for all Arabs and Muslims in the contemporary world came as a shock to a community that expected to see a strong and unified stand against the war—not to mention an appropriate sense of urgency—during a time of crisis.

Even during the U.S. war in Afghanistan, the same organization attempted, together with other groups, to release a position paper that would accurately reflect the sentiments within the community. Even that small effort was to no avail. Apparently, each group had its own obtuse interests in mind, such as the next invitation to a White House dinner or a State Department briefing, or its sources of funding. For other organizations, a joint statement of any kind would have made it difficult for any of them to present itself as the sole organization representing the American Muslim community, a rationale which would have been laughable were the situation facing the community and the world not so gravely serious. The organizations could not even muster as trivial a contribution as a joint press release endowed with meaningful content: the end product was instead a compromised and condensed document that contained little to no substance and was duly ignored by U.S. officials and the media as being of no consequence.

Indeed, a crisis of inaction has hit the American Muslim organizations as they proceed to distance themselves from the disastrous circumstances facing the Muslim community and the Muslim world, as if to pretend they do not even exist or matter. They continue day to day with their trivial business-as-usual pursuits, which properly belong to a bygone era, in the face of global calamity. Even their national conferences are now little more than social events, venues at which people can gather from different parts of the country to greet their many friends.

Many of the sincere and politically aware American Muslims are slowly coming to the opinion that many if not most of these groups exist only for themselves, to sustain their leaders financially, and to promote their "status" in American society. That they are even concerned about their personal or political status in the eyes of a U.S. leadership that is persecuting Arabs and Muslims at home while engaging in the wanton destruction of Arab and Muslim lives and aspirations overseas in itself makes their integrity suspect.

While the American Muslim leaders are quick to defend their own persons or organizations against the slightest attack, they remain unwilling to take a forceful or decisive stand when honest members of the community come under assault by U.S. authorities, or when Arab and Muslim countries come under attack by U.S. forces. The question remains: How long will our institutions be dominated by those who represent a minority view different from that of the community at large, a view that emanates from the small personal interests of a few individuals? How long will these organizations be dominated by individuals beholden to their own personal interests, so that the only time they spring into action is to please their government hosts or advance their own political careers?

The prevailing sentiment within the community, never accurately reflected by these groups, is that the war against Iraq was an unjust war and an illegal occupation, against which the peoples of the world, even non-Muslim populations in other countries, have protested. The average Muslim believes that the purpose of this war is primarily to control the oil resources of the Middle East and also to advance a foreign agenda bent on further weakening the Arab and Muslim world, while strengthening Israel. Since this aggression was undertaken in defiance of all international laws and norms, Muslims regarded it simply as a display of power against a weak and debilitated nation, destroyed by 13 years of a U.S.-enforced global embargo on the country. This was the feeling within the Muslim community across the United States and this is the view they expected to be represented by their leaders, despite the widespread fear and paranoia from which they have been suffering at the hands of the American security apparatus. What the people expected was strong leaders, possessing integrity, who would project this view, and who would voice it loud and clear to the people they know in the U.S.

government and to the world. Instead, American Muslims watched as their supposed leaders went on the air with positions that in no way represented the community's views or opinions. The same has been true of those representatives who have appeared on television or produced statements condemning or distancing themselves from the brave Palestinian fighters who have sacrificed their own lives in pursuit of freedom and liberty for the Palestinian people.

The Arab and Muslim community has entered into the most critical phase of its existence in the United States. For many, this period of fear and uncertainty as to the fate of its members is merely a prelude to the most terrible part of this phase, which has yet to come. Indeed, talk of a more disastrous future ahead dominates many gatherings and late-night conversations as the government has given the community no reason to think otherwise.

From the initial Patriot Act, which invested U.S. authorities with widely expanded powers to spy on and otherwise intrude into the lives of its citizens and legal residents, talk of a Patriot Act II with the potential to strip even native-born Americans of their citizenship is already sending chills down people's spines. Now would be the time for American Muslim organizations to leave their misdirected priorities behind and step up to face these challenges in an attempt to salvage the community's liberties within these borders. But, there is no indication as yet that they are anywhere near up to the challenge. In fact, in January, 2004, Congress stepped up its measures to monitor these groups. In a well-publicized act of boldness, the Senate Finance Committee requested the IRS to turn over confidential tax and financial records, including donor lists, of dozens of Muslim charities and foundations.[8]

While much of these groups had already been targeted, had their assets frozen, and effectively been shut down, this came as part of political maneuvering to attack the Muslim community. Such significant and private information in the hands of reckless Congressional members with clear political agendas sets a dangerous precedent for freedom of expression, sending yet another chill down the spine of potential supporters of Muslim charitable and civic organizations. No doubt, the agents of Islamophobia are already eagerly awaiting the opportunity to exploit and abuse this confidential information.

Looking Ahead

As American Muslims become increasingly familiar with buzzwords like "national security," "secret evidence," and "profiling," their civil liberties as well as their human rights are becoming cliffhanger affairs. The community's freefall into the abyss of mass political persecution and loss of due process is now just over the horizon, as any American Muslim who tries to help his fellow Muslims overseas in any historically meaningful way can now be deemed a "terrorist" with hardly a second thought, and dealt with accordingly.[9] The pro-Israel forces, be it in the form of organized political, intellectual, or social institutions or through the news media, have always been unified in carrying the same inflammatory message inciting people against Islam and Muslims. This message was summarized in a number of statements released by Israeli officials throughout the West in the early 1990s, which clearly labeled Islam as the new enemy. These early statements have been continuously repeated over the years, inducing a fear of "Islamic fundamentalism" threatening the United States. All of these efforts, however, were capped following the attacks of September 11. Among the goals behind this campaign are to:

1. Defame the image of Islam by associating it with fundamentalism, extremism, and terrorism, thereby leading America into a war with the Muslim world from which Israel reaps the benefits.

2. Portray the Islamic movement as a strategic and mortal threat of the first order, and subsequently to remove the political dimension of the Islamic faith as a legitimate alternative to secularism, and ultimately to defeat any chance for Islam to succeed as a political solution to the problems in Arab and Muslim countries.

3. Defeat the Palestinian resistance against Israeli occupation under the guise of promoting democracy in countries that have opposed Israel or its "interests." The ultimate objectives of this strategy have been to divide the Arab and Muslim peoples and re-shape their national and religious identities.

Some Muslim organizations in the United States have responded to the attacks of the U.S. media not head on but with more pandering, and by focusing their televised remarks on issues that are insignificant in comparison with the situation of a world that is caving in on all sides. Instead of trying to buck up their American credentials at such a time, they should be engaging in urgent and vocal efforts to free the community's political prisoners and stop the U.S.-sponsored wars and occupations overseas that are hurting Arabs and Muslims throughout the world. Yet these leaders and spokesmen seem simply to ignore the critical events of the day.

Even on the subjects that are unimportant, relatively speaking of course, the organizations have been impeded by the culture of rivalry that exists among them, a rivalry which results from the leaders of these organizations placing their personal or political ambitions over the interests and feelings of the community they claim to represent. All the while, Muslims both here and overseas continue to suffer the consequences of their silence and inaction in the areas that matter. Today, with the stakes higher than ever before, the community expects, and it deserves, a far different type of leadership than what it is now getting. ■

• Mahdi Bray, Executive Director of MAS Freedom Foundation, leading a protest in front of Justice Department, Washington, D.C.

Chronology of Islam in America Since September 11, 2001

In the weeks and months following the September 11 attacks, the American Muslim community became a target of the growing discrimination and xenophobia that came in the form of hate crimes and other backlash. Though public officials initially cautioned against targeting the innocent community, incidents of racism, some of them violent and others institutionalized, continued in the months thereafter. The following information has appeared in numerous reports compiled by groups such as Human Rights Watch, the American-Arab Anti-Discrimination Committee (ADC), the Council on American-Islamic Relations (CAIR), and the Muslim Public Affairs Council (MPAC). This is a partial chronology of many of the most significant incidents.

▪ 9/11 Terrorist Attacks

September 11: Terrorists attack the World Trade Center in New York and the Pentagon in Washington, D.C. Two hijacked jetliners slam into the WTC and one into the Pentagon. A fourth airliner crashes in a field in Pennsylvania. American Muslim organizations joined the nation in denouncing this tragic and heinous crime. The leaders of nine Muslim American groups said in a joint letter to President Bush on September 11, "American Muslims, who unequivocally condemned today terrorist attacks on our nation, call on you to alert fellow citizens to the fact that now is a time for all of us to stand together in the face of this heinous crime. We hope that the perpetrators of these crimes will be apprehended immediately and swiftly brought to justice. Muslims stand with all other Americans who, on this sad day, feel a sense of tremendous grief and loss. The letter was signed by the leaders of the *American Muslim Alliance (AMA)*, the *American Muslim Council (AMC)*, the *Council on American-Islamic Relations (CAIR)*, the *Muslim Public Affairs Council (MPAC)*, the *Muslim American Society (MAS)*, the *Islamic Society of North America (ISNA)*, the *Islamic Circle of North America (ICNA)*, the *Muslim Alliance in North America (MANA)*, and *American Muslims for Jerusalem (AMJ)*.

▪ Justice Department Names 19 Suspects in 9/11 Attacks

September 14: U.S. Justice Department names 19 suspects in attacks that include 15 nationals from Saudi Arabia, two from the United Arab Emirates, one from Egypt, and one from Lebanon.

▪ President Bush Visits Mosque

September 17: President George W. Bush visited a mosque to urge that Muslim Americans be treated with respect after the terrorist attacks against U.S. targets, saying, "The face of terror is not the true faith of Islam." Slipping off his shoes to respect Islamic custom, Bush sought to quell a surge of anti-Muslim incidents following the September 11 attacks on the World Trade Center and the Pentagon. "These acts of violence against innocents violate the fundamental tenets of the Islamic faith and it's important for my fellow Americans to understand that," Bush said at the Islamic Center of Washington. The visit was part of a broad government effort to crack down on what the FBI said were dozens of "retaliatory hate crimes" aimed at Muslim and Arab Americans, including assaults, threats, arson, and two possibly ethnically motivated murders.

■ Assets of 27 Groups and Individuals Frozen

September 24: Bush orders U.S. financial institutions to freeze assets of 27 groups and individuals suspected of supporting terrorists.

■ Bush Meets Muslim Leaders

September 26: President George W. Bush holds a meeting at the White House with Muslim leaders during which he states, "The teachings of Islam are the teachings of peace and good." The President denounces the hate crimes against Arab and Muslim Americans as "bigotry" and urges the media not to identify the terrorists who perpetrated the attacks in New York and Washington as "Islamic" or "Muslim" terrorists. Instead, they should be identified with their organization or country. The President once again states that "this is not a war against Islam, but against a bunch of criminals." The organizations represented at the meeting include the American Muslim Political Coordination Council (AMPCC), American Arab Institute (AAI), Islamic Society of North America (ISNA), Islamic Institute (II), American Arab Anti-

Discrimination Committee (ADC) and American Lebanese Heritage Club.

▦ Muslim Leaders Hold Emergency Summit

October 23: Leaders from the Muslim American Society (MAS) and the Islamic Circle of North America (ICNA) hold a summit in Falls Church, Virginia to discuss the aftermath of the September 11 attacks. The meeting aims at discussing the new realities resulting from the attacks and what they mean for the future of the Muslim community. According to a statement by the organizers, "the Muslim leaders are required, now more than ever before, to provide the clear vision, the answers to the challenging questions of our time, and the plan to lead our community through these difficult times into its better future." Dr. Souheil Ghannouchi of MAS who presided over the summit, states, "On the one hand, the Muslim community was taken by fear and lived for a while under siege. There are also some signs of shame and guilt among Muslim youth. On the other hand, while the charged atmosphere caused paranoia and encouraged bigotry, suspicions, and backlashes, there is an unprecedented interest in Islam and tremendous support and sympathy, a clear dissociation between Islam and terrorism, and a firm recognition of Muslims as an integral part of the American social fabric." Leaders discuss the need to reevaluate community practices and examine things such as written materials by Muslim scholars and the need to address fundamental issues such as citizenship from an Islamic perspective. A proposal for a Muslim legal defense fund is also made to address the hundreds of Muslims detained post-9/11. Finally, the statement encourages the community to stay engaged, emphasizing "the need for broad and consistent political participation at all levels, not just national elections, and the need to strive for actual access to the political system not just symbolic recognition."

▦ USA Patriot Act Enacted

October 26: the President signs the Uniting and Strengthening America by Providing Appropriate Tools Required to Intercept and Obstruct Terrorism Act, better known by its acronym, the USA PATRIOT Act. The law, which hurriedly passed with little public debate, has been criticized by constitutional law experts who say it erodes the civil liberties that Americans take for granted. In particular, critics have charged that the Act gives the executive branch the power to detain immigrant suspects for lengthy periods of time, sometimes indefinitely. Critics have also pointed out that the Act allows the executive branch to circumvent the Fourth Amendment's requirement of probable cause when conducting wiretaps and searches.

▦ FBI Raids Muslim Businesses

November 7: Federal agents raid Muslim businesses suspected of helping funnel millions of dollars to bin Laden's network. President Bush asks at least nine countries to freeze assets that aid bin Laden and al-Qaida.

▦ 5,000 Young Men from Middle East Called for Questioning

November 9: Attorney General John Ashcroft announces a plan to target for questioning some 5,000 young men of

Middle Eastern and South Asian heritage who entered the country during the previous two years on non-immigrant visas but who are not suspected of any criminal activity.

▪ Racist Comments Made by Attorney General

November 9: In an interview with syndicated columnist Cal Thomas, John Ashcroft is quoted as saying, "Islam is a religion in which God requires you to send your son to die for him. Christianity is a faith in which God sends his son to die for you." Later, the Attorney General declines to clarify his statement.

▪ Dr. Mazen al-Najjar Rearrested

November 24: After being unjustly detained for over three and a half years on the basis of secret evidence, Dr. Mazen al-Najjar was ultimately released in December 2000, following a lengthy national civil rights struggle in which the mass media, Congress, the White House, and the federal courts were heavily involved in lifting the unconstitutional practice and freeing its Arab and Muslim victims. Nearly a year later, however, and in response to the events of 9/11, federal agents once again arrest Dr. Al-Najjar at his home in Tampa, Florida. The Palestinian refugee is hauled off to Coleman Federal Penitentiary's maximum-security wing, where he was kept in solitary confinement until his deportation nine months later. Once again, he is detained based purely on the whim of the national security agencies and denied a fair and open hearing. Rather than secret evidence, this time *no evidence* is used in justifying his abusive treatment.

■ The Holy Land Foundation Banned

December 4: The Holy Land Foundation for Relief and Development (HLF), headquartered in Richardson, Texas, is banned for raising money for Hamas, a Palestinian organization declared by the U.S. government as a terrorist group.

■ Jewish Defense League Bomb Plot Averted

December 11: Irving David Rubin and Earl Leslie Krugel of the Jewish Defense League are indicted in Los Angeles for conspiracy to bomb a mosque, the office of the Muslim Public Affairs Council (MPAC), and the office of US Congressman Darrell Issa (R-CA).

■ Assets of Global Relief and Benevolence International Foundation Blocked

December 14: The Treasury Department blocks the assets of Global Relief and another group, the Benevolence International Foundation, on the grounds that the groups are providing financial assistance to terrorists. Government agents raid Global Relief's offices in Bridgeview and Illinois.

■ Muslim Americans Poll on War on Terrorism

December 19: A systematic poll of Muslim Americans has found that two-thirds agree with the Bush Administration's assertion that America is fighting a war against terrorism, not Islam. The poll results are released by Project MAPS: Muslims in the American Public Square, a project sponsored by the Center for Muslim-Christian Understanding at Georgetown University and the Pew Charitable Trusts. The poll was conducted by *Zogby* International.

Chronology of Islam in America 2002

■ **Muslim Offices and Homes Raided in Virginia and Georgia**

March 20: Federal agents raid a number of Muslim offices and homes in Virginia and Georgia. The raids are launched as part of Operation Green Quest, a task force created to track and disrupt the sources of terrorist finances.

■ **Another 3,000 Individuals from Middle East Under Questioning**

March 20: Attorney General John Aschroft announces second FBI dragnet plan to question an additional 3,000 individuals of Middle Eastern and South Asian heritage. In San Francisco, San Jose, and Oakland police departments have refused to participate in the interviews because the plan violates state laws or local policies against profiling based on race or national origin.

■ **Plan Announced to Register Non-Immigrants from Muslim Countries**

June 5: The Justice Department announces a plan that would require hundreds of thousands of lawful visitors—

including those already in the country—from mostly Muslim nations to provide fingerprints to authorities upon arrival and register with the Immigration and Naturalization Service after 30 days in the country.

■ Florida Terrorist Plot from Jewish Podiatrist Averted

August 23: Robert Goldstein, a podiatrist is charged with plotting attacks on Islamic centers across the state. He was found to have an arsenal of high-powered guns, Claymore mines, homemade bombs, and napalm. Agents also found a typed three-page mission template for a terrorist attack against Muslims in Florida planned for the anniversary of the September 11 attacks.

■ Operation TIPS Scaled Back

August 9: Amidst public outcry, the Department of Justice announces that, "given the concerns raised during the program development phase about safeguarding against all possibilities of invasion of individual privacy, the [Operation TIPS] hotline number will not be shared with any workers, including postal and utility workers, whose work puts them in contact with homes and private property." But, the program will still seek to enlist workers involved in "transportation, trucking, shipping, maritime, and mass transit industries."

■ Fingerprinting Non-Immigrants from Muslim Nations

August 12: The Department of Justice finalizes a plan that requires thousands of lawful visitors—from 24 Muslim nations—to provide fingerprints to authorities upon arrival and register with the Immigration and Naturalization Service after 30 days in the country. Visitors who fail to do either of these things face fines or even deportation.

■ High Court Allows Closed-Door Hearing

October 8: The Third Circuit Court of Appeals in New Jersey rules that immigration hearings involving people detained after September 11 may be closed by the government without the input of the court.

■ President Bush Distances Himself from Christian Right Attacks Against Islam

November 13: In a meeting with U.N. Secretary General Kofi Annan, president Bush says: "Some of the comments that have been uttered about Islam do not reflect the sentiments of my government or the sentiments of most Americans. Islam, as practiced by the vast majority of people, is a peaceful religion, a religion that respects others." He also says: "By far, the vast majority of American citizens respect the Islamic [read Muslim] people and the Muslim [read Islamic] faith. ... Ours is a country based upon tolerance. ... And we're not going to let the war on terror or terrorists cause us to change our values." Media reports quote White House officials as saying that the president's remarks were prompted by recent attacks on Islam, particularly those of Pat Robertson, who said that Muslims are "worse than the Nazis." "He (Bush) wanted (to make) a clear statement," a senior White House official tells Reuters.

▦ INS Special Registration Program Launched

November 15: The Justice Department launches the INS Special Registration Program for male nationals of 24 Muslim countries. The INS Special Registration comes in four stages: (Group 1 Dec.) Iran, Iraq, Libya, Sudan and Syria; (Group 2 Dec.) Afghanistan, Algeria, Bahrain, Eritrea, Lebanon, Morocco, North Korea, Oman, Qatar, Somalia, Tunisia, United Arab Emirates, and Yemen; (Group 3 Jan.) Pakistan and Saudi Arabia; (Group 4 Feb.) Bangladesh, Egypt, Indonesia, Jordan and Kuwait. All male citizens or nationals of these countries age 15 or older are required to register. Registrants are told to re-register again before their registration anniversary date.

▦ Hate Crimes Against Muslims

November 18: Hate crimes and other acts of vengeance skyrocketed nationwide against Muslims and other immigrants from the Middle East after the Sept. 11 terrorist attacks, according to a long-awaited FBI report released today. The FBI found that while attacks against Muslims had previously been the least common hate crime against a religious group—just 28 in 2000—the number of incidents surged to 481 in 2001, an increase of 1,600%. The huge rise comes "presumably as a result of the heinous incidents that occurred on Sept. 11" of 2001, the FBI says.

▦ Hundreds Held for Minor Visa Violations

Hundreds of people from the Middle Eastern countries are arrested by the federal immigration officials in Southern

California when they comply with orders to appear at the INS offices for a special registration program, according to the *Los Angeles Times*.

Chronology of Islam in America 2003

▪ Deportation of Muslims Increased

January 15: The U.S. government dramatically increased the deportation of people from Muslim nations in the year after Sept. 11, 2001, even as it eased up on illegal immigrants from Mexico and other countries. The numbers of foreign nationals expelled to their native countries in North Africa, the Middle East, and South Asia multiplied faster than for citizens of nearly all other nations from October 2001 to September 2002, according to an *Atlanta Journal-Constitution* computer analysis of Immigration and Naturalization Service records. The analysis provides the first comprehensive look at the nationality of people deported since the terrorist attacks.

▪ Muslim Workers in California and Illinois Face Discrimination

February 5: The Equal Employment Opportunity Commission (EEOC) confirms that Muslim workers in California and Illinois have faced discrimination because of their religion. Giving a ruling on the sacking of a Muslim pilot following the 9/11 terrorist attacks, the EEOC says that the airlines fired the pilot because of his religion, race, and national origin. The Muslim pilot, a native of Fiji who lives in the San Francisco Bay area, was fired based on anonymous accusations of impropriety and a call from a person claiming to be with the FBI seeking an interview with the worker.

▩ FBI Plans Counting of Mosque Members

February 3: Newsweek reports that the FBI Director Robert Mueller's top aides direct chiefs of the bureau's 56 field offices to develop "demographic" profiles of their localities—including tallying the number of mosques. On February 20, the Council of American-Islamic Relations (CAIR) urges FBI Director Robert Mueller to offer assurances that American mosques are not being asked to turn over membership lists to local agents. First, the FBI wants a count of all the mosques in their regional field offices. According to the Islamic Society of Frederick, Md., FBI agents who requested a meeting with their leadership "mentioned casually" they would be asking for a list of the society's members. This sent red flags up for the Islamic Society, which immediately informed media outlets, interfaith partners, and civil rights groups. Local FBI officials then said they would not press for the list local agents had requested.

▩ The Arrest of Dr. Sami al-Arian

February 20: Tampa, Florida. After eight years of government harassment due to his activities on behalf of Palestine and his political activism and leading stance on civil rights in America, Dr. Sami al-Arian is arrested by federal authorities on spurious charges stemming from his decades of activism. Three others are also arrested and detained. The same afternoon, Attorney General John Ashcroft hails the arrests as the latest victory in the "war on terror," giving credit to the Patriot Act for making it possible. The men are subsequently moved to the Coleman Federal Penitentiary and kept in solitary confinement under the most oppressive conditions. To protest his political incarceration, Dr. Al-Arian embarks on a hunger strike for 150 days. Months later, a judge sets the trial date for January, 2005, nearly two years following the arrest.

■ Ashcroft Scores Political Points in Idaho

February 26: The Attorney General goes on national TV claiming that another key figure in the war on terrorism was arrested. Sami Omar al Hussayen, a PhD student at the University of Idaho has been waiting 14 months for his trial, mostly in solitary confinement. Initially he was charged with visa fraud. Two weeks before his trial the Government filed a superceding indictment alleging material support for terrorism stemming from his maintenance of an internet website. Finally the Government alleges that the website encouraged financial support of Hamas. The case may be the first case to raise and challenge the USA Patriot Act. If convicted he could face over 100 years in prison.

■ Northwest Airlines Apologizes for Deplaning Muslim Immigrant

May 21: Harris Khan, 28, a Pakistani immigrant, who was removed from a Northwest Airlines flight three months after the Sept. 11 terror attacks, allegedly because he looked

Middle Eastern, receives an apology and monetary damages from the airline in a settlement. As part of the agreement, believed to be the first of its kind in the country, the airline also agrees to train the pilots about the importance of civil-liberties protections for passengers.

U.S. Senate Condemns Attacks on Muslims

May 23: The U.S. Senate unanimously adopts a resolution condemning violence against Muslims and other minorities. The resolution, presented by Democratic Senator Dick Durbin, named Arab Americans, Muslim Americans, South-Asian Americans, and Sikh Americans as minorities targeted for hate crimes.

Supreme Court Won't Review Secret Deportation Hearings

May 27: The U.S. Supreme Court rejects a challenge to the federal government's policy of holding secret immigration hearings of people detained after the Sept. 11, 2001, attacks. The justices decline to review a U.S. appeals court ruling that news media and public access to the deportation proceedings could endanger national security. Without any comment, the high court refuses to hear an appeal by New Jersey newspapers arguing that the government may not keep the proceedings secret without a specific, case-by-case showing that closing the hearing would be necessary. The secret hearings are among the tactics the Bush administration adopted after the hijacked plane attacks on the World Trade Center and the Pentagon. A directive 10 days after the attacks ordered immigration judges to close hearings for detainees whose cases the U.S. Justice Department deemed were of "special interest" to the government's terrorism investigation. During the government's investigation, approximately 766 detainees were designated as "special interest" cases, 611 of whom had one or more hearings closed, the *New York Times* quoted department lawyers as saying.

▓ FBI Criticized Over September 11 Detentions

June 2: Foreigners (Muslims and Arabs) detained as part of the investigation into the Sept 11, 2001, attacks on the United States were held too long without being charged and were subjected to "unduly harsh" conditions of confinement, a U.S. Justice Department audit reports. The audit by the department's inspector general finds "significant problems" in how authorities handled the 762 foreigners who were detained for immigration violations during the investigation into the hijacked airliner attacks. Some detainees were locked up almost continuously, were moved around in handcuffs and leg irons, subjected to abuse, and had their cell lights kept on day and night.

▓ More than 13,000 Arabs, Muslims Face Deportation

June 6: More than 13,000 of the Arab and Muslim men who came forward earlier this year to register with immigration authorities—roughly 16 percent of the total—may now face deportation, the *New York Times* quotes government officials saying. Only a handful have been linked to terrorism. But of the 82,000 men older than 16 who registered, more than 13,000 have been found to be living in this country illegally, officials said. Advocates for immigrants have accused officials of practicing selective enforcement of immigration laws by focusing on illegal immigrants from Arab and Muslim nations. Rather than disrupting communities, they say, the government should improve its intelligence and prosecution of terrorists.

▓ Justice Department Prohibits Racial Profiling

June 17: The Bush administration bans federal law enforcement officers from racial profiling in routine police work, but said agents may use race and ethnicity to identify suspected terrorists. A 10-page guidance drafted by the Justice Department is approved by President Bush and sent to all federal law enforcement agencies. It does not apply to state and local police. Ralph Boyd, Assistant Attorney General for Civil Rights, says the Bush administration is the first to issue a formal policy on racial profiling. Before the terrorist attacks of Sept. 11, 2001, local and state police were accused of racial profiling far more often than federal agents. But that changed after hundreds of Middle Eastern men were detained in the Sept. 11 probe.

▓ Virginia Resident Targeted Because of His Perceived Religious Views

June 9: Singled out because of his views, Majed Hajbeh, a longtime permanent resident of the United States, is charged with fraud and tried in federal court. Although he was found not guilty, Homeland Security appealed his bond before an immigration judge, insuring that he would be incarcerated until the case is finally resolved. Although

Immigration and Customs Enforcement alleged that he was a national security threat and had ties to terrorism, he was charged only with immigration fraud, an allegation that the Government could not substantiate. The pattern has been repeated in dozens of cases throughout the country under the pretext of preserving national security.

▓ Banks Blacklisting Muslims

July 2: American financial institutions are using extreme interpretations of the U.S.A. Patriot Act to justify blacklisting Muslim account holders, reports *An-Nahar*, an Arabic weekly based in Southern California. The Council on American-Islamic Relations (CAIR), says Muslims are complaining that some of the biggest banks and credit agencies in the United States, such as American Express, HSBC, Fleet Bank, and Western Union, are canceling accounts and making intrusive demands for private information. Many of the cancellations seem to be inspired by the similarity of the account holder's name to names that appear on a Treasury Department list of Specially Designated Nationals and Blocked Individuals (SDN). In one high-profile case in early 2003, Western Union denied service and a refund to a Muslim African-American from New York unless he provided photo identification and information about his country of birth.

▓ Judge Accepts Life Ban for "Terrorist" Remark

July 6: A suburban New York judge agrees to a lifelong ban from the bench for asking a Lebanese-American woman if she was "a terrorist" when she appeared in court over parking tickets, officials said. The state judicial watchdog said in a ruling that Judge William Crosbie of Tarrytown, New York, acknowledged he could not successfully defend the charges of using an ethnic-based comment and agreed "he will neither seek nor accept judicial office at any time in the future." Anissa Khoder, a U.S. citizen who immigrated from Lebanon 14 years ago, filed a complaint on May 16 with the watchdog, the New York State Commission on Judicial Conduct. She said Crosbie asked her at her May 15 court appearance if she was "a terrorist." Khoder was challenging two parking tickets that had been left on her dashboard within one hour.

■ Report on USA Patriot Act Alleges Civil Rights Violations

July 20: A report by internal investigators at the Justice Department has identified dozens of recent cases in which department employees have been accused of serious civil rights and civil liberties violations involving enforcement of the sweeping federal antiterrorism law known as the USA Patriot Act. The inspector general's report, which was presented to Congress last week, says that in the six-month period that ended on June 15, the inspector general's office had received 34 complaints of civil rights and civil liberties violations by department employees that it considered credible, including accusations that Muslim and Arab immigrants in federal detention centers had been beaten.

■ AMC Chairman Meets with President Bush

July 24: Dr. Yahya Mossa Basha, Chairman of the American Muslim Council (AMC), meets with President George W.

Bush in Michigan. Dr. Basha was invited to meet with the president as part of the White House outreach efforts. On this occasion, Dr. Basha handed over a letter to the president on behalf of the American Muslim community. The letter outlined Muslim issues and offered comments on peace in the Middle East.

▪ Poll: 44% of Americans Think Islam Sparks Violence

July 24: The Research Center for the People & the Press shows that there has been an important shift in public perceptions of Islam. Fully 44 percent of the American public now believe that Islam is more likely than other religions "to encourage violence among its believers." As recently as March, 2002, just 25 percent expressed this view. "Our findings in this area actually point in different directions," said Melissa Rogers, executive director of the Pew Forum. "On the one hand, there's certainly an increase in the number of Americans who believe that Islam encourages violence. Yet at the same time, a narrow majority of the public continues to have favorable views of Muslim-Americans, and only 24 percent have an unfavorable view."

▪ Dr. Ali al-Mazrui Held for Seven Hours

August 3: Eminent Muslim scholar, Dr. Ali al-Mazrui, who has lived in the United States since 1974, is detained and interrogated for seven hours after he returned from a working visit to the Caribbean. Kenya-born Mazrui, a political scientist who still carries his country's passport, and is the author of many books on Islam and Africa, holds the Albert Schweitzer chair at the State University of New York at

Binghamton. Mazrui told the *Washington Post* in an interview later that he was questioned first by Immigration officials, then by Customs representatives, and finally by agents from the Department of Homeland Security. He commented, "Their questions included 'What is jihad?' and whether I believed in it. I gave them Jihad 101. A basic introduction to a subject at American universities is called 'course 101'. Then they wanted to know what sect of Islam I believe in. When I said Sunni, they asked why I was not Shia. That was definitely a first. That's like asking a Catholic why he isn't a Protestant."

▪ Bush Appoints Anti-Muslim Scholar to Peace Role

August 23: A Middle East expert who has written dismissively of diplomacy is named to the board of the U.S. Institute of Peace. The largely honorary appointment of Daniel Pipes, a gift of President George Bush, has outraged Democratic senators, American Muslims and Arabs, liberal Jews, and a large portion of the academic community, who say his opinions are not conducive to peace.

▪ Rev. Bob Edgar Condemns the Hate Speech of Conservative Christian Leaders

August 29-31: Faced with an increase in hate crimes, threats to their civil liberties, and an assault on their faith, about 40,000 American Muslims gather in Chicago for the 40th annual convention of the Islamic Society of North America (ISNA) on Labor Day weekend. Attending the convention, the Rev. Bob Edgar, head of the National Council of Churches, which represents thousands of mainline

Protestant and Orthodox Christian congregations, condemns what he calls the "hate speech" of conservative Christian leaders who condemn Islam. He commits the resources of his organization to foster respect for the religion.

▓ Abdurahman Alamoudi Arrested

September 28: Abdurahman Alamoudi, an American Muslim and one of the founders of the American Muslim Council (AMC), is arrest on September 28, 2003, at Dulles International Airport in Virginia after a flight from London. According to media reports, he was found to be in possession of large sums of money that he received from the government of Libya in exchange for lobbying the U.S. government. In a statement, the Muslim Public Affairs Council (MPAC) says that he was taken into custody for violations of the law that were unrelated to the War on Terror or to any alleged involvement with terrorism. The MPAC statement said: "The targeting of individuals or organizations by law enforcement should not be politicized, and the alleged crimes of one individual should not be allowed to taint an entire community. Biased pundits motivated by personal agendas, with the support of some in the government, have exploited the tragedy of 9/11 to marginalize the voices of American Muslims, and to prevent the emergence of an effective and independent American Muslim leadership."

▓ FBI Revokes Its Service Award from Arab Leader

October 9: After pressure from a pro-Israeli group and columnist, the FBI rescinds an award it had planned to give to a prominent Arab-American leader this week and raises questions about his connections with men the government wants to deport. Imad Hamad, who heads the local branch of the American-Arab Anti-Discrimination Committee, had been scheduled to receive a prestigious service award today in Washington, D.C., for his work with law enforcement after the Sept. 11, 2001, terrorist attacks. Local conservative columnist Debbie Schlussel and the Zionist Organization of America—one of the oldest pro-Israeli groups in the nation—led a spirited attack last month against Hamad, charging in letters and articles that he is sympathetic to terrorists and unworthy of such an honor. Hamad said the allegations that he supports terrorism are baseless and came from fringe groups with no credibility.

▪ General Boykin Says His God Was Bigger

October 16: Los Angeles reports that The Pentagon has assigned the task of tracking down and eliminating Osama bin Laden, Saddam Hussein, and other high-profile targets to an Army general who sees the war on terrorism as a clash between Judeo-Christian values and Satan. Lt. Gen. William G. "Jerry" Boykin, the new Deputy Undersecretary of Defense for Intelligence, appeared in dress uniform and polished jump boots before a religious group in Oregon in June to declare that radical Islamists hated the United States "because we're a Christian nation, because our foundation and our roots are Judeo-Christian ... and the enemy is a guy named Satan." Discussing the battle against a Muslim warlord in Somalia, Boykin told another audience, "I knew my God was bigger than his. I knew that my God was a real God and his was an idol." On at least one occasion, in Sandy, Oregon, in June, Boykin said of

President Bush: "He's in the White House because God put him there."

■ American Muslim Organizations Call for General Boykin's Removal

October 20: American Muslim organizations denounce the anti-Islam and anti-Muslim comments by Lt. General William Boykin who was recently appointed as Deputy Undersecretary of Defense for Intelligence and called for his removal from this sensitive office. They say that, while every American has the freedom to express his opinion, it is essential that those who hold high policymaking positions should exercise judgment in their public speaking and that Lt. Gen. Boykin clearly lacks such judgment. These remarks feed into an emerging pattern of religious bigotry against Muslims and Islam.

■ U.S. Court Rules It Is OK to Hold 9/11 Witnesses

November 8: In a victory for Washington's anti-terrorism arrest tactics, a U.S. appeals court rules that a Jordanian student can be held as a material witness in a grand jury Sept. 11 investigation. The 2nd U.S. Circuit Court of Appeals overturns a trial judge's finding that the government had wrongly used the material witness statute to hold the student, Osama Awadallah, whom prosecutors later said lied when he denied knowing one of the Sept. 11, 2001 hijackers. The case has drawn wide attention because it questions whether the U.S. government is acting legally when it jails indefinitely people who are not charged with a crime but might be called to testify before a grand jury investigating terrorist activities.

■ Supreme Court Rejects Appeal from Global Relief

November 10: The Supreme Court rejects an appeal from an Islamic charity whose assets were impounded three months after the terrorist attacks. The Global Relief Foundation argued that the government put it out of business without proof that the Illinois-based charity was funneling money to terrorists. Justices refuse to consider whether it was unconstitutional or illegal for the government to freeze the foundation's bank accounts.

■ INS Special Registration Suspended Partially

December 2: The Homeland Security Department partially suspends the special registration program that targets boys and men from 24 Muslim countries. The two changes in Special Registration requirements are the following: (1) The annual re-registration requirement is suspended for all Special Registrants, i.e., for both those who registered under the "Call-In" and those who were registered at a port-of-entry (POE). (2) The 30/40-day follow-up interview requirement (applicable only to POE Registrants) is also suspended. All other requirements for Special Registrants remain in effect including Departure Registration and Reporting Changes of Address, Employment, or Educational Institution.

■ Key Provisions of Anti-Terrorism Statute Declared Unconstitutional

December 3: The U.S. Court of Appeals for the Ninth Circuit declares unconstitutional significant parts of a criminal statute barring "material support" to terrorist organizations, and rejected the government's interpretation of the statute as imposing liability on "moral innocents." The case, Humanitarian Law Project v. Ashcroft, involved a challenge brought by the Center for Constitutional Rights on behalf of a human rights organization in Los Angeles and several groups of Sri Lankan Tamils to a statute that criminalizes "material support" to any group designated as "terrorist" by the Secretary of State. The Administration has argued that the statute makes it a crime to provide material support to terrorist organizations without regard to whether the donor knows that the organization is a designated group, and the statute includes within the ambit of "material support" the provision of "personnel" and "training."

■ Democrats Court Vote of Disgruntled U.S. Muslims

December 21: Three years after Muslim Americans overwhelmingly voted for George W. Bush, democratic presidential candidates court these disenchanted voters in hopes of winning millions of backers in key states. "I want to earn the support of Muslims and Muslim leaders across the United States," Sen. John Kerry (D–MA) tells the annual convention of the Muslim Public Affairs Council (MPAC) outside Los Angeles. "I very much hope for your support," Democratic candidate and former Vermont governor, Howard Dean tells the MPAC convention. The community's favorite remained Ohio Congressman Dennis Kucinich, a longtime champion of rights for the American Muslim community. He polled much higher with Muslim voters than among mainstream Americans.

Chronology of Islam in America 2004

▓ Senate Committee Seeks Muslim Groups' IRS Files

January 14: The Senate Finance Committee asks the Internal Revenue Service (IRS) to turn over confidential tax and financial records, including donor lists, of dozens of Muslim charities and foundations in its investigation of terrorist funding. According to the *Washington Post*, "the request marks a rare and unusually broad use of the Finance Committee's power to obtain private financial records held by the government. It raises the possibility that contributions to charities such as the Holy Land Foundation or the activities of such groups as the Muslim Student Association could be subjected to Senate scrutiny."

▓ Alabama Muslims Denied Right to Islamic Attire

January 15: Muslim women in Alabama report that they were prevented from obtaining or renewing their driver's licenses because they refused to take off their headscarves.

▓ N.Y. Congressman Calls U.S. Mosque Leaders "An Enemy Amongst Us"

February 11: Appearing on pundit Sean Hannity's conservative nationally-syndicated radio program, Rep. Peter King (R-NY) claims that the vast majority of American Muslim leaders are "an enemy living amongst us" and that "(American) Muslims" cooperate in the war on terror. He added, "I would say that 80-85 percent of mosques in this country are controlled by Islamic fundamentalists." When prodded for his sources, King cited noted Islamophobes Steve Emerson and Daniel Pipes. King's comments were condemned by American Muslim organizations.

■ U.S. Freezes Accounts of Large Saudi Charity

February 20: The Treasury Department orders banks to freeze the accounts of the al-Haramain Islamic Foundation. FBI and IRS agents search the U.S. headquarters of the Saudi charity in Ashland, Oregon, alleging that it has been used to finance the al Qaeda terrorist network around the world. These are the latest in the government's crackdown on the charity, having previously closed offices in Bosnia, Somalia, Indonesia, Kenya, Tanzania, and Pakistan. The charity's U.S. attorney, Lawrence Matasar, says "we believe no crimes have been committed." The U.S. branch of the charity has mainly distributed Islamic books and videos to Americans, and also helped establish a mosque in Springfield, Missouri.

■ Supreme Court Will Not Hear Holy Land Foundation Appeal

March 1: The Supreme Court refuses to reinstate a lawsuit over the Bush administration's decision to freeze assets of the Holy Land Foundation, the largest Muslim charity in the United States. The highest court in the land does not provide any comments or reasoning behind its decision in rejecting the appeal. HLF, based in Texas, was shut down in December, 2001, under government allegations that it was linked to terrorist groups. Lawyers continued to deny that claim, stating, "to this day, no court has required the government to present a single live witness or sworn statement supporting its contention that HLF, once this nation's largest Muslim charity, funds the terrorist group Hamas. The government's claim of national security must be considered in light of a history of similar claims that have proven exaggerated."

■ Virginia 11 Verdicts Handed Down

March 5: Following a one month trial, Federal Judge Brinkema hands down the verdicts in what has come to be known as the "Paintball 11." Six of the eleven, including noted Muslim activist Ismail Royer, had previously come to plea agreements with the government, with some even becoming witnesses for the prosecution, while the remaining five members went to trial. Having waived their right to a jury, their fate was left in the judge's hands, who acquits two men of all charges, but convicts the remaining three on some of the biggest counts, including conspiracy and weapons charges which carry long prison sentences. The decision is devastating to the Muslim community, which had come to hope that the young men would be released, as the government's case was unconvincing to all who knew them.

■ Hate Crime Statistics

May 4: The Council on American-Islamic Relations' (CAIR) report outlines 1,019 incidents and experiences of anti-Muslim violence, discrimination, and harassment in 2003, the highest number of Muslim civil rights cases ever recorded by the Washington-based group. According to the report, called "Unpatriotic Acts," hate crimes alone jumped by an unprecedented 121 percent.

CAIR said factors contributing to the sharp increase in reported incidents included a lingering atmosphere of post-9/11 fear in America, pro-war rhetoric leading up to and following last year's invasion of Iraq, a disturbing increase in anti-Muslim rhetoric, and abuses associated with the implementation of the USA PATRIOT Act. ■

PROFILE: THE VICTIMS OF THE
ZIONIST PLOT

• Shukry Abu Baker

• Abu Baker receiving an award for his humanitarian work, AMC Conference, 2000.

• Muhammad Salah

• Salah welcomed home to Chicago after his release from an Israeli prison, 1998.

Chapter 9

THE HOLY LAND FOUNDATION AND THE SAGA OF HAMAS IN AMERICA

Over half of my adult life was spent in the West. The circumstances that have brought me here to the U.S. are not much unlike those of many other Palestinians who because of the Diaspora found themselves in the unlikeliest of places. We seek only to better ourselves through education and a moral foundation that allows us to continue to redress the injustices committed against our people. I do not acquiesce to the theory that human beings are inherently evil, violent or have fallen from grace due to man's nature. Yet, the innocent Palestinians have been assailed based on such pretenses. Stereotyping of Muslims and Palestinians in the West has desensitized the public and policy makers alike.

—Dr. Musa Abu Marzook, Metropolitan Correctional Center,
New York, May 3, 1997.

The true nature of the history of Hamas in the United States and its relationship with American Muslim institutions and individuals has been sorely overlooked in an atmosphere clouded by the geopolitical rivalries of earlier decades and the terrorist attacks of September 11, 2001. Numerous national and international political factions perceive that their interests are served by portraying this history and relationship to be something other than what it is. This portrayal has had serious consequences for Middle East peace, the relationship between Islam and the West, and political rights in the United States. It is, therefore, imperative that we objectively examine the role of Hamas in this country.

The role of Hamas in the United States, to the extent that it had one, is the result of a fascinating dynamic of social and political trends. It is a story of the return of Palestinians to Islam, the travel of Palestinian Islamists to the United States, and their successful efforts to raise awareness of their cause, and Israel's determination to block all expression of solidarity for the Palestinians.

No endeavor of this nature would be complete without a focus on the life of Dr. Musa Abu Marzouq, who epitomizes the historical processes and trends of the Islamic awakening in Palestine and the rise of Hamas, an organization he would eventually help lead. Dr. Marzouq has long been known among his associates and peers for his genius, knowledge, and broad horizons. These characteristics enabled him to be distinguished among his colleagues and guaranteed him leadership positions among the Palestinians. His story is the story of Hamas in America, and the axis around which all future accusations against pro-Palestinian groups in the United States would eventually revolve.

Islamization of Palestinians

The saga of Hamas begins with the origins of the Islamic reawakening in Palestine and the dynamics of that reawakening under the pressures of Israeli occupation and anti-religious Arab secular nationalism.

Islam Suppressed

When Israel first occupied the West Bank and the Gaza Strip, Islamic awareness and dedication among the Palestinian people were weak. Religious discourse had little following beyond the borders of the mosque. The mosques were attended largely by old people who knew they would soon depart this life and now sought Allah's forgiveness in their last days. Because so few Muslims practiced their rituals outside the mosque, the religion's role was very limited.

In pre-1967 Gaza, there were a limited number of Palestinians who belonged to the *Ikhwan al-Muslimeen*, or the Muslim Brotherhood, which opposed the secular regime of the Egyptian government that ruled that area of Palestine at the time. The activities of the Ikhwan were very limited, however, because of constant surveillance and harassment by the Egyptian Intelligence Service (*mukhabarat*) and its agents in Gaza. Because the Brotherhood was perceived to be a threat, Egyptian President Jamal Abdul Nasser imprisoned thousands of the group's members, torturing and executing scores of them. Under Egypt's cloud of repression, fear, confrontation, and execution, the social role of those seeking a revival of Islam was severely restricted.[1]

The situation of the Muslim Brotherhood in the West Bank was much better, however. The area was ruled at the time by Jordan's King Abdullah Hussein, who had built a working relationship with the Muslim Brotherhood in Jordan. His rule carried a sort of religious legitimacy since the Hashemite family perceived religion as a stabilizing factor, necessary for the regime's existence and continuity.

Palestine's Muslims Awake

With the Arab defeat of the 1967 war, Jamal Abdul Nasser's popularity dissipated along with Arab secular nationalism. The ascendance of Anwar Sadat to Egypt's presidency led to a reconciliation with the Muslim Brotherhood. Sadat's legitimacy was threatened by Nasserism and the leftists, and he strengthened his hand in the first few years of his rule by allowing a degree of political and economic openness.[2]

This relative freedom provided the Muslim Brothers with the needed space to express themselves, and the group began to engage actively in political life. It sought to regain the confidence and the popularity it had enjoyed during the twenty years preceding Nasser. As evidence of its status, tens of thousands of its followers and supporters regularly attended the Brotherhood's public events. In some cases, such as its Eid events, more than a million people gathered.

It was inevitable that such an active Islamic presence in Egypt would be reflected in Gaza and in Palestine in general. The Muslim Brotherhood came out publicly to call on the people to return to Allah, to organize and preserve their religious identity, to support national unity, and combat the Israeli occupation. These efforts succeeded in organizing the youth of Palestine, some of whom eventually went to Egypt to continue their education in Egyptian universities.

One such student was Musa Abu Marzouq, a young man raised in a refugee camp in the city of Rafah on the southern border of the Gaza Strip. As a Palestinian, he lived under conditions of deprivation and homelessness in refugee camps for many years. Marzouq lived the tragedy of many Palestinians and never forgot it. On a daily basis and with a watchful eye, he witnessed Israeli brutality against his people. The dramatic scenes of homelessness, life in the refugee camps, occupation, and suffering of the Palestinian people shaped his concept of the "national character." At the same time, he was deeply influenced by his religious upbringing and his attachment to Masjid Al-Huda, the mosque that he visited several times a day. These factors enhanced his feeling of loyalty to his people, to the Palestinian cause, and to the feeling of great responsibility that he has since shouldered. Marzouq realized as a Palestinian that he had to devote his life to this cause, and work hard day and night to liberate his people from occupation.[3]

Marzouq finished his elementary and preparatory schooling at the U.N. Relief and Work Agency (UNRWA). After the 1967 war, he was forced to go to Jordan, and he was never allowed to return to live due to the occupation. Like many Palestinians, he traveled to Cairo where he finished his high school and was admitted to Helwan University. He graduated with a B.S. in mechanical engineering in 1976.

As a result of this wave of travel to Egypt, these Palestinian students began to interact there with the Muslim Brotherhood and their student cadres in the universities, which witnessed a tidal wave of Islamic resurgence during the 1970s. This phenomenon reflected a religious awakening in all facets of Arab society during the 1970s, ignited during the 1980s in part by widespread enthusiasm over the Iranian revolution and the collapse of the Shah's regime. This is a trend that has continued throughout the Arab and Muslim worlds.[4]

Using their newly acquired skills in the propagation of Islam and political organization, the Palestinian graduates returned and contributed significantly to the acceleration of the religious awakening in both the West Bank and Gaza. This awakening heavily influenced the socio-political and economic life in the Occupied Territories.

The building of mosques intensified, expanding the role of the house of worship in the everyday life of the majority of Palestinian Muslims. The mosque became the center of youth activism, where religion, sports, and educational activities were held regularly. Discipline and manners were taught there. Qualified people volunteered their time, energy, and resources to advance the role of the mosque and to establish a grassroots movement, which led to the advancement of the Islamic commitment in the Occupied Territories.[5]

Toward the end of the 1970s, economic conditions stabilized in the Gaza Strip, where they had heretofore been far inferior to that of the West Bank. The number of technocrats and intelligentsia among the Muslim Brotherhood in the area increased considerably, to such an extent that the group was no longer able to absorb the skilled graduates returning from Egypt. As it happened, the Muslim Brotherhood's need to locate gainful employment for its educated members coincided with a critical shortage of educated employees in the oil-rich nations of the Persian Gulf, which at the time were undergoing the petrodollar renaissance—a period of rapid expansion and modernization. These Gulf countries lacked a domestic pool of qualified, trained people to develop and manage their newly expanding infrastructure, which required engineers and other technocrats, educators, entrepreneurs, and administrators.

An idea then gained currency among the leadership of

the Brotherhood in Gaza that some new graduates should be encouraged to travel to the Gulf region where they might secure jobs and the ability to provide financial and moral support for their people in Palestine. Prior to this, the Brotherhood had discouraged travel, as they perceived a need to keep their members at home to contribute to the process of awakening there. Consequently, a number of such graduates made their ways to the Gulf to help build the region's infrastructure.

Musa Abu Marzouq was part of this trend. Shortly after graduating from Helwan University in 1976, he traveled to the United Arab Emirates where he was employed in a number of important well-paying jobs in both the public and private sector, including one with a project of the ministries of electricity and water, and another as a production manager at an aluminum factory. He later worked with the Abu Dhabi National Oil Company (ADNOC), where he was able to save a substantial amount of money.[6]

The Palestinian expatriates in the Gulf benefited from the job opportunities in Kuwait, Saudi Arabia, and the United Arab Emirates. At the same time, they contributed to a process of Islamic resurgence there and interacted with Islamic leaders in the region. Ultimately, they succeeded in securing funds for countless educational and relief projects in Gaza and the West Bank. Marzouq exemplified this tendency when he returned to Gaza from the U.A.E. for a brief visit, where, with a generous contribution, he helped found the Gaza Islamic University.

As these Palestinian professionals in the Gulf finished their undergraduate and graduate degrees, many of them sought and obtained scholarships to pursue their higher education in the West, especially in the United States.

Moving to America

In the early 1980's, a wave of Palestinian students from the Persian Gulf states arrived in the United States, where they were welcomed by senior members of the Muslim Brotherhood who had immigrated after Nasser's crackdown over a decade before. Musa Abu Marzouq and Ismail Abu Shanab, who would later become leaders of the political wing of Hamas, were among many such students who had obtained scholarships from the Gulf countries.

Marzouq arrived in the United States in 1981 on a scholarship provided by the United Arab Emirates, where he had been working for the state-owned petroleum company. His goal was to finish his MA and PhD degrees in Engineering. He also financed his education with the money he had saved in his governmental and private sector work in the U.A.E.

The presence of Marzouq and other Palestinian Islamists in America's Muslim community provided them with the opportunity to rally support for the Palestinian cause. In a short period of time, they succeeded in making the Palestine Question the central concern of Muslims in America. By the time the first Intifada erupted, American Muslims shared with Palestinian-Americans a sincerely held compassion for the Palestinian people in their daily struggle.

"Palestinization" of American Muslims

The Palestinian students arrived in the United States amid a resurgence of Muslim activism. With their efforts stretching over more than a decade, the Palestinian Islamist leadership in the United States leveraged that trend and awakened considerable sympathy for the suffering people of

Palestine in the Muslim community, and mobilized its institutions to such a degree that it became difficult for any Islamic organization in America to neglect the Palestinian cause if it wanted success and prosperity.

Raising awareness

During the 1970s, Islamic activism began to flourish in the American landscape. Muslims established a number of associations and student unions, which then held annual conventions to unite Muslims scattered across the country. Organizers of such conventions invited renowned Muslim scholars from the Muslim world to attend, and the suffering of Muslims in Palestine, Kashmir, and elsewhere was frequently a topic of discussion. The gatherings also served as forums where participants could express their opinions about the injustices committed by the regimes across the Arab and Muslim world against the Islamic reformist movement.

Since Palestine was one of the most pressing and visible causes for Muslims around the world, some Islamists began to consider establishing an association with the primary goal of introducing the Palestine issue to America and mobilizing support for the Palestinian people. This call was well received among Muslims, especially among the Palestinian community in America. Thus, the Islamic Association for Palestine was founded in 1980, and it enjoyed the support of the majority of the Muslim leadership in America.[7]

In the 1980s, the IAP's activities consisted of lectures on the Palestinian issue in mosques and student organizations across the country. They published a popular newsletter that addressed the grievances and suffering of the Palestinian people. The group also worked successfully to make the Palestinian Question a permanent issue on the agenda of the Muslim community's annual conventions in America, ensuring that well-known Palestinian figures were among the Islamic leaders visiting from countries like Jordan, Egypt, Palestine, Tunisia, Sudan, Kuwait, Saudi Arabia, Pakistan, Turkey, and Malaysia.

Marzouq participated quite actively in this burst of activism that was sweeping Muslim communities across the United States. His work was helped by his well-known reputation and popularity during his stay in this country. The warmth of his character, his sincerity, generosity, and hard work earned him the trust and the love of the Muslim community in America. During his years in graduate school, he traveled frequently throughout the United States. He gave lectures and seminars, and actively participated in the activities of the Islamic Association for Palestine. His activism gave him the opportunity to meet students and assess the qualifications of the Palestinians in America as well as their financial capabilities and their willingness to support their countrymen back home.

When the Intifada erupted on December 8, 1987, news coverage of the conflict by the American media, especially CNN, contributed to the Muslims' growing awareness of the suffering of the Palestinian people. On a daily basis, dramatic scenes of children and youth confronting Israeli tanks were shown around the globe. These stirring scenes generated the sympathy of both Muslims and non-Muslims. This coverage rallied Muslims and others to the defense of the Palestinian people and generated a sympathetic trend toward their cause.

This sympathy encouraged Muslim scholars and activists to come to America to talk about the suffering of the Palestinian people and generate financial and moral support for their struggle. Muslims in America were reminded of their religious obligation toward their fellow Muslims in Palestine who were suffering under the occupation. Muslim scholars even issued *fatawa* to encourage Muslims to donate generously to the Palestinian people. In fact, Muslim scholars deemed donating to the Palestinian cause as "an obligation upon every Muslim, everyone according to his ability."

When the Intifada began, Marzouq was still in graduate school. The escalation of the uprising, the Israeli forces' unprecedented brutality in trying to crush it, and the aggravation of Palestinian suffering inspired him to redouble his efforts to mobilize support for the Palestinian cause among Muslims in America. He encouraged them to actively support the Intifada, and his broad network of contacts and the trust he had earned in the Muslim community in America enabled him to mobilize financial and moral support for the uprising.

Intifada and the need for relief

With the escalation and the continuation of the uprising and the increase in the number of the jailed, wounded, and killed, relief efforts were badly needed in Palestine. The six years preceding Oslo witnessed intensified humanitarian efforts by Islamists seeking to relieve the Palestinian people from their suffering. Such efforts extended on a worldwide scale, and were not confined to Islamists in America.

Pro-Palestinian activists in America initiated a campaign for donations to support wounded Palestinians, refugees, and orphans, and to assist the families of those who had died in the fighting, which exceeded thousands in less than two years. Mosques, Islamic centers, and annual conventions were the forums used to mobilize such support and to encourage the people to donate for the cause of Palestine. Donations were sent to charitable organizations to be spent on supporting the orphans, the needy, and the injured. Funds went to purchase ambulances, build health clinics, and to help satisfy other urgent needs of the Palestinians in the occupied territories.

An urgent need was quickly perceived for the establishment of an American relief organization to channel the donations of Arabs and Muslims to the occupied Palestinian land. Activists had begun to realize that traditional methods of donation and financial assistance through individuals were incapable of handling the amount of donations and responding to the severe needs of the Palestinian people. Customs enforcement at airports and limits on money transfers also made it difficult to deposit relief funds.

Eventually, some well-respected Palestinians in the country set about establishing a licensed relief organization to implement the relief efforts professionally and legally. The organization, the Holy Land Foundation, was to be governed by a board of directors to supervise its relief work and determine its relief effort priorities in the occupied land or in refugee camps in neighboring Arab countries like Jordan, Lebanon, Syria, and elsewhere.[8] Shukri Abu Baker, a Palestinian born in Brazil, raised in Kuwait, and educated in the United States, began his efforts with some of his associates and friends such as Ghassan Elashi, Muhammad al-Mozeyen, and other Palestinians to organize, license, and register the foundation in California on January 11, 1989.

At the start of the Intifada, HLF's work was limited by

its meager resources, lack of experience, and reliance on volunteers. As hostilities escalated, the number of casualties increased, and economic conditions worsened, the foundation was forced to improve the quality of its work out of necessity.

A catalyst for the foundation's growth was the leadership and the charismatic character of Mr. Abu Baker, who helped early on to establish its credibility and work. A man of many talents, his intellectual depth was expressed through his writings and poems, which conveyed the inhumane conditions of the Palestinian people. With his eloquent writing, he was successful in touching the minds and hearts of countless Arabs and Muslims in the country. Consequently, the foundation became very well known among Muslims in the United States.

Muslims around the country learned that they could donate their Zakat money to Islamic charitable organizations engaged in relief work. They began to donate these funds to HLF (Zakat is a religiously obligatory annual donation to charity). Such positive developments encouraged the Arab and Muslim community to double their donations and their support to the foundation.

Another key component of HLF's achievements was its success in forming an effective team of employees. Its staff grew steadily, both in the field and in the United States. At the same time, the voluntary aspect of relief efforts remained an integral part of its model in the Palestinian territories and in the United States. In addition, the foundation institutionalized its work with the establishment of its headquarters in Dallas, Texas, and with the opening of branches in the occupied territories and the refugee camps in Jordan, Lebanon, and elsewhere.

The Money Trail

Much has been made of the supposedly clandestine ways in which money made its way from the hands of Muslims in the United States to the needy in Palestine. The reality is much less exciting. Money was raised, processed, and disbursed in an open, transparent fashion consistent with the laws and ethics of the countries in which relief efforts operated.

How funds were raised

The efforts of HLF were boosted by the accumulation of American expertise in the techniques of fundraising and channeling the money to the needy on the ground. It also benefited tremendously from the knowledge and experiences of similar Christian and Jewish relief organizations. Such techniques were reflected by the amounts of money collected. Whereas in its early days the foundation collected several hundreds of thousands of dollars annually, the use of modern techniques helped multiply donations into millions of dollars, to the extent that the foundation collected ten million or more annually particularly near the end of the year 2000.[9]

Islamic scholars and preachers in the mosques had perhaps the most profound impact on the level of support for HLF when they urged Muslims to donate their Zakat to the foundation. The field reports from the occupied territories and the refugee camps in Jordan, Lebanon, Syria and elsewhere also had a deep impact on mobilizing donations. This first hand experience allowed HLF to provide compelling videos and first-hand testimony of conditions in Palestine, which deeply moved the people and convinced them to give generously.

• HLF, the first Annual Charity Conference, 1999.

• Abu Baker attending an HLF fundraising dinner.

• HLF publications: information brochure (left) and monthly newsletter (right).

The foundation often attracted the support of wealthy benefactors. Marzouk, for example, pledged $210,000 of his own personal money and added it to the donations he collected for the Holy Land Foundation in December of 1991. This donation later became the basis of the Israeli government's accusations that the foundation was "connected to" Hamas.

How funds were processed

Funds collected by the HLF were typically transferred by wire from the Dallas headquarters to banks in Jordan, Lebanon, Israel, and the Occupied Territories. These transfers were open and unconcealed, and authorities in all countries were aware of them. HLF employees in those countries then disbursed the funds in the form of grants intended for specific projects to licensed non-profit entities in good standing with the authorities. HLF would screen each project and organization to ensure that they were indeed qualified and authorized to perform relief work. A further requirement was that they be non-profit groups with no political affiliation.

How funds were disbursed

The beneficiaries of the Holy Land Foundation were the poor and the needy in Palestine and those who sought to improve their conditions in order to enable themselves to play vital roles in their communities. The foundation did so through direct relief work and by supporting the work of several nonprofit and charitable organizations that supervised humanitarian aid and social services in Palestine.

The foundation set its relief priorities by sending its envoys to visit the occupied territories and assess the needs, witnessing first hand the catastrophic and inhumane situation the Palestinians lived in for decades. In an interview, Shukri Abu Baker illustrated some of the projects carried out by HLF in the occupied territories. He classified these projects in this way:[10]

Emergency Relief Projects. The goal of this program was to provide immediate assistance to needy families. Such assistance included immediate health care, food, and shelter.

Social Services Projects. This included providing services to orphans and providing financial assistance to needy families. It also provided food, shelter, and rehabilitation services.

Educational Services Project. The goal was to provide needy students with tuition and school supplies, and to build schools to meet the growing needs of the population and to relieve crowded schools. The project also sought to provide teachers and lecturers to work in the different educational institutions in Palestine.

Socio-Cultural Development Projects. The goal was to provide financial assistance for the community, youth centers, and elderly. It also carried out cultural activities to preserve the cultural identity of the Palestinian people.

Health Care Services. This program provided financial assistance for the expansion of health care facilities and hospitals. The program also helped build clinics, purchase equipment, and train health care personnel.

Economic Development Project. The goal was to provide financial assistance, training, and job creation services.

Among the most important of these projects was the Social Services Project. At its peak, the foundation cared for almost 900 orphans and needy families. It also made a deep impact with its developmental projects which supported local charitable organizations, like hospitals and clinics, and community development programs such as skills development for women. For example, the foundation provided substantial support to Ramallah Hospital, the Ahli Hospital in Hebron, and Al-Razi Hospital in Jenin. It also supported schools, youth clubs, and a specialized children's library in the West Bank.

HLF Balance Sheet – 1995 to 1997

1995

Cash Donations	$2.3 Million
Gifts in Kind	$964,000
Total	$3.3 Million
Programs & Grants Disbursement	$2.8 Million

1996

Cash Donations	$3.0 Million
Gifts in Kind	$2.7 Million
Total	$5.7 Million
Programs & Grants Disbursement	$4 Million

1997

Cash Donations	$3.3 Million
Gifts in Kind	$2.2 Million
Donated Services	$30,000
Total	$5.53 Million
Programs & Grants Disbursement	$3.1 Million*

*December 97 disbursements not included
Source: *HLF News*, vol. 5, issue 1, March/April 1998.

The Charges of Terrorism: Fact and Fallacy

By the early 1990s, the increasingly sophisticated activism of the American Muslim community had not gone unnoticed. Pro-Israel activists in the United States who had previously occupied themselves with worrying about the impact of secular Arab groups turned their attention toward Islamic organizations. Operatives of the pro-Israel lobby began to demonize Palestinian Islamists and to argue that all Islamic movements were directly affiliated with or supportive of Hamas.

Hamas was founded in Gaza by leaders of the Muslim Brotherhood at the beginning of the Intifada in 1987, and grew in popularity due to its strategic military operations. At the time of its founding, two things were important to Palestinian society: one was resisting occupation, and the other was improving the lives of people socially and economically. Hamas was able to do this better than any other group. Hamas symbolized the aspirations of Palestinians moving toward the Islamic trend. From the beginning it was a multifaceted organization in which military operations played only one of many important roles. The movement gained a reputation of trust and service through its extensive religious, social and educational activities. Its military operations were the response to Israeli aggression and the oppression of Palestinians on a daily basis.

Hamas did not begin with militarized program. At that time, Hamas for the most part did not carry out military operations. Its activities were confined largely to rousing yet peaceful demonstrations against the occupation. But, with the escalation of Israeli brutality and the general dissatisfaction with the Oslo agreements, the Intifada began to grow more militant. The number of Islamist Palestinians assassinated or killed by Israelis reached unprecedented numbers, even though Hamas at one point had declared a unilateral truce for six months. In doing so, Hamas' goal was to provide the Palestinian Authority with the support it needed to conclude an agreement that would bring about peace and end the occupation.

A fateful event changed the course of the Intifada and Palestinian resistance. On February 25, 1994, an Israeli settler massacred fifty Muslim worshipers while they had congregated for the dawn prayer at the Hebron Mosque during the month of Ramadan, a month of fasting and spiritual contemplation. The Israeli government took no action against this atrocity, and in fact encouraged settlers to lionize him (there is a "memorial" in his honor above the site). In response to the murders, Hamas' military wing, the 'Izzudin al-Qassam Brigades, pledged to carry out five operations that, a Hamas statement said, would "make the Israeli Army and the settlers cry blood for their deceased." Hamas succeeded in carrying out its promise with five devastating attacks on Israeli targets. These operations antagonized Yitzhak Rabin, Israel's prime minister at the time, who then pledged to fight Hamas everywhere and cut off all sources of support to the organization.

Consequently, in 1995, Israel's lobby succeeded in passing a law in the U.S. Congress instituting the creation of an official list of "terrorist" organizations and granting the government broad new investigative and enforcement powers against those groups. Shortly thereafter, the Israeli government and intelligence agencies worked closely with the Israeli lobby in the United States to pressure the Clinton Administration to add Hamas to the list of terrorist organizations. These efforts succeeded at a time when Clinton's popularity was sinking due to the financial and sexual scandals he was involved in. The president issued an executive order in January, 1995, declaring Hamas a terrorist organization. Thus, all individuals who were members of Hamas were subject to arrest.

The designation of Hamas as a terrorist organization had more to do with political considerations than a moral stand against violence. After all, the United States has supported Israeli aggression as its state sponsored terrorism destroyed the lives of tens of thousands throughout the Middle East.

After the outlawing of Hamas, the U.S. Department of Justice began targeting Palestinian activists it said were linked to the organization. One such person was Musa Abu Marzouq. After his graduation in 1993, Marzouq worked in several commercial projects in Louisiana, all the while remaining true to his permanent cause, that of Palestine. His activism had transformed him into an international figure in the Islamic movement. His renown, intelligence, and vision, and his personal connections in Gaza, Egypt, and the Gulf made him a natural candidate for leadership. Several years passed before he declared even to his closest associates that he had been chosen to lead the Political Bureau of Hamas in 1992. He kept this a secret to such an extent that most people were not aware of it before his arrest at the John F. Kennedy Airport in New York on July 25th, 1995. But, some had noticed that his name had become familiar among a group of people who spoke on behalf of Hamas.

During Dr. Abu Marzouq's prolonged incarceration Hamas felt that the movement's long-term interests would be better served if the position of the head of the political bureau were filled, at least pending his release. Khaled Mishal was chosen for that purpose. Mishal has a residence in Damascus and can be reached through conventional channels.

Two months after Marzouk's arrest, the Israeli government presented the U.S. Department of Justice with a petition of charges. The list contained twenty-two charges of murder and attempted murder solely based on his role as the head of Hamas' political wing. The charges alleged that he assisted and encouraged members of Hamas to carry out suicide bombings against Israelis. The Israeli petition also demanded that the U.S. government extradite Abu Marzouq to Israel to face criminal charges. In so doing, the Israeli government based its accusation of Marzouq on the confession, provided under torture, of Muhammad Salah, a U.S. citizen jailed by Israel on charges of membership in Hamas.

The Case of Muhammad Salah

Muhammad Salah, a Palestinian American, is well known, especially in Southern Chicago. He is a naturalized U.S. citizen born in East Jerusalem, and he still has family members living in the city. He is a quiet and well-loved person in the Chicago Muslim community. He used to volunteer for community services, especially cleaning and preparing deceased's bodies for burial, usually at the Mosque Foundation on Harlem Street. The Israeli government arrested Salah in January of 1993 while he was on a visit to Jerusalem distributing assistance to the families of the Intifada victims. After two years of incarceration and twenty-two postponements of his trial, he reached a plea bargain with an Israeli military court and was sentenced to five years in jail. As part of the plea, Salah was forced to admit membership in Hamas and that he had distributed money on its behalf.

Salah's attorney argued at the time that the Israeli authorities were determined to prove something against his client, and predicted that had he not plea-bargained, his trial would probably have been postponed for another twelve years. Since the occupation authorities lacked evidence against him, it had resorted to threatening tactics. He was previously accused of being the international leader of Hamas military wing, responsible for the killing and the disappearance of the remains of an Israeli soldier, as well as of being the mastermind behind the reorganization of Hamas and the financial support of its military operations. The only thing his trial "proved" was his admission, under duress, to membership in Hamas.[11]

After finishing his sentence, Salah returned to the United States on November 10, 1997. The leadership of the Muslim community, which had rallied to his defense while he was incarcerated and lobbied for his release, warmly welcomed him at O'Hare International Airport. Since his return, he has been under constant surveillance and barred from traveling abroad. On June 6, 1998, President Clinton placed him on a list of "Specially Designated Terrorists." His bank accounts were confiscated. The Department of Justice seized his house and his assets, and he was prevented by executive order from doing business with any other American citizen. The government also confiscated the assets of the organization he worked for, the Quranic Literacy Institute, with total assets of $1.4 million.

Ever since, Muhammad Salah has been fighting to get back his money and reestablish his life. His attorney has struggled to refute the Israeli accusations. Hamas itself issued a communiqué that the confiscated money does not belong to it, and that it has no assets in the United States. "Such accusations are silly and have no foundation whatsoever," the statement said.

Flimsy allegations

The statements attributed to Salah during his torture in Israeli prisons were used as the cornerstone of the case against Marzouq and then later scores of Palestinian groups in the

United States. Those statements made no direct connection, however, between Marzouq and the military operations, as the Israeli petition for Marzouq's extradition claimed. Even the petition itself made only scattered claims about Marzouq's role in Hamas, focusing instead on his role in humanitarian relief to the families of Palestinians victims, and in particular those expelled by Israel to Southern Lebanon in the Roses Refugee Field Camp in Southern Lebanon.

In fact, the main issue that seemed to dominate the Israelis' interrogation of Muhammad Salah was the remains of Ilan Sadoun, an Israeli soldier missing for several years. The Labor government sought to find his remains, as the issue was viewed as an important card in the upcoming elections. This observation led some analysts to believe that Israel's insistence that the U.S. extradite Marzouq was an attempt to pressure the Hamas' leadership to provide information on Sadoun's remains.

Another problem with Israel's theory was that the vast sums of money Marzouq allegedly handled for Hamas were inconsistent with any military goal. The cost involved in financing a military operation, about $500, was miniscule compared to that of building the mosques, health clinics, youth centers, and educational institutions which constitute the core of Hamas' mission and, by all informed accounts, were in fact Marzouq's sole concern. Ultimately, despite Israel's allegations, no court has ever found that the money collected by Dr. Marzouq or others in the United States went to any cause other than the promotion of Palestinian civil society that would lead to an efficient and strong government capable of leading Palestinians in a post-occupation phase.

In fact, it is natural for a nongovernmental organization like Hamas to embark on fundraising to support its social and political networks in the occupied territories. Marzouq would have been instrumental in the fundraising process as an ambassador to the outside world, particularly in the Arab world. In his many official trips to Arab capitals, he focused on the wide network of social services that the movement was involved in as a means of meeting the needs of a Palestinian population living under a brutal occupation.

The campaign against Palestinian Muslims also runs into constitutional problems. The Constitution of the United States prohibits *ex post facto* legislation, that is, laws that make lawful activity retroactively illegal. Raising funds for Hamas prior to 1995, the period that Marzouq is said to have done so, was a perfectly lawful act. It is for this reason that during Marzouq's incarceration, the United States failed to bring criminal charges, which they clearly would have done had they been able to. It certainly would have served Israeli interests and justified his U.S. incarceration.

Another key aspect of Israel's mounting campaign against U.S.-based pro-Palestinian groups was the allegation that the Holy Land Foundation was somehow linked to Hamas and supported the group financially. This claim was based partly on Marzouq's $210,000 dollar donation to HLF—made in 1991, about two years before Marzouq became involved with Hamas and four years before such involvement would have been illegal.

Another claim against the HLF was that it supported Hamas by funding its charitable organizations and the families of suicide bombers. In an interview with a Jerusalem newspaper, Shukri Abu Baker of the HLF was asked about these claims.[12] He maintained that the foundation's files were not kept secret, but were open to perusal by anyone who wished to do so, as is the case in similar charitable organizations. The Holy Land

Foundation followed a policy of extreme transparency with regard to donation collection and distribution. Most of its donation collection was documented by video and the distribution was in public. The aim, Abu Baker said, was to deprive the Israelis or other agencies of ammunition that might be used against it in the future. Fundraising occurred through legitimate organizations that were providing humanitarian assistance to Palestinians and had no direct affiliations with Hamas. Even those who may have had indirect relationships did so based on communal, religious, and national affiliation.

Asked whether HLF's files contained information about money paid to the families of Hamas fighters, Abu Baker stated that the foundation supported orphans regardless of the reason of the death of their parents, and that it did not discriminate between orphans for political reasons.[13]

One means by which HLF's activities were portrayed in a sinister light was Israel's tendency to define the word "martyr" as "suicide bomber," and its portrayal of HLF's stated goal of caring for the families of martyrs to mean solely the support of Hamas fighters' families. In Islam, a martyr might be anyone who died in a war zone, regardless of whether that person was a combatant or civilian. In the newspaper interview, Abu Baker said that the HLF did help children whose parents were killed by the Israeli army, but that if indeed some of those orphans belong to the children of the members of Hamas, they were a minority. At the same time, it also helped children whose parents were killed by the Palestinians themselves, accused of being a traitor and an agent of Israel. The HLF did not conduct an inquest into the reason of the death of the parent; rather, it studied the case in cooperation with local charitable organizations.

In the interview, Abu Baker also pointed out that there

is no Israeli law prohibiting the adoption of orphans due to the nature of the death of their parents. Had there been such legislation, he said, then all Palestinian, Israeli, and international charitable organizations would be supporters of terrorism based on such reasoning.

Aside from the Salah and Marzouq cases, Israel's claims against Muslims in America remained for many years on the margins of political discourse. After the terrorist attacks of September 11, 2001, however, the accusations gained considerably more traction. The FBI began raiding Islamic organizations across the country, especially those led by Palestinians, frequently citing the allegations of pro-Israel activists in the United States or Israeli intelligence as the basis of their actions. Some of these organizations were closed, and some of their employees were imprisoned or deported without any evidence of wrongdoing. Palestinian groups have born the brunt of this trend, despite the fact that Palestinians had nothing to do with September 11. The Holy Land Foundation was one of the organizations that were raided. Its assets were seized and it doors shuttered.

Dr. Abu Marzouq's saga culminated in a recent indictment that is plainly politically motivated. In announcing the indictment of the Elashi brothers of HLF and the information technology firm Infocom, Attorney General John Ashcroft used Dr. Marzouq's status as a "specially designated terrorist" to package his indictment of Palestinian Muslim activists. Among the charges in the indictment was that the Elashi brothers through business transactions continued to deal with Dr. Abu Marzouq. The irony is that the U.S. government was aware of and ratified these transactions at the time.[14]

Geopolitical dynamics

The American campaign to demonize and criminalize Muslim and Palestinian activism in support of their brethren in Palestine has its roots squarely in Israel's desire to extinguish the source of any aid and comfort whatsoever to the subjects of its occupation. This desire is part of a strategy to ultimately achieve the surrender of the Palestinians through demoralization and humiliation.

As American Islamic activism grew in scale and sophistication, and as attention turned toward supporting the Palestinians, Israel and its U.S. supporters grew increasingly worried that support from American Muslims would undermine their campaign of military subjugation. It also disapproved of successful efforts to feed, house, and clothe its Palestinian subjects, since this alleviated the despair that Israel hoped would lead to surrender. Consequently, the pro-Israel lobby made the unraveling of American Muslim activism in support of Palestinians a top priority.

In the early 1990s, the Israeli campaign against American Muslims was waged primarily on the sidelines, in the margins of the political scene and by colorful fringe characters like Steven Emerson and Daniel Pipes who enjoyed little credibility outside pro-Zionist circles. The terrorist attacks of September 11th, 2001, altered the rules of engagement of this political battle dramatically. As false as it was, the pro-Israel lobby successfully drew a connection between the unjust attack that Americans had just suffered and the Palestinian resistance. Pro-Israel activists both in and outside of the Bush administration who had long wanted an excuse to dismantle pro-Palestinian groups jumped at the chance, justifying their crackdown by portraying Israel's interests as identical to those of the United States.

The impact of this campaign thus far is glaring. It has led so far to the closing of the major Islamic relief organizations and the seizure of millions of dollars donated in charity by American Muslims. The Holy Land Foundation topped the list of these groups. The Israeli press reported at that time that the Executive Order that closed HLF came as a result of a blunt demand by Sharon to President Bush, who acted instantly.

The Holy Land Foundation was a target of particularly high priority because it enjoyed the overwhelming support of the Arab and Muslim community in the country. Its distinguished relief works made it very trustworthy, and Arabs and Muslims placed their full confidence in its work and its projects.[15] The foundation was a success story and admired by governments in Jordan, Lebanon, and Palestine. The attack on the HLF led to attacks on Muslim organizations, businesses, centers, and mosques. Virtually anyone who ever supported HLF has become vulnerable as a result. One of the most prominent entities to suffer such injustices of late is *Infocom*, a Palestinian Muslim-owned entity that was shut down by U.S. security agencies. So far, the trend is continuing and there are signs in the near future that it will succeed.

This process is quite ironic because the Muslim community in America contributed to the victory of Bush, believing that he would be even-handed in his foreign policy. In another stroke of irony, Muslim leaders were scheduled to meet President Bush on the 11th of September, 2001, to receive his expression of gratitude for their support in the elections. The President was expected to repeat his promises to grant access for the Muslim community and act upon them. In the aftermath of the tragic events, however, and after identifying Muslims as being behind these attacks, the U.S. Department of Justice targeted Muslim activists, agencies, businesses, and homes to such an extent that Muslims currently live in their darkest days. The common feeling in the community is that President Bush has abandoned his promises to American-Muslims. The Zionists, Christian fundamentalists, and Neo-conservative Jewish activists like *Project for the New American Century* (PNAC), pressured Bush immediately after 9/11 to adopt their policies as the U.S. national security strategy.

These principles, memorialized in a report by (PNAC), published in September, 2000, entitled *Rebuilding America's Defenses: Strategy, Forces and Resources,* encouraged the promotion of U.S. world domination, pre-emptive strikes, torture, and the restructuring of the entire Middle East to give Israel dominance and control. They are using the expanded powers they received after 9/11 to combat the Palestinian Intifada, exterminate the supporters of the Palestinian cause in America, and ethnically cleanse the Palestinian homeland of all Arabs, Christians and Muslims alike.

Muslims are now painfully aware that the Israeli agenda, which criminalizes Muslim activists and Muslim organizations in America, has gained overwhelming support within the U.S. legislative and executive branches, particularly in the Departments of Justice, Defense, and Homeland Security. These agencies now openly act upon allegations provided to them by Israeli officials or their proxies. The former fringe agitators like Steve Emerson and Daniel Pipes of the early 1990's in a final irony are now rehabilitated and reenergized in their battle against Islamic activism and Palestinian nationhood.

Conclusion

For a group of Palestinian Muslims, their quest to bring freedom and dignity to their homeland took them from the squalid streets of their Gaza refugee camps, to the universities of Egypt, to the sands of the Gulf, then to the suburbs of America. The success they enjoyed in nearing their goal attracted the attention of the Israelis and their supporters, who chose to import the Middle East conflict to America. For years they tried with limited success to agitate against Palestinian Americans, but September 11th gave them the opportunity to arrange a sweeping crackdown on Palestine's supporters.

The true role of Hamas in the United States is a mere shadow compared to the elaborate theories the pro-Israel lobby and their allies in the Bush administration have constructed. What are the results of the crackdown? Israel may meet its goals of choking off expressions of solidarity for Palestinians. Bush may be able to claim he's fighting terrorism, garner campaign funds, and win an election thanks to the pro-Israel lobby. But the effects are more far-reaching.

The political freedoms of Americans are eroded as confessions under torture are admitted as evidence, vague allegations by intelligence agents are considered proof of wrongdoing, and due process is suspended as people are jailed on secret evidence and property is confiscated without charge—all because the alleged "criminals" subscribed to the unpopular side of a political issue.

Palestinian children suffer as millions of dollars languish, unable to buy a child in a refugee camp some pencils and paper or a backpack. The sick go untreated and the orphans grow up with no one to show concern for them. And then we wonder why young Palestinians feel hopeless about their future?

America's image suffers as the world watches the U.S. government stand in solidarity with the world's last Apartheid state, burning through billions of dollars to stamp out sympathy for an occupied and brutalized people, and destroying its democracy in the process.

The story of Hamas in America is less remarkable on its own merits then for the political chaos that comes from its telling. As long as those hostile to Palestinians tell the story and deny them the right to tell their side, occupation will continue to go unchallenged, peace in the Middle East with justice will not be possible, and both Palestine and America will continue to suffer as a result. ■

• Marzouq attorney Michael Kennedy speaks at a press conference in New York.

• Nadia Elashi, wife of Dr. Mousa speaks to the press in New York, 1997.

Part Four

MUSLIM LEADERSHIP UNDER SIEGE

The suggestion that Arab and Muslim Americans appreciate being singled out and interrogated is a prime example of the Attorney General's wartime propaganda machine in full swing.

—Congressman John Conyers Jr.,
House Judiciary Committee.

PROFILE: AMERICAN INJUSTICE: CASE STUDIES

• Dr. Sami al-Arian

• Dr. Mazen al-Najjar

• Abdurahman Alamoudi

• Dr. Abdelhaleem Ashqar

• Dr. Rafil Dhafir

• Dr. Sabri Samirah

• Imam Jameel al-Amin

• Elashi Brothers

Chapter 10

MUSLIM LEADERSHIP UNDER SIEGE

The growth of Islamic movements and of government appeals to Islam underscored, Faruqi believed, the pressing need for think tanks and experts prepared to bridge the bifurcated world of modern secular elites and more traditional religious leaders. Such organizations could provide the studies and plans needed to address the question of what modern Islamic political, economic, social, and legal systems should look like. At the heart of his vision was the Islamization of knowledge.

—John Esposito and John Voll, *Makers of Contemporary Islam,*
Oxford University Press, 2001.

During the past four decades, the growth and development of a viable community of Muslims in the United States has been a cornerstone in the continuing evolution of America toward a pluralistic and multicultural society. Suffering people from all parts of the world have found a safe haven in this land. Beginning with the Puritans, who were persecuted for their religious beliefs in Europe before they migrated to the safety and security of the New World, America has always opened its doors to such people when the doors closed behind them in their original homes. European Jews suffering from the hands of hatred and intolerance in the mid-twentieth century also discovered sanctuary in a nation that upholds the values of freedom and equality.

Only two decades later, as turbulent times would come to afflict the Islamic world, people from throughout that region of the globe would also seek refuge in the United States. As firm believers in their faith, repressed and shunned by their oppressive, authoritarian, and staunchly anti-religious governments or suffering at the hands of a cruel, foreign occupation, the young men and women of this generation believed in the promise of a nation whose values they admired as children and dreamed of bringing to their own societies. Growing up in the 1950s and 1960s, these individuals were already basking in the glow of American history, traditions, and culture. A young Sami al-Arian was raised in Cairo watching episodes of "Kojak" and "The Fugitive." Mazen al-Najjar was reading the works of T.S. Elliot. Abdurahman Alamoudi was mourning the tragic death of President John F. Kennedy. By the time they reached America, these men were already steeped in the best that America had to offer: the freedom to believe, think, and speak as one wishes, to practice one's faith openly, and to assemble peacefully and establish a community. In the summer of 1975, Sami al-Arian's first days at an American university centered on a civics course in which the professor explained "the two D's: due process and dissent" as the cornerstones of American democracy. The American dream, according to the immigrant Muslims of that era, was to be welcomed in a place where distinctions were not made based on race and ethnicity. America was a place where citizenship was not defined by language or skin color. It was a place they would embrace because it had already embraced them.

Even from within, America's indigenous Muslims believed in upholding the promise of their country, though that promise often went unfulfilled. H. Rap Brown saw the oppression, inequality, and injustice still prevalent in his society. Following his decades of active leadership to overcome those weaknesses in America, he witnessed in Islam a more peaceful and effective way of doing so, becoming Jamil al-Amin. In all, these leaders saw in their faith, whether from birth or reversion, and in their country, whether native or adopted, a bridge between these ideals.

The Muslim activist movement in the United States began with students, young, eager, and devoted to addressing the world's many injustices. The liberties guaranteed to them in America would ensure that no unruly force could disrupt that effort out of hatred, prejudice, and intolerance. It was on the basis of these rights and freedoms that America's growing Muslim community believed it could act in accordance with its deeply held principles to establish itself as a viable community and work toward improving the society and the world around them. While this vision for a better, more equitable, and just world did not always coincide with the policies of their government, it was nonetheless their constitutionally protected right to espouse that vision and work for change. It is in this vein that the young Muslim students established their early institutions, ranging from student activism and charitable work and volunteerism to religious and social leadership.

The youthful exuberance and idealism displayed by these

moral and upright men was not without its share of errors. Some of them, while in their hotheaded younger days, or later while riding the wave of anger and frustration at the further deterioration of an already deepening crisis, uttered words that they would lament in later years as being rash, unproductive, and ultimately inconsistent with their beliefs. It was a part of the learning process. To err was human, but none ever transgressed the clearly drawn boundaries of the law. And speech, no matter how unpleasant or regrettable, was still a right protected by the constitution's first amendment. Most importantly, through all the years, these lapses in judgment, at their worst, were only in contravention of the moral code by which the American Muslim community lived and the society around them that valued many of the same ideals; never were they a clear or even implicit violation of any legal statute or judicial code.

The learning curve for America's Muslim leadership involved the trial and error of young students who sought the most effective and fruitful way to effect change. They were constantly adapting to their surrounding environment and the social climate of their time. This spirit remained with these men long after their academic days were over and well into their professional careers, family lives, and years of public service. This resulted in the building of important institutions to continue their mission of promoting peace and justice in troubled parts of the world while also continuing to enhance and improve the life of their community at home. Mosques and schools became commonplace in every corner of every city. Charities such as the Holy Land Foundation helped hundreds of thousands of suffering people. Institutions such as the World & Islam Studies Enterprise helped expand the intellectual horizons of American academia. The American

Muslim Council built a bridge of peace, unity, and understanding between America's disenfranchised Muslim minority and the powerful establishment. Through it all, there was no written guide on how and where these leaders were to proceed and by what standard. They did not have the luxury of savvy political consultants or expensive legal advice. They simply followed their instincts and worked within the bounds they felt were permissible by the American tradition.

Little did any of these men know that a perversion of the law, would target, vilify, and condemn them purely based on their religious and political beliefs, words, and associations. While the political prosecution of individuals was not new to American society, it remained in the shadows of past historical times, unknown to those who had become familiar only with the shining face of American freedom and tolerance. And so when the assault on American Muslim institutions and their leaders began, with a first wave in the early 1990s, many were unprepared to respond. The secret evidence trials, on their very face antithetical to everything that America stands for, were an ugly adversary, but one that united American Muslims and their neighbors of many faiths to fight for justice and restore the image of America as the protector and guarantor of rights.

Following September 11, 2001, that image was shattered into a million pieces. All of the men in the pages that follow have since suffered irreparable harm. Decades of lawful, vigorous, and peaceable activity were suddenly branded as illicit, subversive, and criminal behavior bent on violence, all under the enigmatic emblem of "terrorism," a catch-all term that denotes any political and social activity (under the label "Islamic") that does not agree with the official political stand of the administration and its policing agencies.

No one could have prepared for the nightmare scenario
that became a haunting reality to the men who prided
themselves on understanding the social and political
realities around them, restrained by an overall American
spirit of justice and the rule of law. Nonetheless, it is
because these principles have been forgone in the name of
security and political expediency that many Muslim leaders
today find themselves imprisoned on charges that would
never have passed muster in any other time. The post-9/11
environment was poisoned with the air of suspicion and
mistrust, with the Muslim community paying the heaviest
price of all, its freedom. Since that day, it has become a
marginalized voice in American society and branded as a
fifth column. Not only have many people suffered, but the
work itself, for which thousands of people have devoted
years of their lives, has been utterly demolished. The Holy
Land Foundation was shut down, with its assets frozen.
The academic host to WISE turned its back on the think
tank, effectively destroying one bridge between East and
West. Following years of harassment and a concentrated
smear campaign, the AMC was forced to close its doors,
thereby depriving the American Muslim community of this
voice among America's political leaders. The present
chapter chronicles the experiences that began in hope and
promise decades ago, but have reached a state of darkness
and despair. The appalling state in which these men and
their families currently find themselves results from a
growing intolerance for independent thought and from a
growing ignorance of the universal wisdom reflected in the
ideals and principles that have been abandoned. It is these
ideals, beliefs, and principles that inspire us to hope in this
dark hour.

PROFILE: IMPRISONMENT OF IDEAS

Dr. Sami al-Arian
- Professor of Computer Engineering, University of South Florida
- Founder, *Islamic Academy of Florida*
- Founder & President, *National Coalition to Protect Political Freedom(NCPPF)*

Dr. Al-Arian and Dr. Al-Najjar participating in a rally for Palestine, New York City, April 7, 2001.

Dr. Mazen al-Najjar
- Ph.D., Industrial Engineering, University of South Florida
- Editor, *Qira'at Siyassiya* (*Political Readings*), World & Islam Studies Enterprise (WISE)
- Imam, Islamic Community of Tampa

Prisoner of Conscience:
The Story of Dr. Sami al-Arian

To be patriotic is to be able to question government policy in times of crisis. To be patriotic is to stand up for the Bill of Rights and the Constitution in times of uncertainty and insecurity. To be patriotic is to speak up against the powerful in defense of the weak and the voiceless. To be patriotic is to be willing to pay the price to preserve our freedoms, our dignity, and our rights. To be patriotic is to challenge the abuses of the Patriot Act.

—Dr. Sami al-Arian, September 2002.

On the surface, the life of Sami al-Arian is like that of many other Palestinians of his generation: born as a refugee in exile from his homeland, forced to endure a secondary status in neighboring countries, and bound to overcome the challenges of being stateless to serve his religion and his nation. The extraordinary nature of the events in Sami's life has made his story a personification of the Palestinian tragedy. As he currently faces trial in American courts for his efforts to bring justice to the Palestinian people, the cause itself has been placed on trial by those who wish to see it denigrated and de-legitimized.

Birth in Exile

Sami's story, like that of most Palestinians today, begins before he was born. In 1948, the establishment of Israel and the subsequent *nakba* saw the creation of one state at the expense of a native population. Nearly three-quarters of a million Palestinian refugees were forced into exile by Zionist forces. Among them was Amin al-Arian, a young man whose family owned a soap factory in Jaffa. He was separated from his two brothers during the war and later discovered that one of them had been killed while in northern Palestine. Between 1948 and 1949, he attempted to discover the whereabouts of his brother, and upon learning that he had died, wanted to find his body. He then moved to Gaza, where he worked for the United Nations Relief and Work Agency (UNRWA) until 1955. A year later, he married Laila, another Palestinian refugee, and the family then fled to Kuwait where Amin al-Arian would settle as an accountant for the Ministry of Education. Nearly ten years after the Palestinian tragedy, Sami was the first of five children born to Amin and Laila, on January 14, 1958. Life in Kuwait was frought with hardships, as the government afforded Palestinians no rights and limited opportunities for education and employment. Sami spent much of his early years with other Palestinian boys who had suffered similar experiences. By 1966, however, his time in Kuwait would come to an abrupt end. The family was ordered by the government to leave immediately after Amin al-Arian refused to become an informant for Kuwaiti intelligence services against other Palestinians. As refugees, the family was vulnerable to the whims of the government, and as such had no control over such occurrences.

A New Beginning

Amin took his family and settled in Cairo, Egypt. He opened a small business there and the children were able to grow in a less restrictive environment. The father placed much emphasis on education as a means for empowerment, and Sami took that message to heart, excelling in both his primary and secondary schools. Moreover, it was during these early years that he began to articulate his views on Palestinian suffering, as a witness to it himself. While Cairo was a welcoming environment and a center for intellectual, religious, and political activity during this period, Palestinians lived nonetheless as second-class citizens. Their residency documents had to be renewed on a regular basis, and access to public services was limited, causing constant feelings of instability and insecurity. As a youth, Sami expressed these sentiments and his attachment to his distant homeland in poetry and essays. At the same time, he found solace in his Islamic faith as a driving force in his life. For most people of this generation, Islam placed their current quandary in proper context and provided the spiritual and ideological tools with which to combat it.

Sami would spend his formative years arming himself with education. He would read countless books on everything from theology, philosophy, and history to politics, law, and literature. By the time he reached his final year in secondary school, he dreamed of going to medical school, the highest educational honor one could have in Arab society. His goal, along with his closest friend, another Palestinian, was to found a clinic to treat Palestinian refugees deprived of proper medical care. In Egypt at the time, medical school entrance required citizens to achieve scores in the 78th percentile or higher in their final exams, while non-citizens such as Palestinians had to perform even higher to stand a chance at acceptance. When the scores were returned that summer, Sami was in the 90th percentile, virtually guaranteeing him a place in the university of his choice. Unfortunately, however, the Egyptian government would decide that year that no Palestinian, irrespective of grades, would be admitted into any medical school. The news came as a devastating blow and yet another example of the double standard consistently applied to Palestinians. The implications were clear: without a state to protect their rights, Palestinians would continue to suffer degradation and humiliation, at the hands of either the brutal occupying forces of Israel or the inhospitable governments in the Arab world. Sami instead chose to leave such a confining atmosphere by accepting an opportunity to study in the United States. His father told him that he would sacrifice their family's life savings for Sami's education.

The Land of Opportunity

His arrival in America in the summer of 1975 was full of hope and optimism. After all, this was a land where for centuries people had come to escape oppressive conditions in their native lands in favor of a free and pluralistic American society that valued such central principles. At Southern Illinois University in Carbondale, Sami's first civics course would be a welcome introduction to American values. The professor began the semester with a discussion of "the two D's," dissent and due process, as the cornerstones of American democracy. These concepts would prove especially important for the Arab and Muslim community in the United States in the decades to come, but held a crucial importance in Sami's life in particular.

While embarking on an undergraduate degree in electrical engineering, Sami still devoted much of his time to religious and political activism. The late 1970s was an era in which permanent Arab and Muslim institutions were being founded for the first time in American history. Among the more significant institutions was the Muslim Students Association (MSA), which by this time had chapters across the country. In addition, loose networks of Arab students from various countries had been formed as a means for intellectual, religious, and social activity. With very few students of Palestinian descent to engage in the cause, the issue was thrust in the hands of young men from other countries, who congregated according to nationality. Much of Sami's time in these early years was spent with students from Kuwait. Ultimately, however, an effort was made to bridge the gap between various small student groups and establish a stronger, unified entity with which to address issues of concern for the entire immigrant student community.

The Muslim Arab Youth Association (MAYA) was born of this effort, with Sami playing a key role in founding the organization and directing its activities. As MAYA's only Palestinian board member, Sami firmly believed that the cause of Palestine must have a central place, not only for Palestinians, but for the entire Arab and Muslim community. The new organization held a number of camps and workshops across the country to engage in the emerging debate regarding the new generation's role in the challenges facing their native lands. It is worth noting that these discussions developed in the language of religious obligation. The direction of the *Ummah*, or global body of Muslims, was always the focal point. As such, Palestine was the de facto frontline of Islam's struggle for freedom, as it suffered directly under Zionist occupation. Sami and others argued that this required the bulk of the Muslim Ummah's energy and effort to go toward this most urgent cause. This view was relatively unheard of at the time, as most Arab and Muslim thinkers were either still grappling with the loss of the "Islamic state" many decades earlier, or drawn more closely to the emergent nationalisms of the time. Though Sami's leadership role ended shortly thereafter, MAYA continued to maintain a position of importance in the community for many years thereafter, taking much of its direction from its original founders.

By 1978, after only three years, Sami had completed his undergraduate degree. A year later, he was already well into his master's degree at North Carolina State University in Raleigh. That summer, he returned to Egypt to visit his family and marry Nahla al-Najjar, another Palestinian and sister of his longtime friend, Mazen al-Najjar. That year, another important event took place, this one of global importance. The Islamic Revolution in Iran sent shockwaves across the Muslim world and completely reconfigured the geopolitics of the Middle East. At once, it placed Islam back on the world stage as a political force, which it had not been in over half a century, and as a solution to social injustice, inequality, and corruption. Sami saw this as a positive step for the Ummah, contending that the energy and will demonstrated by Iranian students were qualities that should be harnessed by Muslims struggling in Palestine. But, many others did not see it this way. Rather the Iranian Revolution, which was Shiite in character, was very often viewed through a sectarian lens by the mostly Sunni Arab Muslims. This led to a very heated and vigorous debate within the American Muslim community, especially with regard to the issue of Palestine.

Moreover, Sami felt energized by these recent events to

continue the effort for Palestinian self-determination, based on Islamic principles, with support from the refugee population and the Muslim community at large. An institution would be needed whose sole purpose would be to address this issue. Following several meetings of prominent Palestinian activists across the country, the Islamic Association for Palestine was established in 1981. As one of its primary founders, having chaired its first steering committee, Sami believed IAP would play an essential role in bringing together academics, activists, and whole communities, Muslims and non-Muslims, at the grassroots level in a unified front to support the Palestinian cause on a number of levels, including humanitarian, political, intellectual, and popular. The main events of the IAP were its regional conferences, meetings, and seminars held throughout the year, during which time thousands of students, families, and young professionals from all different ethnic and national backgrounds would come to attend lectures by dozens of important intellectual figures from around the world. The IAP also organized protests against the Israeli invasion of Lebanon in 1982 at a time when Sami served as editor-in-chief of the IAP's magazine.

For Sami though, this was not the extent of his activities. While in North Carolina, he assisted in publishing and distributing a number of important books, journals, and articles on many topics ranging from religion and politics to the arts, the role of women, and the question of Palestine. He was also asked to speak on Palestine at events across the nation. In 1982, he was invited to be on a panel at the University of Michigan with Professors Ali Mazrui and the late Ismail al-Faruqi. At the young age of 24, Sami was honored simply to be in the presence of such distinguished academics, let alone speaking alongside them at such an important event.

A Moment for Introspection

The following year, Sami journeyed to Palestine for a visit. He and his family traveled through its various cities and sites, seeing the land his parents once called home. When his grandmother passed away in Cairo earlier that year, she still wore the key to her house in Jaffa around her neck. While Sami thoroughly treasured his brief stay in Palestine, praying in its many historic mosques, walking its spacious fields, and climbing its tall mounts, he would not enter into Palestine again in the decades to follow.

Nonetheless, Sami returned from his trip eager to resume his work to alleviate the suffering he witnessed in the occupied territories. For a number of reasons, however, the activist effort in the United States began to experience a weakening lull. For one, Israel's invasion of Lebanon in 1982 and its subsequent devastation of that country and its Palestinian refugee population only further accentuated the impotent and helpless state of the Arab and Muslim world. The regional conflict had expanded further, and the subsequent shock left most people uncertain of how to react. For many activists in the United States, Islamic principles still provided the framework toward success in these issues.

While the prevailing view envisioned the intellectual and political evolution of the Islamist movement, a minority saw the situation as too critical to await such idealistic advancements from within. Rather, a minority view called for immediate action to be taken on behalf of Palestinians struggling to survive against the occupation, regardless of the status of the Islamic political movements. Sami al-Arian was one of the leading figures articulating the latter point of view, leading him eventually to leave his position with the IAP, in favor of more independent pursuits. In addition, his efforts to open the organization to wider involvement from representatives of various other causes and issue areas met with much resistance.

He published a booklet in 1983, entitled "The Fall of the Third Mirage," which criticized the performance of the Islamic movement and called for a non-sectarian approach to the Palestinian conflict that welcomed Muslims of all sects and people of all faiths, including Jews who opposed the occupation. In addition, he asserted that the conflict was not one between Islam and Judaism, as many people on both sides had concluded. Rather, it was against the form of political Zionism and its racist outlook on the conflict. While these opinions were initially viewed with disdain from within the Muslim leadership, leading Sami to leave his post, that rejection would not last. Slowly, such minority views would become the mainstream, as institutions would gradually come to embrace them. Indeed, Sami was ahead of his time on a number of key issues facing the Muslim community. For instance, while most Arab community leaders at that time saw Iraqi President Saddam Hussein as a heroic advocate of the Palestinian cause, and the defender against the spread of Shi'ism and Iranian influence in the Arab world, Sami was a lone voice that denounced his atrocious human rights record and his exploitation of legitimate causes consistently throughout the years as ultimately hurtful to Islam, Muslims, and the issue of Palestine.

Distinguished Academic

Sami's institutional work would not appear again until the late 1980s. In the meantime, he completed his graduate work at North Carolina State University, defending his computer-engineering dissertation in 1985, and worked to establish the Muslim community center in Raleigh. While looking for work, he came upon an offer from the University of South Florida, located in Tampa, a city on the Gulf of Mexico. During his initial visit, the chairman of the Computer Science Department took Sami to Bayshore, which reminded him of the Nile in Cairo. He happily accepted the teaching offer and relocated with his family to Tampa in January 1986. While at the USF, he would have a very distinguished teaching career. He was quickly promoted and ultimately gained tenure in 1992. He would earn the Outstanding Teacher of the Year Award in 1993, another outstanding award at the university level in 1994, and receive the highest reviews and evaluations from students. He authored a number of articles in his field that were published in various books and academic journals. In addition, his research brought hundreds of thousands of dollars in grants to the USF.

Community Builder

Along with a distinguished career as one of his university's top professors, Sami still devoted a vast amount of time to his many interests. He helped establish the Islamic Community of Tampa, which would build one of the largest mosques in the Tampa Bay area. He would be its primary imam and serve as president of its board. The Muslim community benefited greatly from his leadership and influence and implemented a number of progressive and constructive policies. His mosque was one of the first to ensure that women participate in the mosque's leadership by ensuring them positions on the board, while most mosques in America featured all-male boards. In addition, he removed much of the segregation that many mosques enforced between religious practice and moral obligations toward humanitarian and political causes. As such, issues affecting the Muslim community locally and around the world became an integral part of mosque activity.

Not the least of these issues was the cause of Palestine. And though there had been a momentary break in Palestinian activism, the issue would be reignited as conditions worsened drastically overseas. The start of the first Palestinian Intifada in December, 1987, sent a clear message that Palestinians had not been cowed into willful submission by their brutal occupiers. Moreover, images of Palestinian children chased by tanks and of bulldozers plowing through orchards and homes became commonplace on the evening news and on the front pages of American newspapers. Indeed, the whole country was taking notice of the atrocities against Palestinian civilians by the Israeli military.

Intellectual Responses to Crisis

Eager to once again advance the cause of justice in the Middle East through institutions, in Tampa in 1988 Sami founded the Islamic Committee for Palestine. The goals of the ICP were similar to the principles on which the IAP came to being. Simply, they were scholarly progress on the issue of Palestine along with mobilizing the community in America to action. A number of publications emerged to that effect. Also important were the ICP's annual conferences. These gatherings, organized by Sami and other local leaders, drew thousands of concerned individuals, some of whom were neither Palestinian nor Muslim, to spacious conference halls for important speeches. In fact, the ICP was responsible for introducing the

American Muslim community to a number of major intellectual figures, including the Egyptian scholar Dr. Abdul-Wahhab al-Missiri, the Sudanese intellectual Abulgasem Haj Hamed, Shaykh Rachid al Ghanouchi from Tunisia, and others who would eventually become noted speakers at a number of other conferences. Along with the issue of Palestine, ICP conferences were wide-ranging in scope, opening the discussion to a number of topics, some of which were previously taboo within such circles. The Kurdish question in Iraq was one that no institution chose to address, but Sami not only ensured that it would be discussed in honest and open terms, but invited a leading Kurdish figure to speak on the subject. Furthermore, the conferences were quick to address current developments such as the newly emerged Islamic republics in Central Asia following the collapse of the Soviet Union, an issue many organizations neglected at the time, and the crises unfolding in Bosnia and Kosovo, years before anyone else took note of them.

Another portion of the ICP's work was in humanitarian aid. While this program has recently drawn much negative attention from the media and the government, it was actually a very modest effort that generated minimal funds for orphaned children during the Intifada. The program allowed its membership to sponsor an orphan in the occupied territories for a small fee every month. Ultimately, the ICP gained the respect and admiration of people across the country. Because it had the benefit of emerging during a more critical time with conditions deteriorating in Palestine, it was able to establish a solid foundation among the Arab and Muslim community in the United States, while also appealing to Americans outside of the community who were nonetheless concerned about the issue. In fact, its program of matching sponsors with children would be mimicked by many other Islamic charitable organizations.

Between the years 1988 and 1992, the ICP held five conferences, becoming the preeminent organization for Palestine in the United States. It also published an English language magazine entitled *Inquiry*, which addressed issues from around the Muslim world, including Afghanistan, Algeria, Sudan, Bosnia, and its staple topic, Palestine. Its final issue featured a detailed analysis of the Oslo Peace Accords and a criticism of its prospects of bringing a just and lasting peace to the conflict.

While Dr. Sami was proud of his organization's achievements, he continuously wished to respond to ongoing international events. In particular, Iraq's invasion of Kuwait in 1990 and the subsequent Gulf War became an important turning point not only in international affairs, but with regard to activist work in America. With the onset of the first-ever American military campaign in the Middle East, a new era had begun in East-West relations that could jeopardize the status of the Muslim minority in America. This sentiment was best captured in Samuel Huntington's seminal piece "The Clash of Civilizations," which predicted an all-out conflict between the world of Islam and the West. Sami was one of the leaders most ardently opposed to the clash thesis, and understood the need to counter such sentiments, which had already begun to creep into policy-making circles in Washington and the media at large. Moreover, he understood that the notion of an impending war on Islam was being used by some interest groups to bolster U.S. support for Israel. The solution, he proposed, was simply education and dialogue. By informing political leaders, prominent academics, and the American public at large about Islam and Muslims, perhaps future policies and interactions would reflect that deeper understanding.

• Dr. Sami Al-Arian lectures at an IAP conference in 2000 (top). He was also a featured speaker at an International ANSWER anti-war demonstration attended by over 100,000 people in 2002. (center).

• Nahla al-Arian testifies on her brother's ordeal with secret evidence before the Judiciary Committee in Congress along with attorney David Cole, 2000.

A Bridge Between Worlds

The result of this endeavor was the World & Islam Studies Enterprise, or WISE, as it would come to be known. Unlike some of the previous organizations with which Sami was affiliated, WISE operated strictly as a think-tank, without any activist agenda. It received approval from the University of South Florida's newly formed Committee for Middle East Studies and proceeded to co-sponsor major events, symposia, and round-table discussions within the university. Events held by WISE were hailed as a resounding success and an example for the rest of the country's academic institutions. Academics were invited from all over the country and the world, holding a wide range of opinions and positions and sharing their perspectives in a proper setting. The goal was clear: to bring all sides together in a civil discourse in order to foster understanding and proceed on the path to social cohesion. In time, WISE would even receive acknowledgment outside of academic circles and in the realm of policy-making. In 1993, Dr. Sami al-Arian was invited to give a presentation at the U.S. Central Command's annual symposium, alongside the prominent academics John Esposito and the late Edward Said. A decade after his initial appearance with two well-respected scholars, Sami was once again flattered to speak on the same panel with two of the most esteemed professors of their time. What is more, the audience before them consisted of the military's top-brass, including General Norman Schwarzkopf, recently returned from the Gulf, along with many top intelligence and State Department officials. The topic for the program was "Islam and the West." The speakers provided an in-depth and complete picture of this complex relationship and the ways by which it could continue to improve and thrive. The talk met with a warm reception and appreciation by the distinguished audience.

In addition to public events, WISE also published a quarterly journal called *Qira'at Siyasiyya*, or "Political Readings." This journal included academic articles ranging across a wide scope of issues. Although the issue of Palestine was significant, it did not dominate. Out of twenty published issues, only two centered on the Middle East conflict. It enjoyed an extensive readership that included government agencies. The success of WISE and the ICP did not come without a price. While most people recognized that America was at a turning point in its history during the post-Cold War period, many forces wished to exert their influence in assuring that the cause of Islam, Muslims, and by extension, Palestine, would not receive a welcoming status in American society. Rather, this campaign relied on maligning and defaming the Muslim leaders of America and delegitimizing the worthiness of their activism work. The ICP and WISE in Tampa were the first casualties of this intolerant war.

An Intolerant Campaign: Early Beginnings

While at the height of its achievement, Sami's institutional work came under fire in 1994 as part of a documentary by the now notorious pseudo-journalist Steven Emerson entitled *Jihad in America*. As Emerson's personal and professional backgrounds were not publicly known at the time, Sami agreed to be interviewed for his program, which was assumed to be on the topic of Islam's growing prominence in America. Instead, Emerson leveled a number of severe allegations in his report, exploiting the newfound fear of "Islamic terrorism" stemming from the World Trade Center bombing in February 1993. The piece essentially suggested that most, if not all, Islamic activist work in the United States was in actuality promoting violence against America and its interests. Emerson and his cohorts to follow would lay the groundwork for the government's campaign against Islamic institutions by spreading their fabrications and leading the American public and its leaders down the road of hysteria, suspicion, and mistrust.

Emerson would later be discredited with a damning book review by the *New York Times*, which called attention to the numerous lies in his work and his predisposition of being an anti-Arab, anti-Muslim extremist. His real demise, however, would take place in the aftermath of the Oklahoma City Bombing in April, 1995, which he stated on a number of networks to be the work of Islamic terrorists. After such outlandishly blind accusations were proven false, Emerson was banished from the world of responsible investigative journalism, only to return years later.[1]

In the meantime, however, a local Emerson disciple in Tampa would carry on the continued attacks. Michael Fechter of the conservative and sensationalist *Tampa Tribune* began his crusade on April 21, 1995, as he wrote an article contending that the bombing in Oklahoma City was the work of Islamic terrorists.[2] Unlike Emerson though, Fechter would be rewarded for his gross inaccuracies by continuing to author articles accusing local Muslim leaders, especially Sami al-Arian, of ties to terrorism. In all, he produced over seventy articles in the six years to follow, most of them rehashing the same unfounded allegations that the work done by the ICP and WISE was nothing but a "front" for terrorist activity. Without ever producing a single shred of evidence, Fechter relied on the tactics of guilt by association, misuse of facts, and circumstantial evidence. The other local papers refused to partake in the *Tribune*'s McCarthyistic style of journalism. John Sugg, former editor of *The Weekly Planet* in Tampa, concluded, "The *Tribune* has woven together unproven assertions, articles from highly suspect publications, and out-of-context statements."[3] Among the countless absurd allegations by Fechter was that Sami "lured" terrorists to the USF, such as Hassan Turabi, the prominent leader of the Islamic movement in Sudan.[4] What Fechter failed to mention was that during his trip to the United States, Turabi met with many members of Congress, the editorial board of the *Washington Post*, and gave presentations before the Council on Foreign Relations and the Brookings Institute.

By October, 1995, the *Tribune*'s fishing expedition took on a more outrageous tone as reports came about that Ramadan Shallah, a former associate at WISE who had left the United States six months earlier, had suddenly emerged as the leader of the Islamic Jihad movement in Palestine. While the news came as a complete shock to everyone, including American and Israeli intelligence, overzealous reporters nonetheless attempted to assert that the local Muslim community in Tampa had somehow known of Shallah's future status as a leader of the group. Efforts to show that the Tampa organizations had any connection to groups overseas proved fruitless for the *Tribune*. In fact, noted Israeli journalist Ze'ev Schiff acknowledged that Shallah "does not have previous experience in terrorist actions. His background is predominantly political. Nor is he considered a religious fundamentalist."[5]

The Height of Zealotry

Fechter's relentless attacks ultimately spread hysteria across Tampa and the USF, resulting in a massive public outcry. It was at this point that government authorities decided to intervene. An investigation was launched into WISE and ICP's activities, in which their offices as well as the Al-Arian home were searched in November 1995. The next morning, the *Tampa Tribune* ran a front-page photograph of the house, printed the address, and included a map of its location, placing the family in danger. This simply reflected a flagrant irresponsibility that had become standard for the newspaper. The experience of having dozens of armed federal agents rummaging through the house was so traumatic, that Sami's mother would later nearly faint at the sight of a garbage truck outside the home with the letters "BFI" on its side, confusing it with the FBI. Around this same time, a group of sixteen prominent Jewish leaders demanded a meeting with USF President Betty Castor to discuss the ongoing drama. The university responded to their concerns about the investigation by suspending the professor with pay in April, 1996, for an indefinite amount of time. It also began to conduct its own investigation into WISE and its activities at the university. In addition, the Immigration and Naturalization Service derailed Sami's application for citizenship, after he had been living in the country for more than twenty years. The pro-Israeli onslaught was in full swing. He immediately filed a

Freedom of Information petition to the government to learn the cause of the citizenship rejection. After two years, the file emerged—containing nothing but a collection of *Tampa Tribune* newspaper clippings. It became clear that federal authorities were actually following the shoddy journalist's work, and not the other way around.

Seeds of Progress

Despite these unwarranted assaults on what was lawful political expression, Sami did not for a moment halt his commitment to serve the many worthy causes with which he was associated. After helping to establish the Islamic Community of Tampa, he led efforts to found a full-time Islamic school for the community's children. The Islamic Academy of Florida opened its doors in the fall of 1992 with only 23 students. By 1996, it had grown to more than 150 students, ranging in grades from kindergarten to high school. The school was one of the first of its kind, offering high quality education in all standard subject areas, while also including religious instruction and Arabic classes. Overall, the IAF benefited the most from Sami's philosophy on education, which regular schools and many attempted Islamic schools lacked. It offered the notion that an Islamic curriculum was essential to build the complete human being, one whose mind, body, and soul (an area which all standard education systems overlooked) were in perfect symmetry with one another. In addition, the goals for the students were quite unique. Along with the expected individual goals and accomplishments, students were expected to become model citizens, devoted in their service to God, their community, and their country. Ultimately, it was the aim of IAF's founders aimed to help students retain a strong sense of Islamic identity, so they could meet the challenges of life and become productive members of their society. In this way, Islam was treated as more than simply a marginal aspect of a Muslim's daily life, but rather as the guiding light of that life. Students at IAF were taught to be patriotic Americans and to appreciate the rights and freedoms guaranteed to them by their cherished constitution. After the devastating attacks of September 11, 2001, students showed support for their country by attending a public memorial with the mayor of Tampa in which they said prayers and sang patriotic songs with hundreds of their peers.

The school continued to blossom and mature, gaining a reputation across the country for providing the highest quality education and becoming a model for other Islamic schools to follow. As the callous attacks against Dr. Al-Arian heightened in 1995, his involvement with such valuable projects did not diminish. On the contrary, his participation increased considerably, as he became the principal of IAF during his time away from the university, handling all day-to-day affairs of the school and single-handedly raising the necessary funds to keep it alive and growing. Within a few years, the school had grown exponentially, expanding to a 14-acre plot of land and accommodating nearly 300 students and dozens of faculty. Sami would frequently express that of all his many accomplishments in nearly thirty years of activist work, the IAF was his proudest achievement. This school, which shaped the future of hundreds of children, became like a child of his own, which he cared for and nurtured constantly for an entire decade.

An Unexpected Turn

Within months of the local media's assault on Dr. Al-Arian's activities, the smoke began to settle and it became clear that the anti-Palestinian witch-hunt was proving fruitless. The university's investigation was led by the esteemed William Reece Smith Jr., former USF president and previous head of the American Bar Association. In May, 1996, he published a thorough report upon investigating all of WISE's activities. He concluded that WISE had never engaged in any wrongdoing whatsoever, but on the contrary its work was beneficial to the university community at large. This laid to rest many of the university's fears, but it still awaited a response from the government. By the summer of 1998, USF officials informed the government that unless it intended to bring charges against Professor Al-Arian, it would reinstate him that fall. Sure enough, upon receiving no response from law enforcement officials, Sami resumed his teaching duties at the university in the fall of 1998.

In the meantime, however, the community was dealing with a pressing crisis. Since the investigation appeared to be going nowhere and the government was unable to find any indication of misconduct by Sami al-Arian or the institutions he directed, it took a back route. By 1997, federal authorities had yet to bring a single charge or declare any unlawful activity, but following such intense media attention, a vehement public, led by certain interest groups, wanted blood. The government's outlet came in the form of "secret evidence." In late October, 1996, the INS began deportation proceedings for Dr. Mazen al-Najjar, Sami's best friend from childhood, his brother-in-law, and an associate at WISE. The saga had entered into an entirely new stage. ■

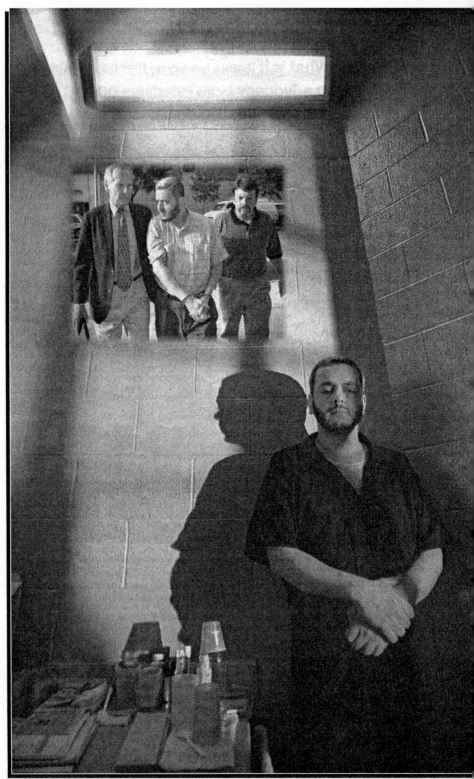

• Dr. Mazen al-Najjar being arrested by federal agents on May 19, 1997 (top), and in his detention cell (bottom), where he was held for three years and seven months on secret evidence.

The Story Within the Story: Secret Evidence and the Case of Dr. Mazen al-Najjar

Mazen al-Najjar was another Palestinian refugee whose life parallels that of Sami al-Arian. Born in Gaza on June 4, 1957, as the oldest of seven children, Mazen and his family were quickly relocated to Saudi Arabia, where his father became an Arabic teacher. They frequently returned to Gaza, however, and spent many summers there. After the 1967 War though, the family was not allowed back into Gaza, as any Palestinian who was outside of the country at the time of the war was now considered a refugee and the Israeli occupying forces did not recognize their right to return. To make matters worse, Saudi authorities expelled the Al-Najjar family for spurious reasons and the family was forced to relocate once again, this time to Egypt. It was in Cairo that Mazen and Sami met for the first time, having undergone similar experiences and hoping to make the best of their current situations. Their professional dreams were shattered when they were not admitted to medical school in spite of their stellar grades. While Sami pursued his education in America, Mazen stayed in Cairo and settled for engineering. Upon his graduation, he received a job offer at an engineering company in the United Arab Emirates, where his family had recently moved. Life in the UAE was frought with hardships. As a Palestinian, Mazen earned one-third the salary of native citizens and was not allowed to apply for a

driver's license. What little money he earned went to paying
the increased costs of living and transportation. Wishing to
leave such a cumbersome and unstable environment, he
applied for a scholarship to complete his graduate studies in
the United States.

A New Life

Mazen first entered the United States on December 11,
1981, as his sister Nahla was giving birth to his niece, Laila.
He immediately appreciated the comfort and freedom that
came with living in America, and settled into the activist
circles of his best friend and brother-in-law Sami in North
Carolina. While Mazen was thoroughly engaged in
intellectual and activist work on behalf of Islam, and
specifically the cause of Palestine, he was not as vocal or
outspoken as other leaders, including Sami. Rather than
found organizations, travel to conferences, or speak before
massive audiences, Mazen instead focused on the important
local work and the publication of topical materials to be
distributed nationally. As the Al-Arian family relocated to
Florida in 1986, Mazen was quick to join them in Tampa,
opting to complete his doctoral work at USF a year later. In
early 1988, Mazen married Fedaa, another refugee from
Gaza. Later that year, she would give birth to the first of
their three daughters.

Aside from his academic pursuit in industrial
engineering, Mazen began to work with WISE on a
voluntary basis from its inception in 1991. By 1993, he had
received official work authorization to become an associate
at WISE. Mazen devoted much of his time to the mission

of WISE. He personally edited every volume of WISE's main publication, the journal "Political Readings." He also spent countless hours in discussions with scholars and academics from across the world engaged in intensive intellectual debates. He translated the works of many noted Middle Eastern scholars to expose Americans to Arabic and Islamic thought. He also became quite active in the local Muslim community, frequently giving the Friday sermons at the mosque and becoming a part-time teacher of Arabic at the Islamic Academy. Mazen was loved by all who knew him as a humble and soft-spoken man who dedicated his life to community service. He could frequently be seen cleaning up after events or playing with children. His thirst for knowledge was unquenchable, and he came to be known as the "walking encyclopedia," because of his ability to discuss at length any topic or subject matter.

When the attacks against WISE and ICP began locally in 1995, Dr. Sami al-Arian became the sole focus of these attacks. As an outspoken leader and advocate of Palestinians, and founder of the organizations in question, Sami was spotlighted by those who wished to destroy his work. The countless defamatory newspaper articles rarely made mention of Mazen or any other of WISE's associates at that time. Nonetheless, finding nothing on which to prosecute the organizations or Sami personally, the government attempted to place pressure on him by targeting others around him. Accordingly, deportation proceedings were initiated against a number of individuals with the most remote ties to Al-Arian. Basheer Nafi, an academic in Virginia who provided temporary volunteer work for WISE was summarily deported in 1996. Hussam Abu Jubara, one of Sami's former graduate students at the USF was also threatened with deportation and entered into proceedings still ongoing today. But of all such cases, the most blatant was the targeting of Dr. Mazen al-Najjar in 1997.

Eye of the Storm

Mazen initially approached the INS voluntarily, wishing to adjust his immigration status to become a permanent resident. As the cloud of controversy descended upon Tampa, the government utilized this move to begin deportation proceedings against him for overstaying his student visa. Mazen and his attorneys fought the government's desire to remove him from the country in court by applying for asylum on the basis that he was a Palestinian refugee with no country to which he could return. Moreover, the INS had seized his refugee travel document, issued by the Egyptian government, and he was completely without any documentation. The document subsequently expired, and Egypt has had a longstanding policy of never renewing expired travel documents, leaving the government's mission to deport him seemingly impossible. Nonetheless, in May, 1997, a judge denied Mazen's application for asylum and he was ordered deported to the UAE, as his last country of residence—over 15 years earlier—in spite of the fact that he had no way of returning there without any documentation.

Before long, the ultimate blow would come. On the morning of May 19, 1997, Dr. Mazen al-Najjar was arrested by federal agents at his home, in front of his frightened daughters. Before he was taken to prison, agents took him to the federal building in downtown Tampa and offered him a deal: full citizenship, a job with IBM, and an otherwise happy future in exchange for his cooperation in investigating his brother-in-law. From the beginning, the arrest appeared to be nothing more than another desperate ploy to intimidate the community and ultimately bring down its leader with whatever means were available. Upon his flat refusal to fabricate lies about the activities of WISE and its associates, Mazen was immediately transported to Manatee County detention facility in Bradenton, Florida, under the pretext of fulfilling a deportation order. The following week, a historic bond hearing would take place, during which America's most core principles would be betrayed outright. The government fought to have Al-Najjar jailed pending his deportation, claiming him to be a "threat to national security," though there was absolutely no reason why he should not be allowed to remain at home. When asked to present evidence of such a claim, the government introduced "confidential information" to the immigration judge, behind closed doors, which neither Dr. Al-Najjar, nor his attorneys could see, let alone confront. The judge returned from his chamber and asked the defense to proceed, based on the evidence he had seen. Of course any defense thereafter would be as difficult as fighting ghosts. What occurred was simply the grossest violation of every constitutional precept in the American system of justice. As a result, Mazen was ordered to continue to be locked away indefinitely, pending his deportation, which was nowhere on the horizon.

This move by the government operated on a number of levels. Internationally, it had already been nearly impossible to find a country to accept a stateless person, even before the immigration judge's decision. The UAE had rejected him outright, along with every Arab and Muslim government. After the American government's allegations that Mazen was "a threat to national security," no country in the world could be expected to take such a person into its borders. In fact, the family would eventually secure a visa for him to be deported to Guyana, which was almost immediately overturned by the Guyana's government when U.S. officials warned the country about their acceptance of a "terrorist." The government's smear campaign effectively halted efforts to find a country to accept him, leaving him to linger in prison without any end in sight.

Nationally, the decision to introduce confidential information to the court was part of a larger campaign against the civil rights of Arabs and Muslims in America. In April, 1996, Congress passed anti-terrorism legislation that allowed the government to contravene certain constitutionally protected rights in order to take a stronger stand against terrorism. Ironically, while the law was supposedly passed in response to the Oklahoma City Bombing of the previous year, an act committed by homegrown terrorists, the law invariably targeted immigrants, specifically those of Arab and Muslim backgrounds. The challenge before that community was immense, but one thing was certain: they would not go down without a fight.

A Community Responds

The struggle to end the ordeal of Mazen al-Najjar as he suffered unjust imprisonment is an epic saga that has become part of the historic American struggle for civil rights. It began with a weak and helpless community, virtually isolated from the surrounding society, anonymous and voiceless. All the forces against it were utilizing the media, the lawmakers, and the public to crush it once and for all. But it is precisely through these channels that the response would come. From very modest beginnings, the community would learn to turn its weaknesses into strengths, ultimately earning a clear victory. Dr. Sami al-Arian became the leader of this effort on a local, national, and even international level. Only a few weeks after Mazen's arrest, Sami founded the Tampa Bay Coalition for Justice and Peace. A group of concerned community members began attending regular meetings to coordinate an organized response to the crisis that had emerged. It became increasingly clear from the onset that while Mazen's fight was ultimately going to be won in a court of law, the case was completely politicized, and the tone for its outcome would be set by current events surrounding the issue. It was with this principle in mind that the Coalition began to pursue its work on several fronts.

The first was the legal route. Capable lawyers were retained to take over the case, including constitutional law expert Georgetown law professor David Cole, who had experience in such cases. Part of the Coalition's mission was to raise the necessary funds to maintain the high quality legal services of Cole and others. Their efforts during the years to follow would prove crucial to the final decision by the court and its outstanding ruling. Secondly, work on Dr. Mazen's behalf would require that the helpless and inexperienced community reach out to others, building bridges and alliances with various other groups that could provide more strength and resources to continue the fight against injustice. Sami was especially successful at developing important relationships with various groups and communities. The Hillsborough Organization for Progress and Equality (HOPE) was one such important bridge toward opening the Muslim community to its American neighbors. The Tampa Muslim community joined HOPE as the first mosque in an organization comprised of nineteen churches dedicated to social issues and important causes. The leadership of HOPE would immediately embrace the Muslim community and continued to work tirelessly toward ending Mazen's imprisonment. It provided grassroots support, leadership, and a show of unity, as this was not a Muslim issue, but an American one. Other organizations were approached that also provided much support. The American Civil Liberties Union and Amnesty International, national and international organizations, respectively, each with local chapters in Florida, were also essential toward any future success.

Third, the Coalition began to work closely with the media, forging important relationships in the process. As the media, and specifically one local newspaper, had been the source of the nightmare for Tampa Muslims, the media would need to be engaged to address the issue in a more sensitive and objective light. It had been evident that many members of the media were promoting their own agenda by continuing the assault on Islamic institutional work. Now was the time for balanced coverage, especially given the seriousness of the situation, with a man's life hanging in the balance. The *St. Petersburg Times* and the *Weekly Planet*, the two other local papers, began covering the case more thoroughly, and approaching it from a point-of-view different from the usual attacks. Additionally, newspapers that issued editorials or published feature articles against secret evidence were widespread; they included the *New York Times, Washington Post, Miami Herald, Chicago Tribune, Detroit Free Press, Los Angeles Times,* and others. More and more, it became evident to most people that this case was a matter of American injustice.

Finally, with all of these areas actively in motion, the fight would be taken to the political arena and the corridors of Washington. After all, it was Congress that passed the horrific law in 1996 that allowed for the government's subsequent abuse of power, and now was the time to put a stop to it in the place where it emerged. With a public and a media that slowly began to open its eyes, members of Congress also began to take note of the civil liberties crisis by lending their support to the case of Dr. Mazen al-Najjar. Political pressure would ultimately prove vital to the result of the court proceedings.

The "One-Man Institution"

All of these activities began with one man: Sami al-Arian. For four years, he made his brother-in-law's case his top objective. The entire case was framed by him, beginning with the mere language of it. What the government proposed to be "confidential information" he called what it really was, secret evidence. That became the sole term used to refer to the unconstitutional practice of introducing evidence to a judge behind closed doors. Throughout the case, secret evidence was the term used by the media, the public, political leaders, and ironically it even became the term that federal authorities in the case themselves applied. The case was framed in the context of historical abuses of civil liberties in the American experience. This was not an Arab issue or a Muslim issue, or even a Palestinian issue, though it encompassed all of these things on one level, but, according to Sami, it was an American issue. The public education campaign that commenced was marvelously successful in that, for the first time, the Muslim community began to define itself, rather than being defined by others in the society, who might have their own interest in portraying it in a certain light. As such, American Muslims began to assert their sense of patriotism toward their country and the ideals on which it was founded. On July 4, 1997, the community held a massive rally at the Tampa mosque celebrating the American Independence Day with an interfaith gathering and a protest against the treatment of Dr. Al-Najjar. Aside from uniting people of many different faiths and backgrounds, events such as these successfully informed all Americans about Islam, Muslims, and even the Palestinian saga, as it was embodied in Mazen's well-publicized ordeal. During the 4th of July rally, a representative of the American Indian Movement, expressing his group's solidarity, made this observation, "Native Americans are the Palestinians of North America, and Palestinians are the Native Americans of the Middle East."

These sentiments continued to be expressed by Christian, Jewish, and progressive leaders, along with the sheer outrage at the secret evidence debacle. Newspaper articles chronicled the suffering of the family, finally putting a human face to this tragedy for the first time. Long pieces in the *St. Petersburg Times* expressed the inhumanity in keeping a father jailed indefinitely as his youngest daughter was growing up without him, spending more of her life without him than she did with him.[6] First-rate investigative journalism by the *Weekly Planet*'s editor, John Sugg, exposed those behind the media allegations as agenda-driven ideological extremists with one thing in mind: defend Israel at all costs by silencing anyone who dares to speak out against it. Sugg put forward the dubious backgrounds of Steven Emerson and the *Tampa Tribune*, its reporters, editors, and its parent company. For the first time since the beginning of the ordeal years earlier, the antagonists were placed on the defensive. Sami's efforts were tireless, as he continued to organize town hall meetings and informational lectures with political intellectuals, prominent journalists, legal scholars, and Muslim community leaders from across the country. In one event, ex-Mossad agent Victor Ostovsky spoke about the Israeli government's plot to stem all Palestinian activism in the United States, even implying that it could be the source of the secret evidence used against Al-Najjar. Legal scholars such as Peter Erlinder, then president of the National Lawyers' Guild, explained the history of civil liberties abuses in America, placing the secret evidence phenomenon in a wider context and shedding light on the struggle to end it.

Ultimately, Sami's success lay in his inspirational efforts to motivate people to action. The Islamic Community of Tampa provided the popular support for the ongoing efforts. Community members were no longer simply regular worshippers, but rather individual activists and advocates on behalf of their beloved brother. Friday prayers were frequently followed by protest rallies in downtown Tampa in which hundreds of people would march and chant slogans decrying secret evidence and the false imprisonment of Mazen al-Najjar. They would always be led by Sami, holding the megaphone and leading the chants. In time, the community began to set its sights on the national political stage. In 1998, a delegation from HOPE went to Washington, D.C., for a meeting with top Justice Department officials to discuss the case.[7] While the meeting itself did not generate any immediate reversal in existing cases, Deputy Attorney General Eric Holden promised that any future secret evidence cases would have to be approved at the level of the Attorney General or her deputy. Federal authorities had finally taken note of the fact that this issue was becoming a growing concern, as a group of important leaders representing thousands of people had come all the way to their offices to express outrage at secret evidence. That historical meeting, on April 15, 1998, effectively halted the use of secret evidence, as no new cases appeared after that date, until after the September 11 attacks.

These efforts continued in Congress, where a massive campaign began to demand the policymakers take a stand against the unjust practice in general and in Mazen's case in particular. Sami's trips to Washington are themselves the subject of much awe and admiration. He proceeded very simply to approach members of Congress and their staffs to inform them of the situation and implore them to take a strong stance. Through patience and persistence, he employed the help of many important people, including David Bonior, a Democrat from Michigan and the Minority Whip of the House of Representatives. Bonior had a long history of standing up for the voiceless, and more recently the American Muslim community, and this issue would be no exception. On the contrary, the issue of secret evidence would go on to define much of his more recent career, as he became the champion in Congress to end its usage. In one gathering, Bonior would refer to the anti-terrorism legislation that allowed for secret evidence as "the worst law ever passed in Congress."

Progress in Congress

Bonior's contributions were manifold. He proceeded to speak out on the issue at major events and national Islamic conferences. He visited the Tampa community on more than one occasion, and even made a visit to Dr. Al-Najjar at his jail as a show of solidarity. Through it all, he and Sami would form a special friendship based on mutual respect and admiration. But Sami's reaching out was not limited to Democrats or liberals. He solicited the support of several Republicans, some of them even staunchly conservative. Representative Bob Barr (R-GA) was one of the original supporters of Mazen's case. Former Representative Tom Campbell (R-CA) had been a constitutional law professor prior to his taking office, and upon hearing about the case from Nahla al-Arian, was astonished to learn that such abuses were taking place in the America of 1998. He soon afterwards lent his support. John Conyers, another Democrat from Michigan and a member of the important Judiciary Committee, also became a leading figure in the fight against secret evidence. By early 1999, these four members of Congress, two from each party, sponsored a bill in the House of Representatives to prohibit the use of secret evidence in immigration proceedings. The bill, known as H.R. 2121, was titled "The Secret Evidence Repeal Act."

Sami's work did not end with the introduction of this legislation. While it was a monumental victory for the American Muslim community and civil libertarians everywhere, the efforts were just beginning. In order to make a serious bid to pass the bill, an immense lobbying campaign was essential. As such, Sami, at times with his wife Nahla, or his oldest son Abdullah, personally visited with hundreds of Congressional offices during his many visits to Washington.

For years, Sami had attempted to involve the American Muslim national political organizations, but with limited success. The secret evidence crisis was initially a "hands-off issue" that most groups feared to approach. It was only upon witnessing the growing interest of non-Muslim groups such as the ACLU, that Muslim groups began to commit to the issue facing Muslims across the country. After all, the secret evidence phenomenon, while personified in the well-publicized case of Mazen al-Najjar, had also afflicted over two-dozen other men in various communities throughout the United States. Thanks solely to Sami's efforts in Tampa, it had now truly become a national issue. But even then, while it was important for groups such as the American Muslim Council and the Council on American-Islamic Relations to lend their names to the growing effort, the bulk of the labor was actually done by the "one-man institution" as Sami came to be known.

During his visits to Capitol Hill, he developed close relationships with a number of other members of Congress and their staff assistants. The bill eventually garnered the co-sponsorship of 128 members of the House of Representatives. After a trip to Tampa, influential Republican Henry Hyde moved the bill to the House Judiciary Committee, which he chaired until its passage. He was taken by the community's plight, and particularly by his host during his trip, Sami al-Arian. Before the bill could be brought to the House floor for a vote, however, it had to go through the necessary channels, in this case, the Judiciary Committee, and specifically the Sub-Committee on Immigration. Sami's keen sense of awareness and understanding of the political process far surpassed that of any Muslim leader in America. Through his experiences, he learned the mechanics of the system and the necessary elements to succeed in the policy-making process. With the knowledge that a vote in the Judiciary Committee was vital to the eventual passage of the bill in Congress, he began approaching and informing members of the Committee about the issue, and gained support from many of them.

While these efforts on Capitol Hill were taking place, Sami never wavered from all the other avenues that were required. During these months in late 1999 and early 2000, the media blitz continued against the use of secret evidence. Over a dozen newspaper editorials, ranging from a number of newspapers in Florida, to national press such as the *Washington Post* and the *New York Times* condemned the government's practice in the strongest terms. Columnists focused on the abuses and supported Congressional efforts to end it. Reporters wrote full-length features in national papers chronicling the suffering of the family and the groundless nature of the government's allegations. Work on the grassroots level did not diminish either. In fact, the number of people involved in the effort increased daily. At its annual conference in 1999, HOPE declared secret evidence and Mazen's imprisonment as one of its top issue items for the coming year. The Islamic Society of North America's annual conference, which draws over 30,000 Muslims each year, held important sessions devoted to the issue, where Sami and other activists would speak. Even Congressman Bonior and others from Washington appeared at the conference to address the community about the issue.

In addition, Sami continuously tried to make in-roads with the Administration itself, whose policy had generated the secret evidence crisis to begin with. In 1999, he attended a private fundraiser for former Congresswoman Cynthia McKinney (D-GA) in Atlanta, where President Bill Clinton was scheduled to speak. Following the event, he briefly met with the President and brought the situation in Tampa to his attention. The President expressed his concern and promised to look into the matter personally. At a separate event, Sami and Nahla were brought face to face with First Lady Hillary Clinton, and also implored her to aid in their struggle. At yet another engagement, Sami briefly told Mazen's story to Reverend Jesse Jackson, who then proceeded to spend much of his subsequent key-note address railing against the government's abuses and sympathizing with Mazen's plight.

Justice Goes National

And though much of Sami's work was individual, he also used this crisis period to continue his trademark institution building. Back in 1997, Sami sought to expand the Tampa Bay Coalition's activities onto the national scene. A subsequent meeting with interested parties in Washington led to the establishment of the National Coalition to Protect Political Freedom (NCPPF). The NCPPF became an umbrella group comprised of over forty local and national organizations, ranging from civil liberties and human rights groups to American Muslim organizations. The new organization was groundbreaking in its efforts against secret evidence by coordinating large events, leading national letter-writing campaigns, and garnering news media and political attention. Sami served as the coalition's first president and was the force behind its achievements for its first few years. In February, 2000, as the Congressional legislation was gaining momentum, Sami coordinated a rally in Congress that drew 700 people from all over the country to the main hall in the Rayburn building in what Rep. Bonior described as the largest public event ever in the halls of Congress. The gathering was addressed by many community leaders, activists, and even several members of Congress. The national Muslim leadership had by then committed to the issue and gave their blessing to the event which was hailed as a resounding success.

That same month, the Judiciary Sub-Committee on Immigration would hold an important hearing about the emerging legislation, during which time Congressmen Bonior and Campbell testified to their support of the legislation. David Cole, Mazen's lawyer and a constitutional law scholar, testified as well. Mazen's sister, Nahla al-Arian, gave an emotional and eloquent statement about the suffering of the family and its firsthand experience with secret evidence. Providing the government's point of view were two federal agents and an immigration official. It was later discovered that Steven Emerson also provided written testimony against the move to repeal secret evidence, citing his usual ridiculous charges. The hearing was extraordinary for a number of reasons. For the first time in the history of the Muslim community, an issue of crucial importance was receiving the type of attention it deserved. The community's top agenda item had taken center-stage and was on the verge of becoming approved into law. Only weeks later, Campbell and Bonior would introduce an amendment to a budgetary bill that included a deduction in INS funds of the amount of money it required to hold secret evidence victims in prison. The bill was passed overwhelmingly, along with the amendment, and though this did not necessarily mean the end of secret evidence (the INS would simply redirect other funds toward the imprisonment of those individuals) this was an important gesture that proved that the majority of members in Congress were on record in support of abolishing secret evidence. Later that fall, the Judiciary Committee would vote on the Secret Evidence Repeal Act, passing it by a vote of 28-2. Although Sami expected the bill to pass, he was surprised by the margin of victory. The legislation was now ready for a vote on the House floor. This was truly an historic moment for Sami personally and the rest of the Muslim community, as the hard work and sacrifice were ultimately coming to bear and the end of their suffering seemed at hand. And while most organizations rushed to their offices to write press releases declaring victory, Sami rushed to the offices of Senators Spencer Abraham (R-MI) and Edward Kennedy (D-MA) to introduce a companion bill in the Senate. Within days, the bill was introduced in the Senate with a promising prospect of passage in light of the momentum.

The Courts Decide

All of this activity served as the backdrop for the court proceedings, which by the spring of 2000 had entered their final stages. Mazen's lawyers had to climb the ladder of appeals before a federal judge would hear the case. As expected, the Board of Immigration Appeals and other appellate bodies upheld the original judge's ruling supporting the use of secret evidence. Finally, after filing a suit that his due process rights were denied, a federal judge in Miami heard the case and chose not to uphold the ruling, nor did she reverse the original judge's findings. Judge Joan Leonard, while ruling that Dr. Al-Najjar was denied due process and issuing her concern at the use of secret evidence, ultimately sent the case back to the original immigration judge for a rehearing, with the recommendation that he reevaluate the case in two phases, one in open record, and an additional secret hearing. If the judge were to rule in favor of the defendant in the first, the government could hold a secret proceeding, providing that it gives the defense a "meaningful summary" of the secret evidence for the judge to consider it. As it happened, after the judge found that Mazen was not a threat to national security, the government held its secret hearing, but failed to provide a meaningful summary to Mazen and his lawyers. As such, INS judge Kevin McHugh heard the case again and, after a two week hearing that involved over 4,000 pages of proceedings, issued a monumental ruling that seemed to lay to rest once and for all the six-year campaign to smear the Tampa institutions. In his October 27, 2000, ruling, he stated:

> The Court finds it remarkable that out of five hundred videotapes that were seized, from which a thirteen-minute composite tape was created, not one excerpt of the composite depicted Respondent engaging in fundraising for any organization. ... Even if the Court found that the evidence demonstrated that the ICP raised money for the PIJ at this event, it was not illegal to do so until 1997. However, in this case, there is

still no evidence that the Respondent raised funds for the PIJ or sent funds to the PIJ. In conclusion, the Court finds that the evidence does not demonstrate that Respondent engaged in fundraising for the PIJ through the ICP. [Page 39]

The Court finds that the Service's claim that the Respondent engaged in fundraising activities for the PIJ, through either the ICP or WISE, is unsupported by the evidence of record. [Page 41]

[T]he record before the Court is devoid of any direct or indirect evidence to support the conclusion that Respondent was meaningfully associated, as required by the Act, with the PIJ. [Pages 45-46]

Although there were allegations that the ICP and WISE were fronts for Palestinian political causes, there is no evidence before the Court that demonstrates that either organization was a front for the PIJ. To the contrary, there is evidence in the record to support the conclusion that WISE was a reputable and scholarly research center and the ICP was highly regarded. [Page 48]

[T]he Court finds, based on the evidence presented at the public portions of the remand bond redetermination proceedings,

that there are no "facially legitimate and bona
fide reasons to conclude that[Respondent] is
a threat to national security." [Page 49][8]

These statements proved damning to the government's
case. In effect, it proved that the government had no case.
As most critics believed, Al-Najjar was simply targeted in
the wave of anti-Arab, anti-Muslim hysteria, attempting to
link all legitimate and lawful political activity of which some
disapproved, with the support of terrorism. In a frantic
attempt to pressure the judge to reconsider his ruling, INS
authorities once again attempted to introduce secret
evidence. But even after seeing that "evidence" for himself
a second time, McHugh maintained the same ruling. The
government appealed to a three-judge panel in Washington,
D.C., which also upheld McHugh's recent ruling on
December 6, 2000, and ordered Al-Najjar released. In a
final act of desperation, INS officials appealed to Attorney
General Janet Reno to review the case, but after evaluating
it and seeing all of the evidence, she too refused to overturn
the decision. Accordingly, Dr. Mazen al-Najjar was
released from detention on December 15, 2000, after 1,307
days and a long and hard battle against seemingly
insurmountable odds. "I hope this is the end of the
nightmare," he said to a large crowd awaiting his release
outside of the prison.

The Next Chapter: The Muslim Bloc Vote

The victory against secret evidence had elevated the American
Muslim community to a new plateau. Dr. Mazen al-Najjar

was the last of the secret evidence victims to be released, and the future seemed bright indeed. Sami's dream was that rather than simply fall back into a lull, the community should gather its energies following its recent success against the civil rights crisis and make a concerted push toward political empowerment. His experiences had taught him many lessons, one of which was that no community, regardless of its status, had ever gained any political weight without first winning its civil rights battle. As 2000 was a presidential election year, the American Muslim community wanted to make its presence felt at the polls for the first time. Previous attempts at creating a bloc vote had fallen on deaf ears, but this time the strategy would be different.

Coming from a position of critical weakness, leaders of the four major political organizations, American Muslim Council, Muslim Public Affairs Committee, Council on American-Islamic Relations, and American Muslim Alliance, declared that they would come to a consensus and urge all Muslims to support a single candidate. While some argued for more long-term strategizing, the immediate need to make a difference far out-weighed the more methodical approach of slowly climbing the political ranks. As such, after an instinctive process, the Muslim leadership endorsed George W. Bush for president in October of 2000, only weeks before Election Day.

For the first time in their history as a community, American Muslims were beginning to reconfigure their political priorities. Known mostly for their deep concerns over U.S. foreign policy, the community was always marginalized as though it were simply another foreign lobby, and not part of the American mainstream political landscape. Through secret evidence, the community's domestic concerns were brought front and center to it, without giving it much of a choice. As such, the civil liberties crisis known as secret evidence became the number one issue item for the community in determining its support. In addition, it evaluated the accessibility of the candidates and how they received the community and its concerns. On all those levels, George W. Bush passed with flying colors. Vice-President Al Gore repeatedly cancelled meetings with Muslim leaders, and his choice of an avidly pro-Israeli Senator as a running mate also chilled support for his campaign. Bush on the other hand, met with Muslims on a number of different occasions, in Michigan, Washington, and even Tampa, Florida.

During a campaign stop in March, 2000, George Bush, along with his brother Jeb, the governor of Florida, singled out one family in a crowd of thousands to stop and talk with for a bit. That family was none other than Dr. Sami al-Arian, his wife Nahla, and their five children. They were pleased when the candidate stopped to talk to them, saying things like, "we have a lot in common," and "we can work together." These messages of unity and support for the oppressed Muslim minority were a welcome change, contrasted with before when candidates would steer clear of any "odd-looking groups." Bush proceeded to pose for pictures with the family and wish them well. Sami of course, took the opportunity to mention that Muslims were eager to lend their support to a candidate worthy of it. In a separate meeting later that fall, Muslim leaders told the Texas governor about their concerns, of which secret evidence was of the highest priority.

They were anxious for a president who would assure them passage of the legislation currently working its way through Congress and also implement a change in policy in the Justice Department itself. Later that week, appearing before sixty million Americans in a televised debate with Al Gore, Bush signaled his support for the community with just one statement. Asked about racial profiling, he gave his standard answer about the issue, and also included the statement that secret evidence was a form of profiling that had to be stopped. The community was beside itself. It expected some commitment from him, but not in so bold a venue as the second of three presidential debates. Within days, leaders had reached a verdict: they would endorse George W. Bush for president and encourage all American Muslims to vote for him. Sami played a critical role in persuading Muslim leaders to endorse Bush. He was working with both campaigns, and Bush's statement at the debate was a result of Sami's continuous effort with his campaign. On the eve of the endorsement, the Gore campaign called Dr. Al-Arian, urging his community to reconsider its decision. Al Gore tried desperately to woo Muslims back toward him with last-minute pledges to end secret evidence and specifically to revisit the case of Dr. Mazen al-Najjar. Sami's response was that this was too little too late.

Sami worked tirelessly toward making Muslims count in the 2000 election. He used his newfound position of national community leader to campaign for Bush on a large scale, working closely with Republican leaders and the Muslim community at large. By Election Day, he had prompted thousands of people to vote for Bush, many of them first-time voters. With his own citizenship status still in limbo, Sami himself was unable to vote, but ironically enough he was personally responsible for thousands of votes going to Bush in

Florida and elsewhere. That night, with the results still hanging in the balance, Sami's phone was ringing endlessly, with individual leaders and representatives of the Islamic Institute, a Washington-based group with close Republican ties, and the head of Americans for Tax Reform, an influential conservative lobby group, all calling to express gratitude to Sami for his efforts, and vowing that his hard work in Florida might have tipped the scale.

A Community Decides

Sure enough, they were right. When the smoke settled a month later, Bush had won Florida by only 537 votes, handing him the presidency. Mazen had been released only days earlier. The Muslim community was riding a strong wave of triumph and was ready finally to take its place on the policy-making table as an equal partner. In order to ensure that their efforts would not go unnoticed, Sami commissioned a scientific study to investigate the number of Muslim voters in Florida and the result of their participation in the recent elections. As expected, results showed that Muslims, who normally tend to vote with the Democratic Party, had voted nearly four to one in favor of Bush. With over 16,000 voters, this gave Bush a clear edge of thousands of Muslim votes in Florida, "plenty more than 537," as Sami was fond of saying.

In the months that followed, Sami continued his work in a variety of areas. Locally, the Islamic Academy of Florida had expanded to nearly 300 students and required much attention. As its principal, Sami had established it as the premier Islamic school on a local as well as national scale. The mosque activities of the Islamic Community of Tampa had increased as well, with frequent community dinners, educational lectures, fundraisers, and religious functions. Nationally, he played an important role in the Muslim community's interaction with the incoming administration. Many initial signs were already discouraging, especially the appointment of known Christian extremist conservative John Ashcroft as the Attorney General. In addition, because the Secret Evidence Repeal Act did not come up for a vote before the end of the previous legislative session, the bill would have to be introduced once again, this time as H.R. 1266. The process began anew, with the push to build momentum in sponsorship of the bill. While it took him 15 months to gain 128 cosponsors the first time, it took him only three months to gather over one hundred this time. Sami and the Muslim organizations maintained their pressure on the government to deliver on its promises. In June, 2001, Sami went to the White House with a delegation of American Muslim leaders for a meeting with Vice-President Dick Cheney, his fourth visit to the White House since 1998. At the last minute, Cheney cancelled, but the President's senior advisor, Karl Rove, instead addressed the gathering about the President's commitment to their issues.

Challenges Arise

Only a week later, Sami's son Abdullah, who had been interning with Congressman Bonior at the time, was ejected by Secret Service agents from a meeting of Muslim leaders with White House officials on the President's new Faith-

Based Initiative. The entire delegation of two-dozen people walked out of the meeting in protest. The community was once again thrown onto the defensive. The incident made international headlines and prompted a personal apology from President Bush regarding the treatment of Abdullah. Secret Service agents admitted they had acted hastily and also apologized for their actions. The Al-Arian family was once again in the spotlight because of this incident, and a subsequent *Newsweek* article chronicling its experiences referred to Sami as one of the nation's "leading advocates" in civil rights, because of his efforts to abolish secret evidence.[9]

By that fall, American Muslims were in a state of peace and cautious optimism. Dr. Al-Najjar was enjoying time with his family and community. Dr. Al-Arian was continuously swamped with his many responsibilities to his family, students, and community. Muslim leaders were hopeful that their efforts were soon to be rewarded. A meeting was scheduled for Muslim leaders with the President for September 11 in which he was expected to declare his support for the bill against secret evidence.

Republican leaders in Congress were awaiting a green light from the White House to continue to move the legislation forward. That morning, however, would redefine America as it had come to be known in the world, and have especially poignant effects on its Muslim minority. The following is Dr. Sami al-Arian's personal account of his experience during the tragedy of September 11, 2001:

> It wasn't quite 9:30 yet on the morning of this dreadful Tuesday when someone approached me as I was speaking to a few students at the Islamic Academy. He asked, "Did you hear

about what happened in New York?" As we rushed to the nearest TV, our hearts sank as we saw horrifying scenes of planes crashing into buildings and people running for safety. Everyone in the room became suddenly speechless. Soon our shock turned to sadness, then to anger. Some were sobbing. It was an agonizing and solemn moment.

Soon after, the media descended on our Islamic center, and before we realized it, we became part of the news. We expressed our deep sorrow and grief. We condemned this criminal act and supported the government in its call for justice against the perpetrators and their benefactors. We joined our fellow citizens in prayer services in many churches starting on the evening of that dark Tuesday.

On Wednesday, the day after the tragedy, seventy-five members of our mosque donated blood. We felt patriotic, but more importantly, part of a national mobilization for doing good. In addition, over $10,000 was collected for the victims' fund of the Red Cross. On Friday, I gave a sermon in the mosque conveying the Islamic teachings in the Qur'an and from the prophet's life that totally reject the logic of indiscriminate killing and hatred. "Whoever kills one innocent life is as though he killed the whole humanity, and whoever saves one life is as though he saved the whole of humanity," the Qur'an teaches. I further reiterated the Islamic principles of cooperation, unity, and tolerance for all faith communities. Needless to say, in all of our interviews with the media, we expressed our heartfelt grief, sadness, and condemnation.

By the following Sunday, our call to an ecumenical service in our mosque the previous day in a full-page advertisement brought over four hundred people—more than half of them non-Muslims. The service was beautiful. All three Abrahamic faiths were represented. We were united in our grief as well as in our determination to overcome this tragedy. I explained in this three-hour service how Islam not only condemned this crime but also called for justice. We said that whoever did this evil act could not invoke religion or use religious texts to justify their twisted logic.

While we were engaging in all of that, our community was suffering from the backlash of misguided people and some media outlets. A gun was fired at a mosque in the area. Several members were harassed with ugly words and acts. Women with their traditional Muslim scarves were especially easy targets for hate-filled comments and gestures. Arab-looking people were taken off airplanes. Others were fired from their jobs. The nonstop talk shows on the radio and television continued to attack the Islamic faith to the point that even some children questioned their parents about why they were Muslim. We had to heighten security at our mosque and school to the tune of $20,000. We felt it was unfair that the Arab and Muslim communities not only had to suffer because of the tragedy at the hands of the terrorists, but also had to endure the hate, distrust, and threats from their fellow citizens. It must be said on the other hand, however, that we received as a community, as well as personally, many heartfelt expressions of love, support, and embrace. They represented the best of America. We made many new friends.[10]

Indeed, the shock suffered by the community in the aftermath of the attacks would be felt for years to come. In Sami's case, however, it would take only a few weeks. While, he undoubtedly understood the risks involved in continuing to be an outspoken activist, he nonetheless knew that there was nothing to be gained from silence. As such, he took to the airwaves in an attempt to continue on the path of progress for American Muslims and the country as a whole. He was often heard saying that as bad as things had gotten for Muslims, with the increased harassment, widespread denials of due process and unjust detentions, they could potentially have been worse if Muslims had done nothing up to that point to improve their status in the years preceding the attacks. This flew in the face of many detractors from within the community, who took this opportunity to argue evermore strongly that America would never accept Muslims, and that any attempt to participate or assimilate was a foolish waste of time and energy. Things would certainly degenerate further in the months to come, but through it all, Sami's faith in the system would stand strong.

Extremism Prevails

On September 26, producers for a conservative talk show called "The O'Reilly Factor" invited Dr. Al-Arian to come on the show to discuss his past work with WISE. He reluctantly agreed, after it was stated that due to lack of time, the show would focus more on the community's reaction to the September 11 attacks. What in fact happened was one of the lowest demonstrations of sensationalistic yellow journalism in American history. The wild-eyed Neo-conservative host Bill O'Reilly proceeded to bombard the professor with preposterous allegations, suggesting that he was a terrorist leader operating a cell within the University of South Florida. His final statement to Dr. Al-Arian was, "All I'm saying is that if I was the CIA, I'd follow you everywhere you went. I'd go with you to Denny's. I'd be your shadow."[11] As is common with most clamorous talk shows, the host controlled the entire conversation, never allowing Sami to complete a single sentence, let alone present any response. He mentioned names of various individuals, including Mazen al-Najjar, implying that knowing any of these people amounted to supporting terrorism. He did not mention that Mazen had never been charged with a crime during nearly four years in prison, or that a judge finally vindicated their institutions in a ruling less than a year earlier. In all, O'Reilly simply rehashed many of the allegations by *Tampa Tribune* reports from six years earlier. In fact, it was later revealed that O'Reilly got his information from the agenda-driven reporter Michael Fechter, who simply fed the ignorant host false data in the hopes of publicly maligning the professor once again and creating a national stir.[12] While this previously might not have had much of a detrimental effect, the post-9/11 national mood changed all that.

Since the program introduced Sami as a "USF Professor," despite his insistence to be introduced as president of the National Coalition to Protect Political Freedom, the axe immediately fell upon the university. The next day, September 27, the university received hundreds of angry phone calls, some of them threatening bodily harm to Dr. Al-Arian. Months later, the university would reveal that one person who called in a death threat that day called back twenty minutes later to apologize. Nonetheless, the university was moved to stern reaction. The university's president, Judy Genshaft, had been at home celebrating a Jewish holiday when she received word of what had occurred the previous evening. Dr. Sami al-Arian was immediately suspended with pay, according to the university officials, for his safety and the safety of the students until the situation calmed down. Sami himself had to change his home phone number to avoid the venomous calls from fuming Americans. His email address was filling up with coarse hate mail from people such as this one:

"IT'S A JOKE YOU'RE A PROFESSOR, YOU RAGHEAD! I SAW YOU SMIRK ON T.V., I KNOW YOUR'E INVOLVED. GO BACK TO STUPID IRAQ OR WHEREEVER THE HELL YOU'RE FROM....U.S. WILL PREVAIL. WE WILL KICK SOME ASS, YOU WILL BURN!... WITH SYMPATHY...AN AMERICAN CITIZEN...P.S. PEACE TO ISRAEL."[13]

For the Zionist schemers behind this entire vicious ordeal, letters such as these were the mark of resounding success. O'Reilly succeeded in confusing his audience by associating Sami with all terrorism in general, including the recent attacks. People did not know that the issues discussed actually stemmed from Sami's days as a Palestinian activist in the late 1980s and early 1990s. His speeches, for example, in which he made certain statements in support of the *Intifada* and its largely peaceful resistance to Israeli oppression, were taken completely out of context, and in the aftermath of 9/11, aired to an understandably sensitive audience. Specifically, the statement "Death to Israel" was continuously mentioned and he would be asked about it for months to come, as though it were a remark he just recently made, and not in a speech over thirteen years earlier. Nonetheless, Sami constantly explained his position that his statement "Death to Israel,' in Arabic, was given to an Arabic crowd that understands what it means. It's death to the occupation, death to the system that has been chasing the Palestinians and making them dispossessed for over half a century, a policy of complete, complete dismantlement of their institutions. It does not mean death to every Israeli."

In addition, he would often add that he would never make such remarks again, in light of more current circumstances. None of that was enough for his detractors. The media onslaught began once again, led of course, by the *Tampa Tribune*. Nationally, Steven Emerson, who after being completely discredited in the mid-1990s, rose from the ashes of September 11 to the status of being a so-called "terrorism expert," was seen on every network spewing his vile defamation of Islam, Muslims, and their leaders and institutions. Specifically, a segment on *Dateline*, NBC's news program, was devoted to Sami's recent debacle with the university, and featured none other than Emerson rehashing his baseless allegations throughout the piece. This added pressure, complete with its unwanted attention for both Professor Al-Arian and the USF, resulted in numerous calamities.

Regression of Justice

As the community across the nation suffered from the media's anti-Muslim propaganda campaign and a Justice Department run amuck, authorities took advantage of the negative attention surrounding the situation in Tampa to once again arrest Mazen al-Najjar in November 2001, as he was enjoying his first full Ramadan back with his community. On the morning of November 24, as he was out getting coins for the laundry machines, several armed federal agents pounced upon him. A witness would later tell reporters that he saw them slam Dr. Al-Najjar to the ground, violently placing him in handcuffs, and literally dragging him away, as he pleaded with them to be able to see his daughters, who were home alone, or at least let someone go and look after them. Mazen was immediately hauled off to Coleman Federal Penitentiary's maximum-security wing and placed in solitary confinement for 23 hours a day. The conditions there were absolutely atrocious, as the facility was designed as punishment for misbehaving inmates with a maximum two-week stay. The official justification of the law enforcement authorities was that he would be kept pending the execution of his outstanding deportation order, which had recently been confirmed by a judge. Once again, he was kept on the ludicrous basis of national security concerns, though this time secret evidence was not used. Instead, the government gave absolutely no evidence, and did not feel the need to back its decision with any actual reasons for doing so. And once again, Mazen was imprisoned for nothing, in an even worse condition than he had ever imagined. After only eleven months of freedom, he was back behind bars, with no end in sight.

Academic Freedom Under Fire

Mazen's second arrest served as a major blow to a community that was already faced with a distressing situation. Its spirits and confidence were at an all-time low. In the weeks following the O'Reilly appearance, USF was no longer accommodating to Dr. Sami al-Arian. Although administrators repeatedly assured him that their actions were taken only for his protection and that the real terrorists —those who had phoned in threats to disrupt campus life—were being investigated, one could not help but suspect that the university was following in those delinquents' footsteps. On October 5, 2004, Dr. Al-

Arian went to the USF campus to attend a Muslim Student Association meeting, a group for which he is the faculty advisor. Days later, he received an angry letter from the administrators, threatening legal measures for supposedly defying their order to stay off campus. The letter stated that it was a "second and final warning" that he should stay away from the school. Of course, while they had told him he could not resume teaching duties, the professor had never been told he could not physically come onto the campus itself. He sent a response claiming that the impolite letter was his "first and only notice" of such a decision, which, he pointed out, would be a source of much hardship for him and his family. After all, his daughter was a student there, his credit union was there, and his office and mailbox were all on the university's campus. Nevertheless, in spite of his protestation, Sami would abide by that decision, and did not set foot on the campus after that single incident. As the pressure mounted, political rumblings within the university's upper tier began looking for a "final solution," as it were, to the "Al-Arian problem."

President Genshaft had only been at the university a couple of years, and was seemingly oblivious to the previous handling of the situation by President Betty Castor, who laid the allegations to rest and reinstated him to his duties in 1998. Rather than follow a similar responsible route, Genshaft took a public position against Dr. Al-Arian and proceeded to suggest that he be fired from his position. As a tenured professor, firing was an extreme decision and unlawful except in the most extreme situations. Even more vocal than the president was the chairman of the university's board of trustees, named Dick Beard. The trustees system was completely transformed under Governor Jeb Bush into a central body chosen by him. As such, the USF board was made up entirely of political appointees, mostly corporate buddies and wealthy businessmen close to the governor himself. Dick Beard, a real estate tycoon, and most others on the board of trustees without any experience in running an academic institution, nor any background in education whatsoever, now held the fate of a well-established professor in their hands. Among Beard's many colorful comments was a reference to Dr. Al-Arian as "a cancer."[14] The university's officials exploited public pressure to advance their own vindictive agenda.

On December 19, 2001, the board called an emergency meeting to discuss the situation. The significance of the date, so close to Christmas, is that the meeting occurred as the entire university community was on its winter holiday. It was clear that USF officials were ashamed of their current course of action, and so chose to do it in as dim a light as possible. At this meeting, Genshaft suggested that the "disruption" caused by Professor Al-Arian's activities warranted his immediate dismissal. Nor did he make clear during his O'Reilly appearance, she argued, that he "did not speak for the university," as though it would ever be interpreted that way. An attorney consulted by the university agreed that enough legal precedent existed to justify the firing. The board had heard enough; it immediately voted 12-1, in favor of firing. The lone vote against the decision was by the sole academic on the board, Dr. H. Patrick Swygert, President of Howard University in Washington, D.C. Meanwhile, Sami was not allowed to attend the meeting, let alone offer any defense. In effect, his due process rights were completely denied as a slap in the face to academic integrity across the nation.

The Professor immediately consulted attorneys in order to wage a legal battle in defense of his rights as a tenured faculty member. The university was in gross violation of its own collective bargaining agreement with its employees by denying him due process. The university's decision set in motion an immense backlash against it, which it did not quite anticipate. The university's faculty union vowed to support their fellow professor, even in helping to cover the costs of the impending legal battle. The Faculty Senate voted overwhelmingly against the president's decision to dismiss the professor. The United Faculty of Florida also became an instrumental group in voicing its outrage over the university's decision. And finally, the American Association of University Professors, the largest faculty organization in the country and oldest defender of tenure and academic freedom, began to investigate the situation and threaten the university with censure, an effective blacklisting of the institution with much negative long-term impact. Student groups also began to take on the fight for Dr. Al-Arian across the country.

Blowback to USF

In effect, following the university's hasty and irresponsible decision, the issue was no longer framed in the way it had been before, but rather was now one of academic freedom. After all, the entire institution of tenure was implemented for professors to be free of any political pressure on the product of their work or the views they espouse. And since there were never any direct allegations against Sami aside from his speech and political activities, which had always been completely separate from his teaching career, any objective observer realized that he was simply being targeted because of those views and beliefs. The cry for academic freedom was heard loud and clear. Newspapers across the country flocked to cover the developing story, as it had become the premier case of post-9/11 discrimination for one's political views, and, according to one editorial the most important infringement on academic freedom since the famous Angela Davis case in the 1960s. Strong statements from the newspapers in Florida, as well as national papers, gave a boost to Sami's case. On January 27, 2002, the *New York Times* editorial stated, "Both complaints [by USF] are groundless and make a mockery of free speech and academic freedom. Governor Bush has compounded the problem by publicly backing the university's approach. ... Free speech and academic freedom must be blind to politics."[15]

The positive response to Sami's unfortunate situation was very welcome indeed. While people had continuously advised him to simply stay quiet and hope things would improve, he had proven them wrong by taking a very sure-footed and proactive approach. After all, he maintained, he had done nothing wrong and was proud of his many accomplishments. His enemies wished him to be silenced into humiliation, and ultimately defeated, but that would not come to be. In the months to follow, Sami was a model of activity unlike any other. He embarked on a speaking tour across dozens of cities. In each visit, he would speak at college campuses, before crowded auditoriums, at local community centers, and at churches and mosques, to the delight of the local community. Everywhere he went, people became inspired to become involved in the growing civil rights campaign against the unjust actions arising from the post-9/11 hysteria. In all, as Dr. Al-Arian became a poster child for political discrimination, he handled his newfound position with grace, honor, and eloquence, as had become his trademarks over the years.

The Campaign Continues

Despite the many advances made in Sami's case, the pro-Israel campaign did not halt for a moment. Frustrated at their inability to bring about a single criminal charge against him, some adversaries attempted to bring civil charges by filing a lawsuit. Such was the case with John Loftus, head of the Florida Holocaust Museum, who sued Dr. Sami al-Arian for allegedly misusing funds he donated to "Al-Arian charities," an entity that does not even exist. The only other problem was that the money Loftus supposedly gave, in the form of a few dollar bills he mailed to the Islamic Community of Tampa, did not even arrive until days after the lawsuit was filed! In his suit, Loftus, who has since been characterized as a lunatic by most Tampa citizens, attempts to link Dr. Al-Arian with virtually every Islamic terrorist organization and terrorist act in the world, including Al-Qaida and the September 11 attacks, the Saudi government, and other outrageous claims. By June, 2002, the suit was summarily dismissed by a court that rightly judged that not only was it frivolous and groundless, but was simply part of a string of attacks against the professor. Indeed, the strategy appeared to be to flood Sami with as many legal proceedings and lawyer fees as possible, in the hopes that one day he would simply be out-funded and overmatched by his detractors.

Meanwhile, the progress of his case against the university was moving forward ever so slowly. With the university expected to make a decision about his firing by the end of the summer of 2002, President Genshaft made a highly unexpected decision, which reflected that she was beginning to rethink her rash judgment in pursue the firing, but she was not ready to reverse course. Rather than complete the firing, or reinstate him, as were her only real options, she instead filed a lawsuit against Dr. Al-Arian in state court, in the hopes of having a judge issue a ruling with regard to the university's decision. In its suit, the university alleged that it sought the "advisory ruling" of a state court on whether firing the tenured professor would be unconstitutional. As it was a constitutional issue, Dr. Al-Arian's lawyers moved the case to federal court, where it was ultimately dismissed. Most observers thought it an odd choice to file such a suit, with the firing still pending. After all, courts were generally not in the habit of ruling on hypothetical situations that had yet to occur. And if the university was so uncertain of its present course, it should not have pursued it in the first place, or at the very least, reversed its decision resolutely thereafter. In effect, this was simply another attempt to stall the process, as most of the pressure now seemed to be on the university to undo its attack on academic freedom.

An End to a Tragedy

It was also during this time that Dr. Mazen al-Najjar's case entered its final chapter. By August, 2002, his appalling detention had entered into its ninth month and the situation was slowly deteriorating further. His health had suffered at the hands of the brutal prison conditions at Coleman Penitentiary, and his family was feeling the renewed pain of his absence from their lives. In the meantime, the family had desperately tried to find a solution to his predicament by attempting to secure him a visa to leave the United States. These efforts proved fruitless for many months, until finally he was issued a temporary visa to Bahrain. The family immediately told the government and the deportation was to be enforced. As a precondition, Mazen's family implored that he be allowed to travel on an ordinary commercial airplane, for fear of intimidating the Bahraini officials, but to no avail. Federal marshals chartered a plane, on which Al-Najjar was placed in his prison garments, handcuffed and with his feet shackled and half a dozen armed guards to escort him on the transatlantic flight. The plane stopped to refuel in Ireland, before continuing on its scheduled path. As Mazen had feared, upon hearing of his being treated as though he were a criminal, the Bahraini government fearfully rescinded its visa to him. The airplane was then forced to land in Rome, Italy, while the agents decided how to proceed. In the meantime, Mazen was left alone, shackled aboard the boiling hot airplane overnight, while the agents rested comfortably in their hotel. The next morning, as they prepared to possibly return him to his U.S. prison, Mazen desperately implored them to attempt to take him to Lebanon, where he had a sister and a potential visa. Thus, their mission was fulfilled as they immediately took him to Beirut and handed him to officials at the airport. That was not the end of the ordeal, however, as Lebanese officials were angered that the Americans could simply "dump their cargo" on their soil without official permission or regard for the nation's sovereignty. In the weeks to come, Mazen would become a political pawn by various members of the Lebanese parliament who wished to denounce America's treatment of its Arab residents and the nations in the Middle East. And so, on August 24, 2002, Dr. Mazen al-Najjar's life in America came to a close, after nearly twenty-one years.

Academic Freedom Defended

Back in Florida, Sami's case was steadily moving through the court system with much progress. His lawyer had represented their side capably, and as a result most of the public and all responsible news media outlets seemed to have been drawn to the side of free speech and due process. More importantly, people began to empathize with Sami on a number of levels, including his religious and ethnic background. He was invited to a number of churches to speak about his Palestinian heritage and his Islamic faith. In addition, his activities on behalf of the Palestinian cause did not halt. He was one of the key figures involved in the recently launched divestment campaign, which sought to halt economic investment in companies that support the Israeli occupation. While the movement was centered among college students in campuses across the country, Dr. Sami al-Arian became a champion of the divestment efforts. He was a keynote speaker at each of the two annual national conferences, at the University of California at Berkeley and the University of Michigan at Ann Arbor. Indeed, as he was approaching his mid-40s, Sami believed that the future of institutional work would rest in the hands of the coming generation. Most people of his age group had given little regard to the community's youth, instead desiring control over national institutions themselves. Sami, on the other hand, became more and more a firm believer that leadership training and increased attention in general was necessary to continue the work that he and his peers had began. The hope and potential no longer lay with him or those of his generation, he surmised, but rather with the rise of a new generation of activists, Muslim and non-Muslim, Arab and non-Arab, and ultimately all American. He instituted a number of leadership seminars at campuses across the country, and was in the midst of founding a new institution, the Democratic Action Research and Training (DART), in late 2002.

Finally, on December 17, 2002, the U.S. district judge in the case against Sami by the University of South Florida ruled to dismiss the case, in another major victory by Dr. Al-Arian against his enemies. Indeed, it appeared likely that the university would lose the case in the days leading up to the decision, but it was used simply as a stalling tactic, in the hopes that the government would step in and aid the university out of its quagmire. By January, 2003, the university declined to appeal the decision against it, and was in the process of beginning arbitration proceedings with the professor. Asked whether he might be allowed to resume his teaching, the chairman of the trustees Dick Beard said, "I'm not even sure that's an option. It's not an option in my view."[16] It became clear from statements such as these that the university did not intend to simply welcome him back into the fold more than a year after the initial hysterical reaction to the O'Reilly interview. Indeed, the arbitration process was expected to last many months, possibly even years, according to most observers.

The Fall of Justice

On February 20, 2003, however, all of that would become a distant memory. That morning, federal agents, accompanied by a *Tampa Tribune* photographer, burst into his home and placed him under arrest. His youngest son

Ali awoke to see his father pushed against the wall with a gun placed to his head. That day will forever live in infamy as the climax of an unjust campaign that lasted nearly a decade. Along with Dr. Al-Arian, three other Palestinians were arrested: Sameeh Hamoudeh, a local community leader, PhD student at USF, and father of six, Hatim Fariz, another local community member, and Ghassan Ballut, an American citizen living in Chicago. The four of them were charged in a bloated 50-count indictment that alleges support of terrorism, specifically the Palestinian Islamic Jihad.

As he was led to the local jail, Sami looked into the many cameras, and said in his soft-spoken way, "It's all politics." Those three words accurately sum up the entire campaign against Dr. Sami al-Arian, and would only be further evinced by the developments of the day. That afternoon, Ashcroft held a press conference watched across the world, in which he announced the arrest of the "North American leader of the Palestinian Islamic Jihad."[17] He further gave credit to the Patriot Act for its help in giving investigators much expanded authority in the case, and continued to plug in the need for yet more such laws to further expand the provision of law enforcement powers. The 120-page document used in the arrest was meant simply to scare the rest of the community into silent submission. It detailed years of surveillance on Sami and the other individuals and on the activities of some of the institutions he founded and ran.

From that day, Sami began a hunger strike to protest his treatment as a political prisoner, for there was no real criminal case, only a highly political prosecution of an esteemed member of the Muslim community. The hunger strike lasted 150 days, as he only drank water and medication for his diabetes. In all, Sami lost over 45 pounds during this period. He ultimately ended his hunger strike upon the dismissal of his court-appointed attorneys and the beginning of his self-representation in July 2003. The bail hearing took place one month after the arrest, and lasted four days, during which time the government was supposed to present evidence that Sami was a flight risk or a threat to national security. Instead, the government introduced no evidence and no witnesses, but simply restated its allegations as they stood in the indictment. The defense, on the other hand, presented over twenty character witnesses on his behalf, from all aspects of his life, as a father, a professor, an activist, an imam, a friend, and so forth. The defense also presented evidence to begin countering some of the allegations in the indictment, while also proving that Sami has never fled in the face of such pressure, and as a Palestinian with only a permanent residency status in America, he was in no way able to travel outside of the country. Nonetheless, weeks later, U.S. Magistrate Pizzo, who was particularly taken by the government's side in the proceedings, ruled against granting Dr. Al-Arian and Sameeh Hammoudeh bail, while the two other detainees, both American citizens, were released.

Human Rights Denied

In the meantime, on March 27 federal marshals moved Dr. Al-Arian from the local jail in Tampa to a federal penitentiary in Coleman, Florida, a city roughly 75 miles north of Tampa. There, he was placed in the "Special Housing Unit," known as the "SHU," which is notorious for its conditions of confinement. The SHU is an area of the maximum-security wing, meant for the punishment of misbehaving inmates. It features the most atrocious living conditions, including solitary confinement in a tiny cell, and only one hour of recreation—in a slightly larger cage. These extremely punitive conditions were even harsher against Dr. Al-Arian than they were on the rest of the prison population. He was allowed only one 15-minute phone call *per month*, whereas other inmates were able to make more frequent calls. Even that privilege was suspended in June, after Sami used his phone call to his home to be connected via three-way with his son in England, apparently a violation of Coleman's policy. He was then punished for six months without being able to make a single phone call. In addition, visits were restricted only to immediate family members. A brother-in-law who came all the way from Egypt was not allowed to see him, despite persistent pleas to the prison's officials. Even visits are non-contact, behind glass, only giving them the ability to communicate through a telephone. Despite this, he was strip-searched before and after every visit, only as a method of humiliation by the prison guards. Medical attention was also severely restricted, while the treatment from the guards has been completely despicable, as they only refer to him as "murderer," or "terrorist," while constantly assaulting him both verbally and at times physically.

Aside from the humanitarian crisis of the Coleman facility, it also worked to severely hamper his case. The psychological torture inflicted upon him by the severe conditions would make it impossible for him to adequately address his case. As the only pre-trial detainees in the entire facility, Hammoudeh and Al-Arian were consistently treated as though they were convicted criminals themselves. Access to evidence was extremely limited, as it resided in Tampa. Then, after taking on his own defense in July, 2003, Sami was still not given the adequate attention despite the fact that he was his only attorney. Rather than pencils, he would be given one-inch pieces of lead with which to write legal motions. With no access to a copy machine, he proceeded to hand-write six copies to submit to the court. Guards would deny him additional pieces of lead for days and sometimes weeks at a time. Furthermore, he was repeatedly denied access to the law library, and even the ability to appear at his own hearings when they were held in Tampa. It was clear from all of these moves by the government, in coordination with the U.S. marshal service and the prison officials, that they meant to psychologically destroy Professor Al-Arian and any chance he might have to emerge triumphant in his case. His family suffered tremendously from this loss, and continues to feel the abuse from the prison officials during each visit. In addition, all the families have suffered from the loss of their sole breadwinner, and have had to depend on the community's help and that of extended family simply to meet basic needs.

Orwell in America

The reaction of the community to the arrests on February 20, 2003, was one of stunned silence. This was the most publicized of all the cases against Muslims in America, and yet there was no resounding cry against the government's actions. On the contrary, most communities were in a state of utter disbelief, shock, fear, and paranoia. In effect, Ashcroft's strategy worked to perfection. From that day on, the community has been in a state of complete debilitation and unable to act in any way to defend against this injustice. Nationally, the major Muslim organizations, under the cloud of suspicion themselves for their various lawful activities, could barely issue a statement supporting Dr. Al-Arian's right to a fair trial. In due time, however, an effort was made to begin organizing toward his case as well as others. In April, 2003, a meeting of concerned leaders and individuals in Washington, D.C., launched the creation of the National Liberty Fund, an organization devoted to raising awareness of the growing cases against Muslim leaders and helping support them throughout the process. An attorney was acquired to take the case, the prominent Bill Moffitt, along with his partner Hank Asbill and the capable veteran Linda Moreno, a local attorney in Tampa who had worked closely with the case since the bond hearing. Together the legal team began, as of October 2003, to fight the case in Florida's federal court.

The Case Continues

While progress in the case as well as Dr. Al-Arian's conditions have been hampered due to a one-sided and bigoted magistrate, their work showed some modest immediate results. In December, 2003, a scandal rocked the case as it was revealed that the search warrants from the

1995 searches were lost. The government explained that the records were shredded and destroyed years earlier, leaving no original documents intact. By January, 2004, attorneys were only beginning to piece together the evidence and make important demands of the government. A January 21 hearing, in which defense attorneys called for the indictment to be thrown out, featured an eloquent Moffitt decrying the charges as politically motivated attacks to silence freedom of expression. Dr. Al-Arian's persecution was compared to the "banning" of figures in South Africa's Apartheid regime.

Unfortunately, however, for nearly an entire year, the government's pressure yielded many awful results as the defenseless Sami lingered in prison for months without proper representation. In April, Judge Moody denied his constitutional right to a speedy trial by setting the court date for January, 2005—nearly two years after the arrest! This was in response to the prosecution, which stated that it was nowhere near ready to present a case against him. In addition, attorneys appointed by the court in March were extremely lacking in their representation of Sami, as they frequently took action contrary to his wishes and to a successful defense. At one point, they even made an appearance on the "O'Reilly Factor," the show that has arguably been the cause of this current nightmare. Even after they were dismissed, however, the rulings in the case have been very detrimental to a fair trial process. In September, 2003, Moody ruled that the defendants and their attorneys could not share the contents of any of the evidence with anyone, including potential witnesses and family members. This was despite the fact that much of the audio surveillance recordings were likely to be exculpatory to Sami and ultimately vindicate him. The media, led by the *Tampa Tribune*, has continued to poison the minds of its readers, which is especially harmful now, given that it is the jury pool from which those who will decide Sami's fate will emerge. Headlines continue to appear almost daily, treating the government's unfounded accusations as fact, while dismissing any defense offered by Sami, his supporters, and his lawyers.

The local community, stunned by the events, did not know how to respond. Most of the members of the Islamic Community of Tampa received intimidating visits from FBI agents, meant to stem any support that Dr. Al-Arian might receive. Again, these tactics proved effective as the community remained virtually silent in the days following the arrests, and only months later began to mobilize into action. Outside of the Muslim community, Sami's many friendships with other groups and individuals proved extremely important, as members of Christian and activist groups came to his support from the onset, writing letters to newspapers and staging modest rallies for him and information sessions on his case. Major organizations also began to take part. In July, Amnesty International wrote a strong letter condemning the conditions of confinement in Coleman Penitentiary, calling them "gratuitously punitive."[18] The letter received much positive press coverage nationally, and even generated editorials demanding that those oppressive conditions be removed, and that he be given full access to the evidence and a real chance at a fair trial.[19] The American Civil Liberties Union also became increasingly interested in the case, and has signaled a willingness to become involved as it progresses into the courts. Nationally, the Muslim community began to show signs of concern and warmly welcomed the National Liberty Fund (NLF) leaders into their towns for fundraising and information sessions. While the present level of involvement must still grow, these early signs are somewhat encouraging.

Ultimately, Sami's case has become the embodiment of the survival of Islam in the United States. He was targeted not for his acts as an individual, but for the effects of his work on a whole community of people. As a foremost leader across a vast array of issues, ranging from justice for Palestinians and the advancement of a peaceful and progressive intellectual dialogue between the Middle East and the West, to the restoration of civil rights for Americans and the pursuit of political empowerment for America's Muslim minority, he has indeed been a groundbreaking pioneer, a one-of-a-kind leader and a model for others to follow. It was because of this that he was targeted, and because he was targeted all of those movements have effectively come to a complete screeching halt. But, while turbulent times have now come to pass, and indeed, lie ahead for years to come, it is ultimately incumbent upon all those who truly speak of justice, equality, and peace to now stand up for those values as they have come under the most severe attack by those who would have them removed. The life of Dr. Sami al-Arian suggests that he would be the first to act during this time, no matter who the victim, and it is because of this fact that he was chosen to languish in prison. To be certain, justice will one day be served, but only once America fulfills its promise to Dr. Al-Arian and all Americans to uphold the values for which it was founded. ∎

PROFILE: AMBASSADOR OF GOOD WILL

Abdurahman Alamoudi

- Founder, American Muslim Council (AMC), 1990
- National Islamic Prison Foundation
- Founder, American Muslim Foundation, 2000
- Goodwill Ambassador, U.S. State Department

It is painful that after 15 years of work to improve Muslim participation in the U.S. government, to improve daily life and help immigrants adjust to this country, to improve the image of the United States with Arabs and Muslims abroad, I am jailed in my own country by my own government on the basis of one sentence spoken years ago in another language to a different audience—badly translated and taken radically out of context.

—Abdurahman Alamoudi, *Washington Post*,
December 12, 2003.

• Abdurahman Alamoudi participates in an international conference in Cairo.

From Bridges to Barriers:
The Case of Abdurahman Alamoudi

Prominent legal activists have characterized the arrest of Abdurahman Alamoudi as a case of selective prosecution driven by political motives. There is great concern among legal and civil rights activists that this case is being tried in the media. The techniques include a misrepresentation of Alamoudi's character, the deliberate omission of the outstanding contributions he has made to the Muslim community and to his country, and the denial of his right to the presumption of innocence through the use of guilt-by-association tactics.

—MAS Freedom Foundation, October 2, 2003.

On September 29, 2003, the state of the American Muslim community descended into uncharted depths at the hands of an out of control government body. Early that morning, as he returned to the United States from abroad, Abdurahman Alamoudi was arrested at Dulles International Airport in northern Virginia. This incident came as such a severe blow to Muslims everywhere because of who this man is and everything he represents. Alamoudi was the premier American Muslim activist on the national and even international level. He was years ahead of his time in everything he did, and accomplished in one decade what no other person could do in a lifetime. Moreover, the unremitting institution-builder, as Alamoudi had been, was also known as the voice of moderation from among American Muslims, one who not only preached tolerance and unity among different faiths, cultures, and peoples, but who also devoted every moment of his life to achieving it. Indeed, the arrest of Alamoudi was a stark signal to the Muslim community in the United States that all bets were off and that there was in fact a war on America's Muslims and their institutions led by many powerful forces in government and the media.

Early Life

Abdurahman Alamoudi was born on March 19, 1952, in Asmara, Eritrea. His mother was Eritrean and his father was of Yemeni descent. Coming from a merchant family, Alamoudi lived comfortably in his Asmara home as part of a large family, with nine siblings. From a young age, Abdurahman held a fascination for the United States. He followed the 1960 presidential election and was elated with the victory of John F. Kennedy. During the celebration, he took a trip to the American library in Asmara to learn more about the country that so interested him. Three years later, when President Kennedy was assassinated, schools in Asmara were cancelled and the entire country was grieving. Abdurahman recalls many being in tears. Kennedy had been a symbol of hope for a better and brighter future, not only for his own citizens, but for all people of the world. From his youth, Abdurahman had a fiery optimism that would mark his character throughout his life. His best childhood friend was an Eritrean Jewish boy. In 1965, Abdurahman recalls that the two talked of accomplishing great things in their lives. His friend dreamed of becoming "president of the Jews," while Abdurahman would become "president of the Arabs," and the two would ensure that their people lived together in peace and harmony.

Relations between Arabs and Jews were considerably better in Asmara than other places in the Middle East until the 1967 Arab-Israeli war. The regional tension spread dramatically, and Abdurahman remembers the steady influx of Palestinian refugees into Eritrea, where their lives would be marked by incredible hardship and suffering. His family tried to help in any way they could. Abdurahman's father would receive mail from Palestinians in the Occupied Territories, which he would then forward to their families in Jordan and elsewhere, as a free service. Abdurahman himself was very affected by the events he had witnessed and the Palestinian predicament would always hold a very special place in his heart.

He had also come to be aware of the struggle of the Eritrean people against the brutal dictatorship ruling their country. Haili Selassi was the source of much pain and anguish for all Eritreans. The tense political climate of the time, complete with its lack of basic freedoms and rights, quickly brought Abdurahman into the realities of the world. In 1968, he went to live in Saudi Arabia, where his older brothers had moved years earlier. There he would be exposed to the origins of his Islamic faith and the traditional Arab society prevalent in their culture. A year later, his older brother Hussein would send him to Egypt to attend college.

Life in Cairo would have a profound influence on

Abdurahman. The spiritual, intellectual, and political climate of the time was both vibrant and turbulent. It was in Cairo that Abdurahman became more closely dedicated to his faith and began to exercise the limited political expression allowed by the Egyptian government to articulate his concern for various Islamic causes. Within a short period of time, he became active in the university's various student groups, including the Eritrean Union and various other foreign student clubs. He would attend conferences and lectures and became engrossed in the events of his time and the issues facing the collective body of Muslims across the globe. A more personal tragic event would come to mark the middle of this period in Alamoudi's life. In 1976, he received word in Cairo that his father had been killed. In the midst of the ongoing turmoil in Eritrea, Asmara was under curfew. A gang of men disguised in military uniforms entered their home that night and attempted to abduct him. When he resisted, they killed him. This traumatic experience would haunt the family for years. None of his siblings would remain in Eritrea for long. The whole family has since moved to Saudi Arabia, while one of his brothers settled in Yemen.

The Land of Opportunity

After ten years in Cairo, Alamoudi left the confines of Egypt for the United States, a nation he had long admired and dreamed of knowing firsthand. Alamoudi arrived on American shores in 1979, went first briefly to Chicago and then to Boston, where he would pursue a master's degree in biochemistry at Boston University. Almost immediately, he recognized opportunities of a social and political nature that could foster further integration of Muslims within American civic society. There was clearly a need for American Muslims to organize themselves as a community, but also to participate in all aspects of American civic life. As a longtime admirer of the United States, Alamoudi was quick to adapt to his new cultural surroundings and accept the many things his adopted country had to offer, as opposed to many of his fellow immigrant Muslims who rejected much of what America represented and instead chose to isolate themselves in their cocoons. This swift embrace of American ideals and values brought about a maturity and sense of understanding in Abdurahman Alamoudi that many of his colleagues would not develop until many years later.

Alamoudi completed his graduate work at Northeastern University, where he was awarded his MBA. In 1996, he became a naturalized American citizen. Meanwhile, he was forging important relationships with likeminded individuals from within the Muslim community, many of whom were the bright young men who would become the future leaders of the American Muslim community. In graduate school, Alamoudi was an active member of the Muslim Students Association (MSA), through which he met many who would graduate from American universities and assume very important positions back home in their own countries, both in the Arab and Muslim nations. For a number of years, he worked with the SAAR Foundation, a charitable organization that oversaw a number of important projects. While Alamoudi was certainly involved in the early institution-building that saw the emergence of many of America's mosques, schools, and charitable and social organizations, he was always one step ahead of the rest of his peers. His commitment to the vision of becoming integrated as a community into the American political landscape led him to establish the American Muslim Council (AMC) in Washington, D.C., in 1990. Considered the first national Islamic political institution in the United States, its purpose was to organize and motivate the Muslim community in America to honor their civic responsibilities and get involved in local, state, and federal politics. Alamoudi would often say that each American Muslim has a duty to share civic responsibilities, and that they should work jointly with Americans of other faiths for the betterment of all.

Becoming a Leader

Serving as AMC's first executive director, Alamoudi would accomplish a great number of things in only a few short years. His work spanned a wide variety of issue areas, including human rights and humanitarian assistance, civic involvement, interfaith dialogue, promoting peace, and protecting civil rights. From the beginning of the crisis in Bosnia, the AMC relayed the concerns of the Muslim community about the Balkans war to the Administration, Congress, and the media. The AMC created the American Task Force for Bosnia. In addition, it coordinated efforts with other organizations seeking an end to the slaughter of Bosnian Muslims who were left defenseless by a U.S.-U.N. embargo, while Serbia and Croatia around them were well armed and using those arms against Bosnia. As the crisis in the horn of Africa unfolded, the AMC headed a Somalia relief effort. It also joined the efforts of Churches for Middle East Peace, a broad ecumenical coalition, and the

Jerusalem Coalition, a multi-ethnic group, focusing on the issues of occupation, dislocation, and economic strangulation which adversely affect the possibility of a just and lasting peace in the Middle East. Indeed, it was the AMC and Alamoudi's activity on behalf of this latter cause that would draw the ire of powerful Zionist groups seeking to maintain their hold over American policy in the region.

Alamoudi, however, would use such hurdles only to push further for integration and coalition building, especially in the area of interfaith dialogue. In 1991, the AMC and the Muslim World League cosponsored a historic two-day conference between Muslim and Catholic leaders at the Washington Retreat House. This was the first national consultation between the National Conference of Catholic Bishops (NCCB) and Muslim leaders. The AMC would also become an active member of Interfaith Impact for Peace and Justice, a coalition of mainline Protestant groups and a number of non-Christian organizations. Concerned about the social challenges faced by Muslims, the AMC held an interfaith round table on Muslims in America, which encouraged interfaith collaboration and called for a common strategy among different religious groups to combat cultural prejudice. Recognizing the stereotypes it faced externally from American society as well as the internal challenges from within its own community, the AMC issued a joint statement with the National Conference of Catholic Bishops (NCCB) in 1993 rejecting all efforts to claim religious sanction for acts of aggression and terrorism. In 1994, the AMC hosted an interfaith luncheon entitled, "The Religious Freedom Restoration Act and Religious Accommodation in America: A Discussion Among Religious Groups," featuring speakers from the Muslim, Christian, and Jewish perspectives.

In the political arena, the Council was successful in fostering strong relationships with members of Congress. After years of hard work, members of Congress began to realize that American Muslims had come of age. Alamoudi's groundbreaking achievements did not go unnoticed. Official and popular Arab and Islamic delegations began to converge from all over the world on Washington, D.C., to visit the AMC and discuss Islamic affairs with American Muslims. Alamoudi was also recognized as the most qualified Muslim leader in Washington who could explain Islamic life in America and the challenges facing American Muslims. His efforts were a shining portrayal of the Islamic teachings of peace among peoples and nations, universal human rights, and tolerance for all religions and cultures. His great success brought him to meet with former President Clinton on several occasions, as well as George W. Bush during the 2000 presidential campaign. It was his enduring commitment to his vision together with the efforts of other Muslim and Arab organizations that influenced the White House under both Presidents Clinton and Bush to acknowledge Ramadan and other Islamic holidays. A postage stamp commemorating the Islamic holiday of Eid was issued in 2001, thanks to the original initiative of the Oklahoma-born convert, Aminah Assilmi, and to the tremendous efforts by the American Muslim Council.

Alamoudi believed not only in working together with other religious communities toward the same goals, but in helping others in the civil rights struggle to protect all Americans. He frequently contended that the Muslim community in the United States would never be accepted as long it was perceived as exclusively focused on its narrow interests, rather than the broad issue areas that concerned the entire society. The AMC endorsed on an annual basis the activities of World Food Day,

Neighbors Who Care (a group for victim's rights), Southern Poverty Law Center, the Center for Constitutional Rights, Children's Defense Fund, Emergency Medical Care for Children, and Green Door (a group providing vocational support for the mentally ill). It also worked consistently with the Coalition for the Free Exercise of Religion, a uniquely diverse and inclusive coalition of American faith communities, resulting in the passage of the Religious Freedom Restoration Act (RFRA) in 1993. Another supported program was the National Islamic Prison Foundation (NIPF). Because of the pressing needs of the estimated 100,000 Muslims who have converted while in prison, and are still serving sentences, or who are re-entering society after incarceration, the AMC supported the launching of the NIPF in the fall of 1993.

As the civil liberties climate in America worsened in the mid-1990s, the AMC became a leading organization in combating the abuses against the community. It had a longstanding relationship with the Immigration Coalition especially following the developments in immigration reform legislation in 1995. The anti-terrorism law passed in 1996 would be the community's main challenge for years to come. With the signing of The Antiterrorism and Effective Death Penalty Act, the government approved the use of secret evidence. Because those incarcerated under this law were ultimately all released without trial or deported, the law eventually proved itself to be nothing more than a targeted harassment of the Muslim community. In its early stages, however, and the selective placement of nearly thirty individuals from across the country behind bars, much of the Muslim leadership was weary of involving itself in their defense. Abdurahman Alamoudi proved himself to be an exception to the general culture of apprehension that plagued ordinary American Muslims. While initial efforts had begun only at the initiative of Professor Sami al-Arian in Florida, without the backing of the community's institutions such efforts would have been fruitless. The American Muslim Council, specifically through Alamoudi's involvement, was one of the first groups to engage itself in the civil rights crisis sparked by secret evidence. It helped launch the massive lobbying effort in Congress that resulted in the introduction in the House of Representatives of a bill to repeal the use of secret evidence. With Alamoudi's support, the AMC would continue to keep civil rights concerns as a top priority for years to come. There came a realization that its true mission to achieve political empowerment for Muslims could not come to pass while such widespread abuses were still allowed to persist.

Alamoudi also pushed the American Muslim Council to be one of the most progressive and free-thinking Muslim organizations in the country. One of the pioneering programs attributed to the AMC was integrating several civic and social community programs into a more or less centralized activity or coordinated function. Among those programs was Muslim Military Members (MMM). The AMC first met with Col. Meredith R. Stanley, Executive Director of the U.S. Armed Forces Board of Chaplains to ascertain the status of Muslim GIs in the Persian Gulf area. The issue of the pressing need for Muslim chaplains was also discussed. As the AMC's Executive Director, Abdurahman Alamoudi joined MMM in an extensive tour of military bases on the East Coast in September, 1993, meeting with Muslim service men and women and members of the military chaplains corp. Alamoudi continued this work through an organization called the American Muslim Armed Forces and Veterans Affairs Council. This prestigious group became recognized by the Pentagon to select and instruct Muslim military chaplains. While Alamoudi's efforts in this regard were important, they would later come into question in the post-9/11 hysteria that swept the country, and especially in various sectors of the federal government.

Challenges Arise

In the summer of 2003, U.S. military officials apprehended a Muslim chaplain, James Yee, on suspicion of espionage. Yee worked at the American military base in Guantanamo Bay, where prisoners of the Afghanistan war were being held. He was accused of taking sensitive materials from the base, charges he denied. As has become customary in all such cases in recent years, Yee would remain imprisoned at a naval base for months without ever seeing his day in court. Of significance to this story, however, is the fact that Yee was ordained as a chaplain by the American Muslim Armed Forces and Veterans Affairs Council, under the tutelage of Alamoudi. The press, in its usual jingoistic fashion, proceeded to link the two men in some fictitious terror plot, though no evidence had been presented toward the guilt of Yee, let alone to some sinister association between the two men. In fact, Alamoudi has never seen or met him and the two men do not know each other. That, however, did not stop two opportunistic pro-Israeli senators, Jon Kyl and Charles Schumer, from capitalizing on the event to question the Pentagon's practices when choosing organizations to select Muslim chaplains. "It is remarkable that people who have known connections to terrorism are the only people to approve these chaplains," Kyl said. Schumer vowed to launch an investigation into the matter, claiming that the Pentagon had given these "extremists," referring to Alamoudi's group and the Islamic Society of North America, the largest Islamic organization in the country, "a monopoly on who becomes an imam in the military."[20]

This incident is entirely representative of every attack ever launched on Alamoudi. His lifelong efforts to promote peace, progress, unity, and harmony among faiths, cultures, nations, and fellow citizens would be continuously mischaracterized and misrepresented by those who wish to destroy his efforts.

Throughout the 1990s, Alamoudi developed strong relationships with policy-makers and statesmen. He could frequently be seen meeting with important members of Congress, ambassadors, and other people in high office. Politicians, advisers, and think-tanks in the corridors of power in Washington, after years of hard work and devotion by Muslims, began to realize that American Muslims had finally come of age. The AMC was the first Muslim forum in the United States interested in providing a positive image of America to the Arab and Muslim worlds. Official and popular Arab and Muslim delegations began to converge from all over the world to Washington, D.C., and visit the AMC to discuss Muslim affairs with American Muslims. Alamoudi was the best man in town to explain Muslim life in America and the role of Islam and the varied experiences of Muslims inside the United States. Reflecting on their interactions following Alamoudi's arrest, Congressman Tom Davis (R-VA), Chairman of the District Committee that governs the nation's capital, wrote:

> I have known Mr. Alamoudi and met with him
> on several occasions. I believe that he will want

to aggressively defend himself in a judicial system that he has helped to promote amongst his community. He has led this same community as an advocate of Arab and Muslim issues, promoting active participation of each member in local, state, and national government. He has helped to establish Arab and Muslim confidence in the political system.[21]

Alamoudi reflected a positive image of the United States to Arab and Muslim delegations. This may have contributed to his making his way into the White House itself, where he met with former president Clinton on many occasions. Now the agenda of Islam figured into the decision-making process at both the White House and the State Department, where Islamic holidays and other occasions were now visible. He even came to be named as "good will ambassador" by the State Department. Letters went out to the Muslim community during the Clinton era that assured Muslims of their acceptance on an equal basis with other Americans. It would be fair to say that the efforts of Alamoudi and the AMC cultivated a positive image of America among the Muslims of the United States during the years when Clinton was in office.

A Zionist Dartboard

He was a centerpiece in bridging the gap between the previously disenfranchised American Muslim community and its political leaders. Alamoudi worked to close that gap by working with leaders to open up toward the community and begin to recognize it as a potential political force, one with manifest needs and concerns. He also worked closely to mobilize the community toward involvement, appearing frequently at events before large crowds at Islamic centers, mosques, banquets, lectures, and even protest rallies. With the increased success and rising eminence of Alamoudi as a national leader, he became a frequent target by some forces wishing to destroy his credibility and burn the bridges he had made with American political and religious leaders. Pro-Israeli stalwarts wrote a series of provocative articles in many newspapers and journals against Alamoudi. These media formats are well known for their anti-Muslim and anti-Islamic prejudice and bigotry. Such notorious writers as Steven Emerson and Daniel Pipes took to the *Wall Street Journal*, the *New York Post*, the *Washington Times*, and the Jewish *Forward* to fan their accusations. They went on the air using *Fox News* to broadcast their anti-Islamic hype. Eventually, this pro-Israeli campaign succeeded in building up enough pressure to have the American administration stop Alamoudi from continuing his peaceful and humanitarian work in preserving the image of a lenient and open-minded America in which Muslims may grow into their civil duties and responsibilities. Alamoudi's mission and efforts to build a bridge of understanding and mutual exchange between American leaders and the Muslim community was being relentlessly undercut.

As the Zionist sledgehammer came down, Alamoudi had to leave his position as the executive director of the AMC, although he continued to be helpful and supportive of its activities as a member. The Zionist nexus began to scrutinize Alamoudi to find any mistake or technicality suitable to condemn him to the political gallows. If this were not possible, they at least sought to put him in a permanent political freeze. These forces brought their eyes and ears to watch and listen to Alamoudi when he spoke at rallies or public occasions that protested certain American foreign policies or supported certain human rights causes. Ultimately, speaking out on behalf of the Palestinians would signal his final death knell, as Alamoudi would be branded a supporter of terrorism, a favorite attack lobbed by Israel's supporters.

It was one such rally that would come back to haunt Alamoudi after his statements were continuously exploited to smear and defame him. On October 28, 2000, Alamoudi was among a number of prominent speakers who addressed a rally on behalf of the Palestinian cause. The issue of Palestine is near and dear to the hearts of all Muslims in America, and usually cited as a primary concern in meetings with political leaders, especially given the American government's role in perpetuating the atrocities committed by Israel. In this rally, staged in front of the White House, speakers gave fiery statements, especially in light of the Al-Aqsa Intifada, which was entering its second month. Alamoudi proceeded to express his outrage at the events in the Middle East, and explained that all Muslims have a duty to support their brethren in the fight for freedom. As was obvious to all, the movement to end the unjust Israeli occupation was being led by Islamic groups, whose goal of bringing a just and lasting peace Alamoudi made clear that he supported. Therefore, he continued, all Muslims were "supporters of Hamas …[and] Hezbollah."[22]

This statement has since been used by the agenda-driven pundits to completely discredit Alamoudi, as though all that he stands for in speech and in action could be completely wiped away with one sentence. Every article published mentioning Alamoudi has attempted to label him a "terrorist-supporter" in a deliberate attempt to drive a wedge between him and the many friends he has made from within the government, Christian, Jewish, and civil rights leaders, and even to alienate him from his own community.[23] These efforts have had mixed success. Within the government, a number of political leaders were heavily pressured by the pro-Israel lobby to disavow any ties to Alamoudi, pointing constantly to his statement as a sign of extremism and fanaticism. In the 2000 election, Hillary Clinton was pressured into returning a $1000 contribution by Alamoudi, after her opponent for the New York Senate seat, Rick Lazio, referred to the contributions as "blood money."[24] Similarly, Senator Arlen Specter (R-PA), in a speech at the AMC conference, chastised its association with someone who espouses such "extreme" points of view.

The vicious assault against Alamoudi was enough to successfully place him in a political freeze with regard to his relationships with members of government. It was a severe blow for all American Muslims that such a charismatic, articulate, and benevolent human being who had made advancements for the entire community by leaps and bounds could be cast aside in this way. The resilient Alamoudi, however, would not allow these attacks to stifle his activism. He recognized the need for more widespread activism and the building of programs and infrastructure within the Muslim community. By strengthening the community from its roots, he reasoned, it could perhaps endeavor to come back much stronger following the widespread attacks against it. With that vision, he had established the American Muslim Foundation (AMF), a group dedicated to promoting important Islamic work in America. Through the AMF, and his involvement with a number of other Islamic institutions in the Washington, D.C., area, Alamoudi fulfilled many of the basic needs of the Muslim community.

In the New World

In the aftermath of September 11, 2001, the entire Muslim community was under attack from all directions, and Alamoudi was one of the most vocal and active American Muslim leaders attempting to rekindle the warm relations between the community and their fellow Americans. He also actively supported the Bush administration's response to the attacks, including the decision to invade Afghanistan and bring to justice those responsible. Alamoudi responded to the persecution of Muslims in America and to the widespread detentions and unlawful searches and harassments by law enforcement officials that followed from the passage of the mislabeled Patriot Act by arguing that the community was in desperate need for leadership. He took it upon himself, along with a few others, to use his position of prominence and that of his organization to develop support networks and active organizations on behalf of those targeted individuals and people who have been arrested unjustly and denied due process.

Though he recognized that his strong leadership and the ire he had incurred from many Zionist groups over the years had made him a vulnerable target, he could not have guessed his fate on September 29, 2003. In late summer, Alamoudi traveled abroad to the Middle East, which he was fond of visiting over the years, developing important relationships toward his work and visiting immediate and distant family. Upon his return, Alamoudi was swarmed by government agents who took him into custody. Later he was charged with defying the Libyan sanctions by visiting the country and accepting funds from a Libya-based charity organization. Moreover, the government attempted to assert that the $340,000 he accepted were intended to be distributed to terrorist organizations in Syria, another country he was to visit after stopping in Britain, where British authorities confiscated the funds. Alamoudi vehemently denies such charges, and has contended that the money was for the AMF, among many other Muslim organizations in the United States, all of which are dependent on foreign contributions due to a constant shortage of domestic fundraising.

The obscure charges against him, which have clearly been applied selectively in this case, considering the hundreds of thousands of Americans who travel to countries, such as Cuba, each year, in spite of U.S. sanctions, have opened up a new angle to Alamoudi's activism over the years, one that is often missing from his record as a domestic leader of American Muslims. In actuality, he had also worked prominently to build bridges between American leaders and the Muslim world. As Mahdi Bray, head of the MAS Freedom Foundation, asserts, "The arrest of Abdurahman Alamoudi, a Muslim leader, activist, and former goodwill ambassador to Muslim countries in former President Bill Clinton's administration, is the most recent example of the government's targeting of Muslim organizations, activists, and institutions."[25]

The Libya Connection

After a decade of appearing on television screens in America and the Arab world, Alamoudi was in effect a spokesman for

• Photo-Op: From L to R, Alamoudi, President Qaddafi, and Shaykh Yousef al-Qaradawi.

• Alexandria, Virginia, jail where Abdurahman Alamoudi is being detained pending his trial.

• Attorney Stanley Cohen speaks about his client's case at a press conference in front of the jail.

American Muslims and a symbol of their continuing struggle for social and political equality. These efforts earned him invitations to participate in Muslim activities across the globe, especially conferences addressing the need for interfaith dialogue and cultural coexistence, which take place on occasion in various Arab, Muslim, and Western capitals. The latest of these worldwide events in which Alamoudi appeared was a conference in the Libyan capital of Tripoli in August, 2003, under the heading "Getting to Know One Another."[26]   In attendance were numerous personalities of fame from various countries in both the Muslim and Christian worlds. One of the main purposes of the conferences was to establish a solid Muslim-Christian front in the face of the growing threat of global terrorism that required a united stand from members of all faiths. After the conference, which yielded a powerful statement signed by all the attendees, Alamoudi went to Yemen to visit family, before proceeding to Syria, where his wife and children were staying at a family home. Upon his return to the United States, Alamoudi was arrested at Dulles International Airport in Washington. He was initially charged with making an illegal visit to Libya and accepting funds from there, contrary to the strict Libyan sanctions passed under President Ronald Reagan in 1986.

Much of this situation centers on the Libyan government's attempt to resolve its long-term quarrel with the Libyan Muslim Brotherhood. These high-level discussions have been ongoing for over four years, and Mr. Alamoudi has been at their margins, dealing with the Libyan representative to the United Nations, Ambassador Abu Zaid Omar Durda. Abdurahman Alamoudi met with the envoy of Libya's permanent mission to the United Nations in

Washington, D.C., at the Woodrow Wilson Center for Political Studies three years ago. The Libyan representative participated in the seminar. The two men had a conversation with regard to Libyan political detainees. Alamoudi had received some petitions to intervene on their behalf in the hopes of releasing them, as some of them were very qualified individuals in their fields and graduates of the United States.

Durda promised Alamoudi to discuss the matter of the detainees with the Libyan authorities. Durda is a well respected and a well-known Libyan politician as he is a former prime minister. Furthermore, Durda promised Alamoudi to facilitate the return of Libyans wishing to return home despite some "security" reservations on them by the Libyan authorities. Alamoudi's efforts proved to be very fruitful as Durda did intervene on their behalf, resulting in the release of hundreds of political prisoners. Though others still remain imprisoned, the Qaddafi International Charitable Organization also promised to intervene on their behalf and close this matter once and for all. Alamoudi further solicited the assistance of well-known Islamic figures such as Shaykh Yousef al Qaradawi who promised to do his utmost best and discuss the fate of the detainees with the Libyan leader, Muamar Qaddafi.

Alamoudi's relationship with Libya involves two dimensions. The first deals with large-scale Islamic activism and the effort to unify Muslim minorities in the West often by seeking assistance from many sources, including the Islamic Call Society, a philanthropic organization based in Tripoli but with a widespread following throughout Asia, Africa, and Europe. Through the Islamic Call Society, Alamoudi received invitations to participate in various activities to address the status of Muslims in America and to exchange experiences with other leaders from minority Muslim countries in Europe and elsewhere in the interest of learning from other communities' successes and failures. The second dimension is humanitarian in nature and deals with Alamoudi's efforts toward freeing political prisoners in Libya who had languished in prison for years in many cases, and were in need of a benefactor to reopen their case and help attain their release. In what modest capacity he could, Alamoudi attempted to help some of these individuals.

There is a possible third dimension of Alamoudi's trips to Libya, the details to which very few people have been privy. This essentially involved efforts by Alamoudi to end the stalemate in U.S.-Libyan relations, which would be to the benefit of both governments, as well as the Muslim community in America. As is common knowledge, American investment in Libya has dried up completely in the past two decades, while Libyan assets in the United States have been frozen by the government, all due to the sanctions imposed on Libya since the 1980s. A staunch advocate of this continued policy of hostility and isolation has been the Zionist lobby, with its unprecedented influence in the halls of Congress and the administration.

Alamoudi tried to find a bridge between the two countries in order to end the soured relations by imploring American political leaders to revisit the matter and consider the benefits of a positive solution. But the size of the problem appeared too large even for Alamoudi to solve single-handedly. It required years of persistent devotion, especially in the face of Israeli opposition to improving relations with Libya, which would provide Libyan leader Muamar Qaddafi an elevated platform from which to support the Palestinian struggle.

Of Alamoudi's many activities, there was one that did not make it into any headlines or onto the radar of much of the American Muslim community. This was his effort to develop a committee of American Muslim leaders whose purpose was to improve relations between Islamists and a host of Arab governments who have traditionally been at odds. This initiative called for a show of good will by both parties to allow Islamic organizations greater freedom in the Arab world, to build infrastructure, provide social services, and operate within the accepted boundaries of national institutions in pursuit of their interests, while such groups would cease the hostile anti-governmental rhetoric and the forceful methods that they had practiced to achieve their political goals, which included terrorism. Another goal of this endeavor was to calm the rising tensions on the Arab and Muslim street against America, which had been fomenting violent sentiments for many years, but especially at the dawn of the 21st century. Alamoudi's vision was to create a cultural, regional, and interfaith exchange among leading religious, political, and intellectual figures in the Muslim world with their counterparts in the United States. It was hoped that this could lead to a better understanding of the deep divisions and causes of hatred and animosity, while searching for effective mechanisms to bridge the divide. These initiatives were addressed by the American Muslim Council under Alamoudi's stewardship in the early 1990s, culminating in an international conference in October, 1993, entitled "Islam and the West: Dialogue not Confrontation." In attendance at this conference were a number of prominent Muslim leaders, along with notable American political leaders and academics. It was an important opportunity for them to meet, consult one another, and come to some understanding with regard to a number of key issues, some of them so complex that they required a continued dialogue.

Following the events of September 11, the old fears and apprehensions rose to the fore once again, as the Muslim community was targeted and harassed, but with special emphasis on the leaders, who were often in the spotlight and on the frontlines in the battle against Islam and Islamic institutions by some forces in society. It was here that Alamoudi's efforts to bring peaceful understanding between sides was undermined by the rash intolerance and widespread prejudice that became standard practice against Muslims in the United States as well as across the ocean in response to the Zionist lobby's influence in the mass media. Such desperate times called for an even more aggressive sector of society to arise and challenge the control recently exerted by neo-conservatives in American policy. Proposals were put forth for a conference in Europe similar to the one that took place in 1993, where leaders from the Muslim world and the West could come together and devise ways to avoid an all-out confrontation waged by the extremists from both sides.

Many of Alamoudi's travels were devoted to convincing Muslim leaders abroad to commit to the interfaith dialogue with figures in the West as being in the interests of all people and as a way to avert a conflict that would lead only to the destruction of all societies. As a witness to some of these meetings myself, I have noted that the heated exchanges among all those concerned usually resulted in agreement on a few key issues. The first was the threat posed by terrorism and the thought of extremist groups, such as Al-Qaida, to mainstream political Islam and the future of Islamic institutions in the West. It was always Alamoudi's position that it was incumbent upon all Muslim thinkers and activists to face the threat of this extremist ideology head-on and combat it internally so that it does not take hold on the mainstream Arab and Muslim street. He called for an emergency summit of Muslim leaders from across the world specifically to address this issue and produce recommendations to be implemented by Islamic movements and enacted into their basic creeds. At the head of these movements was the Muslim Brotherhood, which accounts for over 80 percent of Islamic activism in the Middle East.

Alamoudi's position allotted him the opportunity to meet with most of the Arab rulers and political leaders throughout the Muslim world. He always received the respect and admiration of those he met. He even had a meeting with the Libyan leader following his attendance at the Islamic Call Society summit in Tripoli. The first question posed to Alamoudi by Qaddafi was about the state of Muslims in America, to which Alamoudi responded by listing the many accomplishments Muslims had achieved in the previous decade in politics and the mass media. He pointed out, optimistically, that Muslims could have a significant impact on the 2004 elections, which might even find the first Muslim elected to Congress. The President was listening to this discussion intently, occasionally commenting or asking follow-up questions and obviously very interested in the reality of Muslim life in the United States.

Qaddafi replied by saying that the United States had a great people, but that its government's foreign policy was unjust and wrong toward the Palestinian people, that he personally held no animosity toward the United States, but that he thought American policy was two-faced and heavily tilted toward Israel. He perceived this as the primary cause of hatred from the people of the region. The Libyan president proceeded to spell out his vision to end the Arab-Israeli conflict, the major thorn in the side of Muslim-Western relations. He foresaw a bi-national state giving both people, Israelis and Palestinians, the right to live peacefully, side by side, on the land. Before the end of the meeting, Alamoudi touched on the subject of Muslim political prisoners languishing in Libyan prisons, especially those who had lived in the United States and then returned to Libya upon completion of their academic pursuit, only to be arrested and accused of being members of the Muslim Brotherhood. Most if not all of these individuals had never committed any offense against the state. Qaddafi promised to look into the matter, and soon enough, a large number of those political prisoners were pardoned and freed as a result of the effort by Alamoudi through the Qaddafi International Organization for Charity Work and the continued pleas by the families of those locked away, many of whom live in the United States. Alamoudi continued to promote good faith and progressive work through his ties to the Qaddafi Organization and his contacts within the Libyan government. This called for repeated overseas trips to carry on this shuttle diplomacy and ensure the release of all prisoners of conscience, especially those whose release was put on hold following the September 11 attacks and the subsequent spiraling of world events that has put all of the region's governments into a whirlpool from which it has yet to escape.

Looking Ahead

The arrest of Abdurahman Alamoudi coincides with the difficult circumstances that have overtaken the Muslim

• Alamoudi, AMC's executive director, shakes hands with vice President Al Gore at the White House.

•Alamoudi attends a White House meeting with President Bill Clinton on November 9, 1995 .

• Alamoudi visits an army base in 1993.

community ever since 9/11. Since then, many Islamic organizations and members of the community have come under increasing pressure. It is not an exaggeration to say that most members of the Muslim community in the United States currently feel intimidated, harassed, and threatened as never before. Muslim decision makers and influential members of the Muslim community in the United States were dumbfounded and shocked at the way the authorities have been treating them in this unfolding saga.

Even though the organizations and leaders who speak for the Muslim and Arabic communities have gone on record to condemn and repudiate the events of 9/11 and all acts of random and abhorrent violence, the American authorities and security agencies have persisted in making Muslims and Arabs feel that they are guilty until proven innocent. This is an unbelievable development presaging political regression into a form of autocracy and tyranny in a country that Muslims from around the world have sought out for a better future because of its liberties and rights, both of which are enshrined in its Constitution and Bill of Rights. Freedom, democracy, and human and civic rights are and have been a hallmark of the American Way.

The arrest of Abdurahman Alamoudi will accentuate these latent fears. The message from official America to the Muslim and Arab community will be unmistakable: You are not wanted as a community within the United States! And the more the Muslims are drawn into this official dragnet the more the message is accentuated: Arabs and Muslims take notice! Depart from the United States before you are deported! The United States, now being inundated with a triumphalist Judeo-Christian unholy alliance, has no room for you! Alamoudi, as a man who has done nothing but build bridges between people and nations throughout his life, seems to have fallen into the wreckage of those bridges by those who would seek to maintain cultural and national supremacy and bigotry over peace. ■

• Meeting for landmark interfaith dialogue. Cardinal William H. Keeler (center) meets with Alamoudi and Bassam Estiwani, 1995.

• Alamoudi speaks with U.S. military personnel.

PROFILE: ACADEMIC AND HUMANITARIAN

Dr. Abdelhaleem Ashqar

- Professor, Business Administration, Howard University
- Founder, Al-Aqsa Educational Fund
- Research Fellow, United Association for Studies and Research (UASR)
- Civil Rights Activist
- Hunger Strike, February 23 – August 21, 1998

I support fully my husband's decision to refuse to submit or collaborate with the government by falsely testifying against his colleagues or himself. I know that my husband is a man of principles and courage. I want people to understand dearly that my husband has not committed or been charged with any crime. He has the full support and love of his family and friends.

—Asmaa Ashqar, wife of Dr. Ashqar

• The Muslim community greets Dr. Ashqar at the airport following his release, Aug. 21, 1998.

The Hunger for Justice:
The Case of Dr. Abdelhaleem Ashqar

I applaud Dr. Ashqar's principled stand. Civil disobedience is one means by which Arabs and Muslims can fight government discrimination and harassment. The Muslim community must band together and support Dr. Ashqar.

—Stanley Cohen, New York Attorney and Activist.

The anti-Muslim xenophobia that pervaded much of the 1990s resulted in a widespread crusade against Islamic institutions and their leaders, of which seemingly no one was immune. In most cases, the aim of law enforcement authorities was not simply to target and punish a specific individual, but rather to cast an entire net and attempt to fish out as many victims as possible. This was no more evident than in the case of Dr. Abdelhaleem Ashqar, a Palestinian scholar and activist who would ultimately linger in prison, not for committing any crime, but for refusing to incriminate his fellow activists.

Like most of the recent victims of a malevolent Justice Department, Abdelhaleem Ashqar was not born in the United States. Rather, he was born in the West Bank town of Sayda on August 8, 1958. He came from a prominent Palestinian family of farmers that also devoted their lives to a free Palestine. His father, also a prominent cleric, had been imprisoned by British authorities for opposition to Mandatory rule. His grandfather spent six years in an Ottoman Turkish prison for promoting Palestinian self-rule. After the 1967 War, Abdelhaleem would suffer the realities of life under brutal Israeli occupation. His family's farms were virtually destroyed, first by the restrictive Israeli practice of closing off farmers from their markets and transportation, and subsequently by restricting water consumption, allowing most of the trees to wither and die. As a child under occupation, Abdelhaleem was forced into a school where six grades were taught in the same room by only one teacher. Despite these harsh conditions, Ashqar would continue to pursue education as his sole means of empowerment, attending Beir Zeit University in the West Bank. He also quickly became active in student government and organized peaceful demonstrations against the Israeli attacks on their academic institutions. One protest in particular became a turning point in Abdelhaleem's life and an experience he would never forget.

On November 2, 1981, the Israelis besieged the university from early morning to evening. The university's administration reached an agreement with the Israelis to let the students leave peacefully without Israeli military intervention. Nonetheless, Israeli troops burst in and arrested a number of students, including Abdelhaleem. They accused him of participating in the demonstration and protesting. They handcuffed him and proceeded to beat him with their fists and the butts of their guns. They stomped on his bare feet for hours at the Ramallah Central Jail. By the end of the night he was bleeding badly. They offered the students three choices: plead guilty and go free, identify other students and also be let go, or face jail. Sixteen students went to jail. Abdelhaleem would not agree to plead guilty and would not testify against others. And so he remained in jail for days. Abdelhaleem was placed in an incredibly small cell with five others. It contained a jar for use as a bathroom. After the student leaders were arrested, other students held mass protests in their support and the Israelis closed the university for two months. Finally, pressure mounted on the Israeli government to release them, and they were released on the equivalent of $2500 bail after sixteen days without charges. The prominent Dr. Hanan Ashrawi, a former Chief Minister for Education in the government of the Palestinian Authority and then the head of the English department at Beir Zeit University, posted his bail.

In the face of this and many other setbacks, Abdelhaleem graduated from Beir Zeit University with his bachelor's degree in 1982, and then pursued his master's in business administration upon receiving an opportunity to study abroad at the University of Laverne in Athens, Greece. He completed this program in 1985, and returned to the Occupied Territories to a position at the Islamic University of Gaza as a lecturer. He would shortly take on the added task of Director of Public Relations for the university, which was an arduous job, especially during the volatile time of the first Intifada in the late 1980s. Ashqar's experiences during this period are particularly important, given what was to come later. He utilized his position with the university to speak out against the atrocities of Israeli occupation, much to his own personal detriment. He was frequently subjected to harsh interrogations by occupying officials and threats of prison, deportation, and even bodily harm to himself and his family.

In 1986, he married, Asmaa Muhanna, who came from a prominent Gaza family and had been a student at the Islamic University. With Ashqar's continued activism, came more threats by the Israelis, even against his new wife. As editor of the university's magazine, he oversaw the publication of detailed articles and commentaries on the occupation that reached thousands of fellow Palestinians, much to the annoyance of the Israeli occupation authorities. In one instance, the magazine detailed a recent raid by Israeli troops on the university in April, 1987, in which they broke windows, gates, and doors. The occupation authorities had had enough. According to Ashqar, in May 1987, "[A high-ranking Israeli official in Gaza] Ms. Tamara again called me to the Israeli head office in the Gaza Strip. She told me that I 'had crossed the line and we know how to discipline you.' She said that they knew that I was a newlywed and that they could hurt me. She said that what I wrote was lies, a provocation, and that I should not have written it. She also told me not to refer to the Israeli army as Israeli occupation forces. She threatened me with jail and deportation." A military order was soon issued banning the publication of the university's magazine.

During this period, Abdelhaleem was appointed by the Islamic University's administration to represent the university in an ad hoc committee established by the Council for Higher Education in the Israeli Occupied Territories "to expose Israel's procedures against Palestinian academic institutions." From the beginning of the Intifada in December 1987 until October 1991, Israel closed down all academic institutions—universities, schools, community centers, grammar schools and kindergartens. The committee tried to rally support from Western countries to pressure the Israelis to reopen the schools, but to no avail. Such efforts only further irked the authorities, resulting in unending harassment from Israel's security forces. By 1989, Ashqar received an opportunity that many of his peers only dreamed of: to pursue his graduate studies in the United States. He was awarded a Thomas Jefferson Fellowship financed by USAID and the Fulbright Program to complete his doctoral work at the University of Mississippi from September 1989. That fall, Abdelhaleem was unable to attend classes, however, because the Israelis would not allow him to leave the Occupied Territories. He was finally allowed to depart only through the intervention of an Israeli attorney and former Interior Minister, who convinced the Shin Bet to let him leave. They told him that Ashqar was a political activist and they did not want him to become active in the United States because a Palestinian that would go to the United States and expose Americans to the Palestinian viewpoint could potentially damage Israel's interests in America. That one statement alone stands as an accurate summation of the motive behind not only the future targeting of Dr. Ashqar in the United States, but the widespread assault against the Palestinian population in America as a whole.

At the University of Mississippi, Abdelhaleem Ashqar would begin his doctoral studies in business administration. Meanwhile, he would also become heavily involved in the growing Islamic and especially Palestinian activist movement in the United States. Having lived his whole life and especially the most recent turbulent years in the Palestinian territories, Ashqar would not simply forget the pain and suffering endured by his family and people in his homeland. He quickly became an active figure within intellectual and activist circles across the country. He was employed as a research fellow at the United Association for Studies and Research, a Virginia-based think tank devoted to building bridges of communication between the Muslim world and the West. Ashqar also regularly attended national conferences and seminars devoted to the Palestinian cause. Through it all, however, he was continuously harassed by law enforcement officials.

As early as 1991, only two years after he had arrived in the United States, Abdelhaleem was approached by FBI agents. They asked him about Palestinian activism in America and the presence of groups such as the Islamic Resistance Movement (Hamas), as well as money laundering, and so forth. Abdelhaleem was very cordial in these meetings, which continued for a number of years, but never sought to incriminate anyone. In one meeting, in October of 1994, federal agents admittedly told him that they were acting at the behest of the Israeli government. They continued to ask him the same questions, and even inquired as to his political activities while at the University of Gaza. These interviews were akin to the interrogations he frequently underwent by Israeli occupation officials in Gaza, though the American federal agents would often assure him that he need not worry and that no harm would come to him. Many times, they would even claim to only want to speak to him for educational purposes, to learn about the situation in Palestine and his own experiences.

While these meetings were led by the FBI, other government agencies were involved as well. At times someone from the U.S. Attorney's Office would be present. Other times it would be State Department officials. Through it all, Abdelhaleem would grow less and less comfortable with his inquisitors, and would soon have good reason to suspect their malicious intentions.

By late September, 1996, Abdelhaleem Ashqar was completing his studies at the University of Mississippi and on the verge of submitting his dissertation for approval. His wife had found employment in New Jersey, and he was in preparations to move there shortly. With seemingly all going well and a bright future ahead of him, in spite of the harassments, Abdelhaleem did not expect what was to come. Following a bad fall down the stairs in which he severely injured his back, Abdelhaleem began receiving intensive treatment toward his recovery. He received a call from the U.S. Attorney's Office, which demanded to meet with him, and continued to insist even after being told that Ashqar was bedridden and in severe pain. That evening, John Hailman, Chief of the Criminal Division, informed him that the investigation had concluded. He also told Abdelhaleem that he now had four options: 1) to be deported; 2) to be charged with crimes and face a possible prison sentence; 3) to help them build a case against Mousa Abu Marzook; 4) to be portrayed by the FBI as an informant on Palestinian groups. Hailman also told him it would not be wise to move to New Jersey.

On October 2, Hailman called once again and arranged a meeting in which several FBI agents were present. They threatened Abdelhaleem with deportation and told him they were trying to build a case against Hamas in the United States, specifically its spokesman in America, Mousa Abu Marzook. They offered Abdelhaleem a number of incentives, including full-time employment, U.S. citizenship, money, and even a ministerial post in the Arafat government of the Palestinian Authority. They wanted his help in proving the existence of a money-laundering scheme that they suspected had taken place, but he simply said that he could not help them and could not incriminate anyone. Abdelhaleem continued to willfully meet with agents for several months more, meeting new players each time, including agents from the Washington Metropolitan field office of the FBI who solicited more information and offered to help pay for treatment for Abdelhaleem's back injury.

During this same time, Abdelhaleem was experiencing odd things. He had known that his telephones had been tapped and there was constant electronic surveillance of his every move. He was also receiving strange phone calls and his mail was being tampered with almost regularly. In addition, someone was canceling his doctor's appointments, and his credit cards were being used. It was clear that someone sought to intimidate him and instill in him a sense of fear and paranoia. As had become Abdelhaleem's custom, however, he would triumph in the face of adversity. In May, 1997, he received his PhD from the University of Mississippi in business administration. Dr. Abdelhaleem Ashqar was ready to begin his teaching career, when the worst thing imaginable happened.

Shortly after being awarded his doctorate, in November, 1997, Abdelhaleem was subpoenaed to appear before the Grand Jury in the United States District Court for the Southern District of New York, which was investigating money laundering. He complied with the subpoena voluntarily, but refused to answer any questions posed to him.

Dr. Ashqar instead gave a prepared statement explaining his position. It stated, in part, "I respectfully refuse to answer any questions put to me other than my name, address and occupation on the grounds that to do so would violate my long-held and unshakable religious, political, and personal beliefs and that my answers will be used against my friends, relatives and colleagues in the Palestinian liberation movement. I would rather die than betray my beliefs and commitment to freedom and democracy for Palestine. I will never give evidence or cooperate in any way with this Grand Jury, no matter what the consequences to me."

Also during this time, as his visa had expired, Dr. Ashqar applied for political asylum in the United States on the basis that returning to the Occupied Territories would result in guaranteed harassment, torture, and possible incarceration by Israeli authorities. That application never got off the ground, however, as the grand jury investigation was heating up. As a result of his refusal to testify, Dr. Ashqar was held in civil contempt by Judge Denise Cote in an effort to force him to testify. Individuals can be held in civil contempt, which is not a criminal charge, for up to 18 months, or until the judge is convinced that the person will not be swayed to offer testimony. And thus Dr. Ashqar was arrested and imprisoned on February 23, 1998. On that day, he began a hunger strike that continued until his eventual release six months later.

During his incarceration, Dr. Ashqar endured the harshest treatment and abuse. He was continuously insulted by prison and hospital officials, who referred to him only as "terrorist." Once he began his hunger strike, he was placed in solitary confinement at the Metropolitan Correctional Center, where he was humiliated by a number of tactics, including constant unnecessary strip searches, shackling of his hands and feet, and placing him in extremely unsanitary holding cells. Furthermore, prison officials were clearly upset by his decision to stop eating, and so they responded in the cruelest of measures. First they continuously kept many trays of food in his presence to add to his suffering. He was denied regular visitations from friends and family. And once Ashqar's health began to deteriorate, he was moved to a prison hospital where he was fed forcibly by hospital officials. This included primarily intravenous feeding through IVs placed in his veins, which was an incredibly painful procedure, as he describes it. Furthermore, as the months passed and his health deteriorated further, it became increasingly difficult to even find veins through which to feed him. In one instance, he endured dozens of needles injected into him in an attempt to find an open vein through which to feed him. Another time, hospital officials went through a vein in his neck, another incredibly painful procedure. Even at the hospital, Ashqar was kept in complete isolation, with only armed guards around him, and not allowed frequent visits.

Through it all, Ashqar had lost much weight, and was becoming increasingly weaker. His back injury had become especially acute during this time, and he suffered from many other ailments. His ability to endure the pain was due to his strong faith, immense patience, and determination to stand for what he believed in. Ashqar frequently thought of those who had suffered throughout history much more than he had, and attempted to place his current ordeal in the context of a much wider struggle that involved pain and sacrifice. He understood fully well that the result of this might be his own death in the custody of U.S. officials, but that was a sacrifice he was willing to make. The famous phrase attributed to him during his appearance before the court, "I'd rather die than testify," was becoming more likely to be fulfilled as the months wore on.

During his agonizing incarceration, Ashqar garnered the support of his entire community. The Free Dr. Ashqar Committee (FDAC) was founded to take on his case. It solicited donations for his legal fees, while also mobilizing the community to action. As Ashqar's case was receiving more media attention, the committee's work was covering much ground. It circulated petitions, contacted government officials, and published articles and brochures. Soon most of the American Muslim community and many non-Muslims were aware of Ashqar's situation and were lending their support. In asserting his position, Ashqar released a statement distributed by FDAC that read, "I will not participate in an unethical plot to incriminate Muslims because of their political views. The government is making lawful activities into crimes. Israel is trying to convince American authorities that Palestinian charitable, humanitarian, and other lawful political acts are a terrorist network. This if far from the truth. Just because many people disagree with the terms and application of the peace process is no cause for political persecution. The Muslim community must understand that this witch hunt is a campaign to silence the voice of dissent and an attempt to isolate the Muslim community from its Muslim activists and Islamic institutions."

Finally, on August 21, 1998, Judge Cote became convinced that Ashqar would not testify and was even willing to die in custody. And so after six months in custody, he was released. Ashqar was finally able to end his hunger strike after 180 days. It would be months before he would regain his physical strength and overcome the painful effects of his hunger strike. In some ways, the strike left him with permanent health problems from which he would continue to suffer, including severe arthritis in his joints, an ulcerated stomach, and chronic migraines. Nonetheless, Ashqar was determined to resume his life, and settled in Virginia. He took an adjunct position to teach business courses at Strayer University in Loudon, VA. Simultaneously, he also became a Research Fellow at the United Association for Studies and Research, in Springfield, VA, where he conducted research on development and technology transfer; in addition, he reviewed and edited articles for UASR's Journal, and consulted with the organization on its business management practices. After a truly trying experience, it seemed that Abdelhaleem Ashqar had successfully begun to move on.

In the fall 1999, he was employed as an adjunct instructor at the University of the District of Columbia, teaching undergraduate business classes. During the spring 2000 semester, he also taught operations management at Towson University in Maryland. Also within his busy teaching career, Ashqar took a position with Howard University in Washington, D.C., as an Assistant Professor, where he would teach several courses over the next three years. After it seemed that his life had gotten back on track and the endless harassment had ceased, the unthinkable happened. As with all other cases, September 11 provided a cover for malicious forces within the world of law enforcement to pursue their political targeting of certain individuals. Ashqar would soon become one of these targets, given his previous experiences with government authorities.

The asylum application which Ashqar had filed many

years earlier was immediately derailed following the September 11 attacks. In fact, he had gotten wind of the government's attempt to press criminal charges against his lawful activities on behalf of Palestinians by concocting claims regarding associations, money transfers, and so forth from their surveillance of him and discussions they had with him over the years. While these efforts did not yield any criminal charges, by mid-2003 it appeared the government would attempt to destroy his character as well as recycle its old methods. After the spring of 2003, Howard University declined to renew Dr. Ashqar's contract and he became unemployed, due to the cloud of suspicion that the government had generated around him in its smearing campaign.

In June of that year, a hearing was held to determine Ashqar's application for asylum. Though his request was initially approved several years earlier, that decision was reversed in the light of September 11. Rather than focus on proving the legitimacy of his claim, the hearing instead went into his political associations and an all-out bashing of Muslim activity in America. The government solicited testimony from known Israeli agents operating as "terror experts," including Reuvan Baz. The government then attempted to have Ashqar answer questions regarding several Muslim leaders and institutions in America, which he had declined to answer during the initial grand jury proceedings in 1998. This asylum hearing was effectively exploited by the government and twisted into an interrogation into the American Muslim community's activities. Wishing to stand by his principles, Ashqar decided to withdraw his application for asylum, and decided that the legal harassments by the American government had been enough to make him want to leave the country. His deportation was scheduled for mid-August. Before that was to happen, however, an Illinois grand jury subpoenaed him on the same day he withdrew his asylum application. He was to appear before another grand jury in Chicago investigating terrorist financing. His deportation was postponed pending the outcome of the grand jury.

Twice Abdelhaleem Ashqar appeared before the grand jury, and both times he refused to answer any questions that would incriminate his fellow activists. His statement to the court this time was just as powerful as it was in his previous experience. He stated, in part:

> My experience with the Court five years ago came at a time of relative calm and hopeful, if illusory, progress in Palestine. It seemed for a brief moment that the Israeli military occupation might soon come to an end. Yet even then, I was adamantly unwilling to testify before the Grand Jury. Today, in the third year of the new intifada against the racist Israeli army and its relentless brutality against Palestinian men, women and children, my hopes for a just resolution to the conflict have been all but shattered. And while many in the world welcome the recent Bush Administration's so-called "Roadmap to Peace," it is viewed largely by Palestinians as a vehicle to ensure Israeli security and little more, calculated to make the illegal settlements permanent, and achieve the expansionist aims of the occupation under the fraudulent guise of a "peace process."

Because of this, I am more resolved than ever
to resist any attempts to force me to testify. I
will never acquiesce in the Court's coercion
to make me violate my religious and political
beliefs. If my incarceration in 1998 taught
me anything, it is this: I possess the inner
strength of mind and spirit, even if the body
should fail, to withstand iron bars and stone
walls. No amount of jailing by the Court will
compel me to testify against others
struggling for Palestinian freedom. Let me
be clear: I view this grand jury, as I did the
one in 1998, as a vehicle of the United States
government to further the aims of Israel. As
in 1998, my refusal to testify here is not the
expression of a desire to obstruct justice or
otherwise to interfere with an "investigation."
I view this proceeding as an illegal abuse of
process designed to chill dissent and to
criminalize legitimate and lawful resistance
against the Israeli designs on my homeland.
As in 1998, the prospect of jail does not
diminish my resolve in any way.

As expected, Charles P. Kocoras, the chief judge in the
grand jury, held Ashqar in civil contempt for his refusal,
once again, to testify. Ashqar immediately appealed that
decision, and returned to Virginia while he awaited that
decision. During this time, he had to check in twice each
day by phone with federal marshals in Chicago, visit his
local immigration office twice a week, and agree not to leave
the state. In this particular grand jury, the government had

granted him full immunity in his testimony, meaning that nothing he said could be used to prosecute him later. But this did not matter to Ashqar, who saw that this was simply another method by which the government halted Palestinian and Muslim activism, while intimidating the community. In addition, he realized that no matter what he said, the Israeli government would use that information to persecute his friends and family, as well as him once he returned. As such, Ashqar was completely firm and set in his beliefs to not comply with the aim of his grand inquisitors. By early September, 2003, the appeal was denied and Ashqar was ordered to return to Chicago, which he did voluntarily, to be jailed yet again on civil contempt charges. So on September 5, he was jailed again, this time in an Illinois prison, and as before, resumed his hunger strike to protest his treatment and as a demonstration of his resolve in the matter.

His case immediately drew national attention, as newspapers in Chicago, Washington, D.C., and elsewhere covered it from the outset. In the post-9/11 climate, however, few dared to speak out in the face of the spreading injustices against Arab and Muslim leaders. Even from within the community, Muslims feared to take on the case of their beloved Dr. Ashqar as they had done before with courage and devotion. National Muslim organizations were eerily silent on the blatant injustice committed against him, with the slight exception of a few modest press releases. It seemed the civil rights crisis of the new era was just too much for most leaders to combat head on. As such, Abdelhaleem Ashqar would linger in prison for weeks, while his health once again deteriorated as a result of his hunger strike. Only three days after he was jailed, on September 8, prison officials cut off the water to his cell and kept it off for six days, until September 14, in another attempt to coerce him through torturous hardships. That day, Ashqar was moved to a prison hospital where he was force-fed through IVs in his veins as before. Even at the prison hospital, he was denied visits and phone calls, and was under constant guard by three officers. Because he was five years older and had still been suffering from his previous hunger strike, Ashqar's health status was worsening much more quickly than before. After a few weeks, it seemed as though the government was going to let him die in their custody.

Then, on October 10, barely a month after Ashqar was arrested, the U.S. Attorney dropped the civil contempt charges and instead indicted him on criminal contempt charges. For the first time during this five-year tribulation, and with already seven months of imprisonment behind him, Dr. Abdelhaleem Ashqar was charged with a crime. This charge was simply the government's attempt to raise the stakes involved in the case, whereas there was no actual crime committed. Once it became apparent that being held in civil contempt would not coerce Ashqar into testifying, the government determined that a criminal trial and a longer prison term would punish him for his lack of cooperation and serve as a warning to the rest of the American Muslim community to never defy the requests of the government.

Upon his being charged, Ashqar's lawyers appeared before a judge who considered allowing him to be released on bail pending the trial on the newly filed charges. Ashqar's supporters came together to provide assurances of up to $1 million to cover the costs of the bond. Ashqar

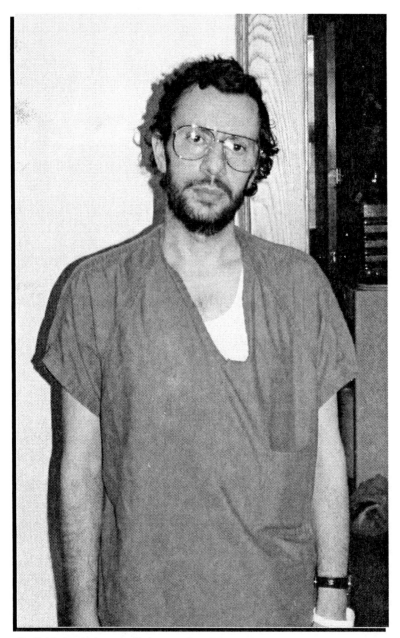

• Dr. Abdelhaleem Ashqar after his hunger strike, 1998.

himself, however, was barely conscious, instead confined to the prison hospital bed while the proceedings went on in his absence. The judge insisted that he end his strike and appear before the court before she would allow his release. And so on November 3, 2003, Abdelhaleem Ashqar was finally released from prison and ended his second hunger strike. He returned to his home in Virginia, to which the court confined him pending the 2004 trial.

Like all of these cases, Abdelhaleem Ashqar's stems from a government that has chosen to take a political debate and give it a legal face. Dr. Ashqar, like many other Palestinians, Arabs, and Muslims in America, is being persecuted for being a Palestinian, an Arab, and a Muslim in America. The ominous words of the Israeli interrogation officer who initially denied him leave from the Occupied Territories have shown themselves to be true. The Zionist forces both in Israel and in the United States are threatened by the thought of a professional, intellectual, and dedicated individual who can well articulate the Palestinian cause before an American audience. Moreover, Dr. Ashqar is not being punished for anything he has done, but rather for what he supposedly knows. It would not even be enough for him to simply take the stand and tell the truth. The government has repeatedly expressed that unless he actively incriminates others, he will be punished with a prison sentence stemming from some small crime or another. It is this despicable practice of pitting friends, colleagues, and community members against one another that pro-Israeli forces hope will generate the break up of all activity that opposes them. Dr. Ashqar has served as a shining example, however, in his hunger for justice, that such a resolve cannot be broken. ■

PROFILE: FROM REVOLUTIONARY TO REFORMER

Imam Jamil al-Amin

- Imam, Community Mosque, Atlanta, Georgia
- Chairman, Islamic *Shura* Council of North America
- Founding Officer and Vice-President, American Muslim Council, 1990.
- Chairman, Student Nonviolence Coordinating Committee
- Author, *Revolution by the Book*, 1994.

No longer can America only acknowledge Judaism and Christianity as its only major faiths. Islam must also be included and recognized for its worth. America must respect its own diversity. Our nation's inclusion and future in the world community may count on it.

—Imam Jamil Al-Amin

- Imam Jamil joins with American Muslims from all part of the country in 1994 in Washington to demand lifting the Bosnian arms embargo.

421

The American Legacy of Justice and The Case of Imam Jamil al-Amin
— H. "Rap" Brown —

To be successful in struggle requires remembrance of the Creator and the doing of good deeds. This is important because successful struggle demands that there be a kind of social consciousness. There has to be a social commitment, a social consciousness that joins men together. On the basis of their coming together, they do not transgress against themselves and they do not transgress against others.

—Imam Jamil Al-Amin

Imam Jamil has struggled against injustice and oppression most of his adult life. Before accepting Islam, he was a prominent leader of the Civil Rights Movement in the United States. On a visit to Howard University in the early 1960s, to see his elder brother Ed Brown, the younger Brown was introduced to civil rights struggles already underway. That visit very much changed his life because from that time onwards Hubert Brown has ceaselessly struggled alongside the oppressed and given voice to the voiceless. In fact, his eloquent, articulate, and insightful style of speech-making won him the title "Rap."

Imam Jamil Abdullah al-Amin is no stranger to controversy. He has been an active public figure all of his adult life, and over the years his activism has taken many twists and turns. During the 1960s, as H. Rap Brown, he came into national prominence by way of his vigorously aggressive approach to America's critical need for societal change. After his embrace of Islam in 1971, the methodology of his struggle became Islamized and more focused, but his struggle for societal change continued.

The Making of H. "Rap" Brown

Hubert Geriod Brown was the youngest of three children born to a working-class family in Baton Rouge, Louisiana, in October 1943. His parents, Eddie C. Brown, Sr., and Thelma Warren Brown were a common laborer and a maid, and instilled a sense of justice and a fear of God in their children. According to Ed Brown, Imam Jamil's oldest brother, "We were taught that you had a responsibility to make things better for the next generation. It was part of the overall orientation of the African-American community at that point in time."

Like his brother before him, Hubert Brown fully embraced this orientation, leaving Southern University before graduating and traveling to Washington, D.C., to join what was then officially known as "The War on Poverty." In 1966, he jumped into the front lines of the Civil Rights Movement as a project director for the Student Nonviolent Coordinating Committee (SNCC) in Greene County, Alabama, acquiring in the process a reputation for being, in the words of a fellow worker, "a fearless and great organizer." He led its campaign to organize black people to overthrow Jim Crow segregation. He and fellow SNCC leader Stokely Carmichael became spokesmen for the radicalization of this movement— advocating anti-imperialism, Black Power, and a spirit of "struggle is necessary." Danger was all around. The previous year, civil rights workers Jimmie Lee Jackson, Rev. James Reeb, and Viola Liuzzo were brutally killed in the struggle to win voting rights for African Americans in rural Alabama.

By 1968, many of the young activists became disillusioned with the nonviolent approach proffered by mainstream civil rights organizations. In the face of a growing avalanche of officially sanctioned brutality, much of SNCC's leadership merged with the newly established Black Panther Party for Self Defense. He emerged as a leader of the black liberation struggle, known for his outspoken advocacy of armed self-defense and inner city revolution. He was targeted by the FBI's COINTELPRO program. Congress passed a notorious law, the "Rap Brown Amendment," specifically aimed at stopping Al-Amin and radical activists like him from organizing resistance among the people. Rap was sentenced to prison for his militant activities, where he served five years.

As many young activists stopped upholding non-violence as an absolute principle, they came under attack for this. Rap answered these attacks—pointing out that Black people were fighting a system that had used massive violence for centuries to keep them oppressed, and that was using such violence on the other side of the world against the Vietnamese people. He mocked the hypocrisy of pro-system critics, saying, "Violence is as American as cherry pie." This famous quote now appears in virtually every article reporting on Al-Amin—as if this undoubtedly true political statement was proof of his guilt in the Atlanta shooting 30 years later. As powerful rebellions broke out in cities across America in the late 1960s, Rap Brown supported these uprisings—as a just and powerful form of resistance.

He tirelessly traveled the United States, speaking on campuses and in Black communities, organizing people to take the struggle higher.

One FBI memo called for writing unsigned letters to create distrust between Stokely Carmichael and Rap Brown. Another FBI conspiracy was aimed at creating bad blood between Southern-based SNCC and the Black Panther Party that was emerging in California. The FBI was determined to prevent the unification of revolutionary nationalist forces—and ceaselessly worked to create divisions, mistrust, and even violent feuds. Rap, who actively supported an alliance of Black revolutionary forces, briefly accepted honorary membership in the Black Panther Party in 1968. These unification efforts ultimately collapsed under an intense-but-secret FBI campaign. In 1967, H. Rap Brown spoke at a Black community rally in Cambridge, Maryland, and proclaimed, "Black folks built America, and if America don't come around, we're going to burn America down." A rebellion followed—during which Rap was wounded in the forehead by a shotgun pellet. Several buildings were burned down. Rap Brown was charged with inciting riot and arson.

When reflecting upon that period several years ago, Imam Jamil contemplated it for a moment and then declared, "It was war." The unwritten record shows that on at least two occasions during the course of that undeclared, high-intensity civil war, attempts were made on his life by members of the "law enforcement community."

The Evolution to Islam

Some critics believe that upon embracing Islam, Imam Jamil lost his revolutionary edge. As one such person stated, "He went from revolution to rhetoric." In fact, nothing could be further from the truth. As the essential meaning of the word *revolution* denotes "a complete change," any knowledgeable and objective observer would have to conclude that with his embrace of Islam and transition from H. Rap Brown to Jamil Abdullah al-Amin, quite the reverse was true. The Imam became a true revolutionary in the fullest sense of the word; and along with his personal transformation, his revolutionary potential as a genuine agent for societal change deepened. In his 1994 book, *Revolution by the Book*, Imam Jamil writes:

> It is criminal that, in the 1990s, we still approach struggle [by] sloganeering, saying, "by any means necessary," as if that's a program ... or, "we shall overcome," as if that's a program. Slogans are not programs. We must define the means that will bring about change. This can be found in what Allah has brought for us in the Qur'an and in the example of the Prophet. Our revolution must be according to what Almighty God revealed. ...
> The mission of a believer in Islam is totally different from coexisting or being a part of the system. The prevailing morals are wrong. Their ethics are wrong. Western philosophy ... has reduced man to food,

clothing, shelter, and the sex drive, which
means he doesn't have a spirit. ... Successful
struggle requires a divine program. Allah has
provided that program.

This is the revolutionary perspective that caused Imam
Jamil Abdullah al-Amin to be among the few American
born Muslims singled out by one of America's most virulent
anti-Islam demagogues, Daniel Pipes, in a report published
in the Feb 21, 2000, edition of *The National Review,* less
than a month before the horrific tragedy unfolded on the
West End of Atlanta. This is also the man that the opinion
shapers endeavored to keep hidden from the public in the
two-year period leading up to the trial. From the time that
the March 16, 2000, tragedy unfolded until the present,
there has been a consistent emphasis on Imam Jamil's pre-
Islamic past, but comparatively little attention given to the
ideological wellspring from which this respected leader has
drawn since 1971, when H. Rap Brown became Jamil
Abdullah al-Amin at the Rikers Island prison in New York.

A National Leader

Imam Jamil al-Amin has served as one of the most
committed and respected leaders in North America. He was
one of the founding officers of the American Muslim
Council (AMC). He served as vice-president of the
organization and after the death of its first president briefly
served in his place. In fact, after his arrest, the principal
founder of the AMC, Abdurrahman Alamoudi said, "I love
Imam Jamil, and I owe him a lot." Imam Jamil was one of

the principle leaders and organizers of one of the largest and most successful Muslim demonstrations ever held in America—the demonstration on behalf of Bosnia in the early 90's which attracted over 50,000 participants as part of the Bosnia Task Force, USA. For an entire generation, he, along with members of his community, planned and carried initiatives to fight violence, drugs, and prostitution in some of America's most troubled inner cities. For years, his was one of the most consistent and visible voices providing education and inspiration to significant numbers of impressionable young Muslims at major conferences and conventions each year, becoming a staple at gatherings of ISNA, ICNA, and the MSA.

In 1992, secretary-generals of four major Muslim organizations in North America, ISNA, ICNA, the Ministry of Imam W. Deen Mohammed, and Imam Jamil's Community met in Chicago to discuss the idea of an Islamic Shura Council of North America. Within a year, the four organizations announced the Shura Council formation in California. In 1995, Abdullah Idris Ali was elected to be its first chairperson, followed by Imam Jamil Al-Amin and later by Imam W. D. Mohammed. Imam Jamil is the organization's last chairman.

A Favorite Target

In his many years as an outspoken advocate of civil rights and a Muslim preacher who reached people across the land, Imam Jamil became a target of local law enforcement authorities eager to defame him and possibly put him in prison. A number of significant incidents arose, especially during the 1990s when he attained much prominence. In fact, his arrest and subsequent trial on murder charges in 2000 was the result of a longstanding campaign to subdue him. These disturbing episodes are a testament to the lengths that authorities have gone in their attempts to destroy a decent and respected man.

In 1995, a young black male was used in an attempt to frame Imam Jamil for a shooting that occurred in Atlanta's West End. The effort backfired when, to the consternation of authorities, the victim publicly stated that he had maintained from the beginning that he did not know who shot him in his leg. He then proceeded to reveal that law enforcement authorities had pressured him to pronounce that Imam Jamil al-Amin was the assailant. Before this disclosure, Imam Jamil was arrested on suspicion of aggravated assault and paraded before the court on August 7, 1995. He was released on bail the following day, and later the charges were quietly dropped, with the police department deeply embarrassed. Since then evidence emerged of a five-year undercover investigation of Imam Jamil initiated by a special FBI-led task force set up within the Atlanta Police Department. Surveillance went on from 1992-1997, and included paid informants planted within the West End's Community Mosque. With the exception of the August 1995 incident, however, the Imam was never charged with any crimes. Finally, on May 31, 1999, Imam Jamil was the subject of a traffic stop in Cobb County, Georgia. To this day, many wonder whether the stop was legitimate. It may very well have been another case of racial profiling, as has been common, especially in the south. Or perhaps he was even stopped because of who he was specifically. Imam Jamil was subsequently placed under arrest for receiving stolen goods, which the officers asserted was the vehicle he was driving. He was booked also for impersonating a police officer, on the basis of the badge he had in his wallet, and for driving without insurance. A few hours later he was released on a $10,000 bond. By September, 1999, he was indicted on all three charges. It was this incident which eventually led to the tragic events in which Imam Jamil would find himself six months later. The charges were clearly unfounded. Imam Jamil provided the police with a bill of sale for the used vehicle. The mayor of White Hall, Alabama, sent a letter to authorities acknowledging legitimacy of the badge that the Imam was carrying in his wallet, as he had been appointed an auxiliary member of the town's police force. As for the minor infraction of driving without insurance, he was willing to pay a fine, and even agreed to community service.

None of that mattered for the police department. In January, 2000, a bench warrant was issued for Imam Jamil's arrest after it became known to them that he had missed his court date. In fact, court proceedings had been cancelled on the date he was to appear due to an ice storm that hit the Atlanta area. About two months later, Deputies Ricky Kinchen and Aldranon English were to serve a warrant for his arrest on the spurious charges. In light of the aforementioned facts, one is forced to ponder whether Imam Jamil Abdullah al-Amin's predicament is the logical end result of a government-orchestrated conspiracy.

The Night of March 16

The events of March 16, 2000, are at best hazy, and at worst veiled from public view. What is known about this infamous day, on the eve of the Muslim Eid celebration, is that a shootout occurred on the West End of Atlanta in which two Fulton County sheriff's deputies exchanged gunfire with a lone assailant. One of the deputies, Ricky Kinchen, would die the next day, while the second deputy, Aldranon English, would sustain serious, life threatening injuries and remain hospitalized in the critical care unit of Atlanta's Grady Memorial Hospital. Between surgeries and while heavily sedated, the surviving deputy would identify Jamil Abdullah al-Amin, through what some experts have opined was a "contaminated photo spread" as the lone assailant. Both deputies claimed to have shot the lone assailant in the stomach area.

Police radio transmissions within minutes of the tragedy recorded the following: "*[911] Caller advises perp in a vacant building on Westview bleeding begging for a ride.*" Police reportedly surrounded this abandoned house five blocks from the shooting scene where fresh blood was found, but found no one inside. Finally, while media reports nationwide issued reports of a wounded "former Black Panther" on the run, Imam Jamil was apprehended four days later in White Hall, Alabama, with no injuries.

The Government's Case

The government's case against Imam Jamil al-Amin was predicated on a number of supposed facts, evidence, and testimony, all of which were easily contested by the defense. The government presented the eyewitness testimony of the surviving deputy, Aldranon English. It presented the fact that both deputies were on the West End of Atlanta to serve a warrant for Imam Jamil's arrest. In addition, officers who arrived at the scene allegedly acquired a description of the shooter from both Kinchen and English that "matched the defendant." The government also stated that Imam Jamil fled the city of Atlanta, thus becoming a fugitive, and when he was apprehended four days later in a small town called White Hall in Alabama, he had a passport in his possession, $1,000 in cash, and was wearing body armor. Prosecutors alleged that Imam Jamil fired shots at law enforcement officers on the night of his arrest, and that an automatic pistol, assault rifle, three spent shell casings, and two .223 caliber magazine casings were recovered from the wooded area from which Imam Jamil emerged on the night of his arrest. Ballistics tests would tie this "evidence" to the March 16 crime in Atlanta, Georgia.

A black 1978 bullet-riddled Mercedes Benz, registered to Imam Jamil was allegedly recovered in White Hall days later. In closing arguments, Prosecutor McBirney asserted, "I can't suggest to you that the state has answers for every single question. ... Where was the defendant at 10:00 PM on March 16? They had an opportunity to call witnesses to corroborate where he was—and that he wasn't there [at the crime scene]—but they didn't." In other words, he instructed jurors to find guilt because the defendant didn't prove his innocence.

The Defense's Case

Imam Jamil's defense attorneys based their case on the background to the events as well as on the details of the ordeal itself. Lead defense attorney Jack Martin would contend, "A fundamental mistake was made by layers of law enforcement when the assumption was made that they had their man, and the impartial investigation that should have ensued was never done." In fact, the government had been pursuing Imam Jamil for a long time. The traffic stop that occurred in Cobb County, Georgia, in September, 1999, began the process for "a bogus indictment" which became the basis for a warrant "that never should have been issued." The surviving eyewitness was inconsistent in his description of the assailant, and refused to be interviewed by defense attorneys prior to the start of the trial. The defense had to rely on English's accounts given to State investigators. Deputy English identified Imam Jamil from what the defense characterized as "a contaminated" photo spread only hours following the incident, and after being given 4 milligrams of morphine. The defense contended that he was in such a hallucinogenic state that English imagined being visited by several people standing around his hospital bed who were never actually there. Both deputies insisted that they shot the assailant in the stomach area, though Imam Jamil was clearly never injured, and Deputy English maintained throughout that the assailant was 5'8" tall with gray eyes, while Imam Jamil is 6'5" tall and has brown eyes.

In fact, the government's practice throughout the entire case should have been enough to throw the case out of court. The bullet-riddled squad car that was involved in the shootout was repaired and returned to service before defense experts could even examine it. A car that was parked on the street at the time of the shootout, also hit by gunfire, was sold at auction, also before defense experts could examine it. In addition, the defense successfully showed that the physical evidence at the crime scene, such as the position of shell casings, did not match English's account of the incident. A law enforcement officer reportedly found large droppings of blood at the crime scene, leading to an abandoned house, probably from the true assailant, who was badly injured. The defense also introduced the 911 emergency call about a bleeding person who pleaded with motorists for a ride, about a half a mile away from the crime scene. A number of West End witnesses testified that someone other than Imam Jamil was the assailant. Federal law enforcement personnel lied outright about what took place during the course of Imam Jamil's arrest. In the words of lead attorney Martin, "reasoned logic would suggest that they would also lie about far more important matters." "Big John," a local sheriff's deputy, along with two other black officers, reportedly spotted Imam Jamil and ordered him to lay on the ground, where he was subsequently handcuffed behind his back. A white FBI agent, Ron Campbell, would arrive on the scene and proceed to kick Imam Jamil and spit on him, while he lay handcuffed on the ground. Finally, Imam Jamil had suffered no injuries during the alleged incident. There was no damage to the vest he was wearing. His fingerprints were not found on any of the guns, and no evidence of gunshot residue was discovered on his person. In fact, there was absolutely no physical evidence to place Imam Jamil at the crime scene. The entire case was built upon the eyewitness account of a police force with clear motivation to put him in prison. It has also been strongly suggested that evidence was planted in Alabama to secure a conviction.

The Trial

Imam Jamil was tried in the court of Judge Stephanie Manis, who in the opinion of many observers took a strong position in favor of the prosecution throughout the trial. The trial was consistently followed by strong supporters of Jamil al-Amin, both Muslim and non-Muslim, from throughout the United States. A charged atmosphere permeated the court proceedings. Armed security personnel were stationed in the courtroom and around the courthouse. Attendees had to pass through two phases of security checks before entering the courtroom, and a surveillance camera was placed to continuously monitor the visitors' section. A special viewing area in a separate room was set up for the print and broadcast media. A significant number of mainstream and alternative media representatives were a constant presence in this room, as well as in the courtroom itself. On the opening day of the trial, the court was abuzz with Court TV's decision not to broadcast the trial. Its officially stated reason for reversing its decision was that there would be diminished public interest in the trial of this controversial figure, because he changed his name from H. Rap Brown to Jamil Abdullah al-Amin. In place of this very important trial, Court TV decided to air a "Dog Mauling Case." At the end of an unfair political proceeding, in March, 2002, Jamil Abdullah al-Amin was convicted on all 13 counts of the criminal indictment. He was sentenced to *life in prison without the possibility of parole*, though Fulton County District Attorney Paul Howard had pursued the death penalty.

The Community Response

One of the most common refrains one heard throughout the course of this troubling ordeal—from Muslim and non-Muslim acquaintances of the Imam—is that the charges were totally out of character with the person they knew.

During the extradition proceedings in Montgomery, Alabama, on April 21, 2000, the courtroom was packed, with an almost even split between Muslims and non-Muslims, many of whom had traveled considerable distances to show their support. Many White Hall residents spoke out about the case. What they had to say was quite revealing. A 45-year-old black male and lifelong resident of White Hall spoke passionately about the man he called "Mr. Brown." He said, in part, "I didn't know the man was no criminal. The only thing I know is that he was in the Black Panther Party back in the 60s, and as far as I know, in my opinion, I haven't seen nothing that he done. I mean ... you're innocent until you're proven guilty. And as far as I'm concerned, he's innocent. From the ties that I have with this man ... within my heart I don't believe what they say he done ... and from what he says ... that it's a conspiracy, yeah, I do believe that." When asked if he thought his opinion was representative of most of the towns' folk, his response was, "In my opinion, yes, if they are older heads like I am, and grew up with and probably knew the man as well as I have, and broke bread with him. He's no stranger to me, Stokely Carmichael, and even the mayor here, he's no stranger. They have close ties, they know one another; Bob Mass, there's other people in the neighborhood, they all know one another."

Beyond White Hall, Alabama, there has been a tremendous amount of good will for Imam Jamil, due to the deeply committed person he has been all of his adult life. Since 1976—when he relocated to Atlanta (Ga.) after serving five years in prison for his previous civil/human rights activism—he and the Community Mosque have been transformative agents on the West End; receiving the lion's share of the credit for improving the quality-of-life for residents in that previously besieged part of the city. His quiet, mild-mannered, Islamically grounded persona has made him a stabilizing force in other respects as well. A 73-year-old neighbor, Ms. Hattie Stegall, commented after his arrest, "I never saw him angry. When someone would die in my family, he would come by an offer his hand. And when the Muslim children would fight my grandchildren, he would make them come to me and apologize." It has also been reported that people from different walks of life would often make "pilgrimages" to his little Community Store. Conservative syndicated columnist George Will made such a visit in 1985, and later wrote, "His shelves are sparsely stocked, but his customers are buying only cheerios and milk, a few dollars worth at a time, and anyway, commerce is not the point. The Koran is the point—every point!"

This is the Imam Jamil al-Amin that many Muslims around the United States have come to know for the past quarter century. This is also why a significantly high level of support for the Imam has continued to come from the non-Muslim community, particularly from activist-oriented, African-American circles, notwithstanding the deliberate and easily discernible efforts that have been made to drive a wedge between the Muslim and African-American communities in and outside Atlanta. This involved manipulating certain facts surrounding the case, and emphasizing that both sheriff's deputies were black males, in a city where the governmental bureaucracy, at least on the surface, is led largely by African Americans.

On the first day of the trial, Mrs. Coretta Scott King, the widow of one of America's most prominent and respected civil rights leaders, the late Rev. Dr. Martin

Luther King, Jr., released a statement to the press. One excerpt read:

> For justice to be faithfully served there must be no rush to judgment and the defense must be allowed to present all of its evidence, just as the prosecution must uphold the highest standards in meeting the burden of proof. ...This tragedy must not be compounded by a flawed trial or a rushed verdict. ... If these standards are scrupulously observed and reflected in the outcome, then the healing process can begin.

Unfortunately, the record shows that the defense was not able to present all of its evidence, nor did the prosecution uphold the highest standards in meeting the burden of proof. Mrs. King was attacked in the media for "interfering" in this troubling, highly politicized case while Imam Jamil's very capable team of highly competent attorneys allowed themselves to be hamstrung by a judge who was more concerned with order than with the dictates of justice.

Many people came to Imam Jamil's defense. Former Attorney General Ramsey Clark made one of the most powerful statements in his support:

> Let me say first, I remember Rap Brown well from the 60s; I thought that he was a splendid human being and leader of the civil rights movement, with a strong touch of nobility and commitment. I remember when

Congress passed the H. Rap Brown law, just to try to get people like him; and finally he was indicted under the law that he honored with his name. ... There can be no question that the United States government—through its intelligence agencies and most of its appointed leadership, and a great deal of its elected leadership—considers Islam, not just militant Islam, but Islam, to be the greatest threat to the domestic and international security of the United States.

The Struggle Ahead

At present, Imam Al-Amin is being held at the Reidesville Maximum Security Prison in the state of Georgia, at the highest level of security, in 23-hour lockdown. He, like numerous other political prisoners in America, is a victim of a multi-faceted failure: failure within the "system" and failure from within his own racial and religious communities. Not long before the commencement of his trial, the internationally renowned political prisoner and award-winning journalist, Mumia Abu-Jamal, released a statement in support of Imam Jamil wherein he noted:

> The struggle for the freedom and liberty of Atlanta Muslim leader Imam Jamil Abdullah al-Amin must take place now, before the cold fingers of the state can close around his neck. ... Al-Amin's freedom lies in people who express their support now, instead of

later. Fairness does not lie in reversing an
unjust conviction; rather it lies in preventing
one in the first place.

The outpouring of visible support that Imam Jamil should
have been able to receive in such a critical life-and-death case
never materialized in the way he deserved. The collective
failure of the entire community of civil rights activists to
respond appropriately in this case has made the atmosphere in
America more untenable for all. Imam Jamil's wife, Karima
al-Amin, as well as his brother Ed Brown, have become vocal
advocates for his case, traveling across the country to speak at
events and fundraisers to help his cause. Meanwhile, his
attorneys have pursued appeals in the hopes of receiving a new
trial. If given a fair trial, they believe Imam Jamil, at 60 years
of age, can finally be vindicated and freed from the shackles of
American prejudice. Until then, he will remain a symbol of
the injustices America has inflicted upon those whose lives
were committed to ensure that it lives up to its ideals. ■

• Imam Jamil (left) and Yusuf Islam (Cat Stevens, right) at a Bosnia rally in May 1993.

PROFILE: HUMANITARIAN DOCTOR
BEHIND BARS

Dr. Rafil Dhafir

- Oncologist, Camden Medical Center, New York
- Founder, *Help the Needy Endowment Inc.*
- President, *Islamic Society of Central New York*
- Founder, *Islamic Assembly of North America* (IANA)

What is he accused of?

On February 26, 2003, Dr. Dhafir and three other employees of *Help the Needy Endowment Inc.* were arrested and falsely charged by members of the Ashcroft Department of Justice with sending money to starving Iraqi families without a license to do so following the 1991 Gulf War in violation of crippling U.S. sanctions.

By July, 2003, the government largely abandoned its false Iraq claims. But having gone through his seized files for five months, it remanufactured the case, charging him with Medicare over-billing of an insignificant amount. Such a tactic proves that the government is determined to use any and all methods to persecute him.

In a sign of desperation, unable to find any evidence of wrongdoing on the part of Dr. Dhafir, prosecutors bullied both his wife and accountant into pleading guilty. Such a tactic is unheard of in a case involving a relatively minor over-billing.

—*Why Justice Matters*. National Liberty Fund.
Vol. 1, no. 1, January 2004.

441

Guilty of Helping the Needy:
The Case of Dr. Rafil Dhafir

Dr. Dhafir is a great guy. Soft spoken, kindest man we ever met. He has many patients that need him. My husband is one. ...He is so gentle and concerned. He always praised God for healing, never himself. We do need Dr. Dhafir to come back and save our loved ones.

—Terry Martin, New York.

A number of cases that emerged in the post–September 11 sweeps of Attorney General John Ashcroft have worked to confirm the perception that the American government has truly embarked on a war against Islam, not terrorism. The onslaught suffered by Muslim leaders and institutions across the country has almost invariably been unjustified. In nearly every case thus far, the government has attempted to tie legitimate activism, humanitarian work, and free speech with terrorism. The case of Rafil Dhafir goes further, in attempting to prosecute work that is admittedly humanitarian in nature, according to the government, but contravening its foreign policy. Recent developments in the case add to the widely held perception by American Muslims that the Justice Department will go to any and all lengths to ruin a person politically, financially, and legally. The Dhafir case has left a particularly dark spot on the American system of justice in the past few years.

Inspired Beginnings

Rafil Dhafir was born on July 1, 1948, to Fatima Thabit and Abdullah Dhafir in Baghdad, Iraq. Of his six surviving siblings, three still live in Iraq, two reside in England, and the other, Dr. Mazin Dhafir, resides in Orchard Park, New York, where he is a dermatologist.

Dhafir was raised as a Sunni Muslim in a hardworking middle class family in Baghdad. He graduated with high honors from high school at age sixteen. He ranked tenth out of 45,000 graduating seniors in the nation. After high school, Dhafir entered Baghdad Medical School in Iraq and completed his study in general medicine in 1971, at age 23. Following medical school, Dr. Dhafir practiced medicine in Baghdad for a few months as service to the government before migrating to the United States in 1972. He settled in Highland Park, Michigan, where he met and later married Priscilla. The couple has no children.

In 1973, after completing his residency at Highland Park Medical Center, Dr. Dhafir began treating patients in an impoverished and crime-ridden area of Detroit, Michigan. In Detroit, he trained in the emergency rooms of Detroit General and St. Joseph's Mercy Hospital. As a result of Dr. Dhafir's emergency room duties he witnessed first hand the impact of poverty and violence. Dr. Dhafir not only treated trauma victims, but counseled victims of rape long before it was standard practice.

It was in the emergency room at Detroit General that Dr. Dhafir had his first experience with a cancer patient. He saw a man, draped in a hospital gown, sitting alone in a hallway of the hospital. A physician approached the man and said, "Sir, you have cancer of the mouth and you are going to die." After the physician gave the man the devastating news, he turned and walked away, leaving the man hopeless and bewildered to cope with the news of his impending death alone. This incident deeply affected Dr. Dhafir. He credits his religion of Islam with teaching him that there is a cure for every illness, except senility, and his desire to hold true to his religion motivated him to devote his career to working with cancer patients.

In 1976, motivated by his desire to treat and care for cancer patients and his faith that these were not hopeless causes, Dr. Dhafir enrolled in the University of Michigan to become certified in oncology. Frances E. Bull, Professor Emeriti of Internal Medicine at the University of Michigan Medical School, remembers Rafil Dhafir as a soft-spoken, skilled physician, who related to his patients in a gentle manner:

> The Section of Medical Oncology had, at that time, three junior faculty members and myself, Professor and Head of the Medical Oncology Section of the Department of Internal Medicine, University of Michigan Medical School, in Ann Arbor, Michigan.

We had a total of two trainees per year when Rafil was with us. With this small number of faculty trainees, we basically worked shoulder to shoulder caring for patients with advanced cancer and grew to know each other well.

I can characterize Rafil as a well-trained, skilled physician, who related to these anxious and ill patients with a gentle kindness. He was soft-voiced and calm in demeanor. He was a practicing Muslim, and therefore did not smoke or drink, and observed the fasting of Ramadan. I held him in the highest regard.

From time to time since his departure for practice in New York, I would see him at the oncology meetings, but our conversations were brief.

I wrote him after 9/11, when there were anti-Muslim demonstrations around the country, hoping he was faring all right. His responding letter, which I cannot now locate and may not have saved, indicated he had reduced his flying because of airport security hassles, but that prior to 9/11 had been doing a fair bit of flying to raise funds to help the children of Iraq. He felt the children were suffering and dying from the sanctions imposed on Iraq, a view which I think is generally agreed upon. This activity would be in line with my knowledge of him as a compassionate human.[27]

Medicine for the Soul

In 1977, Dr. Dhafir passed his medical and oncology boards and went on to practice medicine and teach oncology at Texas Tech University in Amarillo, Texas, in 1978. Upon his arrival in Amarillo, there was no mosque where Muslims could congregate to practice their religion. In order to help fill this void, Dr. Dhafir made a part of his personal residence available as a place of worship for the Muslims in the Amarillo area.

In 1980, after living in Amarillo for two years, Dr. Dhafir relocated to Syracuse, New York, to become Associate Director of the cancer research project at Bristol Labs. He was able to help the company speed up the process in delivering vital cancer medication to seriously ill patients. Despite Dr. Dhafir's busy schedule at Bristol Labs, he assisted the Muslim community in building a mosque on Comstock Avenue in Syracuse. Ayesha Abdulazeem, one of the founders of the Islamic Society of Central New York, describes Dr. Dhafir's participation in building the mosque as follows:

> Dr. Rafil Dhafir, was invited to join our community of fledgling and predominately indigenous Muslims as an Amir. At first, he presided over our weekly meetings held on Sundays, wherever the University had a vacancy. Eventually, as the community grew in size Dr. Dhafir developed experientially in his ability to orchestrate the business of a not-for-profit. ... He along with several other community members began to

formulate the plans to secure land and fund-raise to achieve the building of a permanent place of worship.[28]

After construction of the mosque was completed in 1981, Dr. Dhafir saw a need to provide spiritual leadership in addition to financial support to his Muslim community. In that spirit, he served as president of the Islamic Society of Central New York. As Dr. Dhafir grew spiritually, his desire to treat cancer patients grew stronger. He felt compelled to return to his medical calling. Driven by his compassion to deliver oncology services to those in need, Dr. Dhafir opened his own practice in Rome, New York, in the spring of 1982. Dr. Dhafir was known and loved by his patients as a compassionate practitioner dedicated to saving lives. Peggy Tosti, a former patient of Dr. Dhafir, describes his unique qualities:

> I have been a patient of Dr. Rafil Dhafir for about eight years. He has shown me he is a man dedicated to saving lives. His compassion and care and relentless studying for cures of the horrible cancers his patients have to endure are unmatched by any other doctor who has treated me. I had the misfortune of suffering two totally separate cancers—nearly back-to-back—and, despite the discouragement I felt, Dr. Dhafir would not allow me to be despondent. He and his kind staff, which includes a Roman Catholic nun, have been totally devoted to my comfort and that of my fellow patients.

When patients undergo therapy for cancer, they inevitably get to know others who are in the same boat. I chatted with many of Dr. Dhafir's other patients and never heard a negative word about him or his staff. To me, this was an amazing fact. Not one of us felt mistreated or questioned the doctor's dedication.

Dr. Dhafir never denied his devout Muslim roots. In fact he often talked of his pilgrimages to his homeland (Mecca). But he never flaunted or attempted to convert anyone. His hiring of a Roman Catholic nun as his nurse practitioner exemplifies his love for all of humankind.[29]

In addition to Dr. Dhafir's private medical practice, he has been on the medical staff of Rome Memorial Hospital since 1982. In a press release issued by the hospital, following Dr. Dhafir's arrest in February, 2003, Darlene Burns, chief executive officer of Rome Memorial Hospital, stated that Dr. Rafil Dhafir has been a respected member of the medical staff since 1982. Over the years, Dr. Dhafir became acutely aware of the financial problems faced by many of his elderly patients. Quite often these elderly patients who received Medicare could not afford the co-payments associated with their insurance plan. Dr. Dhafir continued to provide his services, waiving the co-payments when his patients were unable to pay.

In 1991, Dr. Dhafir recognized that there was a dire need for medical services in the rural community of Camden, New York. Dr. Dhafir took up this challenge. He established the Camden Medical Center in addition to maintaining his private medical office in Rome, New York. Through his hard work and dedication he was able to recruit a number of doctors to join his effort to provide medical services to the Camden community. Doctors from a wide array of special areas such as internal medicine, family practice, pediatrics, and gastroenterology came to the Camden Medical Center. The Camden Medical Center continues to provide valuable medical care to more than 20,000 patients a year.

A Humanitarian Heart

Dr. Dhafir's compassion and generosity did not end with the cancer patients that he cared for. He also has a special place in his heart for the children of Iraq. His concern for the children of Iraq was, of course, in no way an endorsement of any nefarious activities of the former regime of that country, which he vocally opposed. Many American and Christian groups have provided relief to the Iraqi children who suffered greatly during the 1990s as a result of the economic blockade. In 1997, the United Nations commissioned a study that looked at a range of health related issues in Iraq. The study found that almost one million children in southern and central Iraq were chronically malnourished:

> The most alarming results are those on malnutrition, with 32 per cent of children under the age of five, some 960,000 children, chronically malnourished—a rise of 72 per cent

since 1991. Almost one quarter (around 23 per cent) are underweight—twice as high as the levels found in neighboring Jordan or Turkey.[30]

Phillip Heffinck, a UNICEF Representative in Baghdad, responded to the findings of the study as follows, "What we are seeing is a dramatic deterioration in the nutritional well-being of Iraqi children since 1991." Heffinck further stated: "It is clear that children are bearing the brunt of the current hardship." Finally, the study points out that there has been no sign of improvement in the nutritional health of the Iraqi children since the U.N. Security Council passed the oil-for-food program.

As people outside of Iraq became more aware of the developing health and medical crisis, Dr. Dhafir felt compelled to help in whatever ways he could. He still loved the people of Iraq, although he did not care for the leader of their country. After the first Gulf War in 1991, many families in Iraq were displaced and many children suffered from malnourishment. In 1993, in response to the suffering of the Iraqi children, Dr. Dhafir was instrumental in establishing the Help the Needy Endowment Inc. (HTN). HTN assisted children and their families by providing food and related items. It also collected and distributed the Zakat on behalf of Muslims. Zakat is an Islamic requirement, which orders observant Muslims to give 2.5 percent of their wealth to the poor each year.

Uneasy Target: Philanthropist Doctor

On February 26, 2003, Dr. Rafil Dhafir of Manlius (a suburb of Syracuse) New York and 3 individuals involved with the charity *Help the Needy Endowment Inc.* were arrested and charged with breaking the International Emergency Economic Powers Act, which established the Iraqi Sanctions, and with twelve counts of money laundering and one count of conspiracy to commit money laundering.

As part of its raid upon Dr. Dhafir and HTN, federal agents interrogated up to 150 predominately Muslim families that had donated to HTN. They were intimidated and asked inappropriate questions about their faith. It was the largest interrogation of Muslims ever conducted by federal authorities at one time. Not only was this raid egregious and a gross violation of the deeply held American principles, it also indicates the government's targeting of innocent humanitarians. Arguably it was an act to intimidate potential character witnesses for Dr. Dhafir.

This massive blitz of local Muslims was made public only thanks to the efforts of the community's religious leaders and one local reporter. This same reporter would go on to write about other (non-Muslim) charities that similarly helped those in need in Iraq in defiance of the sanctions, but yet were not investigated. This reporting stood in sharp contrast to local television coverage that focused on the supposed terrorist link indicated by Attorney General Ashcroft. On the evening of Rafil's arrest, viewers saw streaming headlines, frequent breaking news interruptions, and on the scene coverage by local networks. Imam Kobeisy of the Islamic Center would later say it was the worst day in his life to be a Muslim.

Support for Rafil would be growing, however slowly. Within the weeks and months that followed, the terror of war and the hysteria created by federal agents on February 26, 2003, was dissipating. Local Muslims pledged over one million dollars for Rafil's bail. He was, however, denied bail three times. The government would never prove its standard assertion, as has been the case in all similar situations, that Dr. Dhafir was involved in terrorist acts or posed a threat to the community. The Court found that "the government is unable at present to demonstrate with any degree of certainty the existence of danger on the part of this defendant, and indeed it may be ultimately shown that the government's suspicions in this regard are unfounded. On this basis, not surprisingly, I find the government has not proven by clear and convincing evidence that if released Dr. Dhafir would constitute a danger to the community." On the other hand, while prosecutors failed to show that Dr. Dhafir posed a danger to the community, the Court found that he had a powerful incentive to flee the country and the resources—both financial and otherwise—to do so if desired. The Court further reasoned that the government's strong case against Dr. Dhafir, coupled with a potential lengthy prison sentence if convicted, is a strong incentive for him to be a flight risk.

Attorneys continued to contest that claim strongly. Just as the government was hopeful it will prove its case, they argued, Dr. Dhafir was every bit as confident that he would be acquitted of all charges against him. The belief that Dr. Dhafir would prevail against the government's claims was seen by supporters as proof enough that he would have every reason and intention to remain in the Northern District of New York, the site of the trial. In addition, Dr. Dhafir's significant family ties to the United States made it highly unlikely that he would flee before trial. Dr. Dhafir presented even stronger community ties than defendants in similar cases who were granted bail. As a 54-year old man, who has been married for thirty years, he has significant ties to the Syracuse community. Dr. Dhafir owns a home in the Syracuse area. Although he no longer had his medical practice, he was still a licensed physician in good standing. He entered the country legally, and had been a United States citizen for decades. He has no criminal record and no record of drug or alcohol abuse. Finally, all of Dr. Dhafir's passports were seized at the time of his arrest, thus, making his ability to travel, especially at a time of heightened security, virtually impossible.

At the time of Dr. Dhafir's detention hearing the Court reasoned that although the Department of Homeland Security had done a wonderful job of securing the borders, there was still a possibility that Dr. Dhafir could drive over the frozen St. Lawrence River into Canada and disappear into a country that has no extradition treaty with the United States. Playing into the bizarre reasoning of the judge, attorneys waited until spring to reissue their demand for his release, with the possibility of his driving a two thousand pound vehicle across the St. Lawrence River being quite remote. It was still denied, nonetheless.

Sudden Change of Course

By July, 2003, after the case of Dr. Dhafir was exhausted by a government body parading it as the latest victory in its war on terrorism and a sensationalist mass media had regurgitated that notion endlessly on the airwaves, a remarkable breakthrough took place. Recognizing that the charges were completely unfounded and that there was little chance that Rafil Dhafir could ever be convicted, the government dropped all terrorism related charges against him. This was not the end of Dr. Dhafir's ordeal though. In order to save face, the government instead charged him with Medicare over-billing in his medical practice, a rather trivial accusation, meant only to come away with something from the government witch-hunt. Gone was the talk of terrorist plots, money laundering, and supporting starving Iraqi children. Now Dr. Dhafir was being charged solely in his capacity as a doctor of faults in his accounting. In addition, his wife Priscilla and his accountant were coerced by government authorities into entering guilty pleas on the new charges, in order to rid Rafil of the more serious accusations. In this way, the government attempted to protect its reputation from the widely held belief that it was targeting innocent people.

In spite of the drastic change of course by the Justice Department, little or no attention was given to this extraordinary development. The media sat quietly as the assertions that it had reported as fact for many months had just been tossed out the window. No public outrage emerged to protest the grotesque abuses by law enforcement officials in their fruitless fishing expedition. As a result, Dr. Rafil Dhafir would remain behind bars without being granted bail, despite the fact that only minor charges remained against him. The injustice would persist for many months, as the government had done the damage it hoped to do in arresting him, detaining him, and adding to the public's misconception of its "war on terror." In fact, what the government did on February 26, 2003, was to close down the only full-time oncology practice, valued at over $3 million, in Rome, New York. It halted the distribution of badly needed humanitarian aid to Iraqis suffering from Saddam Hussein's regime and crippling U.S. sanctions. It raided the homes of over 150 donors, everyday law-abiding Muslims, none of whom were subsequently charged with any crime. It also incarcerated a man who committed no crime as he provided aid in a legal, humane, and efficient manner simply because he was perceived as a threat to America.

On November 14, 2003, press conferences were held in eight cities across the United States to protest the fines and arrests of individuals who had provided humanitarian aid to Iraq in defiance of the sanctions. At the Syracuse protest, a statement by Dr. Rafil Dhafir was read to the gathering of media and protestors. It read, in part:

> We are fortunate to live in this great place on earth that our maker made prosperous and unique. Noble people are always grateful for any act of kindness extended to them. We should show our thanks and gratitude to our maker. Words and lip service [are] not enough. How can we pretend that we are grateful when the silent majority is not lifting a finger to change and improve our surroundings peacefully?
> Are we grateful when the liars are allowed to defame the truthful ones?
> Are we grateful when we [acquiesce] to the bigots and racists masquerading as law enforcers and keep silent?
> Are we grateful when we allow the good to be portrayed as evil and evil portrayed as good?
> Are we grateful when we keep silent when the greedy continue to exploit the needy?

Are we grateful when we allow the mischievous few to ruin this beautiful country of ours under many guises?

Are we grateful when the news media work in concert with dishonest government officials by not exposing them in asking the tough questions?

Are we grateful when people are allowed to prosecute those who act to save and preserve the lives of the less fortunate?

Those who impede the good deeds of others and make no effort to save the lives of their fellow human beings actively, directly, and indirectly are responsible for the death of innocent children, women, and men whose only crime is that they are not like us and they are not of us.

How can we claim that we are grateful when the silent majority don't even care, let alone do something, to alleviate the misery of fellow human beings?

O our maker, the Generous One, we beg your forgiveness for our shortcomings, for our neglect of the needy ones and our ineptitude towards the corrupt ones. For we realize that unless we improve our surroundings we risk being deprived of your generosity.

These powerful words put in plain words the notion that there is indeed something wrong with American society in the post-September 11 world. Cases such as his are emblematic of a larger problem that persists in persecuting the few who hold minority views and who express them in lawful ways. Moreover, in this particular case, it appears as though Dr. Dhafir simply held that view at the wrong point in time. After all, in the lead up to the war on Iraq, which began only weeks after Rafil's arrest, government officials ranging from the President and Secretary of State, to seemingly everyone below them, were drawing upon the humanitarian crisis in Iraq as one of the main justifications for their preemptive war. All around Washington, the theme of "helping the oppressed Iraqis" became a popular trend in the months that Dr. Rafil Dhafir languished in prison for doing precisely that. The bitter irony in this case is self-evident. And it is only once the halls of power face up to this hypocrisy that this nation can heal the wounds of hate and mistrust that have since sprouted in all its corners and across the world. ■

PROFILE: A UNITED STATES SECURITY RISK?!

Dr. Sabri Samirah

- PhD, Political Science, University of Illinois
- MS, Economics, DePaul University
- Founder and President, *United Muslim Americans Association* (UMAA)
- Board Member, *Islamic Association for Palestine* (IAP)
- Director, *American Middle Eastern League for Palestine* (AMEL)
- Board Member, *Council of Islamic Organizations of Greater Chicago*

I want a hearing before a judge to be able to hear all the charges leveled against me. I want to defend myself in court. I deserve due process.

—Dr. Sabri Samirah

Congressman Henry Hyde meeting with Muslim delegation in Chicago, Illinois.

Due Process Denied:
The Case of Dr. Sabri Samirah

> The government cannot short-circuit the rights of an alien who
> has long lived in the United States by revoking his parole and
> then treating him as if he had never been here at all.
>
> —US District Judge James B. Moran, March 25, 2003.

On January 18, 2003, while traveling, Sabri Samirah was handed a three-line paper by an immigration officer at Shannon Airport in Ireland, stating that he was a "security risk to the United States." How Dr. Samirah is a risk and why are only a few questions that the United States government has failed to answer, and most likely will never answer.

Who is Sabri Samirah?

Friends have described Sabri Samirah as "Sharp yet polite, smart yet humble, with an everlasting smile." Holding a Ph.D. in Public Policy and Economics, and dedicating all of his life to his community, Sabri became a well-known and respected leader in the Chicago-land Muslim community through his hard work and sacrifice. One of his main goals was to help integrate Muslims into mainstream American society. In addition to that, he has spent a great deal of time in leading national and local organizations that advocate the right of Palestinians to live a free democratic life and educate the public about the Palestinian/Israeli conflict.

His Early Life

Sabri Samirah was born in Amman, Jordan, to Palestinian parents in 1967, the same year that the Israeli occupation began. With the exception of three years in Bahrain early on, he spent all of his life in Jordan until his arrival to the United States in 1987, prior to his twenty-first birthday. Sabri was raised in a typical Palestinian family dreaming of one day returning to their grandparents' home in Jerusalem's Old City. He was a very bright young man with many dreams and performed well in his academic life. He obtained his bachelors degree and was ranked first of his class at the University of Jordan. From an early age, Sabri also took on an activist role, becoming very involved in his community and in youth activities. Among other things, he led neighborhood kids and won prizes in Qur'anic competitions at local mosques and schools, organized the "Aqsa Eagles," a local soccer team, and was the treasurer of a big local *zakat* committee helping the poor. In addition, Sabri was an active member of the Student Government for his department at the University of Jordan, where he worked hard to conduct popular student educational seminars, hold book fairs, and organize *umrah* religious visits to Makkah.

Being the top of his class he was offered a full scholarship by the Jordanian Royal Court to complete his higher education in Amman but his ambitions were higher than what he could accomplish in Jordan. That led to his decision to travel to a land of new opportunities, America.

Life in America

Sabri, like many other young Arab Muslim immigrants who dream of coming to America in search of a good education and a better life, was faced with many difficulties and challenges. He managed to successfully complete his master's degree in Economics at DePaul University and continued on to a doctorate program at the University of Illinois at Chicago. In 2001, Sabri graduated with his PhD in Political Science. While all that was taking place, Sabri was working to raise and support his family as his wife obtained a master's degree in special education.

In spite of the many challenges faced by immigrants, Sabri remained optimistic about his future, believing that his hard work would be rewarded. While adjusting to life in his new country, he became enamored with American freedoms, democracy, and human and civil rights. He valued the privilege of voting and worked to encourage American Muslims to exercise their right to vote in elections, which he himself would not have the opportunity to practice as a non-citizen. He established and served as president of the United Muslim Americans Association (UMAA), in Palos Hills, Illinois, from 2000 until late 2002 when he was not allowed back to his home in Orland Park, Illinois. This organization was instrumental in developing relations between the

Muslim community and members of Congress. In June, 2001, alone, Dr. Samirah was among a number of dignitaries to meet with influential Congressman Henry Hyde (R-IL) on two separate occasions. The meetings addressed a number of issues that concerned the community. Issues were raised ranging from Palestine to Lebanon, American foreign aid, and racial profiling in the United States. Hyde listened attentively to their issues, promising to work in his capacity as their congressional representative to investigate them. "We stressed to him that House hearings on issues relevant to the situation in the Middle East should include experts from both sides. The public forum-like hearing is the only way the American representatives can reach a fair decision after being clearly informed of all the facts." said Samirah of his encounter.[31] In addition to these efforts, Dr. Samirah was heavily engaged in interfaith dialogue groups in the months following September 11. He often specifically focused his attention on improving relations between local Muslims and Jews. He recognized that progress must be made not only in the region undergoing conflict, but in the United States as well. His accomplishments were featured in an article by the *National Journal* which stated in part, "[Dr. Samirah] does recognize that the United States plays a central role in resolving the Palestinian question. 'Unless the U.S. gets involved,' he says, 'we will not see peace.' Further, he believes that dialogues between American Jews and Muslims are crucial because these two groups can bring the American principles of freedom and equality for all peoples to the debate."[32] Dr. Samirah has also been an active member of the Islamic Association for Palestine and its efforts to bring about a just resolution to the Middle East conflict.

Among UMAA's other accomplishments under the leadership of Dr. Samirah was the passage of a state law requiring certain businesses to declare whether food they sell is Islamically acceptable. The Halal Food Act was passed unanimously by the state senate, following the testimony of Muslim leadership, including Dr. Samirah.

Friends recall that, "to any person that met him, Sabri was more American in heart and action than many Americans. He loved America because he valued freedom." Throughout his stay in the country, he traveled only once, in 1990, to visit family back in Jordan and to get married to his wife, Sima Srouri. Shortly after their marriage, the couple was blessed with their first American born child, Ibrahim. The birth of Sabri's first child deepened his attachment and belonging to America. Today, Sabri has three American born and raised children.

Sabri's Designation as a "Security Risk"

After spending many years in the United States and establishing a family, Sabri was attached to what he lovingly called his country, the United States. He came as a young man and spent all of his adult life in America, becoming attached to its culture and norms. After the completion of his academic program, he applied for an adjustment of status for both himself and his wife. His applications were repeatedly refused or "lost." Finally, after years of delays of his adjustment for no reason by the INS, the couple was approved and started the process of obtaining their permanent residence status.

In December of 2002, Sabri received news from his family in Jordan notifying him of his mother's deteriorating health. Almost immediately, Sabri, who is very passionate about his family, decided to travel to see his mother, and based on that emergency, he applied for an advance parole document, a reentry document granted to aliens to be able to enter the United States.

Sabri was pleased with the government's decision allowing him to leave the United States and did so on December 28, planning to return on January 18, 2003. On that day, his plane stopped at Shannon Airport in Ireland and while going through an INS inspection, Sabri was handed a decision by the local INS office that was sent exactly one day prior to his scheduled arrival in the United States, stating that he cannot enter the country because he is a security risk for the United States. Sabri objected and showed the officers the advance parole issued by the INS, but this was not honored. Being designated as a security risk caused fear among the Irish police and they forced Sabri to stay in an Irish jail rather than wait in the airport until arrangements could be made for him to fly back to Jordan.

Facing Humiliation at Shannon Airport

Sabri was handcuffed and taken by the Irish Police in a very humiliating and embarrassing way for such a respectful man who has never been arrested nor committed any crime at any point in his life. He always lived as a role model spending his time between his work, family, home, and college and suddenly found himself sitting in a jail cell.

Back in the United States

While Sabri was being held in jail, his wife Sima and their three children were getting ready to see him. Decorating the newly bought house, the four were anxiously waiting to go to the airport for his arrival when suddenly his wife received a call from him telling her that he was not allowed back and he is in jail. His wife initially took it to be a joke as he is known for his sense of humor but later shocked to learn otherwise. Sima did not know what to tell their three children who were separated from their dad for the first time in their life. She was in tears waiting by the phone, wishing and praying that Sabri would soon come home to his beloved family, friends, and community. Confused and puzzled by all this, his wife, with the help of community members, decided to do their best to support Sabri's decision to fight for his right to return to his adopted country.

The Legal Case

News of Sabri's inability to return affected the local community and rallied many to offer their help to his family and to work on his case. Sabri's lawyers started filing objections and contacting the local INS offices but no one ever returned their phone calls. Others in the Muslim community contacted the INS and no result was ever achieved.

The community stood behind Dr. Samirah in his fight for due process, holding an important town hall meeting on October 17, 2003, sponsored by a wide coalition of organizations, including Amnesty International and other civil and human rights groups, as well as Arab and Muslim organizations. The event, which launched a commission to investigate racial profiling and civil rights abuses, featured a number of important speakers, some of whom told the story of Dr. Sabri Samirah. Jesus Garcia, former Illinois State Senator who is part of the commission said, "This event, these testimonies, help us put a face on the suffering that is becoming wide spread in this country, especially in light of the increasing pressure that is making it harder for immigrants to come here or to seek asylum. The most important challenge we face is to continue breaking the silence."[33]

On March 25, 2003, U.S. District Judge James B. Moran issued a ruling in favor of Dr. Samirah stating, "The government cannot short-circuit the rights of an alien who has long lived in the United States by revoking his parole and then treating him as if he had never been here at all." But, the government delayed sending Sabri the reentry form and the next day government lawyers filed an appeal with a higher court district to uphold the lower court decision.

On July 2, 2003, the 7th District Court, the highest judicial body in Illinois, upheld the government decision to deny reentry to Dr. Samirah on the basis that his designation as a security risk was made at the discretion of Attorney General John Ashcroft and it is not subject to appeal. Dr. Samirah appealed the federal ruling on August 15, 2003. Finally, in January, 2004, Dr. Samirah's attorneys appealed his case to the United States Supreme Court. "This case has serious implications for a million immigrants living in this country," said one of his lawyers, Mark Flessner.[34] The court is expected to decide whether to hear the case in April 2004. In the meantime, unable to cope with life without him in the United States, Dr. Samirah's family relocated to Jordan to join him while the case is settled.

Currently, disregarding the struggles and the scrutiny facing American Muslims in America, Dr. Sabri Samirah continues to hope to return one day to the United States due to his faith that the system will vindicate him. In a statement following his appeal to the Supreme Court, he said, "The time will come where all people will see that the government is politically motivated. I reaffirm again that I will do all I can until my rights are restored and my name is cleared. This experience has taken a devastating toll on me, my loved ones, and my community, both emotionally and financially."[35] Time and again, Sabri has demanded a fair hearing to be given the opportunity to challenge the U.S. Government in its false accusations against him. In spite of his bad experience, America remains a country very close to his heart, and his faith in its values has not been shaken. ■

• Dr. Sabri Samirah at an Islamic Association for Palestine convention in 1996.

PROFILE: THE VICTIMS OF XENOPHOBIA

• Ghassan Elashi

• An artist's rendition of the Elashi brothers at a court hearing in 2002.

Attacking Muslim Communities:
The Case of the Elashi Brothers

The government's statements regarding the arrests are neither indicative nor proportional to the frivolous nature of the allegations detailed in the indictment. It is clear from the indictment, and from the statements made by Attorney General Ashcroft, that the charges are exaggerated and leave one to wonder if the Justice Department is attempting to scapegoat the Elashi brothers for the perceived government ineffectiveness in the war on terrorism.

Waseem Nasrallah, president of
Muslim Legal Fund of America (MLFA).

In its attack on Muslim charities in the United States, the Justice Department has gone to great lengths not only to destroy these institutions by freezing their accounts and shutting down their offices, but to make sure that such events receive as much national attention as possible in the government's propaganda war against Islam and the Muslim community. Such was the case in Dallas, Texas, on December 16, 2002, when federal agents, to much fanfare, arrested four brothers and charged them with terrorism. Only hours later, Attorney General John Ashcroft held a news conference in which he boasted of the Justice Department's success in cracking down on terrorist cells across the country.

The case of the Elashi brothers was one of the first to receive widespread national attention in the post-September 11 atmosphere. Many within the media hailed it as an unquestioned victory in America's war against Islamic terrorists. In contrast, any observer with regard for the values of due process and equality understood this to be a fishing expedition by the government and a symbolic case meant to instill a sense in security among Americans while spreading a wave of fear and panic in America's Muslim minority. It was also viewed by some as a test case, for if the government, based purely on the atmosphere of hysteria and emotionally charged anti-Muslim and anti-Arab sentiments, could get away with prosecuting this family based purely on charges that hold no weight whatsoever, there would be nothing to stop it from continuing that assault on various other leaders, organizations, and communities throughout the United States.

Biographies of the Brothers

Thus, the Elashi case came as a devastating blow to a community already beset by the heated climate in the aftermath of 9/11. To add insult to injury, the Elashi family is a well-known family in the Dallas/Ft. Worth area as well as throughout the country. They are a very well respected family and devout Muslims. Most people in the community were shocked by the arrests of some of their most esteemed brethren. The eldest brother, Ghassan, came to the United States in 1978 and finished his master's degree in professional accounting from the University of Miami in 1981. He worked as a financial manager for Research Computer and Technology Corporation in California between 1982 and 1986. He then joined

International Computer and Communication, Inc. in California as International Sales Manager, before joining InfoCom Corporation in Texas as the Marketing Director in 1992. In 1989, he co-founded the Holy Land Foundation and served later as the chairman. Ghassan is married with six children and has been a U.S. citizen since 1992.

Bayan came to the United States in 1977 and received his master's degree in computer science in 1980 from Purdue University. He served as the President and Chief Technology Director for Research Computer and Technology Inc. in California. Of his many accomplishments, he led the company to introduce the first Arabic personal computer in the world, called "Alraed". He incorporated International Computer and Communications Inc. in California and served as its president from 1986 to 1992. Bayan incorporated and has served as the president of InfoCom Corporation in Texas. He is married with five children.

Basman came to the United States in 1979 and completed his bachelor's degree in mechanical engineering from Ohio University. He worked as a manager of an automotive service station in California from 1985-1988 and joined International Computer and Communications Inc. in California as Operations Manager. He has served as the Operations Manager of InfoCom in Texas since 1993. Basman is married with 3 children.

Hazim came to the United States in 1979 and graduated with a B.S. in computer engineering from Portland University in 1988. He joined International Computer and Communications Inc. in California as Network and Personal Computer Manager from 1988-1992. He joined InfoCom Corporation in 1992 and has served in the same position until 2000. Hazim is married with four children.

All of the Elashi brothers have held leadership positions in some capacity, whether in the local mosque, school, charities, or activist organizations in the area

A Community Unites

InfoCom Corporation, the business in which all four of the Elashi brothers were employed, became the focal point of the federal investigation and the subsequent indictment of the Palestinian American men. The charges, detailed in a 33-count indictment issued on December 16, 2002, allege criminal conduct by the Elashi brothers through InfoCom. Twelve of the counts allege that exports to Libya and Syria were made in violation of U.S. export control laws, and the remaining counts allege that financial transactions were made in violation of the International Emergency Economic Powers Act (IEEPA).

Though still in a state of devastation following the arrests, Dallas Muslim community leaders banded together in defense of the Elashis. On January 24, 2003, several area Muslim organizations, along with other local civil and human rights groups in North Texas, announced the formation of the Liberty Task Force to help coordinate community efforts aimed at ending what the group calls "racial and religious scapegoating" involved in the charges against the Elashi brothers. In a statement released that day, Liberty Task Force members said:

> The government's statements regarding the arrests are neither indicative nor proportional to the frivolous nature of the allegations detailed in the indictment. It is clear from the

indictment, and from the statements made by Attorney General Ashcroft, that the charges are exaggerated and leave one to wonder if the Justice Department is attempting to scapegoat the Elashi brothers for the perceived government ineffectiveness in the war on terrorism. The Attorney General's statements are unwarranted and inappropriate given the nature of the alleged trade violations (which involve obsolete and out-dated computer equipment), therefore bringing into question the government's real motive behind the arrests of these men.

The statement continues:

Regardless of the government's rhetoric, the Elashi brothers must be presumed innocent and have an opportunity to present evidence of their innocence in a court of law. The government's investigation and prosecution of these men have been conducted in a way that violates the principles of fairness and due process that are fundamental in the American judicial system.

By supporting their defense, American Muslims, along with other people of conscience, are stating unequivocally that their love for this country and its security should not come at the expense of their civil rights or due process of law. Racial and religious scapegoating should never be tolerated.

The Liberty Task Force characterized this case as the latest in a series of initiatives by the Justice Department that target U.S. Muslims. During that same period, the Department of Justice launched four rounds of "Special Registration" for citizens or nationals of Muslim countries. Civil rights groups filed a lawsuit against the government challenging the constitutionality of identifying people for "Special Registration" based on their countries of origin. To many observers, the Elashi case was the foremost high-profile legal battle for the defense of the civil rights of Muslims and all Americans.

Indeed, the Muslim community's stern response to the arrests was in part a reaction to the government's exploitation of the events to advance its own agenda by hyping an otherwise shallow and plain case. The FBI touted the charges by stating, "Today's indictment proves once again that the FBI is committed to aggressively pursuing terrorists and disrupting terrorist networks across the United States. The investigation out of Dallas relied upon an array of intelligence and law enforcement initiatives and tools that have characterized our post 9-11 prevention efforts." In fact, nowhere in the indictment are the Elashis charged with outright support of terrorism. Most of the counts deal specifically with their business practices, which the Elashis contend were always within the bounds of the law. The Liberty Task Force released a document responding to the charges against the four men and their corporation, InfoCom.

Responses to the Unfounded Allegations

Counts 1 through 7 and 12 charge the Elashis with making a shipment of HP color laser printers and personal computers worth $28,000 to Libya in 1997. According to the statement, "evidence would show that InfoCom did not make any shipments to Libya. InfoCom made the shipments to Malta, and the customer instructed a Malta based shipping company to forward the goods to Libya without InfoCom's knowledge."

Counts 8 through 12 charge the making of shipments of personal computer parts to Syria without a proper license between 1998 and 2000. With regard to this issue, the Liberty Task Force contends, "Evidence would show that at that time, InfoCom relied on shipping company documents that showed a license was not needed to ship such parts to Syria. Evidence would show that InfoCom made another shipment of a digital telephone switch and obtained the proper export license from the Department of Commerce."

Counts 13 to 33 charge that in 1992 the Elashi brothers conspired with their cousin, Nadia Elashi, the wife of Mousa Abu Marzook, to hide an investment of $250,000 under her name. In response to this third allegation, the statement had this to say:

> Evidence would show that Mrs. Nadia Elashi, not her husband, invested the money with InfoCom. At that time, she and her husband were permanent residents of the U.S. The government had knowledge of this investment since 1995. In 1996, InfoCom, based on a U.S. court order, handed the government all documents and cancelled checks related to her investment. In 2001, the government froze a total of $105,000 from InfoCom's bank account as an estimate of the

amount of the return on investment paid to Mrs. Nadia Elashi since her husband was added to the specially designated terrorist list issued by the U.S. government in 1996, four years after the said investment deal started. Evidence would show that all the checks InfoCom paid Mrs. Elashi since the beginning of the investment were deposited in her bank account in the U.S. Most of the money deposited was spent by her son, to help pay for his tuition and living expenses.

Uncertain Future in an Uncertain Climate

In spite of the cloud of frenzy surrounding their arrest by the government, Ghassan Elashi was released without bail pending trial. The Muslim Legal Fund of America, a non-profit Islamic organization that began in defense of Muslim leaders and organizations, took on the Elashi case. By early 2004, the case had yet to reach trial but the community remained hopeful and steadfast in the face of the adversity. As head of the most prominent American Muslim charity, Ghassan Elashi was successful in providing the community with the much-needed support it required, and many Muslims believe it was because of this that he and his brothers, who were also very active in the community, were targeted. While the experience has been increasingly draining both financially and emotionally for the Elashis, their families, and their community, hope remains that the climate of hysteria will subside in favor of a just and equitable treatment by the powers that be. ■

PROFILE: A HUMANITARIAN WHO LOST HIS IMMUNITY IN POST SEPTEMBER AMERICA

• Rabih Haddad

• Rabih Haddad with his family

Though he was never charged with a crime, he was treated like an archcriminal, held for most of his detention in solitary confinement. By order of Attorney General John Ashcroft, his deportation hearings were conducted in strict secrecy until a lawsuit forced the government to open the case to public scrutiny. The government refused to release him on bond because it considered him a "flight risk." Yet when it failed to come up with evidence to warrant terror charges, the United States forced his flight, deporting him to Lebanon.

—Ann Mullen, *Detroit Metro Times*, March 17, 2004.

• Salma al-Rushaid, flanked by Nihad Awad (left) and Ashraf Nubani, testifying before Congress on behalf of her husband.

479

Liberty's Forsaken Son:
The Story of Rabih Haddad

I am particularly appalled that the Bush administration would be
championing these proceedings and the use of secret evidence.
During the campaign, Mr. Bush promised to oppose the use of
secret evidence. Now, he is not only using it, but by obtaining
and using new powers for secret evidence for asset freezes in the
so-called USA Patriot Act, he is expanding it. The attacks of
September 11 should not destroy our Constitution. Rather, they
should strengthen our commitment to it. Imam Haddad is entitled
to the full disclosure of any evidence against him.

—Congressman John Conyers (D-MI).

As the highly populated Muslim Midwest braced
itself in the aftermath of 9/11, it would come to
face a number of high-profile cases that exhausted its
resources. Not the least of these was the case of Rabih
Haddad, which revolved around activist work in Chicago,
Illinois, and Ann Arbor, Michigan. Haddad was a
Lebanese immigrant who had been in the United States on
and off for some twenty years. His arrest came on
December 14, 2001, as part of the government's shutting
down of Global Relief Foundation, one of the most
successful Islamic charities in the United States. As in every
other case, government investigators accused the ten-year

old humanitarian organization of having terrorist ties, though no one in the organization nor the organization itself was ever charged with a crime. According to Detroit's *Metro Times*, Jeffrey Collins, U.S. attorney for the Eastern District of Michigan, "no evidence was ever brought before his office to warrant criminal charges against Haddad."[36] He was officially being held because of an expired visa, a common immigration violation.

Background

Born in 1961 to a Christian family in Lebanon, Rabih Haddad was encouraged by his parents to pursue his own path toward God in the midst of the sectarian strife of the Lebanese civil war, and at the age of 18, he was drawn to Islam and embraced the religion. From an early age, Rabih began writing poetry, following in the footsteps of his grandfather, Abdallah Kobersi, a well-known poet in Lebanon. Later, while in prison, Haddad would chronicle his ordeal in eloquent prose and poetry. After high school, he enrolled at the American University of Beirut for one year, before his parents sent him and his brother Bassem to the United States to escape their war torn country. He came to the United States to pursue his engineering degree at the University of Nebraska. In 1987, he married Salma al-Rushaid, also a student.

　　Becoming increasingly more devout in their beliefs, the couple traveled to Pakistan the following year as volunteers hoping to help relieve the suffering being caused by the expanding humanitarian tragedy. Fallout from the Soviet war in Afghanistan caused an influx of refugees into Pakistan who were in desperate need of food, clothing, shelter, and medical care. Following the family's time in Pakistan, Haddad was intent on creating a permanent charity that would address the needs of humanitarian crisis situations throughout the Muslim world. In 1992, he co-founded the Global Relief Foundation (GRF), a humanitarian organization devoted to such issues. He served as chairman of GRF's board from 1992, and as its CEO between 1992 and 1996. At the time of his arrest, Haddad served as GRF's public relations director and chief fundraiser for its extensive projects. In only its first year, the GRF raised $700,000 to distribute more than 400,000 pounds of rice, sugar, and flour to 10,000 refugees in Pakistan. The organization also sponsored a school for 130 orphans and a medical lab that same year. As is the standard with most American Muslim charities, funds were raised through private contributions from group members and the larger Muslim population in the United States, usually following speaking engagements on the refugee crisis at mosques and community centers, as well as through publishing and distributing brochures.

By 1993, Haddad and his family had settled in Chicago, where the GRF was based. There he became an active member of the expanding Muslim community. He also lectured widely and wrote many articles, mostly on topics related to relief work and the Islamic faith. In the ensuing years, the GRF would expand widely, opening international branch offices in several countries. In 1998, Haddad returned to the United States following a failed attempt to seek work in his native Lebanon. But after deciding he would rather not settle his family in Chicago's urban environment, Haddad moved to the small town of Ann Arbor, Michigan, an area known for its large Muslim minority. There he continued his activist work, building on his leadership of the Global Relief Foundation, which, by its tenth year, had raised a total of over $20 million. It had become one of the largest American Muslim charities, second only to the Texas-based Holy Land Foundation. While in Ann Arbor, Haddad became a popular member of the community. Among his many activities, he volunteered as a teacher at the Michigan Islamic Academy in Ann Arbor. Rabih Haddad made a name for himself within the community as an effective fundraiser for the mosques in Ann Arbor and Ypsilanti and for the Ann Arbor chapter of the Council on American-Islamic Relations (CAIR). He has represented the Muslim community at town hall meetings and interfaith panels.

Haddad had been in Ann Arbor for two and a half years at the time of his arrest in December, 2001, with his wife Salma and the couple's four children. According to other leaders in the local Muslim community, he had always been a model upright citizen. His students have testified that he stated unequivocally that the attacks on 9/11 were not the acts of true Muslims.

On the afternoon of Friday December 14, 2001, three INS agents arrested Rabih Haddad. The INS refused Mr. Haddad bond on the basis that he would be a flight risk and would pose a danger to the community, but the agency had not offered any credible basis for these allegations. The justification for the arrest was a minor visa violation, one that thousands of others have incurred without any repercussions. Mr. Haddad's visa had expired, but he was applying for permanent resident status. In accordance with a visa amnesty law passed under the Clinton administration, this did not require him to leave the country. His INS hearings were closed and secret.

An Open Letter to "Lady Liberty"*

My Dear Sweet Lady,

You don't know me, yet I am one of your forsaken sons. In my dreams you come to me with promises of freedom and great aspirations, in a land far away. "One nation, indivisible, under God," you said. "Life, liberty, and the pursuit of happiness were guaranteed to all, " you said. "A land where justice is blind," you said. Your words swept me up in a tornado of hope, dreams, and inspiration. I answered your call and came to you with open arms, and oh, what a sight you were! Standing tall over the world, holding your torch like a beacon, calling stray ships on a turbulent ocean to safe harbor.

It was then that I pledged to you that I will uphold and practice the values that you stand for. Little did I know that I will be persecuted in your name, and little did you know what your children were doing behind your back, some wittingly, but most unwittingly. They are afraid, my dear Lady, and fear almost always begets hate. I have done my best to preach and explain. I made every effort to promote and expedite healing among all of your children who are still anguishing and agonizing over the national tragedy of Sept. 11. I condemned and denounced those barbaric acts of horrific terrorism. I called upon your children to come together and embrace one another. I implored them to triumph over adversity and flock to your side in a show of unity and defiance to those who would rob us of the values that define our way of life.

Someone once said, "There is nothing as strong as real gentleness, nothing as gentle as real strength." When I think of this, I think of you! Take a look over your shoulder and whisper gently to your children not to be afraid. From my jail cell, and because of my faith and trust in Almighty God, I tell you that my spirit is free! Free as the meadowlarks of Nebraska, proud as the bold eagles of Alaska. You do not have to worry about me; just keep your torch burning high, and remain in the dreams of the oppressed and persecuted around the world. Continue to be the beacon of hope and an oasis of prosperity for so many.

Come what may, I will hold true to the pledge I made to you. "Truth" and "justice" will ultimately prevail!

With love and hope,
Your forsaken son,
Rabih Haddad
Monroe County Jail

* Published in *Ann Arbor News*, January 13, 2002

Civil Liberties Denied

Haddad was denied bond and labeled a "flight risk," after which he was immediately placed in solitary confinement under very strict conditions. His wife and four children were devastated, as was their entire community of supporters, both in Michigan and back in their native Chicago, where Global Relief's offices remained. As GRF's cofounder and chief fundraiser, Haddad was targeted because of his work as a humanitarian provider to impoverished refugees in war torn lands across the globe. Haddad's imprisonment lasted nineteen months until July 14, 2003, when he was ultimately deported to Lebanon, to be followed by his family. The ordeal had a devastating effect on the Muslim community as a whole, but on the victim's family especially.

On January 11, 2002, Rabih Haddad was transferred to the Metropolitan Correctional Center in Chicago without notification to his wife or his lawyer, Ashraf Nubani. He was held in solitary confinement, and his access to the outside world was made as difficult as possible. His wife, Salma al Rushaid, attempted to visit him and was turned away with a variety of excuses until February 4th, which was her first sight of Rabih since he had disappeared from Michigan. Ten days later, Salma was notified that the INS was commencing removal proceedings against her and three of their four children (the fourth is an American). This case was combined with Haddad's hearing, rescheduled, and postponed repeatedly.

After weeks of solitary confinement, on approximately March 13, 2002, Rabih Haddad was allowed to join the general prison population, and finally to have non-contact visits twice a week with his family for two hours at a time and one 15-minute phone call per week to his family. This option was offered to him following intense protests from supporters and a prison visit by Congressman John Conyers. The prison's explanation that it was keeping Rabih in solitary "for his own protection" was shown to be baseless.

Over a year later, however, the family was subjected to even more inexcusable humiliation. On February 9, 2003, Salma was turned away from visiting her husband at Monroe County Jail. The guards cited heightened levels of security as the reason she was denied her visitation rights. The Attorney General had recently raised the national threat level from yellow to orange.

A *Michigan Daily* article chronicled these abuses. Haddad's attorney was quoted as saying "They gave her some spiel about the national security being raised to code orange during the pilgrimage. It would have been nice if they had called her before, but even then I'm not sure it would have been justified. What does the rise in national security have to do with their family?"[37] According to the article, "He [Ashraf Nubani] added that he felt it was very inappropriate to suggest that religion would have anything to do with that type of violence. Nubani said that Haddad's wife was very upset when he spoke to her over the weekend. 'He's been in jail for 14 months with no criminal charges pending,' Nubani said. 'I feel so sorry for her because no matter how you look at it, she's innocent and is being punished.' Nubani added that he could not verify that this was a national policy and would affect all INS detainees, but said he felt that in Haddad's case, it was being used selectively. He said that Haddad has been a model inmate, despite the fact that he has no criminal charges and his family made weekly visits and were always model visitors.

'This is just one thing in a series of actions used to justify the federal government's unjust incarceration of Haddad,' Nubani said. 'They could say code orange until doomsday—but time will tell and I believe Haddad will be vindicated'."[38]

Civil Liberties Defended

Rabih Haddad's ordeal was highly publicized as it received the backing of the Muslim community, as well as America's civil rights leaders. Mass demonstrations were taken before the jail, even prompting Haddad's move from his Michigan cell to a prison in Chicago, before being sent back to Michigan, without any notification to his worried and perplexed family and community of supporters. Present at one of these rallies was Congressman John Conyers (D-MI), a longtime champion of civil rights, who declared, "I am particularly appalled that the Bush administration would be championing these proceedings and the use of secret evidence. During the campaign, Mr. Bush promised to oppose the use of secret evidence. Now, he is not only using it, but by obtaining and using new powers for secret evidence for asset freezes in the so-called USA Patriot Act, he is expanding it." Conyers proceeded to visit Haddad in prison in March, 2002, becoming the first person apart from immediate family to visit him in his jail. Following the meeting he said, "The attacks of September 11 should not destroy our Constitution. Rather, they should strengthen our commitment to it. Imam Haddad is entitled to the full disclosure of any evidence against him."[39]

The deportation proceedings against Haddad were conducted entirely in secret, with no access given to the family, community, or the media to witness what was being done. Even Haddad himself was not allowed into the courtroom. Following a lawsuit by Conyers, the American Civil Liberties Union, and several media organizations, a judge ruled that Haddad's hearings must be opened to the public. Judge Nancy G. Edmund's decision on *Detroit Free Press et al v. John Ashcroft, et al* and *Rabih Haddad v. John Ashcroft et al* effectively denied the Justice Department's claim that secrecy was more necessary than individual rights. The government immediately appealed, but in the meantime the hearings had to be open. On April 10, 2002, the 6th Circuit Court temporarily stayed the portion of Judge Edmunds order and instructed defendants to hand over the INS hearing transcripts. On April 19th, however, the government announced that it would no longer seek a stay of Judge Edmund's ruling. According to defense lawyers, this meant that:

> Any hearings in Haddad's case that are held before the Sixth Circuit must be open (absent a showing by the government to the immigration court that a portion of the hearing must be closed to advance national security interests);
> The plaintiffs are entitled to the transcripts or tapes of the previous immigration hearings that were wrongfully closed. Subsequently, on April 22, 2002, the *New York Times* reported on the newly opened records, and stated that the main suspicion against Mr. Haddad appears to have been that he had traveled to Pakistan as part of his humanitarian work.

In early June, 2002, Haddad was transferred to the Monroe County Jail in Michigan to await the rescheduled INS hearing. As the first proceeding to be opened to the public following the April court rulings, it was a momentous event, despite the short length of the hearing and the fact that it did not address any of the substantial issues. An eyewitness detailed his account of what took place:

> The hearing was open and the courtroom, with approximately thirty spectators, was full. Three rows were reserved for the media. Most print and television sources from Detroit and Ann Arbor were present. Approximately fifty supporters of the Haddad family were at the building, although only twenty or so could fit in the courtroom. The others held signs in front of the Brewery Park Building (in the rain) during the proceedings.
>
> The hearing lasted only about ten minutes. Rabih's lawyer, Ashraf Nubani, presented an application for political asylum on behalf of Rabih. Rabih was not in the courtroom but was present via closed circuit television from the Monroe County Jail. Judge Elizabeth Hacker had Rabih swear to the authenticity of his asylum application and swear that the application was not "frivolous."
>
> The judge set the asylum trial date for August 27 at 9 am. She waived the presence of Salma's and Rabih's children.
>
> Ashraf Nubani then requested a reconsideration of bond for Rabih. The judge replied that

this setting was inappropriate for that request. Nubani stated he just wanted the judge to be aware that the bond redetermination request had been filed.

The judge then adjourned the hearing and the lawyers requested to speak with Rabih over the closed circuit television. Nubani informed him of the paperwork formality and Saleh said he was coming to see Rabih. We, in the peanut gallery, requested that the camera be turned toward the audience so that Rabih could see his supporters were there. He smiled and waved back at us.

Following a Justice Department appeal to the Sixth Circuit Court of Appeals, Judge Damon Keith upheld the decision to keep the proceedings open. He stated, "Democracies die behind closed doors. A government operating in the shadow of secrecy stands in complete opposition to the society envisioned by the framers of our Constitution."[40] On August 26, 2002, a three-judge panel of the Sixth Circuit Court of Appeals upheld Judge Edmunds' decision and ruled that the federal government cannot hold secret deportation hearings without giving justification. During a PBS interview, commentators expanded on the significance of the ruling. Lucy Dalglish, a media lawyer and director of the Reporters' Committee for Freedom of the Press responded, "I was overjoyed. I thought it was a marvelous decision. The opinion itself reads like a textbook on how to run a democracy. And it really reaffirms our faith that we really can get through everything; everything we've been through in the last year is not a reason to abandon the way we operate in this country. And I thought it was very affirming of the court process, the immigration process, and actually reassuring to the public as well. And perhaps, from my perspective, the best result is that for the first time in almost 20 years we have a decision from a significant court, the 6th Circuit, that clearly says that the media has a very important role in democracy and informing the public."[41]

On September 17, 2002, Federal District Judge Nancy Edmunds, having reviewed the evidence presented by the government arguing for a closed hearing, ruled that Haddad must have a new, open bond hearing with a different immigration judge or else the government must release him. This ruling on his detention did not change his deportation hearing, scheduled for October 7. Meanwhile, jail officials threatened to transfer Haddad if his family and supporters continued to gather at the jail. The bond hearing was attended by many supporters and news reporters, who were surprised when Immigration Judge Robert Newberry closed the detention hearing despite Judge Edmunds ruling. Appeals were immediately filed by the *Detroit Free Press* and others. The newspaper's lawyer, Herschel Fink, commented "I'm shocked that Judge Newberry ignored the rulings and orders of Judge Edmunds and the U.S. 6th Circuit Court of Appeals by refusing to allow the media to be heard on the issue of exclusion, and making no findings whatsoever before throwing the press and public out of the courtroom." According to press reports "Fink said an open hearing is necessary to allay fears among Arab-Americans that Haddad is being railroaded by the government and to let Americans know why the government allowed Haddad to remain in the U.S. after his visa expired. Fink said he would not have filed the motion had Newberry made any attempt to make the government justify its request to close the hearing."[42]

On October 15 and 16, 2002, the immigration judge in the case held a hearing to consider Haddad's asylum request. On the first day of the hearing, his friends and supporters were not allowed into the building, but, after considerable protests, the following day the immigration court administrator claimed there had been a "misunderstanding" and acknowledged that the hearings were supposed to be open. Asylum was denied on November 22, 2002, and soon after that his lawyer filed an appeal. On January 22, 2003, the U.S. 6th Circuit Court of Appeals rejected the Justice Department's request that the entire court review last year's decision by three of its judges allowing the press and the public to attend deportation hearings.

Conclusion

Once the proceedings were opened to public scrutiny, it became apparent that the government had no case against Haddad or the GRF. The cloud of suspicion it had so successfully created in the previous year had virtually disintegrated. Haddad was looking forward to proving that he was wrongfully targeted so he could be released once again. Though the government agents continued to try to muddy his reputation by providing false links to any terrorist groups, up to and including Al Qaeda, it was only successful in not granting him asylum in the United States, but not in charging, let alone proving, any allegations against him. Finally, in July, 2003, without any notice to his family or his attorneys, Rabih Haddad was secretly deported to Lebanon, confirming the widely held belief that the federal government had no genuine belief that he was at all a threat. According to Georgetown University law professor David Cole, "It [the deportation] means the FBI cleared him of any terrorist connections. ... The stated policy of the FBI was to not deport anyone who might be connected to terrorists. So that means he was not connected."[43]

In essence, however, the government achieved what it set out to do. By arresting and deporting Global Relief's chief fundraiser under the cloud of suspicion, and further by searching its offices, confiscating its files, and freezing its assets, the FBI successfully shut down an important humanitarian institution. The group attempted to sue the government for its wrongful designation of it as a terrorist organization without providing any evidence of its claims. The United States Supreme Court rejected a similar suit by the Holy Land Foundation, another Muslim charity. Roger Simmons, attorney for Global Relief said, "They blacklisted us and didn't tell us why. We want to eventually get a court to give us what every other American corporation or citizen gets, which is the right to confront your accuser. We believe when we get to see the evidence, the so-called evidence, we will be able to show it is unreliable, inaccurate, or false."[44] Haddad similarly contends, "All we have been asking since December, 2001, is to show us a shred of evidence and give us a chance to defend ourselves."[45] Counterterrorism expert Juliette Kayyem maintains the position of most American Muslims that Haddad was deported because government officials wanted to "wash their hands of what was clearly a mistake."[46]

The family resettled in the Lebanese capital, Beirut, reuniting with Haddad's extended family. He was overwhelmed with joy at returning to his country and enjoying the freedoms afforded to him there, which were unjustly taken away at the hands of the American government. His family, and especially his children who were deprived of his love and guidance for years, were relieved to have him back in their lives. In many ways it was a happy ending to an otherwise stressful ordeal. Though Haddad was never afforded any justice by the American system or given the opportunity to prove his innocence, he was nonetheless relieved to have survived the torment of nearly two years imprisoned without trial. Many others remained in similar circumstances hoping for their day in court, something so few Muslims in America were afforded in the weeks, months, and years after 9/11. ■

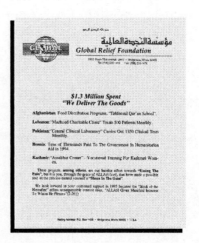

• A Global Relief Foundation publication.

PROFILE: MUSLIM AMERICANS ON
THE FRONTLINE

• Imam Siraj Wahhaj

• Imam Wahhaj speaks at the Dar Al-Hijrah Islamic Center.

• Imam Hamza Yousuf

• Imam Yousuf at an ISNA convention.

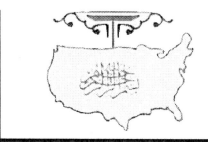

• Sheila Musaji

• Logo of The American Muslim invoking the blessing of Allah on America.

Chapter 11

IMPROBABLE TARGETS: INDIGENOUS MUSLIMS

But as I have documented at greater length on other occasions, much if not everything about the conduct of these organizations points to their essential agreement with the "conquor America" agenda. ... It is not accurate to say, as President Bush said of the Islamist leaders with whom he met on September 17th, that they "love America as much as I do."

From Daniel Pipes, "The Danger Within: Militant Islam in America," *Commentary*, November 2001, pp. 19-24.

During the previously documented accounts of the targeting of American-Muslim communities, a specific pattern was seen to have evolved. This pattern primarily involved a number of key features, the most significant of which is that in nearly every case, the targeted Muslim leaders were immigrants. This segment of society has historically been an easy target for a number of reasons. For one, immigrants are generally accused of having pre-existing loyalties to their native lands in preference over their adopted homeland. In recent years, this was especially expressed against immigrants from the Arab and Muslim worlds, who were viewed as valuing their native societies, cultures, and especially religions, over that of the United States. Considering that the policies and statements of Muslim governments often clashed with those of the United States, this was viewed with particular suspicion. Unfortunately, few critics of the Muslim immigrant community would even attempt to reconcile their bias with the fact that these people had left their homelands, which implied a respect and admiration for the United States and its opportunities and what it offered in terms of freedom and quality of life. Nevertheless, as with the previous experiences of minority immigrant communities, they would become the targets when tensions arose between their host nation and their countries of origin.

With the deepening tensions in the Middle East, it was inevitable that Muslims in America would bare the brunt of the attacks against their religion and people. This was true of the whole immigrant Muslim community, especially those who were public figures. In addition to these reasons, immigrants are also particularly vulnerable, not only because of their official status as "outsiders" but also because of their initial ignorance of the cultural norms around them. In many cases, immigrants were in an inherent state of weakness and unable to respond to the assaults on their rights and their reputations by the government and the media. With only loose networks and outsider organizations that had yet to crack into mainstream America, there was little room for maneuvering following the unprecedented attacks against them. Their legal experience and public relations savvy were still in an infantile stage, and, lacking the necessary resources and knowledge to mount a defense against the assault on their rights, they were vulnerable.

Immigrants were also a convenient target because of their particular interest in certain issues, which often conflicted with mainstream American views. This has been the case with all supporters of the Palestinian cause, facing the response from pro-Israeli groups, whose influence on media reporting and government policy is unrivaled by any special interest group in America. In fact, it is usually activism in the area of Palestinian rights that lands most American Muslims in hot water with the media and government. The same holds true for Muslim activists for Kashmir against whom a more powerful Hindu lobby has solidified the U.S. position of non-engagement in India's atrocities against Kashmir. While many international Muslim causes were originally limited to the immigrants from those lands, the past two decades have seen an expansion of the movement in favor of a more inclusive approach to dealing with the crises of the Muslim world. This has included all Muslims, immigrants and indigenous, and non-Muslims, Christians, Jews, and leftist progressives, as well as traditional or principled conservatives. As such, the attacks, which were initially levied only against immigrants as the weakest and most vulnerable link in the American Muslim chain, have since spread to include other Muslims, and even non-Muslims who are vocal on certain issues. This section will explore the abuses against indigenous Muslim communities and their leaders.

Indigenous Muslim Leadership

As the defaming of Muslims and Islam escalated after 9/11, the last group of Muslims in America to be targeted was the African-American and also the European-American community, together with their Christian supporters. These two groups have maintained identities separate from the immigrant Muslims partly because of language and ethnic heritage, but primarily because the indigenous Muslims focus on issues of conscience that concern all Americans and affect Muslims in America primarily as Americans. In other words, they have an American agenda independent of any foreign agendas from abroad.

The African-American Community

African-American Muslims prior to 9/11 were in some sense "off-limits" for Zionist ideologues because their loyalties to America are generally accepted without question and because collectively they have half a century of experience in the American political process and therefore are more knowledgeable on how to respond to attacks. Furthermore, a benign racism among many immigrant Muslims has hindered African-American integration with Muslims from abroad, so a broad-brush attack on them as part of a monolithic Muslim threat is not credible.

Nevertheless, the last twenty years have seen an important breakdown in barriers between the African-American Muslim community and their immigrant counterparts. This has occurred primarily in the area of institution building, in which many leading organizations such as the Muslim Students Association (MSA) and the Islamic Society of North America (ISNA) have worked to integrate indigenous Muslims in what was previously an immigrant oriented organization. Past presidents of MSA chapters included countless African-American students. Even ISNA has had a number of noted African-Americans in upper leadership positions and on the board. This trend of integrating communities continued even more with the development of political organizations such as the American Muslim Council (AMC), the Council on American-Islamic Relations (CAIR), and the American Muslim Alliance (AMA), all of which have had officers who were African-American. In many ways, this integration of communities has also featured an integration of agendas, as both communities have adopted a singular platform with both domestic and international concerns. And though there exists an inevitable tug between the priority that such issues receive, there has nonetheless been legitimate interest and involvement from African-American Muslims in issues like Palestine, Iraq, and Kashmir, and involvement in domestic social concerns such as crime, drugs, and education from the immigrant Muslim leaders. This integration of communities has benefited both sides tremendously and has served to empower and unite them toward a common mission.

Nonetheless, this transition has drawn the ire of those who have previously devoted all of their energies to attacking immigrant Muslims and undermining their efforts by curtailing their rights. As such, African-American Muslims have also become targets of these campaigns. Top leaders include Imam Siraj Wahhaj of New York, who has been a leading religious leader for many decades. Imam Siraj has been a longtime spokesperson for the American Muslim community, and is a fixed feature at major national conferences such as ISNA's, on whose board he has served for many years. In June, 1991, he was also the first Muslim to deliver a prayer before the U.S. House of Representatives, reciting verses from the Qur'an and praying for God to bless America and grant its leaders wisdom and guidance. This event was initiated by efforts from the American Muslim Council whose goal it was to integrate Islam into America's rich religious heritage. Imam Siraj has earned many honors, both within the American Muslim community and from mainstream America. He has become a leading figure in interfaith dialogue on the national level, as well as a popular leader for African-Americans.

After September 11, 2001, as the onslaught came down on virtually all of America's Muslim leadership, Imam Siraj became a favorite target of many Islamophobes, including the ubiquitous Daniel Pipes, whose never-ending condemnation of American Muslim leaders has been noted for its vile distortion of the facts in favor of spreading hysterical allegations. In an article for *Commentary* in November, 2001, Pipes assails Imam Siraj in a piece entitled *"The Danger Within: Militant Islam in America."* The critique's central theme paints a sinister picture of a fifth column of Muslims in America bent on destroying the nation from within and replacing its political institutions with a militant Islamic state that enforces "more radical and intrusive actions like prohibiting conversion out of Islam, criminalizing adultery, banning the consumption of pork, formalizing enhanced rights for Muslims at the expense of non-Muslims, and doing away with equality of the sexes"! The sheer assertion of such outrageous ambitions is laughable, but Pipes notes it in all seriousness, all the while implicating African-American Muslims in propagating ideas such as replacing "[America's] constitutional government with a caliphate." Pipes attacks Imam Siraj for his alleged support of such revolutionary goals, which would require the overthrow of the same government before which he delivered an opening prayer.

Furthermore, Dr. Pipes attempts to establish guilt by association by noting the increasing cooperation between immigrant Muslims and indigenous Muslims. As all immigrant Muslims are generally implied to be suspected of terrorist ties, so too must all those black Muslims who associate with them, according to the logic Pipes establishes. He cites Imam Siraj's testimony in the trial of Shaykh Omar Abdel Rahman in 1995. While Pipes has already implied his intent, he goes on to state it explicitly, saying, "The disparity between Wahhaj's good citizenship in the House and his militant forecast of an Islamic takeover—not to mention his association with violent felons—is only one example of a larger pattern common to the American Muslim scene." In other words, the unification of communities among Muslims and with the larger American community is viewed by pro-Israeli ideologues such as Pipes as an inherent threat to their perpetuation of a one-sided foreign policy. He goes on to castigate explicitly Imam Siraj Wahhaj's ties to previously immigrant-dominated institutions, painting such involvement in as sinister a light as possible. "As for Siraj Wahhaj, he is a top figure in the Council on American-Islamic Relations, the Islamic Society of North America, the Muslim Alliance in North America (MANA), and the Muslim Arab Youth Association (MAYA), and his views contaminate every single one of them." These statements, taken together, best summarize the nature of the attack on the African-American Muslim community.

Another major theme prevalent in these works is that of conversion. As nearly all African-American Muslim conversion took place over the past four decades, and continues to do so in great numbers today, Pipes and his cohorts recognize the importance of conversion rates and the implication they hold for an American Muslim community that is prominent in its numbers. The tendency then is to proceed to vilify converts and imply that by adopting their new faith, they automatically maintain loyalty only to it and abandon their country. Converts are often portrayed as mentally unbalanced and fanatical. Such was the case with a number of important figures within the community, including Imam Jamil al-Amin, who upon his conversion and leadership of a prominent Atlanta Muslim congregation became a frequent target of law enforcement for decades, until his unjust prosecution for which he was sent to prison.

Since September 11, such situations have risen dramatically, as numerous African-American Muslims have also been the subject of government harassment and imprisonment. Caliph Basha ibn Abdur Raheem is one of the "Paintball 11," in Northern Virginia, and was treated no differently than the immigrant Muslims with him during the raids, arrest, and trial. He was ultimately acquitted of all charges in that case, but the damage done to his reputation has ensured that his life will never be the same again.

Even Hispanic Americans, a growing segment of the Muslim population, have not been exempt from these arrests. Jose Padilla, a Hispanic convert to Islam, gained national notoriety for an alleged plot to set off a "dirty bomb" in the United States. Padilla, an American citizen from birth, was not only arrested by military officials, but was the first American ever to be designated as an enemy combatant on American soil and threatened with trial by a military tribunal. The government has continued to hold him indefinitely for nearly three years, and refuses to disclose the evidence against him. Questions over the legality of his treatment have reached federal courts that have been highly critical of the government's procedure.

The European-American Community

The European-American community of Muslims did not coalesce as a mutual support group until the mid-1980s, even though there have been outstanding "white" spokespersons for Islam in America dating back to Alexander Russell Webb in the late 19th century. He was a senior official in the U.S. Department of State and introduced Islam to mainstream America at the first World Parliament of Religions in 1893 in conjunction with the Chicago World Fair, the Colombian Exposition, which commemorated the 400th anniversary of Columbus's "discovery" of America. Webb published a Muslim magazine for several years in New York. This first Muslim periodical in America has been a basic source for Euro-American Muslims in the burgeoning research into their own history.

The principal force in the rise of European-Americans to prominence as leaders of Islam in America is Sheila Musaji, who founded a scholarly periodical, *The American Muslim*, in 1989 as a forum to bring together the various competing factions of Muslims so that they could cooperate in promoting an Islamic social agenda in America based on their common purpose as seekers of truth and stewards of justice.

This, in turn, gave rise to the First American Muslim Pow-Wow in 1993, held at Dar al Islam near Abiquiu in northern New Mexico. The pow-wow is a traditional Native American institution that brought together the leaders and members of diverse tribes to discuss common challenges and agree on common strategies to address both threats and opportunities. This pioneering effort foundered a year later at the Second Muslim Pow-Wow when the Administration of Dar al Islam, under the influence of its Saudi funders, succeeded in taking over Sister Sheila's inclusive project in order to channel it into the exclusivist mindset of Muslim factionalism. The suppression of its central mission killed the project.

The journal continued for another two years, until it died because of lack of funds, because the European-Americans, almost all them intellectuals, were poor, and because the immigrant Muslims refused to support a group that was founded to overcome factionalism. At its peak just before its demise, *The American Muslim* had twenty associate editors, each responsible for a different subject area. These ranged from academics, like Abdallah Schleifer and John Comegys, poets and artists, like Abdul Hayy Moore and Mohaned Zakariya, and professional politicians, like its founding Associate Editor for Political Affairs, Dr. Robert Dickson Crane, who was Director of Publications at the International Institute of Islamic Thought (IIIT) in the mid 1980s and Director of the Legal Division in the American Muslim Council in the early 1990s.

Immediately before 9/11, a few of these original editors decided to revive *The American Muslim*. Sheila took action by restarting the magazine on-line a few days after 9/11 in order to help meet the need for enlightened understanding of Islam, including both its contribution to America in the past and its potential for the future.

Although many of its hundreds of lengthy articles published on its website, www.theamericanmuslim.org, during the first two years after 9/11 were critical of American foreign policy, it did not become a target of the Islamophobes until February, 2004. At this time a running battle commenced between Daniel Pipes and the editors of *The American Muslim* in response to Pipes' accusation on his personal home page, www.danielpipes.com, that the logo of the magazine represented a blatant intention to destroy the U.S. constitution and replace it with the imposition of Islamic law. The logo consisted of calligraphy forming the *"Bism Allah"* superimposed on a map of the United States. Although this invocation of God's blessing had been the logo of the magazine for fifteen years, Daniel Pipes suddenly discovered in it an evil design to destroy America.

The raging battle, both on and off-line, escalated when one of the four "co-owners" of the website inadvertently copied Pipes with a private letter from Jeremy Henzell-Thomas that analyzed Pipes' paranoia from the perspective of professional psycho-linguistics. This analysis of Pipes concluded:

> Daniel Pipe's misreading of the TAM logo is one of the best examples I have ever seen on the psychological phenomenon of confirmation bias—seeing what you want to see. It's the extreme version, in cognitive science terminology, of top-down or script-driven processing—i.e., fitting input into existing conceptual frameworks and failing to admit data that contradicts them. If I were still lecturing at Edinburgh University on

psycholinguistics for graduate students, I'd take this as my prime example, because it demonstrates all too clearly how confirmation bias induces a state akin to blindness. We know also from studies in visual perception that ambivalent images tend to be disambiguated not by logical analysis but on the basis of familiar assumptions—seeing what we are used to seeing.

Of course, we have to ask whether Pipes has simply misread the image, or deliberately misread it to promote his own agenda.

If the former, then he is a poor thinker and needs to go back to school to learn how to think (Alvin Tofler said that the illiterate of the 21st century will not be those who cannot read and write but those who cannot learn, unlearn, and relearn—which is a simpler way of saying that poor learners cannot admit new data, cannot refine their existing scripts by admitting new information).

If the latter, then he is a manipulative demagogue who adds intellectual dishonesty to his deficits in thinking.

The correct response to primitive distortions of this kind is not to become emotional and defensive but to expose them for what they are through superior knowledge and argument. This is what the Muslim ummah needs to renew.

At an early period of your history I guess that people like Pipes were the ones who saw Reds under every bed. Anyone who has studied the discourse of propaganda knows that the language used in the USA to denounce the Reds was strikingly similar to that used by the Reds to denounce the USA. The language of demonisation is always mirrored by both sides: the Axis of Evil vs. The Great Satan. This is the nature of the dischotomising tendency which underlies all undeveloped human thought and which is the cause of so much unnecessary conflict. Pipes betrays his own projections in the way he reads an innocuous image showing the Muslim presence in America as an explicit statement of intent by the Muslims to take over the USA and replace the Constitution. The irrational scope of this distortion and the vehemence with which it is uttered are themselves evidence of Pipes' primitive mental processes. What anyone with a modicum of psychological understanding reads from that is that Pipes himself harbours an intent to promote the takeover bid of which he accuses the Muslims. I don't think we need to ask ourselves who and what he wants to take over, and on whom he wants to impose his own brand of ideology, so obvious is the answer.

It also takes few powers of deduction to realise that had the TAM logo showed any country other than America, Pipes would be interpreting it as threatening evidence that Muslims in America are unpatriotic fifth-columnists incapable of integration into American society. Confirmation bias is remarkably robust (even, incidentally, among many scientists who pride themselves on objectivity).

What I suggest is that instead of defending the American constitution from an imaginary take-over bid from Muslims, he might address the fears of those who are already witnessing the take-over of all that is best in the American system (including the constitution) by a cabal of ideologically motivated extremists in the White House who have not only undermined your constitution but shamed America in the eyes of the world. A more apposite image of the current take-over bid for world domination might be a map of the world with "God Bless America" stamped on it.

And let's throw in the Moon and Mars for good measure now that the President has declared his intent to colonise the solar system."[1]

Pipes shot back with an attack in his widely-distributed homepage branding Dr. Henzell-Thomas as "a British Islamist with a totalitarian mind."[2]

Sheila replied by comparing Pipes' accusations with the original statement of purpose of The American Muslim, which reads as follows and has been observed scrupulously ever since:

> The American Muslim is dedicated to the promotion of peace, justice, and reconciliation for all humanity. It's purpose is to: 1) provide an open forum for the discussion of ideas and issues of concern to Muslims in America from various points of view (based on Qur'an and Sunnah) representing no one school of thought, ethnic group or organization, but to encourage all to be represented in these pages and to speak for themselves; 2) provide a forum for and encourage inter-community dialogue particularly on divisive issues, and to encourage interfaith dialogue to find common ground for cooperation on issues of mutual concern; 3) provide the most comprehensive information possible about individual and group efforts and projects to enable networking and cooperative effort; 4) offer support and encouragement and provide shura (consultation) to those who are speaking publicly on behalf of the Muslim community; 5) help Muslims with a deep

personal commitment to Islam and to
America to locate each other; 6) help people
of faith (Muslims, Christians and Jews) who
share our concern for dialogue and peaceful
resolution of problems to find each other so
they can work together; and 7) provide a
balanced, moderate, alternative voice
focusing on the spiritual, dimension of Islam
rather than the more often heard voice of
extreme political Islamism.[3]

Dr. Pipes' failure to retract his accusations against Sheila
and Henzell-Thomas prompted other editors of *The
American Muslim* to expose Pipes' behavior in this affair as
the clearest example of the totalitarian mentality that has
motivated the entire campaign of Zionist aggression against
Muslims and Islam in America. ■

• Imam Siraj Wahhaj, the first Muslim ever to give an invocation in the U.S.
Congress.

PROFILE: AMERICA'S CONSCIENCE
IN ACADEMIA, POLITICS, AND MEDIA

• Antony Sullivan   • John Esposito   • Paul Findley

I have recently learned that your organization (campus-watch.org) is compiling dossiers on professors at U.S. academic institutions who oppose the Israeli occupation and its brutality, actively support Palestinian rights of self-determination as well as a more informed and intelligent view of Islam than is currently represented in the U.S. media. I would be enormously honored to be counted among those who actively hold these positions and would like to be included in the list of those who are struggling for justice during these times.

—Joel Beinin, former president,
Middle East Studies Association (MESA), September 22, 2002.

• Cynthia McKinney   • William Baker   • John Sugg

Chapter 12

THE INTELLECTUAL SPARTANS

...And then they came for me, but by that time there was no
one left to speak up!

—Martin Neumuller, a German clergyman,
Auschwitz-Birkenau, 1944.

Despite the overwhelming negativity that has
emerged in the past few decades with respect to
the American Muslim experience in the general American
society, it is important to note that there have nonetheless
been some people who have welcomed these new neighbors
with more open arms, and have been instrumental in
solidifying a place for the Muslim minority on the grand
stage of American social, religious, intellectual, and political
life. These individuals have withstood much personal
sacrifice and the lobbing of attacks and accusations against

515

them from the leading Islamophobes for their determination to support the basic principles in which they believe. They are motivated by a desire to speak only the truth, and stand up for the freedoms of religion, speech, and association for all people, while promoting the notions of good citizenship, social pluralism, and interfaith and inter-civilizational dialogue, all the while hoping that understanding among people of different backgrounds will ultimately provide for a better society for all.

These individuals have come from all walks of life, and include academic scholars, journalists, politicians, and religious leaders who have devoted their careers to defending the American Muslim community in the face of gratuitous abuses and assaults. All of them have achieved considerable success in life but never at the expense of their deeply held principles, and so have continued to lend their voice to a community left without a voice in the wake of the massive hysterical campaign against it.

• Antony T. Sullivan

Professor Antony Sullivan is a distinguished senior scholar who holds an honorary position as an Associate at the Center for Middle Eastern and North African Studies at the University of Michigan in Ann Arbor. Before his retirement in 2000, Sullivan was affiliated for 30 years with the Earhart Foundation, most recently as Director of Programs. Throughout his prestigious career, Sullivan has maintained a profound interest in the affairs of the Muslim world and its community in the United States. Over the past three decades he has traveled frequently to the Middle East in connection with his professional responsibilities and research interests, speaking before many international conferences and meeting with top officials. From 1962-1967 Sullivan taught at International College in Beirut, Lebanon. He has written two books and some 80 articles and reviews, and has lectured widely at universities in the United States and abroad.

In addition to his professional achievements, Sullivan has had a longstanding relationship with the Muslim community in the United States, frequently addressing large and small gatherings at mosques, conferences, and lectures. As a traditional conservative, Sullivan appreciates the commonalities Islam has with traditional conservative views, especially with regard to social issues. He has frequently spoken of the benefits that Islamic values could have on American society if given the opportunity. As such, Sullivan has brought many Muslims into the fold of political activism under the traditional conservative wing of the Republican Party. Unfortunately, after September 11, many of the initiatives that were pledged to be pursued by Republican leaders from President Bush on down were scrapped in favor of a highly hostile posture toward American Muslims led by the adoption of the neoconservative ideology and its anti-Muslim agenda. Sullivan has valiantly opposed the policy of alienation and recrimination, writing an article in the November 5, 2001, issue of the popular conservative *Insight* magazine entitled "Should policymakers see Islam as an enemy of the West?"

He answered the question posed to him in strong terms, stating, "No: Islam, Judaism, and Christianity historically produce societies with like characteristics. Islam—as a religion, culture, and society—most emphatically is not an enemy of the West. Those who argue the contrary slander not only the third and last of the three great Abrahamic revelations but make all too likely the outbreak of either a religious war pitting Christianity (and perhaps Judaism) against Islam or a war of civilizations pitting the West against the entire Muslim world. And be assured: Any wars of religion or civilization will not be wars that the West—or the United States—will win."[1]

Sullivan does not hesitate to mention the civil rights violations against Muslims embodied in the secret evidence trials, blaming the likes of Bernard Lewis, Daniel Pipes, and Steven Emerson for the phenomenon. "Their work, implicitly or explicitly, prepared the ground for the U.S. Anti-Terrorism Act of 1996 and the consequent jailings without charge of up to 19 Arabs or Muslims in the United States. No evidence of culpability of any of these individuals ever was adduced publicly. Ideas—particularly those of distinguished scholars—do have consequences, and bad ideas may indeed have very bad consequences."

Furthermore, he does not shy away from stating what few in the United States have the courage to say, that is, placing the culpability for such perceptions of global enmity squarely where it belongs. "It is not by chance that those most frequently proclaiming that Islam is an enemy of the West are themselves fervent partisans of Israel or Israelis themselves. Islam is in no way a challenge to the West, but in its political form it may well present a threat to Israel. If so, that is Israel's problem, not ours. Israel alone can mitigate any Islamic threat only by dealing justly with all its neighbors, and most specifically with the Palestinians. As a Republican and a conservative, I call on my philosophical comrades in arms to reject the anti-Islamic triumphalist warmongering of neoconservative ideologues. And I urge all Americans to repudiate any belief that Islam is an enemy of the West. This idea is wrong. Worse, it is dangerous. To all of us. Especially now."

Only a month after the events of September 11, Sullivan spoke at the annual conference of the American Muslim Alliance (AMA) in San Jose, California, in which he delivered an especially riveting speech in support of the American Muslim community's efforts to dispel the hysteria against it. He also spoke about the hugely unbalanced U.S. foreign policy, the Palestinian plight, and the genocide of Iraqi children in clear and unequivocal terms.[2] Indeed, throughout his life and career, Dr. Antony Sullivan has displayed the courage and conviction to stand up for truth in the hope that the truth may prevail.

• John L. Esposito

One of the most consistently outspoken individuals on Islam and East-West relations is Professor of Religion and International Affairs and of Islamic Studies at Georgetown University John L. Esposito. Esposito is also Founding Director of the Center for Muslim-Christian Understanding in the Walsh School of Foreign Service at Georgetown. Throughout his decades of scholarship, he has been a beacon of hope for people of all faiths and cultures yearning for greater understanding. He has been a tireless speaker on every continent delivering a consistent message of a possible peaceful and harmonious world.

Indeed, his contributions are too numerous to mention, but one can immediately note the dexterity with which he has conducted himself over the years. Esposito has served as a consultant to the State Department as well as corporations, universities, and the media worldwide. His specialization includes Islam, political Islam, and the impact of Islamic movements from North Africa to Southeast Asia. He has served as President of the Middle East Studies Association of North America and the American Council for the Study of Islamic Societies and is Vice Chair of the Center for the Study of Islam and Democracy in Washington, D.C. His publications are profuse, including many of the top texts on Islam in the world today. Esposito is Editor-in-Chief of the four-volume *Oxford Encyclopedia of the Modern Islamic World*, and *The Oxford History of Islam*. His more than twenty-five books include *Unholy War: Terror in the Name of Islam*, *The Islamic Threat: Myth or Reality?*, *Islam: The Straight Path*, *Islam and Democracy*, and *Political Islam: Revolution, Radicalism or Reform?* Esposito's books and articles have been translated into Arabic, Persian, Urdu, Bahasa Indonesia, Turkish, Japanese, Chinese, and European languages.

Moreover, Esposito has not confined himself strictly to the world of academia. With the knowledge that conditions can only change once all people become affected by a better understanding of things, and not only the intellectual elites, Esposito has been a very vocal participant in the mainstream forum of public opinion. Throughout the last three decades, he has been interviewed or quoted in the *Wall Street Journal*, *New York Times*, *Washington Post*, CNN, ABC Nightline, CBS, NBC, and the BBC and in newspapers, magazines, and the media in Europe, Asia, and the Middle East.

He acknowledges his main mentor to be Palestinian Muslim scholar Ismail Faruqi, with whom he studied at Temple University. From his early years, Esposito has understood the essence of Islam better than anyone else in his position. He recalls his experience of learning about what most Americans have little or no knowledge. He was asked once what Americans should know about Islam, and responded:

> There are two things. One is an awareness that there is, in fact, not just the Judeo-Christian, but a Judeo-Christian-Islamic tradition. That's what got me interested in Islam. I had studied Christianity; I had studied Judaism. I had studied Hinduism and Buddhism. And when I studied Islam, I thought that I was going to be studying the religion that was "over there." Because in those days, in graduate school, and even in undergrad, you talked about Judaism and Christianity, and then you put Islam with Hinduism and Buddhism. Suddenly, I discovered a religion that, in fact, recognized the revelation of the Torah and the New Testament; recognized Moses and Jesus; traced itself back to the patriarch, Abraham, and back to the "one true God"; shared a vision of moral accountability, human responsibility; had a vision of God, human beings, angels, devils, judgment, etc. That was beyond what I could appreciate.
>
> The second thing is for Americans to realize the similarity, in many ways, in emphasis of Islam

and Judaism. Islam and Judaism, in contrast to Christianity, emphasized religious observance. You talk about an observant Jew, an observant Muslim, more than dogma or doctrine. In Islam, recognizing the Five Pillars and what they call upon a Muslim to believe in—absolute monotheism, belief in God, prophecy, and revelation; prayer five times a day; fasting; pilgrimage; paying the tithe to support those that are poor—all of that is there, along with dealing with the issues of violence, radicalism, and extremism.[3]

Throughout his distinguished career, Esposito has reflected this deep understanding of the Islamic religion, as well as the Muslim community on the local and global level. He has been an honored guest at many of the national and international conferences and gatherings held to discuss Islamic issues, and has built a strong relationship with Islamic scholars that most Western academics can only envy. Within the mainstream American media and political circles, he has time and again risen to defend Islam against those who would defame it and promote the notion of an ongoing conflict between civilizations. He has done this at his own personal sacrifice, becoming himself a frequent target of Islamophobes wishing to silence any voice of reason emerging within the forum of public opinion and policymaking. In September, 2002, one of the many articles against Esposito emerged in *FrontPageMagazine*. Entitled, "Esposito: Apologist for Militant Islam," the article is mysteriously attributed only to "Campus Watch," the McCarthyite group founded after September 11, 2001 by

Daniel Pipes and Martin Kramer to intimidate and silence voices on the Middle East and American foreign policy with which it does not agree. In fact, the article itself proceeds to quote the attacks on Esposito from Kramer's book, *Ivory Towers on Sand*, as though it were using an outside source, and not simply rehashing the same diatribes of the article's authors. Following the standard method of attack, the author(s) distort a number of statements made by Esposito over the years attempting to show him as a radical, while also attempting to convey that he is anti-American, unpatriotic, and possible even anti-Semitic. It then proceeds to malign him by showing his "sinister" associations with American Muslim leaders, such as citing his defense of Professor Sami al-Arian. Campus Watch concludes by saying, "While Esposito works for a center designed to create Muslim-Christian understanding, he only creates obfuscation. And unfortunately, many others take his lead. The American university system, therefore, should reexamine their Middle East specialists' explanations of modern day Islam—particularly, the violence associated with its radical and extremist interpretations."[4]

Ultimately, however, Professor Esposito has attained a status of respect and professionalism unrivaled by others in his field. His prominence in the area of Islamic scholarship has offered Americans a more reasoned and moderate voice that paints a more promising portrait of a peaceful and prosperous future of cooperation between the Islamic world and the West. He has also been a great source of support and inspiration for the American Muslim leadership and its efforts to realize this grand vision of a greater America renewing the civilization inherent in its Judeo-Christian-Islamic heritage.

• Paul Findley

Another major non-Muslim figure that has nonetheless had enormous impact on the state of the American Muslim community is former Congressman Paul Findley (R-IL). Born in 1921 in a small town in Illinois, Findley served in the U.S. Navy during World War II, before returning to work as the editor of a local newspaper. In 1960, he decided to run for his local 20th District congressional seat. He was elected to the U.S. House of Representatives and remained there for over two decades from 1961 to 1983. Though for many years, Findley would have no direct connection to Islam, later in his career of public service, he would become gradually exposed to Islam through his interaction with Muslim people from across the world and his particular interest in certain international issues. In his last book, *Silent No More: Confronting America's False Images of Islam*, Findley recounted his personal experience that drew him toward learning more about the people and their faith. He narrates how three decades ago he, like many Americans, harbored misinformation and stereotypes about Islam and its followers until an unexpected journey to South Yemen to plead for the release of an imprisoned American put him unwittingly on the trail to discover Islam and the Muslims. He has since examined the false images of Islam that linger in American minds and the impact of these stereotypes on U.S. national interests.[5]

Findley's real accomplishments would follow this journey, which inspired him to reevaluate U.S. relations with Arab countries in terms of a better strategy for America. He saw that nothing was being accomplished by the state of enmity that it had developed with the Syrians, Egyptians, Lebanese, and Palestinians, while committing unconditional support to the Israelis. By the mid-1970s, Findley naively began to argue for a more balanced approach, completely oblivious to the consequences. "I began to speak out in Congress. I argued from what I considered to be a U.S. viewpoint—neither pro-Israel nor pro-Arab. I said that our unwillingness to talk directly to the political leadership of the Palestinians ... handicapped our search for peace."[6] Of course Findley would soon learn that the American political sphere had no room for talk of a balanced approach to the ongoing conflict, and that the only acceptable view was an unflinching support of the Jewish state. As such, in 1982, Findley had earned the ire of the Israeli lobby, which proceeded to pour incredible amounts of money into his unknown Democratic opponent who pledged unconditional support for their interests. Thus, Findley was defeated and removed from his congressional seat of 22 years. The American-Israeli Public Affairs Committee (AIPAC), Israel's chief lobby in the United States, publicly took credit for Findley's defeat. He later wrote, "I naively assumed I could question our policy anywhere without getting into trouble. I did not realize how deeply the roots of Israeli interests had penetrated U.S. institutions."[7]

From his stunning upset at the hands of the Israeli lobby, Findley would devote his life to revealing the truth of the situation to the American public based on his experiences and his research on the issue. In 1985, he published *They Dare to Speak Out*, his best-selling book on the demise of public figures based on their drawing the vehemence of the Israeli lobby. The book was the first of its kind to examine the pull of Israel's supporters in the United States from the White House to the halls of Congress and the Pentagon. It provided a thorough analysis of the phenomenon and in-depth accounts of politicians, journalists, and academics who had suffered due to their speaking out in the face of a Zionist juggernaut.

In the years ahead, the American Muslim community would come to recognize Findley's efforts to bring justice to their region of the world and praised his work in Congress and his outspoken attitude since leaving. He began to receive invitations to national Islamic conferences, which he graciously accepted. At conferences such as the Islamic Society of North America (ISNA), which provided the largest gathering of Muslims in the country, Findley became a featured keynote speaker, and would ultimately attain celebrity status within the rapidly growing American Muslim community of millions. Moreover, he gave the community insight into the workings of the American political process, with which they were unfamiliar, and provided American Muslims with hope that they could one day have an impact on the policies being issued by Washington.

During the early 1990s, as political institutions such as the American Muslim Council (AMC) began to be established, Paul Findley would begin to have a more important role within the community as a guide and mentor for the voiceless minority wishing to attain some foothold into the decision-making process in their nation's capital. Workshops and seminars organized by groups such as AMC featured Findley and others wishing to impart their experience in the political process. In the meantime, Findley continued his activities, authoring a follow-up book to his groundbreaking success. This book, called *Deliberate Deceptions*, chronicled the distortions by Israel's supporters in their pushing of policies favorable to their interests at the expense of innocent lives in the Holy Land and American interests abroad. Though Findley was widely regarded within the Muslim community, he reached across the American landscape, frequently speaking at churches, synagogues, and community centers, while making television appearances and authoring many articles for mainstream publications. He was in effect an ambassador for truth to the American public and had a reach beyond which any American Muslim leader could attain.

In the late 1990s, though Findley's interests had always been directed more toward American foreign policy toward the Middle East, he began to develop more concern for the status of civil liberties of America's Muslims. During the "Secret Evidence" trials, Findley was one of the more outspoken public figures against the phenomenon, writing frequently about it and visiting communities to encourage their action against it in an otherwise intimidating climate. By the 2000 election, Findley was well in-tune with the American Muslim community's platform and chronicled their experience in building political institutions and establishing a voting bloc in his book *Silent No More*. Through his three decades of interaction with Islam and Muslims, Findley developed a true affinity for the culture and norms of Islam, and had devoted much of his time simply to educating Americans about their brethren in faith. He developed a popular pamphlet entitled "A Friendly Note From Your Muslim Neighbor," which he personally distributed to thousands of people to break down the barriers between mainstream America and the disenfranchised Muslim minority.

As with all other courageous supporters, Findley suffered constant attacks even after his ousting from Congress. As recently as 2002, the usual rabble of Islamophobes has attempted to paint him as anti-Semitic and a terrorist sympathizer. One noted anti-Muslim writer, Robert Spencer, commented scathingly against Findley's most recent book, specifically its depiction of AMC founder Abdurahman Alamoudi as an "early pioneer in Muslim political activism," but "quotes none of his statements supporting terrorist groups." Spencer concluded, "Alamoudi's inclusion in this book as a normal guy and a good American is a sign of the blinders people have on."[8] Others have similarly attempted to smear Findley because of his associations with American Muslim leaders.

In the final analysis, however, Paul Findley remains as a testament to his country as a true patriotic American who has served his nation from his younger years as a navy officer in World War II, through his days as a Congressman from Illinois, and onto his later years as an advocate of peace, equality, justice, and human rights for all. He has maintained a courage, strength, and resolve throughout his life that few others have shown.

• Cynthia McKinney

In recent years, no one has suffered more from supporting the American Muslim community than Cynthia McKinney. The Democratic Congresswoman from Georgia suffered at the hands of a concerted campaign to remove her from office in 2002. Her experience is yet another telling example of the forces operating within the United States with ulterior motives contrary to the American way. It stands as a lesson to all concerned citizens on the abuse of power to silence the lone voice of dissent.

Cynthia Ann McKinney was born in Atlanta in 1955 and was rooted in the civil rights struggle of the 1960s. From her early days, she was a conscientious individual who was unafraid to speak out against injustice, a quality that stayed with her throughout her career. In 1988, she was elected to the state legislature, where she produced monumental work on behalf of minority rights that attracted national attention. In 1992, she became the first African-American woman elected to the House of Representatives from Georgia and was the only woman from the Georgia delegation at the time. Throughout her tenure in Congress, McKinney held fast to her principles of producing a more just and equitable society, especially for her constituents who continued to suffer from racial inequality, lack of economic opportunity, and troubling education and healthcare provisions. In time, however, her interests expanded globally, as McKinney became heavily involved in international relations, an area in which she maintained a strong interest, having pursued her academic studies in it for many years. She was appointed to the powerful Armed Services Committee in the House of Representatives, as well as the International Relations Committee, on whose Subcommittee on Human Rights she was a ranking member.

Throughout her decade in office, McKinney became a more vocal speaker on certain issues that endangered the status quo established by certain elements in society. McKinney was critical of American arms deals with foreign nations, especially those with atrocious human rights records, and in 1997 after a five-year effort she succeeded in passing the Arms Transfers Code of Conduct aimed at curbing U.S. arms sales to dictatorships. In time, McKinney became critical of U.S. policy toward the Israeli-Palestinian conflict, and was a vocal opponent of Israel's policy toward the Palestinians. She made frequent statements to that effect, especially during hearings and other briefings by the Foreign Affairs Committee, often drawing attention to herself from staunch supporters of Israel wishing to silence her. With unwavering support from her constituency behind her, however, McKinney felt free and secure to speak her mind no matter the consequences from the powerful Washington elites.

In due time, McKinney would not only became a strong advocate of a more balanced approach toward the Arab and Muslim worlds, but became entrenched in the ongoing civil rights struggle of the Muslim community following the passage of the anti-terrorism bill in 1996. McKinney was one of the earliest opponents of the use of secret evidence, speaking out to that effect among her colleagues and at major gatherings and civil rights rallies. The American Muslim community approached her for support and was not to be disappointed. Over the years, she would become one of the strongest advocates of Muslim rights in Congress, never failing to speak out on behalf of a community that was heavily out-muscled by the pro-Israel and anti-Muslim lobbies. From the outset of the push to repeal the use of secret evidence, McKinney was one of the first individuals to sign on to the bill put forward by David Bonior (D-MI) and Tom Campbell (R-CA), as well as to solicit the support of her colleagues, especially those in the Congressional Black Caucus, most of whom eventually co-sponsored the legislation. In the process, McKinney always made herself available to the Muslim community, who had received little or no access from the majority of legislators. She even attended a number of Islamic conferences and spoke about the need to integrate Muslims into the American political process, not only for the protection of their rights, but for the betterment of their country as a whole. In many ways, McKinney became a hero for the American Muslim community and a champion for its cause.

The events of September 11 and the ensuing prejudice had a way of making the once impossible not only possible, but probable based on the intensity of underlying motivations. The Cynthia McKinney saga provides a great example of such malicious intent given new voice under the cloud of suspicion and hysteria. What many pro-Israel activists had tried for ten years to accomplish was now well within their reach. McKinney was immediately put on the fringe of the Washington policymaking scene because of her outspoken views on American foreign policy, especially now as it seemed to coincide with those of the perpetrators of the attacks. In one eloquent speech on the implications of the ongoing conflict, she stated, "We must honestly ask ourselves what is the root cause of this war being waged on our people and our country. I suspect that we will need to look at altering some of our foreign policy positions in some parts of the world. Unless we do this I fear that a military campaign, unsupported by sound foreign policy strategies, will only cause immeasurable civilian suffering throughout the world and may well actually lead to more terrifying attacks upon our cities and our citizenry." Such words were often treated with careless abandonment by her detractors. McKinney maintained her resolve and was consistently critical of the handling of both the attacks themselves and the subsequent "war on terror" waged by the Bush Administration:

The world is teetering on the brink of conflicts while the Administration's policies are vague, wavering, and unclear. Major financial conflicts of interest involving the President, the Attorney General, the Vice President, and others in the Administration have been and continue to be exposed. This is a time for leadership and judgment that is not compromised in any fashion. This is a time for transparency and a thorough investigation.

McKinney simply would not relent, calling upon the Bush Administration to defend Palestinians against Israeli terrorism in the wake of the massacre at Jenin in April 2002. That same year, America's pro-Israel lobby decided that it had had enough, and developed a strategy to defeat McKinney once and for all. For one, they decided to pool their resources behind another Democratic contender for the seat who would meet the incumbent McKinney in the primary later that summer. The lead-up to that primary would exhibit some of the dirtiest politics ever exhibited on American soil. McKinney was subjected to a campaign of lies, defamation, and assassination of character on a national scale. She was thrown into the limelight during a very tense debate about the White House's knowledge of certain facts before the 9/11 attacks. Repeatedly, McKinney was quoted as saying that the Bush Administration had foreknowledge of the attacks and allowed them to occur because of the political and financial gain that the President and his associates would receive as a result. This charge was castigated publicly by all politicians, Republicans and Democrats alike, and McKinney was severely marginalized even from her own supporters. The only problem was that the statement was ultimately revealed to have been a fake report whose source remains unknown, but speculated to be the same people working to unseat McKinney, led by the pro-Israel interests in Washington. Unfortunately for McKinney, the false quotation made its way to every major news outlet as fact, from NPR to the *New York Times* and *Washington Post*, with numerous commentators exclaiming that McKinney was a "loose cannon," "loony," and "dangerous."[9] Suddenly, a small race for a suburban Georgia congressional seat turned into one of the most-watched contests in the nation during the 2002 midterm elections. The American Muslim community rallied its support behind McKinney, with frequent fundraisers by groups such as the Council on American-Islamic Relations (CAIR) held in communities across the country. Efforts by CAIR were not sufficient, however, in combating the manifold support McKinney's opponent, a staunchly pro-Israel African-American woman named Denise Majette, received from Jewish groups.

By the time the results came in, McKinney had lost her seat to Majette, much to the dismay of her American Muslim supporters, who lost a true champion of justice and freedom in McKinney. The unified effort between Jewish groups and Republicans, who were allowed to vote in Georgia's Democratic primary, proved to be too all-powerful for the weak and debilitated post-September 11 American Muslim community. The loss of this hero did, however, serve as an important lesson to them about the need to support their leaders, especially in times of crisis. While American Muslim supporters in Congress have since been few and far between, the loss of McKinney was a devastating blow, and will remain on the shoulders of her supporters as an example for years to come.

• William W. Baker

For over two decades, Muslims have had a dedicated friend and supporter in Christian leader Dr. William Baker. A well-traveled Christian theologian and Biblical archeologist, Baker most recently has been the founder and Executive Director of Christians and Muslims for Peace (CAMP). The organization, based in Southern California, has branches in North America, Europe, Africa, the Philippine Islands, and the Middle East. His career has been devoted to enhancing his knowledge of his Christian faith. Upon completing his studies at Ozark Christian College and Oxford University, he spent time at the Near East Institute of Archaeology in Jerusalem, where he came to discover the cross-section of the three Abrahamic faiths. Moreover, as a professor of ancient history and sacred literature, Baker began to appreciate not only the Judeo-Christian texts which he had studied his whole life, but the Islamic scriptures as well.

His experiences in the Holy Land led him to write his first book in 1982. Entitled *Theft of a Nation*, the book is an eye-opening account of the situation, especially the atrocities committed against the Palestinians and the terrible suffering they were undergoing as a result of military occupation and the unending land confiscations. It further examines the conflict in the historical context of the creation of the Israeli State with emphasis on biblical hermeneutics of fulfilled prophecy, the Israelis and the Palestinians. The book became a hit with many communities, including the growing American Muslim community that had the opportunity to learn about an issue so near and dear to its heart from an entirely new perspective, that of an American Christian. The book has since been republished in two subsequent editions and translated into several languages.

Throughout the subsequent years, Baker became a popular spokesperson for these issues from a religious perspective, traveling throughout the Middle East and becoming recognized in America for his efforts to bring peace to a troubled region. Baker became a prominent media analyst, appearing on numerous national and international networks, including ABC, CNN, C-Span, BBC, MEB (Middle East Broadcasting), and was a frequent guest on many of the top-rated radio talk shows. His prominence resulted in his being invited to the White House to discuss U.S. policy in the Middle East, and he received multiple invitations to address the House of Commons in the British Parliament throughout the late 1980s and 1990s. Additionally, Baker has personally met with numerous world leaders, including the late Anwar Sadat of Egypt, the late Hafez Assad of Syria, Nawaz Sherif, former Prime Minister of Pakistan, PLO Chairman Yasser Arafat, and former Vice President Al Gore. Baker also testified before the United Nations Human Rights Commission in Geneva, Switzerland. In fact, during the mid 1980s, Baker was the only American citizen invited to Beirut, Lebanon, to discuss the release of Western hostages. For his many efforts he received the King Faisal Peace Award in 1996 and was nominated for the 1997 Nobel Peace Prize.

Throughout his years of incredible service, William Baker became a close friend to the American Muslim community. As the national organizations began to open up their conferences to more non-Muslim speakers, Baker was one of their most important guests for many years, and remains a fixture at ISNA's national gathering each year. For his Muslim audiences, he has been a source of hope and inspiration for continued dialogue and cooperation toward peaceful coexistence and conflict resolution between different faith communities, but especially the predominant Christian majority in the West. Especially for many conservative Muslims who were weary of working with Christians, Baker forced them to rethink their perceptions of other faith leaders and begin working toward a cooperative effort on various issues. Baker continued his speaking engagements, addressing hundreds of crowds, including many churches in which he delivered a message of unity and understanding of Islam. He was also a frequent guest of many Muslim Students Association chapters, as younger American Muslims were especially drawn to his gentle nature, eloquent style, and hope-filled message.

In 1998, Baker published his third book, based on his years of interaction with Muslims. Entitled, *More in Common Than You Think: The Bridge Between Islam and Christianity*, the book was an important work that was timely and pertinent to advancing society's understanding and tolerance by shattering stereotypes and misconceptions that have often been raised between followers of the world's two largest monotheistic faiths. In this clear and concise text, Baker introduces laypersons to Islam, the fastest-growing religion in the United States. Baker's central theme throughout is mapping the common ground between Islam and Christianity.

But despite his message of peace and understanding, Baker has paid a heavy price in recent years. Following the success of his books and speaking engagements, the respected theologian became a target of a concerted campaign to mar his reputation as a tolerant voice of reason. Especially in the aftermath of September 11, this campaign was aimed at blacklisting Baker from speaking on college campuses and at Islamic functions. The episode began with a series of articles in a small weekly newspaper in Baker's native southern California. The heavily conservative and staunch anti-Muslim publication lobbed outrageous accusations at Baker, labeling him a "neo-Nazi" and citing his involvement with a small political party in the early 1980s as proof. Aside from engaging in guilt by association, the paper's attempts to paint Baker with the brush of extremism in order to denigrate his many accomplishments were seen as a vindictive effort to silence him as a voice of unity between Muslims and Christians. He was seen as a threat to the Jewish community, which has built a strong alliance with many Christian groups and solidified widespread support for Israel as a result. Baker's efforts to provide Christians with an alternative perspective on the issues and at the same time encourage Muslims to build bridges with their Christian neighbors was viewed as a major threat to many of Israel's staunchest supporters, who launched malicious campaign to discredit Baker completely. The articles even went so far as to question his credentials as a theologian and scholar, while branding his books anti-Semitic. The campaign against Baker specifically targeted his strong relationship with Dr. Robert H. Schuller of the Crystal Cathedral Ministries in Garden Grove, California, a congregation he frequently addresses.

In subsequent weeks, these articles were picked up on a

national level as a result of the work of Daniel Pipes, who continued the defamation campaign against Baker, leading to protests against his lecturing at a number of events, most notably one in Ontario, Canada, where he was invited to speak on Christian-Muslim relations, only to be met with a mob of protestors from the Canadian Jewish Congress shouting at him and calling him a Nazi. These hurtful cries could not be more inappropriate and appalling to someone who throughout his life has done nothing more than speak the truth as he saw it, and has sacrificed much in order to promote peace and unity among nations, peoples, and faiths. American Muslims are fortunate to have the support of a courageous, faithful fellow believer in the form of Dr. William Baker. They can only marvel at his tremendous efforts for the unity of the Christian and Muslim communities in the face of conflict. Like them, he too has suffered much adversity as a result of his speaking the truth.

John F. Sugg

In the world of popular media, the American Muslim community has suffered tremendously in the past decade. The general impression according to most Muslims has been that the news media have been a bitter aggressor, taking every chance to distort the religion of Islam and mischaracterize its adherents. People differ as to whether this is simply a result of a profound ignorance that American news agencies have about the new kid on the block, or if it is actually part of a concerted effort by powerful forces to marginalize Islam and cast it out from the fold of a pluralistic

American society in order to advance their own political interests. While the latter has certainly shown itself to be true in many instances, most notably those cited in previous chapters, for the most part the media has demonstrated an interest in pursuing the popular story and riding the wave of public opinion on a given topic, including Islam. While there has been an overwhelming amount of negative publicity for the American Muslim community's activities in recent years, there has been a subtle undercurrent of good press attempting to show American Muslims as part of the overall cultural makeup of society and as a positive contributive presence for the country. In addition, there have even been those within the media who have come out in defense of Muslims targeted by the government and mainstream media and have suffered unjustly as a result.

Of this latter group, no other person has been consistently on the frontline of the attack against Islamic institutions than investigative journalist and newspaper editor John Sugg. This longtime journalist was the editor-in-chief of the *Weekly Planet*, based in Tampa, Florida, in the mid-1990s, at the same time that the attacks against that Muslim community's leadership was in full swing. The one-sided approach of the *Tampa Tribune*'s "Ties to Terrorists" series, which condemned the Florida institutions, had no counterbalance from any other news outlet, and so the community was left defenseless against the onslaught. But then just as the attacks were reaching their peak, John Sugg's interest in the story peaked as well. He began his own thorough investigation into the matter, and eventually uncovered some deeply disturbing information.

Sugg's brilliantly exhaustive investigation was published in a series of articles in the *Weekly Planet*, which were of significant importance, especially after the situation in Tampa was worsening following the arrest of Mazen al-Najjar on the basis of secret evidence. Among other things, Sugg pursued the causes of these frivolous investigations to their root, the media manipulator in the form of Steven Emerson, who was secretly behind the *Tribune* series. Sugg revealed Emerson's dubious past and began to slowly lift the air of suspicion from around the Tampa community in as best a fashion as he could. During this time, Sugg also took on a number of speaking engagements, most notably a journalist forum at the University of South Florida that discussed the recent allegations against the Muslim community in particular, with emphasis on the overall paradigm of the Arab-Israeli conflict.

Sugg's work was especially important in beginning to shift the tide against the unjust incarceration of Al-Najjar and setting a trend within the media to take a strong stance against secret evidence. Even in their coverage of the issue, other newspapers began to tread more carefully. Most notably, the *St. Petersburg Times*, the other local newspaper, began to have more balanced coverage of the Muslim community and its ongoing ordeal with the government. As a result of Sugg's work, which is chronicled in other chapters, secret evidence would eventually become a national issue and Emerson and his cohorts were exposed as agents working toward a sinister agenda. In fact, Emerson attempted to counteract Sugg's work by filing a lawsuit claiming that Sugg libeled him in his work. This was a clear attack against Sugg's journalistic integrity and an attempt to silence and intimidate him. Sugg's subsequent legal battle with Emerson lasted several years, before a court ultimately cleared Sugg of any wrongdoing, a decision Emerson failed to appeal.

Sugg has since moved to Atlanta, Georgia, where he has

• American Muslim leaders at a fundraiser for former Congresswoman Cynthia McKinney (D-GA).

• Veteran investigative journalist John F. Sugg accepts an award at an American Muslim Council banquet.

• Former Congressman Paul Findley (R-IL) addresses the national convention of the Islamic Association for Palestine.

taken on editor-in-chief responsibilities at another newspaper, *Creative Loafing*. His work has continued unabated, as he has uncovered other agents of Islamophobia operating as legitimate investigators or journalists, most notably self-proclaimed "terrorist sleuth" Rita Katz. Throughout his career, Sugg has acted as the conscience of the mass media, frequently calling its irresponsible behavior to task, and questioning the methods and intentions of those who would manipulate the news and public opinion to advance their nefarious causes. He has also given voice to a community without any power to articulate its views in the public forum. ■

• Tony Sullivan speaking at a UASR-Georgetown University conference, 2000.

• John Voll addresses the audience at the joint CMCU-UASR Conference.

Part Five

BANKRUPTING MUSLIM INSTITUTIONS

It is time for active measures against the spread of Islam in the United States.

> —Alex Alekseyev, Pentagon and CIA consultant on national security, *Pravola*, November 21, 2003.

PROFILE: SPREADING HUMANITARIAN AWARENESS

• Rafiq Jaber, IAP President

• Members of the Jewish community participate in IAP convention in Chicago, Illinois, December 2001.

• Prominent Muslim figures sitting with Rabbi Weiss at an IAP Convention.

• Panel discusses Palestinian rights before large audience.

Chapter 13

DAVID BOIM vs. QLI
THE $600 MILLION
CASE

I think the Boim case is like so many other cases that have been brought, either criminal prosecutions or civil lawsuits, on behalf of or directed by Zionists and pro-Israeli groups. The strategy is to bring frivolous prosecutions and law suits to frighten the community, to bankrupt the community, to harass and intimidate the community. It is part of a broader Government and even private strategy to divide, punish, and intimidate the community.

—Stanley L. Cohen, a renowned New York attorney,
and civil rights activist, March 2004.

During the mid-1990s, a new phenomenon emerged in the attack on Islam in America. On the heels of the media campaign against them, Muslims were increasingly vulnerable to assault from all sides. And while this often resulted in gross abuses by federal officials and law enforcement authorities, some forces in society resolved toward swifter action that came in the form of civil complaints and lawsuits. Powered by the Zionist lobby and its many institutions, a concerted effort was undertaken to destroy Islamic charitable organizations in the United States, especially those that aided Palestinians in need. Following the intense scrutiny that was given to most Islamic institutions after the onslaught by the agents of Islamophobia, led by Steven Emerson and others, certain individuals attempted to exploit the widespread negative media attention to plunge these organizations into financial ruin and public disrepute.

These lawsuits were helped greatly by existing legal statutes that provided loopholes for such frivolous measures, along with new anti-terrorism legislation in 1996, which also gave lawyers wider legal precedence to pursue suits against legal organizations. In May of 2000, one such suit was filed in a federal court in Chicago. Stanley and Joyce Boim, parents of David Boim, who was killed in a West Bank attack in 1996, filed the suit against a number of American Muslim organizations and individuals. The documentation in the case cites a number of legal precedents that allow for the suit against these groups to be taken up by a court. The first is a law passed in 1992 that allowed victims of terrorism to sue for damages in civil court. Then, in 1995, an executive order signed by President Bill Clinton placed Hamas, the group that was allegedly behind the attack on Boim, on a list of terrorist organizations. By 1997, following provisions in the 1996 anti-terror bill, the President and the Secretary of State issued orders that made it illegal to provide material support to any listed terrorist organization, such as the groups operating in the Occupied Territories, including Hamas. The Boims claimed that a number of Muslim groups in the United States were actually "front" groups for Hamas, providing them with material and logistical support to carry out attacks such as the one that killed their son.

The groups in question included the Quranic Literacy Institute (QLI), an organization based in Chicago that translates and publishes sacred Islamic texts and other scholarly research. Also included was the Holy Land Foundation, one of the largest providers of humanitarian aid to needy Palestinians. The Boims, who have lived in Israel for many years and have dual American-Israeli citizenship, contend that both these and other organizations knowingly sent money to Hamas and helped plan terrorist attacks, including the one that killed their son. The lawsuit demanded $201 million (later augmented to $600 million) as compensation for their loss. In fact, the plaintiffs in the case would bear a tremendous responsibility to prove their allegations in court, something that even the federal authorities have not attempted. In fact, when the action was filed against them, none of the organizations or individuals had been charged with any criminal wrongdoing by the government. They had all been operating openly and legally for many years. Legally, it would be a real challenge to allege such outrageous offenses when law enforcement authorities, whose job it is to investigate such crimes, had not brought any charges.

The bulk of the Boims' case centered around Mohammad Salah, a Palestinian-American living in Chicago, who was investigated by a Justice Department inquiry into financing of Hamas. Salah was also included in the lawsuit, after spending five years in an Israeli prison after pleading guilty to a charge of illegally channeling funds to Hamas. He returned to Chicago after his release in 1997, and has repeatedly denied supporting Hamas or being in any way involved with the group. The guilty plea, he stated, was the product of a forced confession after being tortured by Israeli authorities. Israel's use of torture against Palestinians is well documented and most foreign nations often dismiss such confessions as illegal and crudely attained while the subject is under duress. Unfortunately, the United States is an exception to that rule, treating Salah's conviction as proof of his involvement in sending funds to Hamas from 1991-1993, and, according to the lawsuit, making him at least indirectly responsible for the terrorists' ability to undertake the attack in 1996.

In June, 1998, over a year after his return to the United States, the FBI seized $1.4 million in assets from Salah and QLI, including a home, van, and bank accounts. An FBI affidavit suggested a relationship with Hamas, supported only by Israeli intelligence, probably derived from Salah's prior false confession.

The lawsuit of May 12, 2000, includes a list of prominent American Muslim organizations, mainly charities, which the Boims claim directly supported the attack on their son. This included the Texas-based Holy Land Foundation for Relief and Development (HLF), the premier American charity on behalf of impoverished Palestinians. In fact, the HLF was instrumental in providing funds for relief efforts in Bosnia, Kosovo, Turkey (following the devastating 1999 earthquake), and domestically in Oklahoma City, as well as for Palestinian refugees throughout the world. The Holy Land Foundation has vehemently denied any connections to terrorist groups, and until the slipshod policies emerged post-9/11 it was largely untouched by government authorities.

The Islamic Association for Palestine (IAP), a two-decade old organization devoted to domestic activism on behalf of an issue central to all Muslims, was also cited in the complaint. Like other organizations, the IAP had never been targeted by government authorities, let alone charged with any wrongdoing. On the contrary, it was in good standing with the government as an established American corporation, and was openly conducting its many activities, which largely included national conferences, grassroots activism, and community and media outreach. Again, however, as with other organizations, the lawsuit aimed to drag this group into the mud. Also included was the United Association for Studies and Research, based in Springfield, Virginia, a think-tank specializing in Islamic and Middle Eastern issues, known widely within the community for its important publications, many of which focus on the issue of Palestine. The significance is that none of the entities named in the lawsuit was ever involved in any fund-raising or providing support to any group overseas, including Hamas.

The lawsuit went on to name countless other entities, ranging from the Palestinian Authority, headed by Yasser Arafat, to Mousa Abu Marzouk, the Palestinian organizer deported by the United States in 1996 for representing the Hamas media office abroad. In all, the plaintiffs attempted to link a wide array of American Muslim institutions, individuals, and international organizations together and brand them as supporters of terrorism. This strategy worked to perfection in most cases, as each institution faced a tragic end, bankrupted by this and other costly legal proceedings as well as negative media attention and public outcry. The government seemed to work on the heels of the Boims in their selective prosecution of the Holy Land Foundation, which was forced to shut down following September 11. With its assets seized and reputation marred by the baseless allegations, the Quranic Literacy Institute reached a state of permanent dysfunction almost immediately following the Boim case. Even the Islamic Association for Palestine cancelled its annual conference in 2003, for the first time since its inception twenty years earlier, and was on the verge of closing its Chicago offices by winter of that year.

The causes of Islamic activism and humanitarian work have suffered most, as America's Muslim community of 7 million strong have been left without credible outlets to voice their political concerns and provide the charitable work for their kin across the ocean. The Zionist stranglehold on these ventures was in full effect, with the dual partnership of U.S. government persecution as well as private lawsuits by Israel's domestic proxies. ■

• First annual HLF charity conference, Dallas, Texas.

PROFILE: THE COMMUNITY OF BIG HEARTS

• Chicago Muslims protest Israeli atrocities in the West Bank and Gaza.

Chapter 14

WORKING IN THE AMERICAN HEARTLAND: THE MUSLIM COMMUNITY IN CHICAGO

Our Arab community in Chicago, which is a majority Palestinian community, considers its humanitarian support for the people of Gaza and the West bank in their struggle to end the occupation a charity, and a stand for their rights, and the rights of all people to be free. We will not be intimidated or turned back in this effort. This is the American way, and it is our right because we are Americans.

—Rafiq Jaber, President,
Islamic Association for Palestine (IAP).

The story of Islamic activism in America and the growth of the Muslim community cannot be adequately told without a discussion of the major areas of such activity. The city of Chicago has been of historical importance to the saga of Islam in America, especially as a center of dedication to the Palestinian issue. Because of its central geographic location, as well as being one of America's largest urban midwest industrial and business centers, Chicago, Illinois, has been of particular importance to the growth of America's Muslim community. As early as the late nineteenth century, the Midwest was the original site of migration for peoples from the Middle East, many of whom settled as blue collar factory workers at plants such as the Ford Motor Company. These small communities would grow in the decades to follow, as relatives and family members would flock to these areas to join those who had already settled in these centers. By the mid-twentieth century, Chicago was not only a city heavily populated by Arab Americans, but was also the site of the rise of the Nation of Islam, led by Elijah Muhammad, and, until his departure from the movement, Malcolm X. In the years to follow, as Muhammad's son, Warith Deen, took control of the movement, merging it with mainstream Sunni Islam, Chicago would become home to hundreds of thousands of Muslims, a huge percentage of which was African-American. Muslim institutions, especially mosques, were established in the city as early as the 1950s.

The influx of young Muslim students from all over the world to the Midwest began in the late 1950s and early 1960s, with the official establishment of the Muslim Students Association in Urbana, Illinois, in 1963. From that point on, the Midwest was an important center of Islamic activism, and every national MSA conference was held in the region for the first two decades of MSA's existence.

Subsequently, and with the establishment of the Islamic Society of North America (ISNA) as the largest national Muslim organization, Chicago became the site of more than half of ISNA's annual conferences. At their peak, these conferences attracted more than 35,000 attendees from across the country. They were the largest gathering of Muslims in America. Many other organizations also regarded Chicago as an ideal location for their activities and national conferences, including the Islamic Circle of North America (ICNA), the Islamic Association of North America (IANA), and most recently, the Muslim American Society (MAS).

Chicago and the Question of Palestine

The city of Chicago has also been on the front line of support for the Palestinian cause. The Palestinian issue has experienced a series of transformations from the earliest days of pro-Palestinian activism in the United States. During the 1960s, Palestinian nationalists from the Popular Front for the Liberation of Palestine (PFLP) were the dominant activists and providers of political and financial support to the cause. These nationalists were secular by nature, and therefore had little to do with the Islamic movement taking root in America at that time. The Palestinian issue itself was thus consigned to the small population of non-religious Palestinians living in the area. Later, in the 1970s, it was Fatah and the Democratic Front for the Liberation of Palestine (DFLP) that became the chief active organizations on the Palestinian political landscape in Chicago. As with the PFLP, this organization was also secular nationalist in nature, and while working actively to promote the cause and rally support for Palestine, it did little to entice the growing Muslim population, either Arab and non-Arab, to make the issue a priority in their communities. These movements never really took off in the United States, and would slowly fade away as larger movements adopted the issue with a more universal and unifying message. The Islamic discourse being articulated by many Muslim leaders soon became more appealing to the Palestinians, who made up a huge percentage of Chicago's Arab population.

The 1980s witnessed a revitalization of the Islamic movement on the issue of Palestine. The MSA and its leaders were beginning to place the issue at the forefront of important Islamic causes. As those organizations solidified themselves, other groups who were specifically focused on Palestine emerged from the support built through the student movement in general. The emergence of the Islamic Association for Palestine (IAP) in 1981 gave a new direction to the dynamics of Palestinian activism. Based in Chicago, the IAP consolidated efforts on behalf of the Palestinian cause and utilized the numerical strength of Muslims, Arabs, and Palestinians, which had grown in the city and its outlying suburbs. There was positive interaction with other groups in IAP activities, as support grew. During the next twenty years, the IAP would hold most of its annual conferences in Chicago, attracting thousands of people to lectures focusing on the events in Palestine and the enduring occupation. The organization flourished, becoming a leading voice for the Palestinian rights movement in America. Another important organization during this time was the Muslim Arab Youth Association (MAYA), which branched off from the MSA. MAYA also wanted to devote its activities to important global political issues, especially the Middle East conflict, which had paralyzed the region. As a national organization, MAYA had support from throughout the country, but found a home in Chicago, where it derived much of its base support and held most of its functions. Both of these groups engaged in similar activities, such as conferences to educate their constituencies and fundraising projects to help the needy Palestinians in the occupied territories and refugee camps. There were also outreach programs to protest the inhumane occupation and efforts to educate the American people and leaders.

None of the activities of either IAP or MAYA would have been possible without the establishment of a viable Muslim community in the Chicago area. Though the Arab community existed in Chicago as early as 1912, very few were observant Muslims.[1] Even between 1933 and 1951, a period of heavy Palestinian migration due to the initial conflict in the Holy Land, there was hardly a single mosque or religious center for the steadily expanding population.[2] This changed in the 1970s, with the migration of new communities to the Chicago area, as well as the integration of pre-existing communities into a more religiously inclined population. Mosques began to sprout up throughout the city and its outlying areas. The expansion of the Muslim community in the Chicago metropolitan area would come to include schools, mosques, and businesses, reflecting the growth of the community to nearly 300,000 people, including more than 100,000 Palestinians.

Faith Into Action

With the increase in the number of people attending regular religious functions, the Palestinian issue and the Islamic movement slowly merged. This process was embodied in the establishment of the Mosque Foundation, one of Chicago's largest and most important Islamic centers. Another significant factor was the sheer increase in the number of mosques and Islamic centers in Chicago's metropolitan area generally, totaling about forty mosques and Islamic centers. From the mid-1980s, the establishment of these organizations would come to represent a community's desire to put its religious beliefs and principles into practice. Many imams and scholars from the United States and overseas participated in fundraising campaigns to collect money for needy families and orphans and to provide medical supplies to hospitals in the occupied territories.

The financial support for these humanitarian causes reflects the economic demographics of the Chicago area. Most Islamic centers depend on the owners of small private businesses as their primary source of contributions. Nearly 3,000 businesses, mostly grocery stores, fast food restaurants, and gas stations were owned by Arabs in the Chicago area, nearly 70 percent of whom were Palestinian. The income derived from these self-employed community members, as well as a small segment of professionals and a growing base of blue-collar laborers and cab drivers, formed the entire basis of the fundraising efforts for charitable causes. Charitable projects depended solely on local support and did not have the backing of wealthy individuals, institutions, or states. With the help of many respected organizers of fundraising activities in Chicago, the Muslim community was able to support the efforts of the Holy Land Foundation (HLF), one of the most successful Muslim charities in America. Through the help of Chicago's Islamic centers, the HLF was able to adopt thousands of Palestinian orphans and send tons of food and school supplies to needy families. Due to Chicago's generosity, the HLF succeeded in its campaign to help even Palestinian refugees in Lebanon, Jordan, and Syria. The Holy Land Foundation was so well received in Chicago, it opened a branch office there to continue its humanitarian aid projects on a more regular basis.

The Intifada (1987-1993)

When the Palestinian Intifada, known popularly as "the Intifada of Stones," erupted in December, 1987, Chicago was one of the first cities to respond to the Palestinian need for financial support. Efforts went toward paying for medical expenses, sending much-needed supplies to the territories and supporting orphans and widows who lost their loved ones due to violence in the heated conflict. This period was particularly important as Palestinian Islamic activism reached new heights. The deepening crisis was spreading a sense of urgency throughout the community for more action, more participation, and more high-profile involvement. As a national center for such activity, Chicago was the premier location for much of the pro-Palestinian activism. Institutions such as the IAP and MAYA continued their activism for Palestine at an even greater pace, holding important sessions, fundraising events, and even demonstrations in downtown Chicago that attracted much media attention. Also during this time, new organizations, such as the Islamic Committee for Palestine (ICP), were founded to address the issue and further mobilize the community's support for the Palestinian people. Though established in Florida, the ICP held most of its annual conferences in Chicago, where it was widely received and credited with pumping new blood into the lifeline of the Palestinian movement, adding a human rights dimension to the conflict. These conferences brought some of the most important religious and political figures and academic scholars to address the Palestinian issue to large audiences, establishing a bridge between the occupied territories and the expatriated Palestinians in the United States. Moreover, many more Palestinians had recently arrived in Chicago as refugees and contributed much of their experiences and expertise to the already established groups, increasing everyone's resolve to combat the human rights abuses.

Even Muslim activity on the national level joined in on the action. All ISNA conferences during this period, along with IANA, another national organization, devoted time to addressing the issue of Palestine, a central priority for all Muslims. Being in Chicago, the home of tens of thousands of Palestinians, the Muslim organizations tried to accommodate this important constituency by placing the Palestinian issue as a main item on these conferences' agendas. This added to the political awareness of the Palestinians and enhanced their sense of Islamic duty toward Palestinians in the West Bank and Gaza, while also galvanizing the widespread support of the American Muslim community at large. More recently, the Muslim American Society (MAS)-ICNA joint conferences held in Chicago have had a similar effect, rejuvenating a wave in popular support for Palestinian activism resulting from government intimidation. All of these organizations have had a lasting impact on the establishment of the American Muslim community vis-à-vis the rest of the world, specifically with respect to their relationship with issues such as the Palestinian question.

The Peace Process (1993-2000)

Following the dramatic rise in activism that emerged in the United States as a result of the first Palestinian Intifada, a period of calm began to set in during the early 1990s. The Gulf War had a dramatic impact, serving as a distraction from the situation in Palestine, and a shift in focus to the ongoing battle between the United States and Saddam Hussein's regime in Iraq. One of the after-effects of the Gulf War was the signing of the Oslo Peace Accords between Palestinian and Israeli leaders in September 1993. This agreement, which most Palestinians regarded as an unjust and unrealistic resolution to a lopsided conflict amounted to a capitulation of their rights as guaranteed by international law. But while Muslim and Palestinian leaders and their millions of constituents were highly skeptical of the so-called Peace Process, the voice of opposition was completely drowned out and marginalized by the mainstream American political and media scene. As such, the 1990s featured a derailment of Palestinian activism, based not only on this agreement, but also on a new policy of opposition from pro-Israel forces within America leading the charge against those who dared to confront Israeli aggression.

While this campaign targeted Islamic institutions throughout the United States, it had a particular impact on the most active of cities hosting many involved in the movement. The Muslim community in Chicago came under attack from 1993, following the arrest of Mohammad Salah and Mohammad Jarad by Israeli authorities. During a trip to the region when they were intending to distribute contributions among impoverished Palestinians in the West Bank, the two men were apprehended by Israeli soldiers.

The Israeli government jailed Salah for five years and released Jarad after a few months in a prison hospital. Israel claimed that both men had ties to Hamas and were delivering their funds to support military operations against Israel. While Israeli officials failed to provide evidence of their claims, Salah was convicted and jailed for five years. Under torture, Salah was forced to sign a confession in Hebrew of his involvement with the Islamic Resistance Movement, though he had never been involved in it. Following the end of his sentence, Salah left Israel for the United States, and the Muslim community welcomed him back to Chicago.

During this period, however, the Salah story would generate unwanted attention on Palestinian activism in Chicago, as press reports began to attack Chicago's Palestinian population as sympathizing with "terrorists" and to charge their institutions with illegal activities, though the government never alleged such accusations during this period. Behind this campaign were the usual suspects, anti-Muslim propaganda attempting to de-legitimize the position that these organizations had attained, not only in the Muslim community, but in mainstream America as well. Legal troubles began to surface in the late 1990s, as the nation as a whole suffered from new anti-terror legislation that allowed for expanded law enforcement authority and legalized practices such as the use of secret evidence to detain Arabs and Muslims. In 1993, Muhammad Jarad, the vice president of Muslim Community Center, would be one of the first from the Chicago community to suffer as a result of the anti-Muslim campaign. Along with Salah, Jarad was arrested and detained by the Israeli authorities, who would attempt to link the most reputable organizations and individuals with illegal groups, in spite of the facts to the contrary. He was released nearly six months later on July 24, 1993, ostensibly for medical reasons, but what most commentators have described as the Israeli government's inability to find any wrongdoing. Others, such as Sharif Alwan, a Palestinian resident of Chicago, would suffer a similar fate, though this time from the American government. Alwan was jailed for refusing to testify in July 1999. He was later released and left the United States to return to the West Bank. Also in 1998, more fallout from the Salah case resumed when government authorities shut down the Quranic Literacy Institute (QLI) as part of their ongoing intimidation campaign. Information from the Israeli government was already used in the case against Musa Abu Marzuq, which ended in his deportation from the United States following a lengthy detention and a highly politicized fight.

Though these attacks were prevalent throughout the country, the Chicago community was considered to be on the frontlines of the Islamophobic campaign to shut down its institutions and silence its people. Viewing it as a center of activity on behalf of Palestine, and a population center for Palestinian Americans, the agents of Islamophobia in government and the media sought to destroy its charitable organizations and activist groups and the popular support they had enjoyed over the years. By successfully marginalizing these movements and designating them all as supporters of terrorism, the pro-Israel forces in America hoped to do away with any opposition to their policies and continue the land appropriation and subjugation of the Palestinian people in the occupied territories.

The community, however, had other ideas. They

admirably rose to the occasion and fought back against the governmental targeting. In the summer of 1998, the Council of Islamic Organizations of Greater Chicago formed a special committee called the Committee for Legal Defense and Civil Rights to combat the ongoing abuses. They proceeded to raise money for the defense of unjustly jailed individuals and held two demonstrations in their support in August 1998.[3] These events brought out hundreds of supporters from more than sixty local Islamic centers. By the turn of the century, it appeared that perhaps the battle for civil rights was on the verge of being won. Chicago area Palestinians and Muslims demonstrated that they would not be intimidated and that their dedication to those suffering even greater injustices in the Palestinian territories would outweigh any threatening harm posed by America's political police apparatus.

In the late 1990s, the voice of Islam toward Palestine became more dominant after the failure of the Peace Process became apparent and because of the apologetic perspectives of the Palestinian nationalist leaders in Chicago. This dominant Islamic discourse, especially in light of the response to ongoing attacks, gave momentum to the Islamic leadership in Chicago and elsewhere in the nation to increase their volunteering and charitable contributions to the Chicago-based organizations. During the years of the so-called Peace Process, living standards in the West Bank and Gaza deteriorated further into a humanitarian crisis. Employment levels were at an all-time low. Starvation, poverty, and illness were reaching alarming heights. In addition, Israel's illegal settlement activity was setting record highs. During the seven-year period of the Peace Process, Israel built more illegal settlements than in the entire 45-year period of its existence prior to that. It became increasingly clear to leaders of the Muslim community that the brutal occupation and oppressive conditions were only worsening, and that the community must continue to lend whatever support it could muster to those in need. In spite of the continued attacks, institutions such as the Holy Land Foundation continued to seek the support of the Muslim community, which gladly gave it in record amounts during the period leading up to 2000.

Al-Aqsa Intifada (2000-Present)

Though it had suffered tremendous attacks during the previous decade, the Chicago area Muslim community continued its pledge to help the premier Islamic cause of the time. By the fall of 2000, Chicago's many organizations and institutions were still in full swing, maintaining humanitarian support from tens of thousands of local people. A number of publications, in both English and Arabic, were also being published to inform the community of ongoing events in the United States and abroad. Newspapers such as *Al-Zaytoonah* and the *Muslim World Monitor*, were becoming extremely popular among Chicago's Muslim community. Other newspapers were specifically Palestinian-oriented, such as *Al-Bustan*, *Al-Quds*, *Al-Mahjar*, and *Philisteen*. Publications would play an even more important role with the outbreak of a second Palestinian uprising, the Al-Aqsa Intifada, in September 2000. As the Palestinian opposition to the occupation made itself apparent on television screens across the world, showcasing the tragedy such as the death of the young

Muhammad Al-Durra, American Muslims were among the first to lend their support to the accumulating list of injured Palestinians, orphaned children, and widowed women. Fundraising events were held to raise money for ambulances and medical equipment, along with food and clothing. Protest rallies were also organized to denounce the Israeli aggression and its support by American taxpayer dollars.

Only one year later, however, as the activism was continuing to rise on behalf of the humanitarian crisis in Palestine, which was worsening each day, the September 11, 2001, attacks completely changed the course of the community's direction. With the devastating fallout from the terrorist attacks in New York and Washington, any tolerance for pro-Palestinian activism from government agencies was soon cast out for a more pro-active policy of ending all such support. The campaign began once again, completely re-energized and with the full backing of many Americans unable to distinguish between the horrific attack on their country and support for an occupied people. New laws, in the form of the Patriot Act, allowed the Attorney General to clamp down on all Islamic institutions. The propaganda war was waged by Steven Emerson, Daniel Pipes, and many others who had waited for years for such an opportunity to end the support by Palestinian Americans for their families back home.

In swift fashion, the process began. First, the Holy Land Foundation was labeled a supporter of terrorism. Government agents shut it down and seized its assets. Former victims were once again targeted, as Abdulhaleem Ashqar found himself once again before a grand jury, refusing to testify and incriminate Chicago area activists. He was placed in jail again, and ultimately charged with criminal contempt. The Enaam Arnaout case gained national attention, as a prominent member of the Chicago Muslim community and head of the prominent charity *Benevolence International* was arrested and charged with the most heinous of associations: working with Al-Qaeda leader Osama bin Laden. Though these preposterous charges were later dropped, the intended effect had already been achieved. American Muslims were ostracized from mainstream society and their activities were de-legitimated and ultimately destroyed. The chilling effect was clearly visible, as no Muslim dared contribute to causes that might land them in prison without cause. Even if they had wanted to continue their support, most of the charities had already been shut down.

Though these attacks following 9/11 took place throughout the country, Chicago in itself is a good example of the many types of government abuses against a community that was the leader in humanitarian support for Palestinians living in the occupied territories and refuge camps in neighboring countries. Other incidents included random detentions of immigrants, many of whom are stateless Palestinians with no country to which they can be deported. Also along with mass arrests were bouts of harassment and intimidation by FBI agents questioning members of the community about their lawful activities and widespread surveillance to the extent of promoting mass paranoia among Chicago's vulnerable Muslim minority. Through it all, the media were entirely complicit in the government's action. Even the Mosque Foundation, one of the preeminent religious centers in all of Chicago, was targeted by a vicious media campaign that began in 2003 with a series of articles in the *Daily Southtown*. These articles suggested that federal authorities were investigating the Mosque Foundation and its leaders "for possible involvement in terror-related money laundering."[4] The media campaign continued into 2004 with the publishing of a front-page series in the *Chicago Tribune* entitled "Hard-liners Won Battle for Bridgeview Mosque."[5] The lengthy article proceeds to malign the respected community by attempting to marginalize its honored leadership and its thousands of worshippers by claiming that a small handful of people who oppose the Mosque Foundation's policies are in fact the mainstream moderates. The article is a clear attack against the mosque's public service activities, which include its support of Palestinian causes and opposition to the unjust detention of American Muslim leaders. A clear aim of the piece was to deter any support that might be given to legal defense funds and thus prevent these political prisoners from having a fair trial by implying that supporting an accused individual is somehow unlawful. Especially considering the heightened tensions since 9/11 and the merciless attacks on American Muslims, this article simply reinforced those policies and legitimates the government's lawless use of it's policing authority to spread fear and panic.

Steadily, the community in Chicago, despite all the anti-Muslim campaigns in the post-9/11 era, has still been actively supporting the Palestinian cause and the recently jailed American Muslim leaders. Even with new law enforcement measures in place and authorities egged on by Islamophobes in the media to undermine the community's activities, there has still been a strong resistance to remaining silent and cowing in fear. Though the scare tactics have had a measurable effect, many leaders and institutions are uniting in opposition to the political persecution of their beliefs and

• Al-Sakhra Entertainment Group performs at IAP convention.

activities in the hopes that they can prevail over this terrible wind in the years ahead, and never be forced to relinquish their support of the just and peaceful cause to which they have devoted their lives. As noted Muslim activist and leader Jamal Barzinji notes, "The alliance of Muslims at large with the Palestinian cause has been the primary reason for the anti-Muslim campaign waged by Zionists worldwide. But, the Palestinian issue will always be something that will help to hold Muslims together."[6] ∎

• Mr. Jarad is welcomed home at O'Hare International Airport on Tuesday, July 27, 1993.

PROFILE: THE VISION AND PIONEERS

• Dr. Isma'il Raji al-Faroouqi   • Dr. Jamal al-Barzinji   • Dr. Anwer Ibraheem

• Dr. Taha Jaber al 'Alwani   • Dr. Fathi Milkawi   • Dr. Hisham al Talib

Chapter 15

THE RAID ON THE IIIT: ASSAULT ON MUSLIM AMERICAN INTELLECTUALISM

The IIIT sought to provide an Islamic vision that would Islamize knowledge by Islamizing contemporary academic disciplines. In this way, Muslim societies and communities could modernize without becoming Westernized. They could borrow and benefit from the best of science and technology while basing their development on Islamic principles and values. The Institute has throughout the years of its existence promoted its vision and agenda through publications, seminars, and conferences and the creation of a network of offices in Europe, the Middle East, and Asia.

—John Esposito and John Voll, *Makers of Contemporary Islam*, Oxford University Press, 2001.

The raid on the International Institute of Islamic Thought (IIIT) in the state of Virginia by Federal law enforcement officials on March 20, 2002, came as a shock to many Americans, Muslims and non-Muslims alike. The

Institute is an academic center as well as a research institution. It has to its credit two decades full of endeavors and publications that help fill the gap and bridge the divide between the civilizations of Islam and the West.[1] It has always been known for its moderation and centrist positions. The Institute's Muslim personnel are known to be anchored within academic circles. They stand out for their strong character and mission of inter-civilizational cooperation. They have a track record of openness to official and political establishments and are motivated by political freedom, media objectivity, and interfaith effort. Since they established this Institute in the early 80's, their record shows that they are as far as anyone can be from religious extremism or bigotry. They have maintained fair and balanced relationships with American religious, political, and academic figures. But, it appears that in the aftermath of September 11, there was a drive to put an end to all sorts of Islamic activities. The purpose seems to be to deflect Muslims from access to the political and media levers of American society. In light of this, the IIIT and other similar Islamic foundations have become targets. Since 9/11, these organizations have been exhausted and depleted of any resources to pursue their vital programs. They are now consumed by responding to legal issues, attending court sessions, and expending much valuable time trying to ward off accusations of extremism and terrorism.

Sorties Out of Hollywood

After September 11, U.S. authorities, in their drive against all establishments thought to be supportive of terrorism, raided a number of Muslim organizations in Virginia and

Georgia. These forces seized huge loads of documents and financial records. This operation, code-named *Green Quest*, was carried out by 150 agents from Customs, the INS, and the FBI, along with local police forces and came down hard on fifteen organizations in Virginia alone.

The federal agents also raided the Marjac operation which dealt with investments, along with the Graduate School of Islamic Social Sciences, known as the Academy or GSISS, in Leesburg, Virginia. Dr. Taha Jaber al-'Alwani commented on this by saying: "The Academy is an independent, American institution, that has no ties to foreign interests. Rather it has close affinities with the American academy. It also is affiliated with George Washington University." He added, "What happened was that a [contingent of] security forces raided the academy and immediately occupied it. They took up positions within it. Then they rounded up the academy personnel along with some students who were placed in the academy's auditorium for interrogation. Then the security agents began scanning the computers and taking documents. They must have carted away more than sixty boxes of computers, CD's, and files."[2]

The IIIT's vice-president, who has been working in a research capacity in the United States since 1981, said that no one told him why these agents were searching the Institute.

All this was justified as a security sweep against Islamic institutions in Virginia and Georgia because these institutions were involved in procuring finances for "terrorist organizations."

The FBI agents entered the premises of the IIIT at 10:00 AM on March 20, 2002. They ordered the employees to evacuate their offices immediately; no one was permitted to touch anything before it was subject to a search. They instructed all employees to go to the Institute's library and not to leave it without prior permission. During that time, these agents minutely examined everything in the offices, even the book titles in the library. The FBI did not allow any employee to leave the Institute until very late in the evening that day. When the employees requested access to their attorneys they were rebuffed by the FBI. The FBI's response was that the Institute's employees were not under arrest. But if they were to be arrested, then they would be permitted to contact their lawyers, as is guaranteed by the Constitution.

Preceding the FBI raid was another visitation on that same day by the Immigration and Naturalization Service (INS). These agents asked IIIT employees for documents that would indicate that they are working legally in the United States. One FBI agent threatened the employees by saying he would take them to the INS offices—even though most of the employees working there are American citizens.

When the IIIT employees reviewed the search order presented by the FBI, they realized that it was issued in connection with some investigations relating to the Institute, as well as other Muslim institutions, based on an allegation that they were involved in collecting money for organizations deemed to be terrorist by the U.S. government. The warrant was issued by a court in Alexandria, Virginia.

The IIIT is one of the oldest Muslim institutes in the United States. It is strictly an academic enterprise. It has many branches around the world. It is not known to have pursued any political activity.

As part of this same investigation the FBI raided the home of Dr. Taha Jaber al-'Alwani, the ex-president of the IIIT, and his wife, Professor Mona Abu al-Fadl. The house was searched from files to furniture to furnishings. They confiscated CD's, research dissertations, and personal documents belonging to Dr. al-'Alwani and his wife. Dr. Mona was shocked and scared by the way these agents broke into their home. Their abuse of household belongings was so outrageous that she could not believe something like this could happen in a country known for its respect for civil liberties and human rights. This whole obnoxious episode led her to leave the United States and return to her country of origin, Egypt, after having spent more than twenty years writing, publishing, and teaching at American colleges and universities. Dr. al-'Alwani is considered to be one of the most outstanding Islamic figures and scholars in America.

FBI agents also searched a number of homes belonging to the leading personnel at the IIIT and other Muslim institutions. Their entire families were subject to such intrusive searches in Virginia and Georgia. Many people were astonished to know that such encroachments could take place. Of all places, the IIIT is very well known for its liberal and open-minded policies. Its motto can be summed up with the words: dialogue, understanding, and cooperation. Many people (Muslims and non-Muslims) who are familiar with the IIIT were appalled at these law enforcement measures. They were shocked to learn that the IIIT had been subjected to the accusations and propaganda that was generated by individuals in the United States who are known to be politically aligned with the pro-Israeli agenda.[3] The whole public assault on Muslim organizations—left and right—is egregious and offensive when it is meant to serve Zionist interests that want to undermine all Muslim activities and close down their well-grounded institutions in North America.

These search and seizure campaigns were launched at the

same time Attorney General John Ashcroft announced that the authorities would be conducting "voluntary interviews" with a wide segment of foreigners residing in the United States in order to obtain national security information.

The renowned Islamic scholar, Dr. Yusuf al-Qaradawi, criticised these search-and-pursue procedures that targeted scholarly institutions. He considered such offenses an eye-opener for those who accepted at face value American policies that have been misleadingly spun around democracy and human rights.

He said that the American administration's search-and-seize procedures toward academic institutes and the mistreatment of Dr. Taha Jaber al-'Alwani reinforce perceptions around the world that the United States preaches one thing and does another. It demonstrates that U.S. actions are at odds with human rights, democracy, and the U.N. charter.

A broad range of American Muslim organizations assailed the raids on Muslim academic, commercial, and philanthropic institutions in the United States. Muslim organizations put out a communiqué condemning these raids because they convey a message of hostility and antipathy toward Muslims in America. They contradict President George Bush's oft-repeated statements that the war is against terrorism and not a clash with Islam and is not intended to intimidate Muslims.

The communiqué requested the American authorities to rely on clear legal evidence in its procedures and practices and not on conjecture and dubious information.

Attorney Nancy Luque explained how these government agents exceeded their legal boundaries when they burst into places and institutes that were not mentioned in the judicial warrant. In addition to that, they expropriated many items that were not included in the search warrant.

Some families were harassed by these authorities in an unprecedented way. In one incident, these agents handcuffed a mother and her daughter in a cruel way for three hours. The agents berated them with vulgarities and threatening language.

The search raids targeted the IIIT, the *Fiqh* Council of North America, the Graduate School of Islamic Social Sciences, the Muslim World League, The Educational Heritage Association, Safa, SAAR, the Success Foundation, and a number of other Islamic financial and charitable organizations.

This American security dragnet against American Muslim institutions displayed the disproportionate influence of special interests over American decision-makers. Journalist Douglas Farah wrote, "The raids prompted widespread protest among the Muslim community. Muslim leaders accused law enforcement officials of carrying out a witch hunt and said the raids, in which computers and other office equipment were seized, was hurting legitimate businesses."[4] It also shows how interests that are opposed to any Muslim influence in America do not differentiate between extremists and moderates.

> The events of March 20th have cast a dark cloud over the government's willingness to build allies. They show a clear bias against various ethnic and religious groups that have spoken out against terrorism long before and since the 9/11 tragedy. This sensational and McCarthyistic approach is unjustified. Like millions of other Americans, the families

raided came to this country to pursue higher education, embrace greater opportunities, and to build a better life—to live the American Dream. They not only enjoy American freedoms but also have undertaken enormous responsibilities to make America even greater. The institutions they have established promote citizen awareness, civic participation, and promotion of the democratic process.[5]

The post 9/11 events revealed the power of Jews of the Zionist ideology who claim they are experts on terrorism and the extent to which they exercise a virtual media monopoly on the subject and have wide-open channels to the Congress. These include Steven Emerson, Judith Miller, Daniel Pipes, and Rita Katz, along with far-right Evangelical Christians. The likes of Franklin Graham, Pat Robertson, and Jerry Falwell harvested the terrible fallout from 9/11 to strike against a budding Muslim effort that was coming of age in a significant way in American society. They could not tolerate a future in which Muslims participated on an equal par politically, socially, and culturally with the rest of America, so they marshaled all the doubts and misinformation about Islam and went after these Muslim institutions.

One consequence of 9/11 was the hot-pursuit of Islamic movements everywhere. Individuals belonging to Islamic movements were threatened in their possessions, their livelihood, and their very survival. The broad and blind sweep against Muslims did not distinguish among Islamic movements working for liberation from occupation, movements that are working peacefully to secure human rights, and movements that are active in intellectual reformation. The Islamic presence in America that began as a student organization in the 1960s gave way to the establishment of the Islamic Society of North America (ISNA) in the 80's and was on its way to enriching civic government through charitable organizations and political outreach programs all benefiting from a community that was growing in economic power faster than any other in America. All this was unacceptable to people paranoid about Islam. Muslims themselves—to a certain degree—may be victims of their own success throughout the last two decades. Muslims became a social and economic force to be reckoned with. Muslims also became a recognized minority competing to have a say in the democratic American process. The group who felt most panic-stricken by Muslims stepping up to the American plate was the Jewish minority that has the Zionist lobby pulling its cords.[6]

It is no secret to say that think tanks favorable to Israeli interests in the United States have been and continue to be watchful and sleepless about the spread of Islam into the fabric of American life. This has been especially so within the past three decades. But today they have come out into the open.[7] September 11th offered them a media bonanza as well as an "intellectual horizon." Zionist front-groups capitalized on fears and harvested all the benefits of an Islamophobic post 9/11. The targets were all aspects of organized, institutionalized, and politically-active programs.

These holier-than-thou Zionists began by what they called "draining the financial pool." They went after every donor in the Muslim world, the Persian Gulf states, and particularly Saudi Arabia. They were successful beyond their own expectations.

The American Muslim community had been viewed favorably by popular opinion. American Muslim institutions were financed increasingly by American Muslims. But, then came 9/11. And with it came an era of improvised laws to curtail Muslim activities in the name of combating worldwide terrorism. Many American Muslim charitable organizations were felled by these almost ad-lib laws. The assumptions that these charitable organizations were in a legal safety zone proved to be unfounded.

An observer of this assault on Muslims in America detected a bothersome synchronization of the media and government authorities. First the media threw accusations and uncertainties into the public mind through the newspapers, many of which are in the grip of the Zionist current. In the second stage, the mainstream newspapers and TV networks hype these accusations and uncertainties until the core content of the news items gains something of a factual aura. This is followed by pressure on investigative departments of the government to take action. The *casus belli* is the media's assertions that Muslim organizations are linked to international terrorism. At this point the authorities are shoved into raid formation. The raid materializes and the institutions that have been raided are now immobilized by having their bank accounts frozen, their files usurped, and their activities reduced to legal battles and media defense positions. The constantly repeated method begins with dubious information and is followed by suspicion, media hype, accusations, raids, and investigations.[8]

Dr. Jamal al-Barzinji, one of the Institute's founders and

directors, commented on the increasingly harsh conditions, saying:

> There is no doubt that the campaign which began in the mid-1990s aimed at drying up the sources of income for Islamic activity has had a huge effect. This accelerated after the passage of the anti-terrorism laws, which unfortunately targeted legitimate Islamic institutions and affected Islamic activism on a national scale. I do not believe there is a single Islamic institution that was not affected. This particularly affected the financial support given to these organizations coming from abroad, nations in the Gulf for example. This has become a very sensitive issue even in their support of intellectual activity, for the resulting fear has stopped them from continuing their support. The scrutiny and pressure have affected all Islamic activity, because each institution has become suspect and is expected to prove its innocence before it can resume its work, be it social, intellectual, or in the mosques. The Institute was affected more than others. The forces wanting to put a halt to Islamic activity targeted the leaders of the Institute, because historically it has been the chief organizer of Islamic activity and ahead of its time, and because the community gained much guidance and help from it in times of crisis. The worst parts of this harassment

were the raids that occurred on March 20, 2002, which targeted our homes, offices, equipment, and computers. But thank God, we are still functioning, even if at a slightly lesser level than before."[9]

The International Institute of Islamic Thought [IIIT]

How can one counter all the accusations and innuendos against the IIIT that have been advanced by Zionist centered authors, media organizations, and pundits, most of them liberal and self "righteous" in their attacks against a growing Islamic presence in America. We can counter them by telling the truth about its nature, its beginnings, and its contributions in an expanding intellectual endeavor to open up channels of dialogue between Islam and the West, and its attempts to present a centrist perspective about Islam far from fanaticism or extremism.

The Islamic Climate in the 1960s

The core people who put together the Muslim Student's Association out of youthful zest in the 60s, and who later coordinated the World Assembly of Muslim Youth (WAMY) in the 70s, in addition to other professional associations and numerous scientific symposia, felt an urgent need for an institute dedicated to an intellectual reformation that would have to extend to all corners of the earth. This reformation of thought required organized efforts among all strata of university students and faculty, as well as outreach to intellectuals wherever they might be in Muslim countries and elsewhere. According to Dr. Barzinji, "The development of the Institute was a natural step in the evolutionary process of the Islamic movement's leadership. The leaders of the Institute are themselves former leaders of the Islamic movement. They grew and developed within it, met each other in the United States, and began reviewing the essence of the movement and evaluating the best ways to realize its goals, generally within the latter half of the last century, and especially during the last twenty-five years."[10]

"This envisaged institute would have to be independent in performance and in resources—not because of any political or partisan agenda, but because intellectual independence is necessary for its integrity and to protect it from political and partisan currents. This core group went to the Islamic world seeking to secure the necessary resources and finances to put together such an institute, and to spare them future efforts of going around and virtually begging for assistance. The whole idea was to financially secure such an institute from falling into the hands of individuals or governments who would like to take it in their own partisan or political direction.

"An initial intellectual conclave at Lugano, Switzerland, was arranged and sponsored in 1977 by the long-established Cultural Committee of the Muslim Students Association (MSA). Its recommendations, resulting from a diagnosis of the crisis in the Muslim realm, were forwarded to the scholars and intellectuals of the worldwide Muslim community. This core group registered the International Institute of Islamic Thought (IIIT) on November 6, 1980, in Pennsylvania. The founders were the five members of the Board of Trustees: Dr. Isma'il al-Faruqi [now deceased], Dr. 'Abd al-Hamid Abu Suleiman, Dr. Taha Jaber al-'Alwani, Dr. Jamal al-Barzinji, and Dr. Anwar Ibrahim. The Institute embarked on its course of responsibilities at the beginning of 1981. The Board of Trustees then decided to move to the suburbs of Washington, D.C., in Reston, Virginia in 1982 and in 1986 to nearby Herndon. The Institute was legally registered in Virginia on June 25, 1985." This was a truly landmark event, as many commentators would later note the importance of the contributions by innovative scholars like Al-Faruqi.

> The growth of the Islamic movements and of government appeals to Islam underscored, Faruqi believed, the pressing need for think tanks and experts prepared to bridge the bifurcated world of modern secular elites and more traditional religious leaders. Such organizations could provide the studies and plans needed to address the question of what modern Islamic political, economic, social, and legal systems should look like. At the heart of his vision was the Islamization of knowledge.[11]

The Institute's Prospectus

The Institute's prospectus and projection was encapsulated in *Islamiyat al-Ma'rifat* (The Islamization of Knowledge). The fundamental purpose was to articulate a world-view that explains in a rational way the validity of an Islamic order decreed by God to man as the Last Testament of an orderly individual and social system.

The attempts to construct such a vision were represented by the Institute's programs, activities, and research hubs. These broke down into five pivots or goals:[12]

1) Construct an Islamic paradigm and an Islamic methodology that would eventually operate the Islamic system to address and adjust contemporary social and behavioral sciences and generate pertinent new information.

2) Develop a methodology for interaction with the basic Islamic sources and references (the Noble *Qur'an*, the Notable Sunnah) so that divine revelation becomes applicable to practical innovation.

3) Develop a methodology capable of engulfing and interacting with both the Islamic and humanly devised heritage.

4) Devise a methodology capable of shedding light on the current affairs of the Muslims and the contemporary world in order to address issues and attendant civilizational challenges and opportunities in the light of Islamic wisdom.

5) Detail an educational system of guidelines capable of applying the Islamic paradigm of thought in civilizational renewal.

These objectives are still the Institute's points of reference and inform its field of research. The Institute considers that this prioritization of goals is best suited to emancipate the Muslim intellect so that it can understand and apply the breadth and depths of Scriptural revelations.

The Institute reiterates that the Islamization of Knowledge project is a methodology for intellectual development, a methodological analysis for research, and a system of methods defining social interaction.

The second dimension of the Institute's generally accepted perspective provides a diagnostic view of individual disciplines in order to understand the mental "whereabouts" of the intellectual elites and determine why they have been unable to change and reform.[13] In order to help us understand certain currents and influences as they ebb and flow, the Institute points to two problems troubling the collectivity of Muslims in the world.

First: A cleavage between political leadership on the one hand and the intellectual and scientific leadership on the other. This schism began after the days of the Prophet Muhammad (ﷺ) and his four immediate successors. In the course of time this left a devastating imprint on the Muslims until they finally succumbed to colonialist control.

Second: An intellectual gap between the secular educational syllabi and the religious educational syllabi. This continues to be the case even after what is called independence [from colonialism]. There have been some efforts in some Muslim societies to integrate the two, but the political leaderships educated under the influence of secularism have managed to stifle such reconciliation.

The Institute's message is that the fundamental reform involved in civilizational renewal requires a paradigm shift, which, in turn, requires a foundation and a diagnostic method to interpret reality. This all is complemented by a third dimension which presents a solution designed to complete the reformation process within a universal Islamic educational pattern covering all fields of knowledge and research. Every society to function at its maximum potential must be enriched through evolving ideas and renewed disciplines.

The Institute believes that the renewal, revival, and resurgence of an Islamic social order [the *ummah*] cannot be launched in a sound way except through institutions, whether they are built by individuals or societies, that have the confidence, loyalty, allegiance, and conviction of the Muslim populace [the *ummah*]. These institutions for rehabilitation and resurgence are necessary instruments for qualitative civilizational leaps.

The Muslim social order [the *ummah*] has suffered endlessly from trying to understand the tradition of resurgence. The reason is that resurgence was always understood as the task of an individual person. Muslims have erroneously come to a conclusion that civilizational awakening and renewal are contingent upon one individual who is able to conduct absolute *ijtihad* and trigger a fundamental change!

As a think tank, the Institute introduced into the public mind institutionalization, hoping that this will lead to the much needed reform among the world's Muslims. Since its inception, the Institute has worked hard to lay the groundwork for institutional undertakings.[14]

In its rational and methodical approach, the Institute stands for the reformist trend in Islam that holds human reasoning in high esteem and is very critical of literalist or dogmatic interpretations. The Institute is opposed to mental reclusiveness. It very much encourages *ijtihad* [reasoning], pragmatism, and pluralism. It respects all Scriptural religions.[15] It also is an advocate of closer inter-faith relations and ties. The Institute's "school of thought" envisions the consolidation of all the common values among the three Abrahamic religions so that humanity can better solve its problems and employ its potentials in the service of humankind. It teaches that in the normal course of life the relationships between Muslims and others are based on and produce peace, dialogue, healing, forgiveness, and cooperation in common concerns on a moral basis that respects differing points of view. As Dr. Barzinji notes, "We do not consider ourselves an independent school, but rather a natural extension of the movement for Islamic revival in its various stages, as founded by Shaykhs Muhammad 'Abduh, Jamal al-Din al-Afghani, and Rashid Rida, with the subsequent revival of the movement at the hands of Shaykhs Hassan al-Banna, Abu al-A'la al-Mawdudi, and Abulhassan al-Nadawi. We consider ourselves an extension of these movements and a continuation of where they left off."[16]

This reformist school of thought believes in the application of Islamic law in the cosmopolitan and universal sense that serve the interests of all people and their needs. It follows that divine laws, beliefs, and religions are meant to help humans construct a better world through cooperation and solidarity.

The Institute's reformist school of thought considers the West to be the source of contemporary civilization and its many achievements for humanity. Civilizational cooperation is required to promote progress and deter conflict and clash.

Initiation of Islam Into the West

As the reformist course of the Institution began presenting its concept of Islamization of Knowledge it followed a consistent strategy. It discovered that since the inception of modern Islamic activism dating back to Jamal al-Din al-Afghani and Muhammad 'Abduh it was in the West that Muslims found respect for the opinions and ideas of "the other." This made it easy for energetic Muslims to work within the Muslim community in the West on the premise that Islam is here to stay and is not here merely in transit!

This strategy produced its own plans for an Islamic future. Islam had to be explained to non-Muslims, some of whom later would become self-actualizing Muslims themselves. Thus, the Muslim population in the United States and Canada began to grow. According to surveys in 2002, the number of Muslims in the United States is estimated to be more than 7 million.[17] Muslims in the West have been enriched by a civilization founded on the basis of mutual respect for other people's beliefs—as wild as some of them might be and on the principle that the state shall not impose any political or religious beliefs on its people, so that everyone is free to pursue one's own happiness and all are equal before the law.

In a relatively short time the Muslims in America sank their roots and spread their wings. They now had at their service many Islamic centers, mosques, and Islamic schools. The Muslim Students Association (MSA) could not keep pace with this Islamic blooming. Those affiliated with it were now professionals, legal residents, and citizens. They boldly established the Islamic Society of North America (ISNA).

The *fiqhi* committee within the MSA was transferred to ISNA. This committee continued to produce informative Islamic legal opinions to help the wholesome growth of an American Muslim community until 1988. On March 10, 1988, this committee then became the nucleus of the Islamic

Fiqh Council of North America after consultations with ISNA's Consultative Committee. Since that time the *Fiqh* Council has grown into an independent scholarly committee that works in tandem with other Islamic institutions in North America and the Caribbean and with other institutes that may evolve in the future. This Fiqhi Council applied for and was accepted as a member of the world Islamic Fiqh Council or Majlis, which functions as a subsidiary of the Organization of the Islamic Conference (OIC). It is also a member of the Fiqh Council of India, and the European Council for Ifta' and Research, permanently located in Dublin, Ireland.

The founders of the IIIT were instrumental in establishing the Fiqh Council of North America for the purpose of formulating an institutionalized *ijtihad* of consensus capable of applying the all-inclusive legalities and ecumenical principles of Islam to the American context. This would serve the dual purpose of solving some problems encountered by Muslims living in North America as well as to untangle some problems peculiar to American society itself. Some of these problems pertain to marriage and divorce, or to financial transactions, investments, and shares, or to issues of identity or minority status.

The IIIT's mission involved the establishment of scholarly and religious relationships with many American social institutions, one goal of which was to promote adoption of the Abrahamic trio of religions in place of the traditional Judeo-Christian duality.

Throughout the last two decades and more since its inception, the IIIT helped to deepen the consciousness of Muslim scientists and scholars regarding the nature of the intellectual crisis and the importance of an intellectual dimension necessary for a comprehensive Islamic Civilizational

Enterprise. The IIIT shed light on the manifestations of an Islamic intellectual decline. It sought to draw up methods and programs for a renaissance with the cooperation of many scholars, researchers, and intellectuals from all fields of knowledge.[18]

The IIIT convened hundreds of conferences, symposia, forums, and study sessions at local, regional, and international levels. Thousands of research workers, educational specialists, and scholarly persons from all walks of academia participated. The IIIT published hundreds of books in many languages and distributed them to a wide readership. Its journals in Arabic and English helped expand rational horizons and genuine Islamic ideas. In effect, Muslim logicians and educators were presented with real mental issues and challenges on the road to acquiring knowledge and articulating an Islamic vocabulary responsive to the language of the time.

The IIIT had the distinct advantage in these vital programs of being open-minded and progressive as it sought cooperation and a common denominator with others in scientific committees, university faculties, and official and private research centers around the world.

In addition to the IIIT's well-documented successes in holding conferences and publishing, it was also unsurpassed in approaching scholars from different religious and national backgrounds.

Since the founding of the IIIT, it has cooperated with the Association of Muslim Social Scientists (AMSS) and together they have issued the periodical *American Journal of Islamic Social Scientists* (AJISS). This has served to bridge the gap between Islamic scholars and academic researchers in all fields of the human and behavioral sciences. The magazine *Islamiyat al-Ma'rifah* (The Islamization of Knowledge) was launched to shed further light on the IIIT's project. Its first issue appeared in June 1995.

Since its founding, the IIIT has established a number of branches and offices in different areas of the world to heighten the efforts for research and studies there. Another purpose was to raise awareness among intellectual and academic elites about the goals of the IIIT, in the hope that a pool of academics would come together and move the project and plans forward. The IIIT's ten subdivisions are in Bangladesh, Egypt, France, Indonesia, Jordan, Lebanon, Morocco, Nigeria, Pakistan, and the United Kingdom.

Judicial Solicitation for Reconsideration and Restoration

The IIIT and the Graduate School of Islamic Social Sciences, along with the Sterling Administrative Group in Virginia, together represent the largest American Muslim institution to be raided by agents and officers of American security agencies. In its effort to regain lost ground and to motivate the American Muslim community, this consortium is appealing for the release of its possessions and properties and for the disclosure of the secret evidence that was used to raid the institutes and homes of American Muslims living in northern Virginia. In attendance at this judicial hearing on this appeal, which took place in a court of law in Alexandria, Virginia, in the western suburbs of Washington, D.C., was an overflow of esteemed representatives from the Muslim community who came to show their solidarity with all targeted Muslim institutions. Family members of the defendants also attended.

The American Civil Liberties Union (ACLU) issued a press release in March, 2003, in which it requested that the authorities hand back the seized items to their lawful owners and that they disclose the secret evidence so that the justification [if any] for the raids might stand the test of law, and so that the public might discover who stands behind these actions and who stands to benefit from obstructing and defaming the reputation of Islamic organizations that are known to be moderate and enlightened.

Kent Willis, the executive director of the ACLU in Virginia, said "the Fourth Amendment to the Constitution grants a citizen the right to be free of unreasonable search. As long as the legal warrant for the search remains secret we will never know for certain the extent of the legitimacy and legality of these searches."

Willis added: "a secret government is the worst type of government because it scares people." He concluded by saying: "It is not only the right of individuals and institutions who are harmed by searches to know why they are targeted with such orders; rather such information should be available to all citizens."

An assembly of Muslim and Arab American organizations concerned with civil rights held a press conference on the June 5th, 2003, in the National Press Club in Washington, D.C., to express their support for a case brought by two American Muslim charities, the Heritage Education Trust and the Safa Trust against the American television network CBS and against Rita Katz concerning a defamation program aired on CBS national

TV on May 4, 2003. Katz is the alleged executive of "SITE Institute," which accused these two charitable organizations of being part of a network that supports terrorism.

The two Muslim charities accuse CBS and the executive of "SITE Institute" in their court case, dated June 4, 2003, of fabricating facts without evidence, which resulted in extensive damages to Islamic charitable organizations, specifically damage to their reputation, threats to the safety and security of their employees, and slander by claiming that they support terrorism. They are suing for compensation of $80,000,000.

Nancy Luque, the attorney for the two charitable organizations, said in her press conference to announce the commencement of the legal case that the Muslim organizations asked CBS to withdraw the film and to apologize for the information contained in it. The CBS refused to discuss the matter, which forced the American organizations to resort to legal remedies in order to defend their rights.

The attorney said it is not easy to cancel the effects of [damaging] language over the air and she asked the American public to understand the reasons for these charities to pursue their rights in a court of law. She added that the objective was not to obtain money, but to hold others accountable for their actions and to let journalists at fault know that there are consequences to their aspersions and calumny.

A former member of the House of Representatives, Arlen Udall said that he personally knows many American Muslims, adding that American Muslims are distinguished by a high sense of moral responsibility. He also said that what is happening to Muslims in America in recent years amounts to a dragnet because of their backgrounds, which is

• Roundtable discussion at IIIT with visiting German scholar.

• Jamal al-Barzinji attends meeting of Fiqh Council of North America.

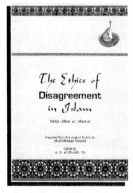  

• A selection of IIIT's publications.

something that should never happen or be tolerated in the United States.

Mehdi Bray, the Executive Director of the MAS-Freedom Foundation, an offshoot of the Muslim American Society, depicted the press conference as a good way to address injustice, because it meticulously expresses the way Muslims feel. He said, "I hope this serves as another serious message to those who, since 9/11, have turned Muslim-bashing, reckless reporting, and defamation into an opportunistic cottage industry. The message is simple: harmful discrimination or mischaracterization of our community will not be tolerated, be it by self-proclaimed 'terrorism experts', the media, academia, or financial and government institutions. Those who insist upon participating in such activities will pay—legally and financially. It's the American way."[19] He added that Muslims are sick and tired of being silent; they want to press their case in court. Bray said CBS has forgotten the impact such programs have on individuals, their reputation, their families, and their kin.

Participants in the press conference included representatives of the American Muslim Association (AMA), the National Association of Muslim Lawyers (NAML), and representatives from the Arab American Institute. Commenting on this, John Abi Nader, representing the Arab American Institute, said that this issue shows how deep Arab and Muslim feelings are running in America when it comes to giving them a bad name in the media. "Truth has become one of the casualties of 9/11; truth is not a relative thing. This is why we have to support this case, because it calls on America to look at the facts within society."[20] ■

Chapter 16

MUSLIMS AND THEIR CHARITIES ON TRIAL

One concern raised about the response to 9/11 was the use of administrative procedures to close down charities without affording them any meaningful opportunity to confront evidence against them or give them any fair day in court.

—David Cole, *Detroit Metro Times*, March 17-23, 2004.

With all the legal push and military pull by the current U.S. administration one might assume that Islamic social and organizational programs in America have been an area of concern by some ethnic groups in America for quite some time now. Indeed, from time to time there were remarks by certain quarters alluding to an Islamic "threat." One of the unspoken concerns by those who were monitoring Islamic activities was the fact that

Muslims may be in America for ever, and their presence might be contrary to well established agendas in the political and social fields. But, these apprehensions never made their way deep down inside the American government.

The notion on the official level was that any danger from the American Muslim community would come from some fringe groups, and therefore there is not much to worry about when it comes to the law abiding character of the American Muslim community. And so for many years the Muslims in America felt at ease and went about their lives as every other American would: an 8-5 workday, nurturing families, and contributing any spare time to the educational or cultural activities of their local mosque. Muslim Americans in such a relaxed atmosphere would pursue their outreach programs, welcome interfaith dialogue, and look forward to the day when Islam is understood for what it is and not for what the detractors say it is. After a full generation of a free exchange of ideas between these Muslims and their non-Muslim compatriots the Muslims were convinced that the United States is the only country where Islam stands a chance to present its teachings and tenets without any cultural bias or historical residuals. America, in the minds of these Muslims, does not have the heavy baggage that Europe has. America is a land that tolerates multiple persuasions and a plurality of faiths and thus Islam can only be at home in America.

In this ambiance of freedom and liberty, some people who were born non-Muslims made the transformation to Islam. "Converts" were on the rise when everyone felt the freedom to exchange ideas and express oneself sincerely and without anyone looking over anyone else's shoulder.

Enter the Contribution and Donation Phase

The flowering of Islam on American soil with all the new converts encouraged other well-to-do Muslims thousands of miles away who heard about the Islamic strides in North America to think about helping out this much welcome development. People with resources and finances were now willing to "pitch in" and help the flourishing of Islam in North America. And American Muslims were in need of any donation they could get. There was a growing need to match the demographic change in America. Muslims are no longer in the hundreds of thousands as they were in the first half of the twentieth century. In the latter half of the twentieth century American Muslims were climbing into the millions. And by the turn of the century there were no less than six million Muslims living in the United States. This meant that these American Muslims would need a community infrastructure—they would need to build new mosques for their daily and weekly prayer services, they would need parochial schools for their children, and they would need other cultural and social services that serve the requirements of Muslims from dietary regulations to getting involved in the American political process.

Word gets around, and many Muslims who are in good financial standing and who are thousands of miles away expressed their willingness to "chip in" and help their American Muslim brethren build an Islamic social network that would eventually contribute to a better quality of life not only for Muslims in America but also for the rest of the American people who are not Muslims.

And with one hand giving and another hand receiving the American Muslim community was able to expand its circle of activities almost exponentially. And so it was: the American Muslim community went from being undeveloped and quiescent in the first half of the 20th century to becoming vibrant and active in the latter half. No longer were the American Muslims a "banana population". They were actually in high gear. And this also raised their budgets. The more activities they assumed the more money they needed. And the more money they received the further they could go in breaking new ground: culturally, socially, educationally, and politically. In actual fact, the American Muslims were experiencing a qualitative jump in their minority status in a pluralistic United States. The makeover of this American Islamic minority caught the eye of several governments in the Arab and Muslim world. Even within the American Muslim community the momentum was so great that it caused many individual Muslims to reconsider their own complacent understanding of an alienated Islam and make a character change to become more involved in interfaith relations and a dialogue of civilizations.

The Coming of Age of Islam in America

The final hurdle to be surmounted was the political one. American Muslims at long last decided to translate their minority status into its political worth. The potentials were unlimited and the resources needed to be husbanded. The task was beckoning and in conclusion the American Muslims moved in to take their positions in the American political process just as was the case with other minorities— to preserve their interests and to secure a better future for the coming generations of Muslims in America as well as for all Americans in a new nation that could be a moral model for the world.

Surveys were speaking about a rapid growth in the numbers of Muslims in America. Catchwords like "Islam: the 2nd Largest Religion in America" were now in the mainstream media. It was at this point in time that alarm bells began ringing. And the hands ringing these alarm bells were well-entrenched Zionist hands that were to be found in their secure positions inside both the media and political establishments. Take it from the horse's mouth: "Undoubtedly the greatest immediate threat to the well being of the American Jewish community and its interests stems from large-scale immigration from the Muslim world."[1]

American Zionists Cross the Threshold

Americans whose loyalty to Israel supercedes their loyalty to America were almost by instinct the first to raise a red flag concerning the minority American Muslim community. These Zionists at heart viewed with fear and suspicion any and all efforts by American Muslims that would translate into something that might one day become a countermeasure to their "Jewish Lobby." The reasoning is that a well organized and substantially financed Muslim Lobby would one day be able to offset all their politicking and un-do their political aspirations in Washington's corridors of power. There is no doubt that the "Jewish Lobby" swings considerable weight on Capitol Hill and there is also no doubt that the well financed and time proven contacts of this Lobby are able to influence local, state, and national elections. With Israel beginning to take a beating in the Middle East, now is not the time to look the other way as American Muslims are making inroads in the American elections through all the channels that are normally and legally open to them.

Lest anyone think these words are the work of a Muslim's imagination gone wild we quote the following:

> I think the organized Jewish community has a great deal of power. And I think that we are watching the high noon of American Jewish power in the United States, and it's moving downwards. We have 52 percent intermarriage. We have young people by every record who do not identify with Israel. We have a community, which is assimilating to a remarkable degree.
> At the same time we have the influx of a large Muslim community with an extremely strong etiological identity and religious identity, which is founded on antipathy to us. The Muslim community is not like any other community. Every single one of their national organizations with the exception of the Islamic Supreme Council is an Islamist Organization.[2]

The 700-pound-gorilla on Capitol Hill swings its weight around; and it will not go light on American Muslims trying to feel their way through the executive and legislative jungle within the Washington beltway. It is naïve and pre-elementary to dismiss the American Jewish Lobby at a time when it throws its weight around in American financial, political, and media circles. The best individuals to acknowledge this fact—even though they will not do so in public—are American politicians and officials running for office. It has become an article of political faith that if an American congressman or president or anyone else who is counted in Washington wants to run for office or re-election they would have to go on record and express their support and fidelity to the state of Israel. Some of them are expected—by the Jewish American Lobby—not only to express their loyalty and aid to the state of Israel but also to recommend or vote for an increase in that support and aid: financially, militarily, and politically.

American presidential candidates are required to praise Israel and underline continued American backing for Israel as they go into their final rounds of debates before the elections in the first week of November every four years. The American political bible has an unspoken commandment to it: Thou Shall Not Criticize Israel. Everyone knows this; but no one wants to say it.

American Muslims Venture Onto Prohibited Political Turf

Frankly speaking, American Muslims were courageous. They did go into the American political arena knowing that eventually they would have to encounter the American Jewish Lobby. They knew that organizing and politicizing American Muslims through Political Action Committees (PAC's) would ruffle Zionist feathers. They knew that if Muslim Americans are going to stand up and be counted politically that they will have to put up with all the pressure that will originate from the American Jewish Lobby. An

American Muslim and an American Jew, if they are frank, will tell you that there is no room for fair competition between the two in the ranks of Republicans, Democrats, or even Independents! The difference is that the American Muslim Lobby wants to prove that its rival will lose in an air of freedom and liberty; while the American Jewish Lobby wants to prove its rival should not exist because it is a threat to freedom and liberty itself! Of course the latter claim is so ridiculous that it does not even qualify to be a fabrication; but the power of the media has placed American Muslims on the defensive in warding off all the accusations that are leveled against all Muslims who are trying to translate their numbers and civic status into political clout.

The Separation of Civics from Finances

The American Jewish lobby knows where to hit in order to cause maximum damage. These lobbyists who are beholden to the Israeli interest want to cut off American Muslims from their financial sources: generous and affluent Muslims around the world. Zionist radars within the American Jewish community all across America zeroed in on American Muslims' fiscal bases and financial resources. After trying to identify these helpful hands, the Zionist American machinery went into full gear. The objective: end all attempts by American Muslims to influence American policies and to have a presence inside American politics.

Muslim Americans as a minority should not be permitted to reach the position of Jewish Americans as a minority. This task is no small one. It needs a strategy. And the stalwarts of the Jewish American Lobby are always ready to do whatever is required for the service and survival of Zionist Israel. And now is the time for all Zionists to come to the support of Israel by rolling back American Muslims into their community shells. The Jewish Lobby mobilized its media and government cadres along with their academic contingents all for the purpose of putting all American Muslim activists who are playing political hardball with their American Jewish counterparts back into the Genie's bottle.

The Israeli assignment that is detailed to the American Jewish Lobby and its derivatives from the Anti-Defamation League (ADL) to a solo pro-Zionist professor on campus is in a nutshell to "neutralize" American Muslim activists and to take "the sting" out of any articulation of an Islamic American Lobby that has the backbone to stand up to and expose all the follies of its American Jewish nemesis.

The Trigger Mechanism

The American Jewish body of interests could not demonize decent American Muslims just because they took issue with Israeli priorities superimposed on the American government. There has to be more to American Muslims than just law-abiding citizens who are beginning to play political tennis and are scoring against the Zionist team in American politics. There has to be a "whipping issue" that will lash the back of this American minority—a thrashing issue that the American Muslims will never forget and that will not only cause them to recede into their minority shell but whose intensity will cause them to go all the way back to their countries of origin; and even there they will live in fear and panic!!!

The American Zionist nexus was about to drop the equivalent of a political nuclear bomb on American Muslims and all other Muslims living in the West. Now was no time for firecrackers and small fry amusements. The American Zionist network was going for the Muslim American jugular. The script was on the wall, and then came manna from heaven: 9/11. This was the turning point that was long anticipated. The media picked up on this unsightly event and began to plant all its image, description, metaphor, and simile seeds in the fertile ashes of 9/11. And all the planted ideas that took root in that day of infamy bore the fruits of demonizing Islam and anyone who would even think of empowering Muslims, be they minorities or majorities! 9/11 was meant and intended to be a knockout for an Islam that aspires to have clout, influence, and weight in America in particular and everywhere else in general.

Before 9/11, Muslims with a self-determination pulse were branded as supporters of Islamic Resistance Movements. Attempts were made to link these movements with terrorism. To this end we observed media campaigns to malign American Islamic charitable organizations and intellectual institutes by linking them to such resistance movements. The obvious reason for this attempted linkage is to taint these American Muslim institutes and councils and to pave the way for law-enforcement agencies to move in and brand them with having ties to suspicious and undesirable Islamic movements. But with all these maneuvers the Zionists behind the scenes were still unable to criminalize legitimate Muslim American foundations or to implicate well-known American Muslims. Was there any damage done? Of course there was. Was it debilitating? Of course it was not.

Now is the Right Time

After 9/11 the world was no longer the place it was before that day. Now the rationale for developing a war against Muslims had the fuel that it always lacked. And now the Zionist plans to exterminate Muslims who want to enter into the political process can be put into operation. We do not think that the word "exterminate" is an exaggerated one in light of what is really happening to American Muslims and non-American Muslims since 9/11. The message is clear: American Muslims have to pay a price for threatening our interests or for even thinking about threatening our interests. How dare the American Muslims think about breaking our Zionist monopoly on the American political process? Measures have to be taken to teach the American Muslim community a lesson they will never forget. And this lesson shall be a lesson for all other Muslims aspiring to empowerment: if you even think about interfering with the Zionist enterprise anywhere, you will meet the same fate!

This chutzpa masks real fears, as shown by the following quote: "But in the next ten years when the final settlement over the Middle East crisis is going to take place, when the deal is going to be cut about Israel, it's going to occur at the time of the maximum Muslim immigration, maximum assertion of Muslim political power, and that's something we've got to watch out for."[3]

After drumming up looming threats by al-Qa'eda and associates these fear mongers turn attention to the financing of terrorism. And now the general public is told that Islamic charitable organizations and all such activities are in one way or another tied into the terrible terror international. This is why it is essential to choke off all assistance going to the Palestinian and Islamic Resistance movement, which is locked in a cruel and unyieldingly belligerent onslaught upon the Jewish people. Unfortunately, the media are guilty of selective representation of the facts on the ground. The financing of Palestinian freedom-fighters after 9/11 has become aiding and abetting terrorism; while the financing of Israeli hostile and deadly assaults and attacks is only presented as "self-defense" or legitimate military operations! The Zionist Israeli encirclement of the Palestinians has more than a military definition. It has become one that is moving in on bank accounts, investments, and charities that act as a virtual support line for the Palestinian people.

An American Hand Out of the Zionist Sleeve

The move forward by the American media was to finger charitable foundations in the Arabian Peninsula and Gulf; and in particular those in Saudi Arabia and Kuwait. Much effort has gone into vilifying these charities and connecting them to al-Qaʻeda. The instigators of this smear campaign came from within the neo-conservative faction of the Republican Party, specifically from closet Zionists. And they are not a tiny faction that can be dismissed as some loony-tunes who should mind their own business; they turn out to be the makers and shakers of almost all critical decisions by America toward the Palestinians, the Arabs, and the Muslims.

This Israeli instigated American offensive against charity money found no resistance from Arab governments who are still caught off balance due to the American military shockwaves that hit both Afghanistan and Iraq. In fact these Arab regimes began to restrict the flow of money from these charities and to monitor them more closely. Some moneys were seized, accounts were impounded, and donations were curtailed. Financial transactions came under closer governmental scrutiny, especially if these donations were allocated for the Palestinians or were earmarked for American Muslims.

Remember, this is what the Zionists all over were looking for since the beginning of the 90's. They never could have been able to get away with such "emergency procedures and loopholes" without the legal pandemonium and the media hype that have taken its hideous shape from 9/11 onwards.

American pressure on the Gulf States served two purposes.

The first one was palpable: to choke off all financial lifelines that feed al-Qa'eda. This was the alleged objective. But the second purpose, which was actually more lethal, was to sever the helping hand that extended from the Arabian Peninsula and Gulf to assist American Muslims empower themselves in the United States.

American Muslims are in a unique position to build bridges between Arab and Muslim countries on the one hand and the United States on the other hand. But that is not what the American Jewish Lobby wants—and so it was not meant to be. This, at least, is the way things have been unfolding so far.

If history were to stop today you would think that the American Jewish Lobby and its stalwarts in Congress and the Executive have the final word on American Muslim affairs—both trans-Atlantic and trans-Pacific. But history has not come to an end. And we don't think it will in the near future. True, official American pressure has paid off in getting both the Saudi and Kuwaiti governments to clamp down on all benevolent and charitable activities. Even contribution boxes at local mosques and Islamic centers have been removed so that the "small change" that comes through this revenue channel is also sealed. Even munificent individuals known for their generosity toward Islamic humanitarian concerns have had their accounts either audited or under very close inspection. All of this, it seems, is to make sure that none of this money ever finds its way into the American Muslim community. Obviously, this has put American Islamic organizations between a rock and a hard place—as these organizations depended to a large degree upon infusions of donations from these overseas quarters. And this makes perfect sense in the minds of the American Jewish Lobby who see a Palestinian behind every curtain or who are gripped by a case of severe paranoia. It is not far-fetched to assume that in the internal thoughts of this Lobby what is Palestinian and what is Islamic are now converging and overlapping to such a degree that they have become—in their minds—indistinguishable. "We could find the issue of the Palestinians being a kind of glue ... among Muslims and Arabs in the United States—that the Palestinian cause and the cause of the Palestinian people could be the kind of cement that helps bring together this incredibly fragmented and diverse community."[4]

Islamic charity foundations found themselves in a pincer position. On the one hand they are being squeezed by American security and revenue agencies, which has resulted in intimidating American Muslims and virtually barring them from contributing to their Islamic charity of choice. The other pincer hand is the virtual cut-off of revenues that used to come from overseas. This will spell the end of many Islamic organizations that used to rely on such funds. Some other Islamic organizations may not close their doors, but they will have to cut back on the number of employees they can pay and on many programs they envisioned for the future.

Congress gets in on the act and orders the Internal Revenue Service (IRS), in effect, to go after almost all Muslim American groups that have a national standing. You know that the current U.S. administration is doing everything it can to dry up Muslim financial sources. "The Senate Finance Committee has asked the Internal Revenue Service to turn over confidential tax and financial records, including donor lists, on dozens of Muslim charities and foundations as part of a widening congressional investigation into alleged ties between tax-exempt organizations and terrorist groups, according to documents and officials.

The request marks a rare and unusually broad use of the Finance Committee's power to obtain private financial records held by the government. It raises the possibility that contributions to charities such as the Holy Land Foundation or the activities of such groups as the Muslim Student Association could be subjected to Senate scrutiny.[5]

This amounts to a severe blow to the networking of Muslim activities. Islamic social services rely on charities; you take away the charities and you almost automatically destroy the social services. This is by no means permanent. Islam is in America in perpetuity. There are times when communities are faced with live-or-die threats. This is one of those times facing the American Muslim community. And it will eventually overcome. American Muslims may have been dealt a setback but it is not a rout. The paranoia about Islam will prove its worthlessness and the Muslims in America will reinstate themselves in the best traditions of freedom, equality, and fair competition. The core of Islam is a message of prosperity, love, and accommodation. This will in due time become obvious even though if you were listening to the media you would think the contrary.

A brief look at the American Muslim institutions and the dates they became an open target for the authorities would give us an idea of the scope and range of this (dare we say) conspiracy that hunts for possible springboards for Islamic social solidarity and the empowerment of Muslims in North America.[6]

■ February 20, 2004
Al-Haramain Islamic Foundation – Oregon
The Treasury Department ordered banks to freeze the accounts of the *Al-Haramain* Islamic Foundation.

■ March 11, 2003
Islamic Foundation – Illinois
Shots fired at the mosque soon after the evening prayer. Windows of the praying area broke. There were around 100 worshippers inside.

■ March 4, 2003
Al-Farooq Mosque – New York
A federal complaint alleged links between the mosque, several Brooklyn businessmen and a cleric in Yemen who,

prosecutors say, claims to have funneled more than $20 million to al-Qaida.

■ **February 26, 2003**
Help the Needy Endowment Inc. – New York
Office raided by FBI. Charity shut down.

Islamic Assembly of North America (IANA) – Michigan
Office raided by FBI seeking information about Sami Omar Al-Hussayen.

■ **February 20, 2003**
Masjid Al-Qassam – Florida
Searched by FBI to collect documents about Sami Al-Arian.

Islamic Academy of Florida – Florida
Searched by FBI to collect documents about Sami Al-Arian.

■ **March 20, 2002**
International Institute of Islamic Thought – Virginia
Federal agents raided the office on suspected links with terrorism.
Graduate School of Islamic Social Sciences – Virginia
Federal agents raided the office on suspected links with terrorism.
Success Foundation – Virginia
Federal agents raided the office on suspected links with terrorism.

National Muslim Leadership Summit – Virginia
Federal agents swept the office due to close proximity of American Muslim Foundation's office, which was actually raided on suspected links with terrorism.

American Muslim Foundation – Virginia

Federal agents raided the office on suspected links with terrorism.

FIQH Council of North America – Virginia

Federal agents raided the office on suspected links with terrorism.

Muslim World League – Virginia

Federal agents raided the office on suspected links with terrorism.

International Islamic Relief Organization – Virginia

Federal agents raided the office on suspected links with terrorism.

International Relief Organization – Virginia

Federal agents raided the office on suspected links with terrorism.

SAAR Foundation – Virginia

Federal agents raided the office on suspected links with terrorism.

SAAR International – Virginia

Federal agents raided the office on suspected links with terrorism.

Safa Trust – Virginia

Federal agents raided the office on suspected links with terrorism.

Mar-Jac Holdings, Inc. – Virginia

Federal agents raided the office on suspected links with terrorism.

Mar-Jac Investments, Inc. – Virginia
Federal agents raided the office on suspected links with terrorism.

Mar-Jac Poultry, Inc. – Virginia
Federal agents raided the office on suspected links with terrorism.

York Foundation – Virginia
Federal agents raided the office on suspected links with terrorism.

MENA Corporation – Virginia
Federal agents raided the office on suspected links with terrorism.

Sterling Charitable Gift Fund – Virginia
Federal agents raided the office on suspected links with terrorism.

York International – Virginia
Federal agents raided the office on suspected links with terrorism.

African Muslim Agency – Virginia
Federal agents raided the office on suspected links with terrorism.

Aradi, Inc. – Virginia
Federal agents raided the office on suspected links with terrorism.

Heritage Education Trust – Virginia
Federal agents raided the office on suspected links with terrorism.

Humana Charitable Trust – Virginia
Federal agents raided the office on suspected links with terrorism.

Grove Corporate, Inc. – Virginia
Federal agents raided the office on suspected links with terrorism.

Reston Investment, Inc. – Virginia
Federal agents raided the office on suspected links with terrorism.

Sterling Management Group, Inc. – Virginia
Federal agents raided the office on suspected links with terrorism.

■ December 14, 2001
Benevolence International Foundation – Illinois
Government shut down the charity on accusations of providing funds to terrorists.

■ December 14, 2001
Global Relief Foundation – Illinois
Government shut down the charity on accusations of providing funds to terrorists.

■ December 4, 2001
Holy Land Foundation (HLF) for Relief and Development – California, Illinois, New Jersey, Texas
Government shut down the charity accusing that group's donations are used to support Hamas terrorist activities, terrorists and their families.

■ December 4, 2001
Quranic Literacy Institute (QLI) – Illinois
Government seized assets worth $1.4 million in cash and property on alleged links with HAMAS.

■ 1995
World and Islam Studies Enterprise (WISE)
FBI raided the office alleging that Al-Arian used WISE and a related Islamic charity to help raise money in the United States for Palestinian Islamic Jihad, a terrorist organization.

Islamic Committee for Palestine (ICP) – Florida (originally Islamic Concern Project)
Shut down by the government. ■

• Professor Sami al-Arian, WISE co-founder.

PROFILE: SCAPEGOATS OF AMERICAN
INTELLIGENCE FAILURE

• Shaykh 'Ali al Tamimi

• Shaykh Jafar Sheikh Idris at Dar al-Arqam.

The Neutrality Act generally allows prosecutions of Americans who go to war to fight against American allies...not Virginians who play paintball and politics in their own backyards.

—Elaine Cassel, *Counterpunch*, March 27-28, 2004.

• Hamad Abdur-Rahman

• Ismail (Randall) Royer

• Sabri ben Kahla

Chapter 17

VIRGINIA JIHAD NETWORK: ALLEGATIONS AND ILLUSIONS

Confused as to how perfectly legal activities can get you 50 years in prison? Welcome to the world of prosecuting Muslims in John Ashcroft's Department of Justice.

Elaine Cassel, *Civil Liberties Watch*,
April 19, 2004.

Anew chapter in the "war on terror" began with the June, 2003, arrests of what federal authorities ominously termed the "Virginia Jihad Network." The Washington, D.C., area and its outlying suburbs, which have served as an important center for American Muslim activity, were still stunned following the March, 2002, raids of dozens of local institutions, charities, and homes of leaders. It became painfully clear to the area's tens of thousands of

Muslims that the Justice Department which had gone to great lengths to disrupt Muslim communities throughout the country was devoting special attention to its own backyard in vilifying the moderate Muslim activity in Northern Virginia. This campaign centered on an important local figure, Shaykh Ali Tamimi, though ironically, he was not formally named in the indictment that targeted eleven others. Nonetheless the national media suggested that Tamimi was the government's "Conspirator No. 1," who masterminded a plot for Americans to wage jihad.

With Tamimi unindicted, the government tried to center its legal case on a blond-haired, blue-eyed civil rights activist and journalist, Randall "Ismail" Royer, who grew up in St. Louis, Missouri. His father is a photographer and his mother a former Catholic nun. In 1994, at the age of 19, he embraced Islam and in 1997 came to Washington, D.C., where he spent several years as a researcher, writer, and investigative journalist for the principal Muslim civil rights organization, the Council on American Islamic Relations (CAIR).

Background
The Case and the Accusations

On Friday, June 27, 2003, a 42-count indictment was brought against 11 alleged members of a so-called "Virginia jihad network." Six arrests took place in Northern Virginia and Pennsylvania, two others were already in custody as a result of an investigation that began in 2000, and three others who were living in Saudi Arabia were arrested there. According to a *Washington Post* article, "Nine are U.S. citizens, several of them registered voters. Three have served in the U.S. military. All but one live in the Washington area. They have varied backgrounds: three are African Americans; five are of Middle Eastern descent; one is a South Korean immigrant and naturalized citizen; two are white. One thing they have in common is a devotion to Islam."[1]

The young men indicted were identified as Randall Todd Royer, Masoud Ahmed Khan, Caliph Basha Ibn Abdur-Raheem, Hammad Abdur-Raheem, Donald Thomas Surrat, Seifullah Chapman, Yong Ki Kwon, Ibrahim Ahmed al-Hamdi, Mohammed Aatique, Khwaja Mahmood Hasan, and Sabri ben Kahla.

Though the arrests were made under the dark cloud of fighting terrorism, none were charged with any terror-related crimes. Instead, the men were accused of a number of weapons and conspiracy charges, the most serious of which was violating the Neutrality Act, an obscure, seldom enforced law that bars Americans from attacking countries with whom the United States is at peace. According to allegations, these young Muslim men were accused of having trained with and fought for *Lashkar-i-Taiba*, a group that seeks to drive India from Kashmir. There was no evidence, nor was there even an accusation, that any of these men were planning attacks in the United States or against Americans living abroad. "Right now in this community, ten miles from Capitol Hill, American citizens allegedly met, plotted, and recruited for violent jihad. These indictments are a stark reminder that terrorists of various allegiances are active in the United States," said Paul J. McNulty, the U.S. Attorney of the Eastern District of Virginia during a well-publicized press conference. But what is the evidence?

The indictment says the men trained at private and military firearm ranges in Northern Virginia to prepare for missions in Kashmir, Chechnya, the Philippines, and other places. Three members of the group had military backgrounds and are accused of instructing the others in small-unit military tactics on private property in Spotsylvania County, using paintball games to simulate actual combat "in preparation for violent jihad." Essentially, the accused Muslims were being branded as terrorists for engaging in the same type of activity that millions of other Americans routinely participate in each weekend. This bizarre aspect of the indictment became the focus of many media commentators, who subsequently dubbed the defendants "the Paintball Eleven" in a number of articles. "The Paintball Case," as it came to be known, revolved around the criminalizing of perfectly legal activities in a less tolerant post-September 11 environment.

The fact that this case at its heart represents an unequivocal example of racial and religious profiling is exemplified by the following observation made by Michael E. Rolince, Acting Assistant Director in charge of the FBI's Washington field office, which headed the investigation. "It is just no longer sound judgment to have people that you believe have engaged in illegal activity and let them conduct an attack before you do something about it. A lot of this is about preemption." The view from the other side is reflected in an observation made by human rights advocate El-Hajj Mauri' Saalakhan. "The Paintball Case represents a twisted form of so-called preemption on the domestice front. The important question is, how far will freedom loving Americans allow the government to go, in the name of a war on terrorism, in distorting the fundamental character of a nation ostensibly predicated on the foundational principle of 'liberty and justice for all'? This is the truly important question."

According to a Washington Post report of June 27,

2003, "The men are accused of gathering at the Dar al-
Arqam mosque on South Washington Street in Falls
Church 'to hear lectures on the righteousness of violent
jihad in Kashmir, Chechnya, and other places around the
world and to watch videotapes of Mujahideen engaged in
jihad.' The Fairfax County home of a Muslim scholar who
has lectured at the Falls Church mosque, 'Ali al-Timimi,
was searched as part of the investigation, according to court
records. He is not charged in the indictment, and federal
authorities would not comment on his role in the case."

The *Washington Post* report also states, "Royer
acknowledged that he worked in Pakistan for Lashkar-i-
Taiba by writing news releases in 1999 or 2000 and that
Yong Ki Kwon, another of the men in custody, was with the
group after September 11, 2001. But Royer said he and
Kwon were not in Pakistan or with the group after
December, 2001, when the State Department declared
Lashkar-i-Taiba a terrorist organization."

When Justice Department officials held a news
conference to say they had broken up the Virginia "jihad"
network, they called the group violent and dangerous and "a
stark reminder that terrorist organizations of various
allegiances are active in the United States." But a week later,
in what was expected to be a series of routine hearings, a
federal magistrate judge, T. Rawles Jones Jr., ordered five of
the men to be freed without bond until trial. Challenging
the Government's allegations, Jones rebuffed the
prosecutors' claim that the men posed a serious threat.
Three of the five were immediately released. A fourth
appeared later before Judge Leonie M. Brinkema in U.S.
District Court in Alexandria, Virginia, to contest the
prosecutors' appeal of his release. Brinkema agreed to let

Seifullah Chapman go free until trial and also released another of his co-defendants. For two judges, from one of the nation's most conservative federal courts, to free defendants in what prosecutors billed as a high-profile terrorism case was a rebuke to the Justice Department. It marked the first time the department had failed in its efforts to hold suspects on terrorism-related charges.

Some legal analysts initially suggested that after a long period since Sept. 11, 2001, during which the government enjoyed broad discretion to bring terrorism cases and to hold suspects, the pendulum is starting to swing the other way, with greater scrutiny of the government's evidence. "The administration is having something of a boy-who-cried-wolf problem," said Jonathan Turley, a law professor at George Washington University who has been involved in national security cases as a lawyer. "The administration has been making these fairly outlandish claims to the public ... and it's caught up with them. The courts are beginning to balk." The court's action follows a sharply critical report issued in July, 2003, by the Justice Department's inspector general. The report found "significant problems" in the seizure of illegal immigrants after Sept. 11. It said many suspects who had no links to terrorists were jailed under severe conditions without access to a lawyer. The inspector general also found that some senior Justice officials dismissed concerns raised by others in the department about whether such actions were legal.

Dar al-Arqam: Fact and Fiction

At the heart of this saga is the Center for Islamic Information and Education, otherwise known as Dar al

Arqam, in Falls Church, Virginia, about five miles west of the Pentagon. It is here that government attorneys claim that young Muslim men in their twenties and thirties would gather to listen to violent rhetoric from the center's leader, as well as plan out actual strategies to wage an armed "jihad." According to the founder of this center, Jafar Sheikh Idries, "At Dar al-Arqam we never raise funds for any charity organization, we don't discuss politics, and there is no recruitment activity for any group. This place is just an institute for soul-purification."

It may be presumptuous to discuss the youth belonging to Dar al-Arqam without speaking about the two most important figures within this Islamic center, who were able to put together a weekly program that attracted many people, mostly university students, for weekly religious educational sessions. This conclave of individuals consisted of students and young professionals. What is remarkable about them is that many of them were Christian converts to Islam. Out of the 150 who attended, about forty percent of them were Christian converts. These educational sessions started in the house of Shaykh Jafar Sheikh Idris in the early 90s. The numbers slowly began to grow. By 1997, Shaykh Jafar moved out of the Washington area, but wanted his class to continue. He asked a young man to take over teaching duties. This young man was 'Ali al-Timimi. Although not as well known to these Fairfax youth, Timimi had by 1997 developed a strong following of African-Americans in the Washington, D.C., area, having taught a weekly class, similar to Shaykh Jafar's, since the early 80s. He also had begun to receive some international recognition due to his frequent trips to Canada and the United Kingdom. With Timimi's arrival, class attendance grew exponentially. Not only did Timimi attract his African-American students from Washington, D.C., but the class also began to have a smoother dynamic because Tamimi was a young American to whom these young men could better relate. He was deeply knowledgeable about Islam, but at the same time comfortable with all things American. Charismatic in his personality, he was also easy going and approachable. On a professional level he was a manager for a top Washington information technology firm, and he had just begun his doctorate in computational biology with a focus on the genetic basis of cancer.

He was being invited to speak about Islam around the world and he intimately understood the day-to-day problems faced by young Muslims in America as he too lived them. After a short while the house could no longer accommodate their growing numbers. Attempts where made to hold the classes at local university campuses or mosques. But, this class was different; these young men (and soon young women) needed their own home. The idea of renting a place was sensible. The idea was to establish a center for Islamic information and education. This, in a nutshell, is what became Dar al-Arqam. The name "Dar al-Arqam" is of rich Islamic meaning. Historically speaking, Dar al-Arqam was a refuge and a haven for persecuted Muslims during the early years of Islam in Arabia. But, more importantly, Shaykh 'Ali al-Timimi points out, "Dar al-Arqam was the first Islamic school established. It was located in central Makkah on Mount Safa, next to the Kaaba. The locality was discreet, yet accessible."

And in a similar humble setting, in the heart of old Falls Church, Virginia, a "new" American Dar al-Arqam was formed. Like the early school founded by Islam's Prophet, the lessons taught consisted of Islam's basic teachings, such as improving and refining the belief, cultivating and disciplining the self, and growing in spirituality. The lessons were appealing to the youth.

The spokesman for Dar al Hijra, the largest mosque in the Northern Virginia area, Al Hajj Johari Abdul-Malik was quoted by the *Washington Post* as saying that at Dar al Arqam, "They're not talking about politics; they're not talking about voting. Their issues are that people should pray, people should fast. They should learn the Arabic language, frequent the mosque, and raise their children to be devout. I've never heard any anti-government rhetoric there."

The Spiritual Leader: Shaykh 'Ali al-Timimi

Ali al-Timimi was born in Washington, D.C., in 1963, the eldest in a family of an Iraqi diplomat assigned to the Iraqi embassy in Washington during the 1950s. His mother was a long time university professor. Ali finished his elementary and part of his secondary education in Washington. He grew up like any typical American kid. Like most boys of his generation, his passions were baseball and rock-n-roll music. He grew up in a predominately Catholic middle class neighborhood and attended a liberal private school whose student body consisted of Washington's elite Jewish community. Shaykh Ali recalls how he never met a fellow Arab Muslim child until he went to Saudi Arabia at the age of fifteen. At age twelve he attended the Bar Mitzvah of one of his best friends, the son of one of Washington's well-known journalists. As is traditional, the Bar Mitzvah was held at Jewish synagogue. Shaykh Ali vividly recalled the event, "We entered the synagogue and all the boys (Jewish and non-Jewish) placed yarmulkes on their heads in accordance with Jewish rituals. After the rituals, the Rabbi began to address the audience. He began to attack the Arabs by saying that they sought to kill young Jewish boys. I was offended that I would be associated with seeking to murder my Jewish classmate and one of my closest friends."

Ali left the hall and waited outside until the ceremony was over. The boy's father later approached Ali and apologized for what was said. Ali says this event had a lasting impact on him. He began to realize that in the larger world, issues of his ethnicity and religion would be something by which people were going to make judgments about him.

After moving to Saudi Arabia with his family, Ali met Bilal Phillips, an individual whose impact on the direction of Islam in both Ali's life and Muslim converts in the West would only appear many years later. Phillips is a Canadian of Jamaican origin. At the time of Ali's arrival, Phillips had just graduated from the Islamic University of Medina. Seeking to complete his graduate studies in Riyadh, Phillips needed a job to support his family. His father (a Christian at that time) taught English at the private school in Riyadh which Ali attended. And here a relationship between a young Muslim scholar and a Muslim youth from the West was established, a relationship that Ali would repeat 15 years later with his students. "What attracted me to Bilal was that he was a Westerner, so he could explain Islam in terms that I and the others at the school could understand." As a result of these teachings, Ali adopted a more traditional concept of Islam idealized in the Salafiya movement. Ali spent only a couple of years in Riyadh with Bilal Philips. It was soon time for him to go back to the United States for college. "I left the United States in 1978 when Islam was at best a passing curiosity; I came back for college in '81 when Islam after the Iranian revolution was now at the center of the news."[2]

During the early 80's, Washington's Islamic Center was the stage for struggle between three competing groups: the traditional leadership of the mosque backed by the embassies, and in particular the Saudis; the Arab youth of the Muslim Brotherhood, which formed the nucleus of what was to become Dar al-Hijra; and the Iranian supporters of Khomeini's Islamic Revolution. Not only was the mosque contested but there was a struggle for the allegiance of Washington's African-American Muslim community. In the end the Iranians not only took over the mosque but also won the hearts of the African-American community due to an articulate Arab American, Imam Muhammad Asi.

Muhammad Asi relates that when he would give a sermon describing the plight of Muslims oppressed in distant parts of the world he would hear someone nearby start sobbing. When he looked down he always saw Ali al-Tamimi sitting below the *minbar* or pulpit with tears streaming down his face. Muhammad Asi says that he has rarely met anyone with such a soft heart.

Ali said, "The gatherings at the Center at that time had little to do with religion and much to do with power politics because this was the time first of the euphoria over the Iranian revolution as a promising model for oppressed peoples all over the Muslim world and then of the wars by Iraq against Iran and by the Soviet Union against Afghanistan. Of course, I got caught up in the politics. But in the end I was hungry for answers to the larger philosophical questions being posed at the university. I flirted with each group, only quickly to become disinterested in their rhetoric and what I perceived as their being out of touch with the questions being raised in America about Islam and Muslims."

Another important influence and friend was Idris

Palmer, the American born son of a Jamaican diplomat. Upon meeting at a religious service, the two spoke at length, Ali recalls, "and the beginning of a twenty-year friendship started." Palmer became more than a friend who also shared a similar background; he was a student of Salafi Islam. He, as Al-Timimi says, "became my second 'Islamic' mentor. Bilal taught me the basics of my religion; Idris showed me how to mingle and address Washington's African-American Muslims." With the relationship between the two men cemented, they began a journey of teaching Washington's African-American Muslims. What they taught was simple, reflecting both their youth and depth of knowledge

As Muslim immigrants began to pour into the Washington area, Muslim activity started moving away from the city toward Washington's growing suburbs. The Muslim Community Center (MCC) was being established in Prince George's Montgomery County to serve the Pakistani community, while Dar al-Hijra was being established in Falls Church to serve mostly the Arab community. The Iranians moved to the Islamic Educational Center in Potomac, Maryland. Washington's African-American Muslims were slowly being detached from the greater Muslim community. The isolated and small study group that Timimi and Palmer had formed was running into more and more complex issues as their numbers began to grow. Timimi decided to spend more time in education, traveling back to Saudi Arabia's Islamic University of Medina.

Here in this holy city, thousands of young Muslim men from all over the world would be given free education, room, and board under the aegis of the Islamic world's leading scholars. Idris Palmer was the first to set out in 1986 to study in Saudi Arabia. Timimi followed the next year. Ali recalled, "It is so odd that today I stand accused of being the 'spiritual leader' of the Virginia jihad network while during the heyday of jihad in Afghanistan, I went to Arabia to study Islam and Arabic while tens of thousands of Muslim youth were leaving for Afghanistan to fight the Soviets."

There is no doubt that the popularity of Islam among African American Muslims encouraged Islamic activists such as the Ikhwan and the Salafis to make inroads into these communities. Budgets were allocated for this purpose. Among the Salafis, the Kuwaitis were the first to enter this race. In 1986, they established The Qur'an and Sunnah Society of North America. A few years later, the Saudi Salafis entered into the picture establishing Dar al Makkah in Denver, Colorado, and the Ahl al Sunnah wa al Bait in Vancouver, Canada, under Mahmud Murad. The Denver group grew to become The Islamic Assembly of North America, or IANA, for short.

Soon both national organizations (the Qur'an and Sunna Society and IANA) began to jockey for Timimi and his Washington African-American following. Timimi and Palmer were being invited to various universities and their campus-based mosques, while Abdul-Khaaliq was being asked to organize the English events. In a short period of time, Al-Timimi was jetting across North America spending two and sometimes three weekends a month speaking. But, his best friend for more than a decade left for the United Kingdom, where he married and settled. With his best friend's departure, a new phase in Al-Timimi's Islamic career was to start.

The national Salafi organizations were being wracked with internal differences reflecting the politics of the Middle East. The Qur'an and Sunnah Society had split in two. The Kuwaitis formed their own organization. IANA, the youngest of all, was now the dominant organization. Al-Timimi saw where the winds were blowing and decided to put his efforts behind IANA. He remarks, "Ideologically I was closer to the Qur'an and Sunnah Society, but they appeared to me as out of touch with reality. In the end, their message was not going to affect Muslims in America, let alone America as a whole. And while I was not as comfortable with the over focus on Middle-East politics found in IANA, I felt that they would be more amenable to my ideas about focusing on Islam in America."

Al-Timimi quickly made his impact on IANA. He proposed that IANA form a delegation to participate in the U.N.'s 4th World Conference on Women in Beijing, China. NGO status was obtained for IANA, a delegation was led by Al-Timimi, and lectures were delivered. Al-Timimi's visionary abilities were used to the fullest. He contacted a prominent Kuwaiti Salafi shaykh of Egyptian background, Abdur-Rahman Abdul-Khaliq, to write a paper on women in Islam. Al-Timimi translated that into English and secured translators for German, French, Swahili, and Chinese translations. A full press staff for the duration of the conference was set up by the Americans. The IANA group had a daily press release in English and Arabic which they would then fax over to the States. The press group in the States would then fax it to over 500 Muslim centers, leading personalities, and the Arabic press. The Arabic media were taking these press releases and re-releasing them under their own names. Thus Al-Timimi with his small band of five was able to direct all the focus on the Muslim participation to his own group.

Dr. Jafar Sheikh Idris was a long-time leader and founder of the Muslim Brotherhood movement in Sudan. He had his differences with Dr. Hasan al-Turabi and left Sudan to teach in Saudi Arabia in the early 70s. But Dr. Jafar had a certain quality that was extremely attractive to Timimi. Having obtained his doctorate in philosophy from the United Kingdom, Dr. Jafar Sheikh Idris was well versed in the intellectual currents of the West. Here, Timimi was able to find someone who could provide the answers to the larger philosophical questions in Al-Timimi's mind. He also influenced Timimi in another profound way, Ali said of his influence, "The contemporary Salafi discourse appeared in the detached and remote areas of Najd (central Arabia) and lacks the ability to address the world as a whole. It tends to be insular and as a result appears to outsiders as xenophobic. So here was this great Salafi scholar who was quite comfortable with presenting Islam by using rational methods. Shaykh Jafar convinced me that I needed to change the tone of my discourse. It is one thing to speak among ourselves where the fundamentals of the discourse is a given; it is another thing to speak before others where there is not only a lack of acceptance but often an initial rejection."

Unfortunately for those who knew him, Shaykh Jafar too would fall under attack following the June 2003 arrests. An October 2 article in the *Washington Post* stated that he was linked to an "extremist Wahabi network," and in the usual course of events, swift government action followed the media onslaught. Later that month, Dr. Jafar was ordered to leave the United States by the Immigration and Naturalization Services, following the rejection of his visa renewal. Following a decade of living in the United States as a researcher, lecturer, and administrator at the Institute for Islamic and Arabic Sciences in America (IIASA) in Fairfax, Virginia, and at the American Open University (AOU) in Falls Church, Virginia, Shaykh Jafar departed without ever being given a reason by the INS.

September 11: The Disaster and Its Aftermath

After the events of September 11, most of the Islamic movements in the world condemned the attacks with a host of moral and political considerations. The Salafis did so equally. When the United States declared its war against terrorism by targeting Islamic relief organizations around the world, followed by a barrage of accusations and instigations against Islamic resistance movements, everyone within Islamic leadership circles realized that the war that was declared against terrorism was expanding to include everything Islamic, regardless of orientation. The difference between one Islamic trend and another was immense, but there seemed to be no distinction coming from the American government.

The new environment created by 9/11 prompted Shaykh Timimi to call for a bold new initiative. Following a series of discussions with prominent Saudi scholars, Timimi put together a white paper entitled, "There has to be an initiative." The white paper stated:

> Any serious dialogue between two contentious sides requires the following: Each side should be able to identify its self-evident deficiencies and faults. The issues of disagreement have to be identified; and a dialogue of reason and objectivity should commence. A dialogue initiative with the West has its legitimacy drawn from the shari'ah. It may be one of the only ways to preclude imminent hostilities with the West.

We suggest the following for doing so: What is required of us in the Islamic world to avoid a clash of civilizations? We should not consider every action by the West with which we disagree to be a hostile or conspiratorial act toward the Muslim umma coming from an ancient crusading hatred meant to shred Islam and the Muslims. Based upon this, we Muslims need to admit that most of the problems that we suffer from today are of our own making, and not made by the West. What is required of the West to avoid a clash of civilizations? The West should not view Islam through the lens in which it viewed its historical experiences with the Church. The West should confess that it bears a portion of the burden in what have become problems in the Muslim World. The West should concede that the role of the Islamic world is not one of exporting raw materials and human labor or potential to the West. We Muslims are heirs of a civilization that has shaped humanity and goes beyond merely conveying Greek heritage. Even today humanity, and the West in particular, should recognize that the Muslims have in their possession real solutions for common human problems.

The white paper went on to suggest positive and productive measures for change and was circulated among more than two hundred Muslim decision-makers, academics, and activists. The central issue again was to avoid any "clash of civilizations" with the West and to disarm those who would rather have Muslims at war with the West. The document ends with a call for an international conference on both the popular and the official levels to jump-start the discussion of these issues.

After September 11, a prominent Saudi cleric, Shaykh Safar al-Hawali sent an open letter to President George W. Bush reminding him of the past relations between America and the Islamic world, advising him not to go overboard in seeking revenge for the attacks, and outlined the reasons for hatred and malice coming from America toward Muslims. He advised Bush to tip the scales in favor of logic and reason instead of reaching for the gun. On October 6, 2002, Shaykh Safar sent another letter, this one to Congress. In it he said that if the Congress goes along with Bush's war against Iraq it would result in a calamity for both sides.

Shaykh Ali's role as a ghost-writer of this letter received much subsequent attention. He remarked, "I had a great deal of uneasiness regarding the march to war on Iraq. Not only was I motivated by purely Islamic and humanitarian concerns for the Iraqi civilian population who, having suffered under Saddam and U.N. sanctions, now faced the might of America's war machine; but more importantly I was deeply afraid that if war was to occur we might end up having crossed the point of no return and truly head for total civilizational conflict. After witnessing the conduct of the Bush administration, I had no hope that there were any voices of reason. My only hope was that in Congress there remained enough independent thinking men and women who would see past the administration's rhetoric. As I am an unknown, what good would an e-mail or a letter from me do? So I thought the best thing to do was have someone on behalf of the world's one billion plus Muslims send a letter to Congress." Tamimi proceeded to edit and write portions of the letter, whose delivery he also oversaw.

Al-Hawali's letter was hand-delivered to all members of Congress and received substantial media attention in the Arab and Muslim world as a sign of Muslims attempting to avoid conflict with the United States. These efforts by Shaykh Ali placed him on the radar of law enforcement authorities, noted for their attraction to popular activists gaining access to political leaders and the media. His contacts with Shaykhs Safar al-Hawali and Salman al-'Awdah could not have gone unnoticed. Safar al-Hawali is very well known for his objections to American policies. He was against his government's reliance on American forces during the Gulf War of 1991. He considered this to be a violation of the country's best interests, as well as a violation of the general Muslim interest. At that time, he wrote his opinion to Shaykh 'Abd al-'Aziz bin Baz and other senior Saudi scholars explaining his point of view and his objection to the way the Gulf crisis was being handled. Shaykh Timimi was convinced that something should be done before the relationship between America and the Muslim world reached a point of no return, especially those relations that touch on the Islamic movement. Shaykh al-Hawali seemed to be more open to understanding the West. He was interested in finding common grounds and fostering mutual understanding for the purpose of peaceful coexistence and the future interest of humanity. Shaykh Ali al-Timimi believed that Shaykh al-Hawali is the most central figure within Salafi circles who looks forward to a dialogue with the West.

Shaykh Timimi's vision of the future of the relationship between Islam and the West was marked by a call for dialogue. In his usual charismatic tone, he stated unequivocally:

> If we are to accept Huntington's basic argument that international relationships in the 21st century will be organized primarily on a civilizational basis, we quickly realize that the closest civilization to Muslims is the American civilization. We can quickly illustrate this by just looking at two civilizational ideals: religion and justice. Unlike any other civilization, Muslim civilization is existentially a religious civilization. And in terms of religion, we find that of all peoples of the world, Americans are closest to the Muslims. Religion and religious symbols are still central to the American self-identity. American society, in general, does not have the atheistic or even anti-religious tone often seen in Europe. I would even further argue that the simple theology of many of the founding fathers like Adams and Jefferson is much closer to Islam than to the theology of today's Christian evangelicals like Bush and Ashcroft or Falwell and Robertson.
>
> When we come to justice, we find that the establishment of justice was the paramount concern in the political philosophy of the founding fathers. It is interesting that the first aim in the preamble of the Constitution— after

its raison d'etre of forming "a more perfect
union" is the "establishment of justice." Justice
is mentioned before "domestic tranquility, the
common defense, the general welfare," or "the
blessings of liberty." And I would argue that the
central civilizational problem for Muslims
today is their sense of a lack of justice.
The Muslim dilemma in my view is not, as
argued by some, primarily a sense of
comparative weakness before the West—
although that is there. The civilizational
dilemma is deeper as it stems from feelings of
oppression and a longing for justice. America
is fertile ground for Islam, and in general
Americans when presented Islam in its true
light generally have positive feelings for it.

These views, expressed candidly by Shaykh Tamimi, are
reflective of the common position of peaceful coexistence
and continued dialogue which typify virtually all strands of
American Muslim thought, including outwardly
conservative movements such as the Salafis. Indeed, it is out
of this newly sprung culture of Muslims originating in
American culture and referring to Islamic roots that the Dar
al-Arqam was founded. The young men targeted as threats
to American security were never shown to have done
anything more than engage in their own religious
awakening, an inalienable right of all Americans. Their
quest for knowledge and spiritual health took them to
weekly classes at their local center and to travels far and wide
across the Muslim world. One of these youths was Ismail
Royer, whose story follows.

The Civic Activist: Randall Royer

Randall Royer, also known by his adopted Muslim name Ismail, was the centerpiece and first person indicted in the groundbreaking case that used the almost forgotten Neutrality Act to prosecute Americans who engage in what they consider to be civil rights actions abroad, but what the U.S. government considers private interference in the internal affairs of countries not at war with the United States. This law was enacted over a century ago to stop American mercenaries from dragging the United States into foreign wars.

Although this act limits penalties to three years in prison, the basket of charges launched against Royer had the potential to incarcerate him for a minimum of 155 years. The central charge was that Royer participated in the actions of a liberation group in Kashmir that opposed the occupation of Kashmir by India, a nation not at war with the United States. This group was subsequently declared a terrorist organization in December 2001.

Royer was also accused of recruiting another American, Seifallah Chapman, a former U.S. Marine who at age thirty had just finished a bachelor's degree in criminal justice in Arlington, Virginia, at Mary Mount University. Chapman went to Kashmir and legally qualified as a terrorist because he was still with the Kashmiri group when it was declared a terrorist organization in December 2001.

According to the search warrants and the FBI's public announcement on June 12, 2003, the men were not indicted for "material support" of terrorism, but for "knowingly setting foot in a foreign state with whom the United States is at peace," and specifically for training to fight abroad and "kill, kidnap, maim, or injure persons or damage property in a foreign country."

In the early days of the court proceedings, the prosecution supported its motion to revoke bail by presenting newspaper stories about the history of acts of terror, the history of the Taliban, and the vulnerability of Americans to religious conversion, noting that, "past perpetrators of terror have often had unique and unpredictable histories." According to Royer's defense lawyer at the time, Stanley L. Cohen, "these submissions constitute a shameless effort to substitute fear for evidence. ... This ignores the particular facts of this man, and his thoughts, words, and beliefs." Cohen objected that, "While this montage of [terrorist characters] occupies center stage in the government's submission, Ismail Royer does not know them, does not like them, and does not respect them. While these characters are ciphers to us ... and therefore convenient to the government's task of constructing a unifying theory of how every Muslim is a potential terrorist, Mr. Royer and his beliefs are no mystery. Rather, we know first-hand from his published articles and writings that Ismail Royer has condemned repeatedly attacks on the United States and Americans; that he considers these groups and their adherents 'extremists' who were not good Muslims; and that he looks upon violence against civilians everywhere as anathema to Islam, be it in New York or Tel Aviv."

Indeed, Randall Royer spoke and wrote voluminously against all forms of extremism and helped to found the internet magazine *A True Word* in which, even before 9/11, he forcefully castigated Muslims who questioned the possibility and need for peaceful coexistence and cooperation between the West and the Muslim world. This applies in particular, he said, to Muslims who live in America, because hostility to America "violates a contract that you have simply by being here."

In a letter to Daniel Pipes sent on February 26, 2002, Royer wrote, "There is extremism among Muslims. Some of what you write as 'Islamism' is extremism. Most of what you describe as 'Islamism' is Islam. Osama bin Laden is an extremist; I've been saying this for years; some members of Hamas are extremists; not because either chose to resist oppression (in the former case, the invasion of the Soviet Union, in the latter, of course, your regime's occupation), but because they suffer from major defects in their 'aqeedah (faith), the effects of which are manifested in the despicable crimes they commit and which erase many times over whatever positive qualities they have or had. For whatever minuscule advantage they might possibly achieve from these misguided activities, they do the most damage to their own souls, to Islam, to their own cause, and not least to innocent people."

The beginning of Randall Royer's alleged career in terrorism begins in what the government brands his crime of "violent jihad" in Bosnia. Stanley Cohen put this in proper context: "Ismail Royer went to Bosnia in the early 1990's for a short time. Like thousands of other Americans sickened by the specter of rape, pillage, and ethnic cleansing, Mr. Royer went not to commit 'violent jihad,' but to resist genocide. He acted at a time when the United States and NATO would not, though he acted with the connivance of our government, which encouraged international resistance to the aggression of Milosevic, Karadzic, and their regime. Indeed, the United States would ultimately lead a NATO force in combat action against that regime, bringing the war to an end and some of its actors to the tribunal of justice. To characterize Mr. Royer's actions as a private citizen in opposing heinous fascism in Europe as 'violent jihad' ill serves the legacy of every American who fought and died in the all-volunteer expeditionary force known as the Abraham Lincoln Brigade in 1930s Spain."

Preparing for Combat in Kashmir

The government's case rested on the illegality of training in small arms for use in supporting the Kashmiri resistance group, Lashkar-i-Taiba. This would hold water only if this group were recognized by the United States as a terrorist organization. It was not at the time that Royer went to Kashmir in 2000. Even after 9/11, the decision to declare it a terrorist organization was disputed within the U.S. intelligence and policy communities. The group, which specialized in social services and religious education, was so close to Pakistan's intelligence agency that many American officials feared such a move could undermine the friendly government of Pakistan.

The saga began on April 10, 2000, when Royer traveled to Pakistan alone. The government charged that Royer fired at Indian positions, but Royer said that he spent only three weeks there, most of the time sick in bed with food poisoning, and that his support of the Lashkar was limited to writing press releases as a journalist.

His travel accounts, however, which were detailed in the government's case as the suspicious gatherings at Dar al-Arqam, enthused Royer's friend Ibrahim Ahmed al-Hamdi, son of the Yemeni deputy chief of mission in Washington, to embark on a similar adventure by visiting Kashmir for a month in August 2000. When he returned, the entire group allegedly decided to start training with small arms in preparation for a similar trip to help in the resistance movement. Their periodic paintball sessions in Spotsylvania County formed the basis of their indictment for allegedly training to "kill, kidnap, maim, or injure persons or damage property in a foreign country."

The government then proceeded to point to gun possession in the indictment, charging many of the defendants with various weapons-related charges. The right to bear arms in America, which is protected by the Second Amendment to the U.S. Bill of Rights, and practiced by millions of American citizens, had to be painted in malicious and threatening terms by the government with regard to these men. In essence, the prosecution was in a predicament in which it had to prove that Royer and the others were terrorists in order to paint their alleged military training exercises in the worst possible light as grounds for a conviction. Instead the government relied on these activities as proof of the former. The government was caught in an obvious circular argument.

In response to the charges, Royer asserted that he was a victim of the government's policy after 9/11 of conducting "fishing expeditions" and incarceration without prior evidence of wrongdoing. Royer affirmed from his prison cell, "The policy is to look for any tiny thing they can bust people on, to arrest them, to have them under control."

Indeed, following the high profile arrests, the U.S. attorneys pursued a strategy of intimidation and coercion of the eleven defendants. Because of the lack of evidence of a crime, the government's strategy to demonstrate the existence of a conspiracy hinged on the necessity to have at least one person from within the group to corroborate their version of events. As such, pressure was placed on various members of the group to enter into plea agreements with the government, in which they would agree to plead guilty to some charges and cooperate with the government in exchange for reduced sentences. In many cases, government lawyers would threaten each of the young men individually, telling them that they would spend the rest of their lives in prison, away from their families, friends, and community. Sentences surpassing one hundred years were declared to be the minimum some of the defendants, such as Ismail Royer, would receive. In spite of their strong belief in their innocence, the men were led to believe that no jury would ever find them innocent, especially in light of the current atmosphere of anti-Muslim hysteria. Moreover, the frightened Northern Virginia Muslim community appeared to have forsaken its wrongfully jailed young men, as few leaders and members expressed outrage at their mistreatment or worked to help resolve their case. Legal fees piled up, and in time, none of the defendants could afford private attorneys, as the popular attorney Stanley Cohen left Royer following the early stages of the case, and local Muslim attorney Ashraf Nubani was forced by the government to leave because of a perceived conflict of interest. As a result, the men were left with public defenders and court-appointed attorneys who were much less competent and unable to promise, let alone generate positive results. The eleven men were left in many ways feeling helpless, confused, and abandoned. And without proper counsel, they became more open to compromising their position of absolute innocence.

The government tactics were successful to a larger degree in forcing six of the defendants to accept plea agreements to an assortment of lesser charges. In exchange for their cooperation they were promised lighter sentences while pressure mounted on the remaining defendants who would go to trial. The government believed the testimony of some of the defendants against the others would ensure conviction, and as such, these other men relented. By the start of the trial in February 2004, six of the eleven men had entered plea agreements, with the remaining five set to go on trial. A trial for the remaining defendants was expected to challenge the government's implausible theories and call for the full acquittal of the remaining Muslim men. At the start of the trial, four of the defendants were set to be tried together, including Masoud Khan, who faced the most serious charges, Caliph Basha Abdur-Raheem, Hammad Abdur-Raheem, and Seifullah Chapman. The fifth defendant, Sabri ben Kahla, was scheduled to be tried separately.

At the outset of the trial, the four men and their attorneys made the deliberate decision to forego their right to a trial by jury, and rest all of their hopes on the unbiased and impartial federal judge before them. Judge Leonie Brinkema, a Clinton appointee, had begun to make a name for herself following September 11 for being wise and judicious in her treatment of terrorism suspects, in the face of an overly bullying and aggressive Justice Department wishing to secure convictions at the expense of fair, open, and just hearings. She had already resisted the government's attempts to jail all of the defendants, releasing many of them without bail. She also expressed doubt at some of the government's allegations and the excessive behavior of government attorneys. Moreover, none of the men or their lawyers believed that a fair and impartial jury could be found in a post-9/11 America, let alone the xenophobic and conservative environment in suburban Washington, D.C. As such, they trusted that Judge Brinkema would see past the smoke screen and into their hearts as misunderstood Muslim youth wrongfully accused in the anti-Muslim hysteria currently plaguing their country.

The trial lasted four weeks. The government laid out its case in what many observers saw as unconvincing fashion, attempting to connect the dots between young American Muslim men devoting themselves to their faith, their recreational activities, and events taking place across the world. The lines were never clear, though the government did not hesitate to inflame the situation by invoking the Taliban, Al Qaeda, Osama bin Laden, and every other post-September 11 terrorism buzzword it could generate, in order to link the men to the worst crimes it could conjure up. In addition, some of the six young men who had earlier entered into plea agreements with the government, had now found themselves in a compromising trap. In exchange for substantially reduced sentences, they agreed to testify against their friends. Some of the witnesses did not hurt the defense, but in one agonizing scene, the prosecution impeached their own witness, as he wrestled with what FBI interrogators had rehearsed with him in more than a dozen sessions in his solitary confinement cell. He was clearly tormented and confused and to the dismay of the federal prosecutor, Gordon Kromberg, he recanted his testimony at the last minute.

The defense put forth two of the defendants to testify in their own defense, at which time they emphatically denied the conspiracy charges against them, professed their love for their country and the innocence of their recreational activities and paintball games. Before the trial was even concluded, Judge Brinkema decided that Caliph Basha Abdur-Raheem had committed no crime, and was cleared of all the charges against him. This was the first major victory of the trial, and many hoped for more such decisions. One week later, however, on March 4, Brinkema shook the Muslim community to its core with her decision to find the remaining three men guilty of the most serious charges against them. In her ruling, she stated that she did not believe the men's testimony in their own defense, and did not appear to find any fault in the arm-twisting of the obviously distraught government witnesses. "Defense attorneys were visibly shaken and shocked by the judge's decision, as the acquittal the preceding week had given the families and their supporters false hope that she would do the same for their loved ones. After scrutiny of the 75-page indictment they said they would appeal the verdict. In contrast to the smug prosecutors, gloating over the victory, family members and friends wept and embraced each other outside the courtroom, while one of the young wives of the convicted men, overcome with grief, was unable to rise from her seat without assistance."[3]

Soon the large crowd of supporters who had come to hear the verdict gathered outside, along with the defense attorneys and some Muslim community leaders who assessed the outcome and voiced their misgivings in a press conference. The attorneys all lamented the verdicts, maintaining their clients' innocence, some saying that they had become very attached to their clients and that it was a very sad day. When asked about possible sentences, Bernard Grimm, the attorney for Masoud Khan, 32, of Gaithersburg, said it could be "in excess of 100 years and he's never gotten a parking ticket." He was convicted of conspiracy to support the Taliban and wage war against the United States. Seifullah Chapman, 31, of Alexandria, was found guilty of conspiring to support Lashkar-i-Taiba and using firearms in connection with a crime of violence and could face up to 60 years, according to his attorney, John Zwerling. Hammad Abdur-Raheem, 35, of Falls Church was found guilty on weapons charges and indirectly supporting Lashkar-i-Taiba. Although he never trained in Pakistan, he, along with Seifullah and Donald Idris Suratt, used the military expertise derived from his service in the Gulf War to train the group members. William Cummings, his attorney did not give an estimate of how many years his sentence could entail. But the weapons charge alone could result in 30 years. Hammad had earlier rejected a plea agreement that would have cut his sentence down to only two years. According to later reports, at the time of sentencing, Khan, 34, faces a mandatory minimum of 90 years; Chapman, 31, faces a mandatory minimum of 35 years; and Abdur-Raheem, 35, could face 15 years or more.

The following Tuesday, the courtroom was again packed with family and friends of Sabri ben Kahla as they awaited his fate with heightened nervousness. To their joy, all charges, including supplying services to the Taliban and firing weapons in Afghanistan, which could have resulted in a minimum sentence of 30 years, were dropped and he was fully acquitted. Tears flowed, but this time they were tears of joy and thankfulness. A radiant and relieved ben Kahla and his exhausted family left the courthouse that day with a bittersweet victory, as they empathized with his three convicted friends, who, only a few days earlier, were immediately taken from the courtroom and thrown into solitary confinement, following Judge Brinkema's orders that they be detained pending their sentencing hearing scheduled for June 2004. They remained in solitary confinement for four days, until their attorneys intervened to have them moved to a less oppressive facility. The remaining six defendants who entered into plea agreements also await a June 2004 sentencing, where they are expected to receive as little as two years in some cases, to as many as eleven and a half in the case of Ismail Royer.

The Fallout

The Virginia case has had a tremendous impact as a watershed case in post-9/11 America. While many high-profile cases have emerged in the months and years since the attacks, this was the first of those cases to go to trial and yield verdicts which many believe have set the tone for justice in the new America. It goes without saying that this case, like many others, featured an unusually high level of politicization, led by "a zealous prosecutor with an overt, transparent agenda."[4] Assistant U.S. Attorney Gordon Kromberg has made no secret of his extremist views that fall to the right of Israel's rightwing Likud Party. Kromberg has in fact traveled to the Middle East, and has been vocal in support of Israel's occupation of Palestinian lands. Back in the United States, Kromberg's associations have included notorious Islamophobe Steven Emerson, whose shoddy investigative work has been at the root of many of the cases currently pending against America's preeminent Islamic activists.

The eye-opening experience of witnessing the denial of justice to this community's young men sent a chilling message to all Americans, and specifically the Muslim community, that these vociferous investigations and widespread arrests were beginning to yield very costly results whose effects would be felt for decades to come, as many of these men were sentenced to prison for most, if not all, of their adult lives. The outpouring emerged immediately following the verdicts, as a press conference outside the courthouse included many of the local community's leaders. Seyed Rizwan Mowlana, the Executive Director of Maryland's chapter of the Council on American-Islamic Relations (CAIR), expressed the despondency of most of the community with his words, "All Americans must remember that we live in the land where justice is designed to be blind in regard to race, religion, or socioeconomic status. Although we find out that the legal system is based on the theory of the presumption of innocence, the perception of the Muslim community is that Muslims and Arabs are automatically considered guilty until proven innocent."[5] Wael Elkoshairi of the Muslim Affairs Council was disappointed, but expressed his resolve, "I want to tell you that the activists, some of them standing behind me and some of them all over the country, will not stop fighting. We, as the Muslim community ask for our rights, we ask to be treated as human beings. And we will continue to work, so hopefully tomorrow will be a better day than today." El-Hajj Mauri' Saalakhan, Director of Operations for The Peace and Justice Foundation, warned, "Rogue elements within the U.S. government have been working overtime to create terror in the collective mind of the American people. The purpose is simple, to facilitate the acceptance of draconian laws which will fundamentally change the character and course of America for the worse. The Paintball Case is just another significant but very unfortunate step in that direction."

Much was made of the plea agreements signed by six of the defendants, which greatly hurt the outcome of the remaining men on trial. Reporters wanted to gauge the reaction of the men and the community to the supposed betrayal by their brethren, but did not receive the divisive words they were looking for. Rather, leaders and attorneys put the blame squarely on the government for putting the youth in such a thorny position from which they could not emerge unscathed. Threats were repeatedly made, it was revealed, to many of the men, of harm to their families, or to themselves, such as being transported to the U.S. military installation in Guantanomo Bay, Cuba, where they would be labeled enemy combatants and denied a trial. Moreover, they were frequently misled, and told that all of the remaining men had already signed agreements, and that they stood no chance going to trial alone. According to Bernard Grimm, attorney for Masoud Khan, many of the men were forced to plead guilty to crimes they did not commit. "These people thought that number one—I'm Muslim—so they already have two strikes against me, and number two—my guess is that they already have some evidence against me, so I'll probably be convicted if I go to trial. So therefore, I'll plead guilty to whatever you put on the table so long as—at the end of the day—when I come for sentencing, you're going to go to bat for me and say I can go home. And unfortunately, that's the way the system works," explained Grimm.[6] These dirty tactics only became apparent in the aftermath of the trial. Attorneys promised, however, that many of these issues would come up during the appeals process, which they vowed to pursue aggressively in the hopes of getting their clients a second chance at a fair and open hearing, preferably in a more tolerant environment. King Lyon, father of Hammad Abdur-Raheem, stated on the day of the verdict, "Let's hope and pray that the last page has not been turned on this so-called trial today, It is a travesty that if these had been young men of a different religion, this trial never would have taken place. So this should be a wakeup call for all religions across the United States that this could happen to your brothers and sisters. We must continue to fight and have faith."

Reflecting on the events, Elizabeth Khan, Masoud's mother, described it as "the worst thing for a mother to have to endure," but remained proud of her son, through all he has suffered. "Masoud does not want to spend the rest of his life in prison, but there is no way he will speak against another who might be innocent, nor will he bear false witness. Masoud said he has to say the truth and accept the consequences."[7] Karen Johnson, Masoud's neighbor, even weighed in with a powerful letter to the media in which she asserted her neighbor's good decency and innocence. "Masoud's trial is an example of the Patriot Act run amok. These convictions are but a smokescreen to cover the fact that no real terrorists have been captured. ... Masoud's conviction proves that McCarthyism is alive and flourishing in our great country and every citizen should be alarmed. ... Remember, Masoud is an American Muslim. Who will be next to have their belongings seized, and false charges levied against them? As an American Jew, I know the answer—Nazism is a lesson Jews are taught never to forget."[8]

Indeed, the reflections that followed were rife with disappointment and regret. One commentator from within the community wrote, "Muslims living in America must come to know and fully appreciate the disturbing reality that the community now exists under a dark cloud of suspicion. No Muslim, regardless of his or her sect or degree of practice, is going to ever be given the benefit of the doubt as far as the American government is concerned. No doubt this is a bitter truth that some Muslims, especially those who immigrated to this land seeking its highly touted "freedom" and "democracy" will find hard to accept, but failure to do so will be met with even more catastrophe."[9] Such were the prevailing sentiments following the ominous results from this verdict, which served a severe blow to the collective American Muslim body's sense of belonging and entitlement. "Obviously, the government does not—and cannot—prosecute every supporter of a cause of which it does not approve. But Muslims today are easy targets. The evidence suggests that these prosecutions and convictions were motivated by discrimination. Terrorism or no terrorism, justice was not done."

Conclusion

The case of the so-called Virginia Jihad Network raises questions about the future of both America and the world. The civil rights question is how much control of the American people the FBI needs in order to prevent terrorism, and how the victims of civil rights abuses can protect themselves from excesses. The tragedy of 9/11 has given rise to bold developments in both international and domestic law. Henry Kissinger stated in his *Washington Post* op/ed piece on August 12, 2002, that the attack on Iraq is needed in order to develop a new international law permitting unilateral preemption against potential terrorism. The same rationale is now being used to override the old laws of civil rights. The requirements of security not only are overriding the established sovereignty of states, but now are threatening the sovereignty of individual persons on which the American system of balanced order, justice, and freedom are based. ■

PROFILE: LIGHT AT THE END OF
THE TUNNEL

IT WAS A DREAM........NOW IT IS A REALITY.......

LET US MAKE IT A SUCCESS......

• Through the storm, the new generation is full of hope and optimism for a bright future.

Conclusion

THE FUTURE OF ISLAM
IN AMERICA

As citizens of this country, we have to defend America in three
ways: militarily, intellectually, and spiritually. We do this by loyal
opposition to unwise policies of unilateral military preemption,
by support of wise foreign policies based on America's founding
principles, and by shared commitment to the spiritual core of the
Abrahamic faiths.

—Professor Agha Saeed, Chairman,
American Muslim Alliance, at Dar al Hijra Islamic Center,
February 21, 2004.

Islamic activism was growing before 9/11 and the
positive impact on the community at large was
impressive. Muslim activists were convinced for the first
time that it was within their reach to enter into the
American political process and stand on an equal footing
with other American legislators in shaping the political
future of the United States.

Developing political access became more important in

Muslim civic organizations as they became more qualified to contribute positively to free and fair elections. Muslim activists and lobbyists were confidently riding the political tide as they were building bridges of understanding and mutual respect with the array of conservative and liberal American political forces. The Muslim political ambition was so high that many involved Muslims were convinced that it was only a matter of time before Muslim Americans would solidify their presence by having an American Muslim elected to Congress. The rapport that had jelled throughout the years between American Muslims and their political interlocutors had persuaded the American Muslim public that they were now solidly within the American political mainstream.

The pro-Israeli lobby and its supporters, always concerned about the growing influence of American Muslims, seemed to have miscalculated. American Muslims were not so naive as to assume that this influential lobby had vanished nor had come to terms with the fact that the Muslims were an up-and-coming political bloc to be reckoned with. Rather, the American Muslims who were active on the American political terrain sensed the magnitude of this Zionist lobby. With all of the obstacles that were placed in the path of this pioneering Islamic thrust into the American political process, American Muslims had for the first time carved a niche for themselves and begun to field candidates and nominees for local, state, and even federal government positions.

Although such progress would have been unthinkable in the past, American Muslim political momentum encountered ups and downs. Like every other interest group they have sympathizers and detractors. There have been media efforts to distort the image of Islamic feedback in the American decision making process. From time to time, innuendo and falsification have been used to try to take the wind out of the Muslim American sail. And there were times when prejudice and the residuals of history kicked in and Muslims felt the effects of discrimination as they tried their best to move ahead and convince all of what they had to say. Truth be told, the active American Muslims have kept their "cool" and "steeled" their nerves and pressed on with their civic duties strengthened with an unblemished character and sometimes with considerable personal sacrifices and selflessness. They demonstrated how responsible and how mature they were even when they had to endure accusations and defamation from expected and unexpected sources.

Throughout those long years, these civic oriented American Muslims developed a flexible political agenda that was able to sit well with potential foes and reticent well-wishers. They were gaining the necessary experience from their political on-the-job-training, they were learning from trial and error, and they were also familiarizing themselves with the details of partisan politics, lobbying, and winning over the "other side." Out of these sequential experiences the Muslims were trying to put together a civic bloc that would be both effective and balanced. And to a great degree they were on their way to doing exactly that. The time had actually come when the Muslims had no doubt that they were finally part of the American political fabric. The key conferences held by major American Muslim organizations reflected this achievement quite accurately. Annual and semi-annual meetings and national and regional symposia were sponsored by such flagship organizations as the Islamic Society of North America (ISNA), the American Muslim

Council (AMC), the Muslim American Society (MAS), the Islamic Circle of North America (ICNA), the Muslim Political Action Committees (MPAC), and others. All of them in the years leading up to 9/11 focused on the mainstreaming of America's Muslims into the political process. The groundwork was done, new terrain was explored, and American Muslims were on their way to civic and political integration into the American political process.

September 11, 2001

As American Muslims were on their way to what seemed to be successful integration into the American political process, pleased with their unprecedented strides into Washington's corridors of power, along came the tragic events of September 11th. September 11th and the political scenario into which it was cast could not have been worse. Suddenly all Muslims were suspect. The American national attitude was defensive. Officials and politicians who before September 11th were open minded and accommodating had now become suspicious. The politically active Muslims who were publicly in the American political arena were made to feel that they were accomplices to September 11th. The American national mindset was now convinced, post 9/11, that American Muslims were kin to the perpetrators of the horrible events of 9/11. Fear began to seep deep down inside the American Muslim community. Hate crimes against American Muslims took a swing upwards. Mosques were targeted, Muslims were receiving obscene telephone calls, public places were no longer safe places for some Muslims in different parts of the country, and years of integration into the American political process were suddenly reversed because of 9/11. The acts of a few fringe Muslims on that horrible day were enough to tar the entire American Muslim community and bring its vital civic participation to a standstill, or, more accurately, to a social setback out of which it has not yet recovered. If this trend continues, there may never be a comeback to the "good old days" prior to 9/11. Due to a hyped up media campaign woven around the events of 9/11, American Muslims all over the world were asking: Where is Islam? How could 21st century America berate American Muslims with mass guilt because of a crime committed by a peripheral and extremist splinter group of Muslims?

American Muslims were now worried about their future in the United States as well as for the safety of their childrens' lives. The question was no longer hypothetical about whether American Muslims are an integral part of American society. It had become a practical question of whether American society is willing to treat Muslims with fairness, equality, and the absence of prejudice and malice. The signs coming from American legislators were not encouraging. With September 11th and the intense scrutiny of American Muslims, the U.S. government enacted laws and rammed them through the legislative process with frantic expediency. Even legislators were suspect as one either was on the side of "right" "against terrorism" or was a terrorist. There was neither room nor time for dissent. The largest department of the U.S. government was created: the Homeland Security Department. The independent INS was dissolved, and would-be foreign visitors, students, resident aliens, and immigrants were given a criminal taint. American intelligence and security agencies reacted hysterically, although it was their own negligence and incompetence in the first place that had allowed such a tragedy to occur. They did too little too late, and then attempted to overcompensate.

Civil liberties were curtailed. The Patriot Act kicked in, and there was talk of Patriot Act II, with profiling, secret evidence, and the worst nightmares of spies and spooks coming out from under their deep cover to roll back the privileges and gains that have been the hallmark of an open, free, and democratic society. All of this sent shockwaves through the American Muslim community because it was made to understand through acts of intimidation and harassment that Muslims were the ultimate target of this combined dragnet and witch-hunt. American laws have been twisted, civil freedoms have been curtailed, and due-process has been violated as a means to stifle future Muslims from ever thinking about equality or competition in what was before 9/11 an accessible American political process. All of this was happening to a conscientious American Muslim community whose spokespersons, dignitaries, and public figures condemned and berated the September 11th attacks against the United States of America.

This "national social catastrophe" for the American Muslim community occurred on the watch of George W. Bush and his administration. The psychological and social wounds inflicted by the Republican Bush administration are deep and extensive. No seasonal politicking going into the presidential rounds of 2004 will be able to heal these profound wounds. Out of a sense of desperation and coupled with an urge for "anything else" the American Muslim community may find itself rooting for the Democratic Party to try to reverse the damages and rearrange the political and social climate in the United States in order to make it possible once again for American Muslims to take their natural position under the American sun. The Democrats are on record as opposing the violation of civil rights and liberties, including those of American Muslims.

It has become evident that the American Muslim community running up to the elections of 2004 are worried that President George W. Bush and his neo-con advisers may be re-elected for another term. This would mean that American Muslims will be exposed to more of the same policies that have reduced them to second-class citizens. Predictions are that, if President Bush is re-elected for another four-year term, American Muslims will leave the United States to avoid his McCarthyite tactics. For American Muslims the neo-cons under George W. Bush are taking the whole American government on a collision course not only with American Muslims, but also with Muslims around the world—all of this as a result of the September 11th inspired war against terrorism.

The obvious question is for whom is this done, and for whose benefit? The immediate answer that comes to the minds of many throughout the world is Israel. American Muslims may pack their belongings, sell their possessions, and go back to their ancestral countries or across the border to Canada. Already, reports have circulated about a considerable number of Indo-Pakistanis who left the United States for a normal life in Canada after 9/11.

There is a sense of anticipation, however, that the wave of anti-Islam sweeping through the United States after 9/11 will recede and in due time American Muslims will regain their civic vitality and rejoin the mosaic of other minorities and ethnic groups, that American Muslims will join their predecessors, the Japanese Americans, American Jews, and

Irish Americans, who also, in times past, endured national intolerance, social prejudice, and legal injustice.

> Some American Muslim leaders are actively encouraging greater effort to make this happen sooner. For example, in dealing with the post 9/11 era, it is critical for the American Muslim community to develop a cohesive leadership on the national level with Islamic vision, establish a functional "think tank" necessary to get a seat at policy making forums, and pro-actively participate in the political process. If it fails to do so, chances are that it will continue to be seen as an alien element and not a part of American multi-cultural and multi-religious society with full rights.
> —Marghoob A. Quraishi,
> Managing Editor of *Geopolitics Review*

This line of thought can see the day when American Muslims will receive an apology owed to them from the U.S. government the same way their predecessors did in the course of American history. There is no question about this: Arab and Muslim Americans are the prime targets of the post 9/11 reconfiguration of American laws, policies, and priorities. And they are feeling the brunt of it.

We cannot say with certainty that the United States of America will regain its balance, return to its original position in which minorities cooperate and coordinate with each other to make America the multi-cultural continent that it was meant to be. We cannot affirm that this anti-Arab and anti-Muslim surge will recede and people, citizens, and tax-payers across the American racial and religious continuum will join hands together without burdening a whole community because of the crime of a very few of its members. We cannot even state with confidence that the future will be free of events as terrible and as offensive as 9/11 is to all of us. Whatever the case may be, and only the future will tell, there still is a very strong probability that the goodness of the American people will carry the day and eventually arrest this decline into national jingoism, international interventionism, and a general deep-seated phobia that justifies its attacks on Muslims everywhere with a religious veneer and a historical atavism.

Probable Scenarios

The first likely scenario concerning American Muslims is the continuation of the current status-quo: more civil rights violations against Arab and Muslim Americans, more new laws to deter any political participation of American Muslims to make a difference in the American decision making process, more social Islamophobia driving American Muslims deeper into isolation and more American military forays into the Muslim world under the pretext that Muslims are acquiring advanced weapons, developing nuclear energy for military purposes, and providing political and popular support for the Palestinians in their struggle against Israel. If this neo-con trend develops toward its natural end it will no doubt have turned the Muslims of the world against this irrational strategy that excludes Muslims from their full civic potential and in some cases reduces them to civilian sub-humans. These neo-conservative marching orders have the potential to drive a wedge within the American Muslim community that will cause immigrant first generation American Muslims to relocate to the Muslim world from where they will not hesitate to oppose American policies by any means necessary, especially when the U.S. government stands lock, stock, and barrel behind Israeli aggression, occupation, and expansion. These neo-con tactics and strategy will also cause indigenous American Muslims to recoil into themselves, keep a low profile, and wait for the time when it becomes possible for them to reassert their social and civic character in the political landscape of a multi-cultural, multi-religious, and a truly pluralistic America. These Muslims may learn through their own experiences that the only party capable of co-opting the aspirations of American Muslims is the Democratic Party. This may happen sooner than anyone would expect. We may see a mass political conversion of American Muslims voting Democratic come November 2004. And if this comes to pass and the American public elects a Democrat as the next president, the American Muslims hope that all the draconian measures that have been taken during the Bush years eventually will be reversed so people can go back to their good human nature and cooperate for the common good of all without pointing to American Muslims as some type of "alien Americans" or "less-than-full" Americans.

Another likely scenario is that the current jingoism will take its course and toll. Official America, in this case, will continue to consider Muslim Americans undesirable and unwanted. These policies may go up a notch and tarnish all American Muslims with the brush of terrorism by harping on the chord that terrorism is a worldwide stain and stigma that has its roots in Islam. We can see this anti-Islamic propaganda developing into best-selling books, blockbuster movies, and riveting television series that demonize Islam and dehumanize Muslims. The common thread that runs through the media will be the "terroristic" origins of Islam and the "Islamic" roots of terrorism. The political imagination spurred on by military and economic setbacks around the globe may finally evoke the images of Armageddon and the Biblical eschatology of the final days with the Muslims occupying the position of the anti-Christ. This is no longer the work of fiction writers. We have been exposed to the inner thoughts of American religious clergymen and military generals who have intimated as much. From Franklin Graham, the son of Rev. Billy Graham, to the highly decorated General Boykin, the religious undertones of a "clash of civilizations" have become ever bolder during the Republican neo-con administration of George W. Bush and his "you are either with us or against us" team of hegemonists.

The imposition of hundreds of thousands of U.S. military personnel around the globe, especially in the Muslim hemisphere of the world, will undoubtedly and regrettably lead to an increasing number of Americans killed in the line of this neo-con duty. Central to all this, as we follow the events nowadays, is the rising death toll of American soldiers in Iraq. Every time an American is killed in Iraq or elsewhere in the Muslim world, there is that much more anti-Arab and anti-Muslim sentiment among the American people; and conversely, every time there are Muslim casualties in their own homelands by occupying American forces there is that much more resentment and hostility toward America by Muslims in that part of the world. This does not bode well for American-Muslim relations. If this trend continues, God forbid, the neo-cons surrounding Bush will drag the United States and the Muslim World to a point of no return. The casualties could become staggering, the losses unquantifiable, and the damage done in human relations could bring the world to the brink of civilizational polarization that will last for centuries to come. This neo-con campaign will breed new forms of terrorism by desperate generations, underprivileged populations, and broken societies. And the American Muslims may become just one segment in this state of affairs. One important and overlooked casualty of 9/11 could turn out to be American Muslims who have been reduced to a status of an American underclass as they see their parents and previous generation(s) humiliated by American diktat and an unrelenting officialdom that degrades and downgrades American Muslims systematically.

Another scenario would have the United States of America bogged down in extended low-intensity warfare in the Muslim world and in the southern hemisphere of the planet indefinitely. With the American armed forces extended around the globe and logistical resources stretched to the maximum along with the reluctance of the international community to foot the American bill, subsequent U.S. administrations will come to realize that they have reached the point of diminishing returns. The United States, it will be recalled, set out during the Bush neo-con administration to check the Chinese economic competitor on the world consumer stage, and to knock out the Euro as a viable currency that was threatening the dollar in the world financial markets. In doing so, the neo-cons used 9/11 as the trigger to its global unilateral position. The neo-cons assumed it would be a cakewalk. The Muslim world would be the first step into a global *Pax-Americana*. But history does not unfold the way the neo-cons around Bush thought it did. America's imperial armed forces will have entered into "Muslim quagmire" for which they have no exit strategy. The American government will be caught between its imperial ego as the only superpower on earth and its enemies' unexpected fierce and tenacious resistance. American service men's body bags will be coming home.

Exploitation of the sea of petroleum between the Caspian Sea and the Persian Gulf has not materialized as quickly and as expeditiously as the original plans called for. Anti-Americanism around the world is reaching all time highs. American intelligence and diplomatic fingers are being burned in Russia, in Southeast Asia, and in Latin America. The United States in the image of the neo-cons has even gone so far as trying to dismember Europe by alluding to Western Europe as the "Old Europe" and the Eastern part as the "New Europe." All of this militarily inspired American bluster and bravado will not result in the expansion of an American 21st century empire but in the humbling of a state destined to relive the mistakes of historically condemned powers such as the Roman Empire and the French and British colonialists of only a few decades ago. Along these lines, and after unmistakable and irretrievable setbacks, the U.S. government may react to its own internationalist follies by spiraling into a self-inflicted isolation. At that time, the American people will have to pick up the pieces and take a closer look at what they were thrust into by the now infamous administration.

In hindsight, the American people will come to realize that a confluence of interests among the neo-con utopians, the American corporate class, the Evangelical Right, and the Zionist Lobby has set America on a disastrous misadventure into the world. A closer scrutiny of the neo-cons will reveal that they were more interested in the security of Israel than with the security of the United States. What was conceived of as the plan for a new American century turned out to be a plot to preserve and protect Israel through the trials and tribulations of that century.

The United States of America and its forward looking people will have paid a dear price to have discovered that within their ranks is an enemy that places Israel above America. American administrations have gone to great lengths to appease this Israeli idol. It began with excluding American Muslims from the channels of political access right after 9/11 and will end with trying to defeat Islamic self-determination half way across the globe. The lessons of antiquity will haunt these die-hard Israeli agents. America, at the expense of its own sons and daughters will have learned the lesson of history: militaries can fight and win over other militaries, especially when they are technologically superior; but militaries cannot fight and win over other fighting rank-and-file people especially when they are ideologically committed.

Muslim Americans are peaceful and peace-loving Americans like the rest of their compatriots. It has been a terrible mistake to let the special interests of the neo-cons call the shots for an administration that will go down in history as one that gambled on the Israeli side of the equation with disregard for its founders' principles and in violation of its own constitution and interests. Neo-con

America has become beholden to the Zionist Israeli interest. This is the truth of the matter that none dare articulate. And the deafening silence about this Israeli stranglehold on America is not in the interest of the United States, it is not in the interest of Muslims around the world, and it certainly is not in the interest of world peace.

Instead of empowering American Muslims to become ambassadors of good-will with their potential to build bridges around the world, the U.S. government against its own interests and in subservience to Israeli interests is mishandling and abusing this important segment of its own population. With Israeli "inspiration," instead of building bridges with the Muslim world via its American Muslim citizenry, the United States is burning those same bridges with the help of its American pro-Israeli citizens. The political potential and capital that is wasted by the Bush administration at a time when it needs its Muslim constituents the most is a supreme act of political folly.

When the American Muslims prior to 9/11 were moving up politically they were doing so for American interests that would have been served best by gaining the understanding of a critical geo-strategic part of the world, i.e., the Muslim bloc. Instead of this, after 9/11 the United States has chosen instead a path full of risks and uncertainties. We can only hope that cooler heads will prevail and an expeditious end is put to this imposing imperialism. If left unchecked, fueled by the irrationality and madness that came with 9/11, this new imperialism will wreak havoc on the rest of humanity who are not within the corporate, evangelical, and Zionist triangle of consent that defines almost all American foreign policy.

A more pragmatic and balanced American administration

must sit back and take a cold and calculated look at the real world and realize that a Muslim bloc even with all its inconsistencies is a region of the world that cannot be colonized or patronized forever. And if the Arab-Israeli conflict seems so intractable it is only wise to approach both the Muslim and Jewish sides with their respective lobbies inside the United States in an air of fairness and evenhandedness. The further the U.S. administrations go in taking the Israeli side without any due consideration for the Arab and Muslim side the more the United States is contributing to further radicalization of this stubborn divide in the future. It may turn out that American Muslims will eventually be prized for their critical and timely position from within a pluralistic America, but only if a fair-minded, evenhanded, and inclusive American leadership has the courage to accept these American Muslims and their trust in the United States of America. ∎

NOTES

Chapter 1

[1] Yvonne Haddad, *Muslims in the West: From Sojourners to Citizens*, Oxford University Press, 2002.
[2] *Ibid.*
[3] George Braswell, Jr. *Islam: Its Prophet, Peoples, Politics and Power*, Broadman & Holman Publishers, 1996.
[4] *Ibid.*, Yvonne Haddad.
[5] Jane I. Smith, *Islam in America*, Columbia University Press, 1999.
[6] Aminah Beverly McCloud, *African-American Islam*, Routledge, 1995.
[7] Arthur J. Magida, *Prophet of Rage*, BasicBooks, 1996.
[8] *Ibid*, McCloud.

Chapter 2

[1] Ilyas Ba-Yunus, "An American Story: Graduating from MSA to ISNA," *Islamic Horizons*, September/October 2003.
[2] *Ibid.*
[3] Omer Bin Abdullah, "MSA Story: Building a Community," *Islamic Horizons*, July/August 2003.
[4] *Ibid.*
[5] "In Spite of Challenges, Our Mission Continues," Interview with Dr. Jamal al Barzinji, *Middle East Affairs Journal*, vol. 9, no. 3-4, Summer/Fall 2003.
[6] Omer Bin Abdullah, *ibid.*
[7] *Ibid.*
[8] *Ibid.*
[9] *Ibid.*
[10] *Ibid.*
[11] Ilyas Ba-Yunus, *ibid.*
[12] *Ibid.*

13 *Ibid.*
14 Sabrina Enayatulla, "MSA Story: The New MSA," *Islamic Horizons*, November/December 2003.
15 Marium Mohiudidn, "Fountain of Youth Renews," *Islamic Horizons*, May/June 2003.
16 Sabrina Enayatulla, *ibid.*
17 MSA National, *Eighteenth Annual Report*, May 1981.
18 Fatima Mirza, "An Evolving Student Voice," *Islamic Horizons*, May/June 2003.
19 "Interview with Altaf Hussein," *Al-Mujtama'*, issue no. 1522. October 12, 2002.
20 *Ibid.*
21 *Ibid.*
22 Richard Lacayo, "A Campus War over Israel," *Time*, October 7, 2002.
23 Yigal Schleifer, "Ready for the Challenge," *The Jerusalem Report*, September 9, 2002.
24 *Ibid.*
25 *Ibid.*
26 "Interview with Altaf Hussein," *ibid.*

Chapter 3

1 *American Muslims in Politics: From Dream to Mainstream*, AMC's 10th Annual National Convention Program Bulletin, Washington: AMC, 2001. See also AMC brochures and *The AMC Report*, its quarterly newsletter.
2 Abdullah al-Arian. "Soul Survival: The Road to American Muslim Political Empowerment," *Washington Report on Middle East Affairs*, March 2004.
3 Paul Findley, "Political Activism by U.S. Muslims," *The American Muslim*, April 2000.
4 Abdullah al-Arian, *ibid.*
5 Issa Smith, "Guilty as Imagined," *Islamic Horizons*, 29,3, May/June, 2000, pp. 22-23.
6 *IANA Link*, 8, 2, March, 2001.
7 Levent Akbarut, "The Role of Mosques in America," *The Minaret*, 5, 7, November/December, 1986, pp. 12-17.

8 A Report from the Mosque Study Project, *The Mosque in America: A National Portrait* (Washington: Council on American-Islamic Relations, 2001), p. 3. Also referred to as CAIR 2001.

9 Shaker Elsayed, "Islamic Schools: Why and How," *The American Muslim*, 1, 1, January, 2000, pp. 42-43.

10 *Media Relations Handbook for Muslim Activists* (Washington: CAIR, 1996). See also CAIR Newsletters.

11 Abdullah al-Arian, *ibid.*

12 *Ibid.*

13 Aslam Abdullah, "Where are the Muslims on the Political Scene?" *The Minaret*, vol. 23, 5, May 5, 2001.

14 Abdullah al-Arian, *ibid.*

15 *Ibid.*

16 Aslam Abdullah, *ibid.*

17 This chapter was inspired by a paper written by Professor Ghulam Hanif and published in the *Middle East Affairs Journal*, vol. 9, no. 1-2, Winter/Spring 2003.

18 Anisa Abd al-Fattah, "Islam in America: A Giant Awakened by Zionism," *Middle East Affairs Journal*, Summer/Fall 2002.

19 A Report from the Mosque Study Project, CAIR 2001.

Chapter 4

1 Joseph Bodansky, "The New Islamist International," *Task Force on Terrorism & Unconventional Warfare, House Republican Research Committee*. February 1, 1993.

2 Ahmad AbulJobain, "Radical Islamic Terrorism or Political Islam?" *United Association for Studies and Research*, Occasional Papers Series No. 1, June 1993.

3 "Officials Distrust Allegations by Israeli-American," *Sydsvenskan* (Sweden), February 2, 2002.

4 "Radical Islamic Terrorism: How Serious is the Threat? What Should Be Done to Counter It?" An American Jewish Committee Luncheon Forum, The Washington Vista Hotel, Washington, D.C., December 6, 1994.

5 Alexander Cockburn, "Judy Miller's War," *CounterPunch*, August 18, 2003.

6 *Ibid.*

7 Zachary Block, "One Man's War on Terror," *Brown Alumni Magazine*, November/December 2002.

8 *New York Times Review of Books*, May 19, 1991.

9 John F. Sugg, "Steven Emerson's Crusade," *Extra!*, January/February 1999.

10 *Ibid.*

11 Ahmed Yousef and Caroline Keeble, *The Agent: The Truth Behind the Anti-Muslim Campaign in America*, UASR Publishing Group, Annandale, VA., 1999.

12 CNBC, *Rivera Live*, August 23, 1996.

13 John F. Sugg, "Stealth Spin Doctor," *The Weekly Planet*, January 28, 1999.

14 *Ibid.*

15 Eric Boehlert, "The Prime-time Smearing of Sami al-Arian," *Salon*, January 19, 2002.

16 Steven Emerson, Prepared Testimony, *House Committee on the Judiciary Subcommittee on Immigration and Claims*, January 25, 2000.

17 John F. Sugg, *ibid.*

18 Steven Emerson, *The Jewish Monthly*, March 1995.

19 John F. Sugg, *ibid.*

20 *Ibid.*

21 *The Jerusalem Post*, September 17, 1994.

22 John F. Sugg, *ibid.*

23 Rita Katz, *Terrorist Hunter* (New York: HarperCollins, 2003).

24 John F. Sugg, "Was CBS Suckered by 'Anonymous'?" *Creative Loafing*. June 12, 2003.

25 *Ibid.*

26 *Ibid.*

Chapter 5

1 "About Martin Kramer," www.martinkramer.org

2 Roger Owen, "Towering Misrepresentation," *Al-Ahram Weekly*, March 28, 2002.

3 *Washington Post*, December 11, 1983.

4 Daniel Pipes, *National Review*, November 19, 1990.
5 Daniel Pipes, "The New Anti-Semitism," freeman.io.com, January 1998.
6 Daniel Pipes, "If I forget thee: does Jerusalem really matter to Islam?" *New Republic*, April 28, 1997.
7 Daniel Pipes, op/ed, *National Post*, August 7, 1999.
8 *Baltimore Sun*, November 24, 1999.
9 Salim Muwakkil, "The Devil and Daniel Pipes," *In These Times*, September 15, 2003.
10 MSANEWS, September 2, 1999.
11 Michael Scherer, "Daniel Pipes, Peacemaker?" *Mother Jones*, May 26, 2003.
12 Edward Said, "A Devil Theory of Islam," *The Nation*, August 12, 1996.
13 William A. Graham, *Arabic-Info*, September 10, 1999.
14 Michael Scherer, *ibid.*
15 *Ibid.*
16 *Ibid.*
17 Reuven Paz, Biography and CV, Global Research in International Affairs (GLORIA), The Interdisciplinary Center.
18 Reuven Paz, "Islamists Abroad," *The Review*, Australia/Israel & Jewish Affairs Council, September 2002.
19 What is PRISM?" www.e-prism.org
20 Reuvan Paz, "Islamists and Anti-Americanism," *Middle East Review of International Affairs*, vol. 7, no. 4, December 2003.
21 M. Shahid Alam, "Scholarship or Sophistry: Bernard Lewis and the New Orientalism," *CounterPunch*, June 28, 2003.
22 *Ibid.*
23 *Ibid.*

Chapter 6

1 Disinfopedia.org, December 10, 2003.
2 Richard H. Curtiss, "Elliott Abrams, Militant Zionist Chosen for NSC Post," *Washington Report on Middle East Affairs*, January/February 2003.

Chapter 7

[1] "The Israeli Lobby," *Prospect*, April 2002.
[2] *Ibid.*
[3] *Ibid.*
[4] Susan Taylor Martin, "Israel Shows its Muscle Dealing with Congress," *St. Petersburg Times*, May 12, 2002.
[5] *Ibid.*
[6] Jihad al-Khazin, "Eyes and Ears," *Al-Hayat*, issue no. 14307, May 22, 2002.
[7] Joel Benin, "Tel Aviv's Influence on American Institutions," *Le Monde Diplomatique*, July 2003.
[8] Jihad al-Khazin, "Eyes and Ears," *Al-Hayat*, Issue No. 14273, April 18, 2002.
[9] Disinfopedia.org, December 10, 2003.
[10] Daniel Pipes, "Canadian Islamists Host a Neo-Nazi," *Worldnetdaily*, January 7, 2004.
[11] www.meforum.org
[12] www.memri.org
[13] *Ibid.*
[14] Brian Whitaker, "Selective Memri," *The Guardian*, August 12, 2002.
[15] *Ibid.*
[16] *Ibid.*
[17] *Ibid.*
[18] *Ibid.*
[19] Ahmed Yousef, *The Zionist Fingerprint on the Post-September 11 World* (Springfield, Virginia: UASR, 2003).
[20] *Ibid.*

Chapter 8

[1] David Cole, *Enemy Aliens: Double Standards and Constitutional Freedoms in the War on Terrorism* (New York: The New Press, 2003).
[2] Anayat Durrani, "American Muslims Coping with the Aftermath of September 11," *Middle East Affairs Journal*, vol. 8, no. 1-2, Winter/Spring 2002.
[3] Yvonne Haddad, Chapter 3, "Civil Rights Concerns in the Metropolitan

Washington, D.C., Area in the Aftermath of the September 11, 2001, Tragedies," District of Columbia, Maryland, and Virginia Advisory Committees to the U.S. Commission on Civil Rights, June 2003.

4 *Ibid.*

5 "We Are Not the Enemy: Hate Crimes Against Arabs and Muslims After September 11," *Human Rights Watch*, vol. 14, no. 6, November 2002.

6 Nedzib Sacirbey, Chapter 3, "Civil Rights Concerns in the Metropolitan Washington, D.C., Area in the Aftermath of the September 11, 2001 Tragedies," District of Columbia, Maryland, and Virginia Advisory Committees to the U.S. Commission on Civil Rights, June 2003.

7 Chapter 5, "Civil Rights Concerns In the Metropolitan Washington, D.C., Area in the Aftermath of the September 11, 2001 Tragedies," District of Columbia, Maryland, and Virginia Advisory Committees to the U.S. Commission on Civil Rights, June 2003.

8 Dan Eggen and John Mintz, "Muslim Groups' IRS Files Sought," *Washington Post*, January 14, 2004.

9 Ahmed Yousef, *The Zionist Fingerprint on the Post-September 11 World*, (Springfield, Virginia: UASR, 2003).

Chapter 9

1 Ahmed bin Yousef, *Ahmed Yassin: Al-Thahirat Al-Mu'jiza wa Usturat il Tahaddi*, International Center for Research and Studies (ICRS), 1989.

2 Ahmed bin Yousef, *Harakat Al-Muqawama Al-Islamiyya: Hamas Hadath 'Abir Am Badeel Dai'm?* International Center for Research and Studies (ICRS), 1990.

3 Ahmed Yousef, *Mousa Abu Marzooq: Al-Rajul wal-Haraka wal-Qadiyya*, Zahratil Mada'in Lil Dirasat wal-Tarjama wal-Nashr: Algeria, 1995.

4 Ibid, *Ahmed Yassin.*

5 Meir Litvak, *The Islamization of Palestinian Identity: The Case of Hamas*, The Moshe Dayan Center for Middle Eastern and African Studies: Tel Aviv University, 1996. See also: Sara Roy, "Hamas and

the Transformation(s) of Political Islam in Palestine," *Current History*, January 2003. pp. 13-20.

6 Ibid. *Mousa Abu Marzooq.* See also: Ahmed Yousef. *The Zionist Fingerprint on the post-September 11 World*, UASR Publishing Group, 2003. pp. 89-97.

7 Ahmed Yousef, "Hikayat Hamas fi America: Al-Ittiham wal-Haqiqa," *Al-Mujtamaa*, No. 1579, December 6, 2003. See: Ahmad Rashad. *Politics and Justice: The Case of Musa Abu Marzuq*, Occasional Paper Series, No. 9, UASR, October 1995. See also: *Al-Mujtamaa*, "Hajma Ala Al-Amal Al-Islami fi America," No. 1298 May 5, 1998. p. 20.

8 Ahmed Yousef, "Mu'assasat Al-Ard Al-Muqaddasa: Masirat Kifah Li-Ighathat Al-Mankubin," *Al-Mujtamaa*, No. 1581, December 20, 2003.

9 *Holy Land Newsletter*, Vol. 8 Issue 3, November 2001.

10 *HLF News*, Vol. 5 Issue 1, March/April 1998. See also: "Holy Land Foundation for Relief and Development," information brochure, 2000.

11 *Filistini Al-Muslimah*, July 1998, p. 11. See also: Gene O'Shea. "FBI Says Salah raised cash for Hamas terror," *Daily Southtown*, June 10, 1998.

12 "An Interview with Shukri Abu Baker," *Al-Bayyadir Al-Siyassi*, 1998.

13 Glenn R. Simpson, "Hesistent Agents: Why the FBI Took Nine Years to Shut Group it Tied to Terror," *Wall Street Journal*, February 27, 2002.

14 "Four arrested in Texas on terror funding charges," CNN.com, December 18, 2002.

15 "Nahwa Banaa Al-Insan wal-Ard, The First Annual Charity Conference", *International Truth*, November 1999.

Chapter 10

1 John F. Sugg, "Steven Emerson's Crusade," *Extra!* January/February 1999.

2 *Ibid.*

3 *Ibid.*

4 Michael Fechter, "Ties to Terrorists," *Tampa Tribune*, May 28, 1995.

5 John F. Sugg, "Stealth Spin Doctor," *The Weekly Planet*, January 28, 1999.

6 Susan Aschoff, "Family of Detainee Feels Like Suspects," *St. Petersburg Times*, April 24, 2000.

7 John F. Sugg, "US Government's 'Secret Evidence' Against Mazen Al-Najjar Has Yet to Produce Indictments," *Washington Report on Middle East Affairs*, July/August 1998.

8 Press Release, Tampa Bay Coalition for Justice and Peace, June 25, 2002.

9 Lynette Clemetson and Keith Naughton. "'Big Dude' Gets Profiled," *Newsweek*, July 16, 2001.

10 Daniel Goldberg, Robert Greenwald, Victor Goldberg, eds. *It's a Free Country: Personal Freedom in America After September 11*, (New York: Akashic Books, 2002).

11 Transcript available at *Foxnews.com*

12 Eric Boehlert, "The Prime-time Smearing of Sami al-Arian," *Salon*, January 19, 2002.

13 Stephen Buckley, "The Al-Arian Argument," *St. Petersburg Times*, March 3, 2002.

14 Ryan Meehan, "Genshaft: Arrest Won't Change Course," *The Oracle*, February 21, 2003

15 Editorial, "Protecting Speech on Campus," *New York Times*, January 27, 2002.

16 Ben Feller, "Judge Tosses USF Suit Against Al-Arian," *Tampa Tribune*, December 17, 2002.

17 Rob Brannon, "Al-Arian Indicted," *The Oracle*, February 21, 2003.

18 Letter to Bureau of Prisons, Amnesty International, July 17, 2003.

19 Paul Lomartire, "Detainee in Fight for Rights," *Palm Beach Post*, August 3, 2003.

20 Jerry Seper, "Arrested Muslim Activist Helped Pick Chaplains for U.S. Military," *Washington Times*, September 30, 2003.

21 Tom Davis, Letter to Judge Hilton, January 2004.

22 Tom Jackman and Spencer Hsu, "Moran to Break with Muslim Activist," *Washington Post*, February 2, 2002.

23 Frank Gaffney, "Preaching Terror," *Townhall.com*, October 14, 2003, and "A Troubling Influence," *FrontPageMagazine.com*, December 9, 2003.

24 Farhan Memon, "Our Money is Not Good Enough," *Washington Post*, October 30, 2000.

25 *Why Justice Matters*, vol. 1, no. 1, January 2004.

26 Documents, "In Time of Turmoil East Meets West: Tripoli Proclamation for *Ta'aruf*," *Middle East Affairs Journal*, vol. 9 no. 3-4 Summer/Fall 2003.

27 "Biography of Dr. Rafil Dhafir," www.jubileeinitiative.org/DhafirBio.htm

28 *Ibid.*

29 *Ibid.*

30 *Ibid.*

31 Dina Rasheed, "American Muslims Committed to Political Empowerment," *Islam Online*, July 6, 2001.

32 Martin Davis, "Jews and Palestinians Begin to Talk, in America," *National Journal*, January 19, 2002.

33 Dina Rasheed, "US Minorities Speak Up on Human Rights Abuses," *Islam Online*, October 19, 2003.

34 Allison Hantschel, "Orland Park Muslim Activist Appeals His Exile to High Court," *Chicago Sun-Times*, January 30, 2004.

35 "Dr. Samirah Appeals to Supreme Court for His Right to Come Back Home," UMAA Press Release, January 27, 2004.

36 Ann Mullen, "Haddad breaks his silence," *Metro Times*, March 17, 2004.

37 Erin Saylor, "Terror alert halts visitation rights for Haddad's family," *Michigan Daily*, February 11, 2003.

38 *Ibid.*

39 *Ibid.*, Ann Mullen.

40 *Ibid.*

41 "The NewsHour with Jim Lehrer", MacNeil/Lehrer Productions. Transcript #7404, August 27, 2002.

42 David Ashenfelter and Niraj Warikoo, "Newspaper asks judge to open Haddad detention hearing to public," *Detroit Free Press*, Wednesday, October 2, 2002.

43 *Ibid*, Ann Mullen.

44 *Ibid.*

45 *Ibid.*

46 *Ibid.*

Chapter 11

[1] Antony Sullivan, "Should policymakers see Islam as an enemy of the West?" *Insight*, November 5, 2001.

[2] Mahjabeen Islam, "Sullivan Speaks Clearly About Why Islam Is Not the Enemy," *Insight*, December 3, 2001.

[3] John Esposito, "Conversations with History," Institute for International Studies, University of California-Berkeley, March 13, 2003.

[4] Campus Watch, "Esposito: Apologist for Militant Islam," *FrontPageMagazine*, September 3, 2002.

[5] Paul Findley, *Silent No More: Confronting America's False Images of Islam*, (Maryland: Amana Publications, 2001).

[6] Richard Curtiss, "Book Review: They Dare to Speak Out," *Washington Report on Middle East Affairs*, April 1985.

[7] *Ibid.*

[8] Julia Duin, "Libraries Revisit Islam," *Washington Times*, October 20, 2002.

[9] Greg Palast, "The Screwing of Cynthia McKinney," *commondreams.org*, June 18, 2003.

Chapter 12

[1] Daniel Pipes, "The Danger Within: Militant Islam in America," *Commentary*, November 2001.

[2] Daniel Pipes, Militant Islam Reaches America.

Chapter 13

[1] Center for Immigration Studies, *The Jewish Stake in America's Changing Demography, Reconsidering a Misguided Immigration Policy*, p. 12, by Stephen Steinlight, October 2001.

[2] Center for Immigration Studies, *The Impact of Islamic Immigration on American Values and the Jewish Community*, Panel Discussion Transcript, June 5, 2002, p. 16.

[3] Center for Immigration Studies, *The Impact of Islamic Immigration on American Values and the Jewish Community*, Panel Discussion Transcript, p. 17, June 5, 2002.

4 Center for Immigration Studies, *Immigration from the Middle East*, Panel Discussion, p. 14, August 14, 2002.
5 *The Washington Post*, January 14, 2004.
6 Muslim Civil Rights Center (MCRC), Attacks on Charities, Organizations and Businesses.

Chapter 14

1 Assad Nimer Busool, "Muslims in Chicago (The Arabs)," American Islamic College, Chicago. Unpublished paper.
2 *Ibid.*
3 "Muslim Community Supports Mohammed Salah as Court Case Begins," *Muslim World Monitor*, no. 104, September 4, 1998.
4 Chris Hack and Allison Hantschel, "U.S. Investigating Mosque Foundation," *Daily Southtown*, September 21, 2003.
5 Noreen S. Ahmed-Ullah, Kim Barker, Laurie Cohen, Stephen Franklin, Sam Roe, "Hard-liners Won Battle for Bridgeview Mosque," *Chicago Tribune*, February 8, 2004.
6 Ahmed Yousef, Raeed Tayeh, "The Issue of Palestine: Motivating Muslim-American Political Empowerment," Maps Project, Unpublished Paper, 2000.

Chapter 15

1 Editorial, *Islamiyat al-Marifah*, "The Raid on IIIT," vol. 7, no. 28, 2002.
2 *Ibid.*
3 *Ibid.*
4 Douglas Farah, *Washington Post*, October 18, 2003.
5 The National Task Force for the Restortation of Constitutional Rights, "The Constitution Assaulted: The Federal Raids of March 20th, 2002 and the USA PATRIOT Act."
6 *Ibid, Islamiyat al-Marifah*, pp. 9-10.
7 Stephen Steinlight, "The Jewish Stake in America's Changing Demography," *Center for Immigration Studies*, October 2001. See: "The Impact of Islamic Immigration on American Values and the Jewish Community," *Center for Immigration Studies*, Panel Discussion Transcript, June 5, 2002. See also: "Immigration from the Middle

East," *Center for Immigration Studies*, Panel Discussion Transcript, August 14, 2002.

8 Ibid., *Islamiyat al-Marifah*, p. 10.

9 "Interview with Jamal Barzinji," *Middle East Affairs Journal*, vol. 9, no. 3-4, Summer/Fall 2003.

10 *Ibid.*

11 John Esposito and John Voll, *Makers of Contemporary Islam*, Oxford University Press, 2001.

12 Information Brochure, International Institute for Islamic Thought (IIIT), June 2000.

13 *Ibid.*

14 Amber Haque, *Muslims and Islamization in North America: Problems and Prospects*, Amana Publications, 1999.

15 *Ibid.*

16 *Ibid, Middle East Affairs Journal*, p. 130.

17 Ilyas ba-Yunus, Moin Siddiqui. "A Report on the Muslim Population in the United States of America," Center for American Muslim Research and Information, New York, p. 25.

18 *Ibid.*, Information Brochure.

19 Press Release, *MAS Freedom Foundation*, June 5, 2003.

20 *Ibid.*

See also: Muhammad Shafiq, *Growth of Islamic Thought in North America: Focus on Isma'il Raji al Faruqi*, Amana Publications, 1994.

Chapter 17

1 Mary Beth Sheridan, "Virginia 'jihad' suspects: 11 men, two views," *Washington Post*, August 8, 2003.

2 Interview with Ali al-Timimi.

3 Iman Potter, "The Muslim Community's Quest for Justice," *Why Justice Matters*, vol. 1, no. 2, March/April 2004.

4 Iman Potter, "Ashcroft's Paintball Jihad Scapegoats in the So-Called 'War on Terror'," *Why Justice Matters*, vol. 1, no. 1, January 2004.

5 "Press conference: Attorneys expose government's tactics," *The Muslim Link*, vol. 4, no. 9, March 2004.

6 "Community Stunned by Paintball Verdict," *The Muslim Link*, vol. 4, no. 9, March 2004.

[7] *Ibid.*

[8] "Neighbor continues supporting Khan family," *The Muslim Link*, vol. 9, no. 4, March 2004.

[9] Abdur-Rahman Muhammad. "Giving Muslims the benefit of the doubt," *The Muslim Link*, vol. 9, no. 4, March 2004.

SELECTED BIBLIOGRAPHY

— Abdullah al-Arian, "Soul Survival: The Road to American Muslim Political Empowerment," *Washington Report on Middle East Affairs*, March 2004.

— Abdullahi An-Naim, "A New Islamic Politics: Faith and Human Rights in the Middle East," *Foreign Affairs*. Vol. 75 #3, May/June 1996.

— Abdurahman Alamoudi, "Abdurahman Alamoudi on the Charges He Faces," *Washington Post*, December 12, 2003.

— "About Martin Kramer" www.martinkramer.org

— Ahmad AbulJobain, "Islam Under Seige: Radical Islamic Terrorism or Political Islam?" Occasional Papers Series no. 1. *United Association for Studies and Research*, June 1993.

— Ahmed Yousef and Caroline Keeble, *The Agent: The Truth Behind the Anti-Muslim Campaign in America*, UASR Publishing Group, Annandale, VA., 1999.

— Ahmed Yousef, *The Zionist Fingerprint on the Post-September 11 World*, UASR: Virginia, 2003.

— Ahmed Yousef, *The Zionist Fingerprint on the Post-September 11 World*, UASR: Virginia, 2003.

— "Al-Arian support by faculty laudable," *The Oracle*, Jan 14, 2002.

— Alexander Cockburn, "Judy Miller's War," *CounterPunch*. August 18, 2003.

— Alex Lynch, "Naked From Sin: The Ordeal of Sami and Nahla Al-Arian," *Counterpunch*, February 25, 2002.

— Allison Hantschel, "Orland Park Muslim Activist Appeals His Exile to High Court," *Chicago Sun-Times*, January 30, 2004.

— *American Muslim Council: Our First Five Years*, American Muslim Council, 1996.

—*American Muslims in Politics: From Dream to Mainstream*, AMC's 10th Annual National Convention Program Bulletin, Washington: AMC, 2001. See also AMC brochures and The AMC Report, its quarterly newsletter.

— "American Muslims: One Year After 9-11," Council on American-Islamic Relations, 2002.

— Aminah Beverly McCloud, *African-American Islam*, Routledge, 1995.

— Amir N. Ali, *Muslims in America: Seven Centuries of History (1312-2000)*, Amana Publications, Beltsville Maryland, 1998.

— Anayat Durrani, "American Muslims Coping with the Aftermath of September 11," *Middle East Affairs Journal* vol. 8, no. 1-2, Winter/Spring 2002.

— Anisa Abd al-Fattah, "Islam in America: A Giant awakened by Zionism," *Middle East Affairs Journal*, Summer/Fall 2002.

— Anis Shivani, "The Warped World of Bernard Lewis: 'They Can't Tell Time and They Don't Like Music'," *CounterPunch*, September 14/15, 2002.

— Anisa Abd al-Fattah, "Review of *God Has Ninety-Nine Names*," 1996.

— A Report from the Mosque Study Project, CAIR 2001.

— "A Review of U.S. Counter-terrorism Policy: American Muslim Critique and Recommendations," Muslim Public Affairs Council, September 2003.

— Arthur J. Magida, *Prophet of Rage*, BasicBooks, 1996.

— Ashraf Nubani, "One Woman's Extremist is Another Woman's Savior," 1996.

— Aslam Abdullah and Edina Lekovic, "Then & Now: The Modern Face of MSA," *The Minaret*, June 2001.

— Aslam Abdullah, "Where are the Muslims on the Political Scene?" *The Minaret*, vol. 23, May 5, 2001.

— Benjamin Duncan, "Arrests Cast Shadow on US Muslims," *AlJazeera.net*. October 8, 2003.

— Ben Shapiro, "Terrorists at our Universities," *Townhall.com*, September 19, 2002.

— Bernard Lewis, "The Roots of Muslim Rage," *Atlantic Monthly*, September 1990.

— Bernard Lewis, "What Went Wrong," *Atlantic Monthly*, January 2002.

— Bill Maxwell, "Quite the odd couple: Al-Arian and Sharon," *St. Petersburg Times*, Feb 5, 2002.

— Brian Whitaker, "Selective Memri," *The Guardian*, August 12, 2002.

— Brian Whitaker, "US Think Tanks Give Lessons in Foreign Policy," *The Guardian*, August 19, 2002.

— Bruce Shapiro, "Florida Witch Hunt," *Salon*, January 8, 2002.

— "Censure is more than black mark," *The Oracle*, Jan 10, 2002.

— "Civil Rights Concerns in the Metropolitan Washington, DC Area in the Aftermath of the September 11, 2001 Tragedies," District of Columbia, Maryland, and Virginia Advisory Committees to the US Commission on Civil Rights, June 2003.

— Dan Eggen and John Mintz, "Muslim Groups' IRS Files Sought," *Washington Post*, January 14, 2004.

— Daniel Pipes, "The Terror-Aiding Prof," *New York Post*. February 4, 2002.

— Daniel Pipes, "Israel May Be Winning," *New York Post*. December 17, 2001.

— Daniel Pipes, "The Defeat of Militant Islam," *Washington Times*. November 23, 2001.

— Daniel Pipes, "Daniel Pipes Explains 'Islamism'," *The Minaret*, September 2000.

— Daniel Pipes, "Canadian Islamists Host a Neo-Nazi," *Worldnetdaily*, January 7, 2004.

— David Cole, *Enemy Aliens: Double Standards and Constitutional Freedoms in the War on Terrorism*, The New Press, New York: 2003.

— Dennis Eisenberg, "The Present Middle East," *Jerusalem Post*, June 29, 1996.

— Derek Montgomery, "Academic freedom threatened," *Badger Herald*, September 11, 2002.

— Dina Rasheed, "American Muslims Committed to Political Empowerment," *Islam Online*, July 6, 2001.

— Dina Rasheed, "US Minorities Speak Up on Human Rights Abuses," *Islam Online*, October 19, 2003.

— Documents, "In Time of Turmoil East Meets West: Tripoli Proclamation for Ta'aruf," *Middle East Affairs Journal*, vol. 9, no. 3-4 Summer/Fall 2003.

— "Dr. Samirah Appeals to Supreme Court for His Right to Come Back Home," UMAA Press Release, January 27, 2004.

— Edward Said, "A Devil Theory of Islam," *The Nation*, August 12, 1996.

— Edward Said, "Impossible Histories: Why the many Islams cannot be simplified," *Harper's Magazine*, July 2002.

— Emelie Astell, "Terrorism Expert Warns of Genocide," *Telegram & Gazette*. April 16, 2002.

— Eric Alterman, "Perle, Interrupted," *The Nation*, March 20, 2002.

— Eric Boehlert, "Terrorists Under the Bed," *Salon*, March 5, 2002.

— Eric Boehlert, "The Prime-time Smearing of Sami Al-Arian," *Salon*, January 19, 2002.

— Eric Boehlert, "The Armchair General," *Salon*, September 5, 2002.

— Eric Boehlert, "The Prime-time Smearing of Sami Al-Arian," *Salon*, January 19, 2002.

— Farhan Memon. "Our Money is Not Good Enough," *Washington Post*, October 30, 2000.

— Fatima Mirza, "An Evolving Student Voice," *Islamic Horizons*, May/June 2003.

— "Florida's black eyes: Two victims of hysteria still paying price," *Daytona Beach News-Journal*, June 18, 2002.

— Frank Gaffney, "Who's 'with' President Bush?" *Jewish World Review*, February 18, 2003.

— Frank Gaffney, "Islamists' White House Gatekeeper," *Washington Times*, February 11, 2003.

— Frank Gaffney, "Preaching Terror," *Townhall.com*, Oct 14, 2003.

— Frank Gaffney, "A Troubling Influence," *FrontPageMagazine.com*, December 9, 2003.

— Gail Epstein Nieves, "Terrorism or Free Speech?" *Miami Herald*, August 25, 2002.

— Gary Rosenblatt, "Monitoring the Muslim Threat," *The Jewish Week*, March 24, 2000.

— George Braswell, Jr. *Islam: Its Prophet, Peoples, Politics and Power*, Broadman & Holman Publishers, 1996.

— Giles Fraser, "The Evangelicals Who Like to Giftwrap Islamophobia," *The Guardian*, November 10, 2003.

— "Greenfield at Large" CNN transcript, January 30, 2002.

— Howard Kurtz, "Right Face, Right Time," *Washington Post*, February 1, 2000.

— Ilyas Ba-Yunus, "An American Story: Graduating from MSA to ISNA," *Islamic Horizons*, September/October 2003.

— "Interview with Altaf Hussein," *Al-Mujtamaa*, issue no. 1522 October 12, 2002.

— "In Spite of Challenges, Our Mission Continues," Interview with Dr. Jamal Barzinji, *Middle East Affairs Journal*, vol. 9, no. 3-4 Summer/Fall 2003.

— Islamic Society of North America (ISNA), 2001 Annual Report.

— Jane I. Smith, *Islam in America*, Columbia University Press, 1999.

— Jason Vest, "The Men from JINSA and CSP," *The Nation*, September 2, 2002.

— Jeff Jacoby, "The Islamist Connection," *Boston Globe*, February 27, 2003.

— Jerry Seper, "Arrested Muslim Activist Helped Pick Chaplains for U.S. Military," *Washington Times*, September 30, 2003.

— Jihad Al-Khazin, "Eyes and Ears," *Al-Hayat*, issue no. 14307, May 22, 2002.

— Jihad Al-Khazin, "Eyes and Ears," *Al-Hayat*, issue no. 14273, April 18, 2002.

— Joel Benin, "Pro-Israel Hawks and the Second Gulf War," *The Nation*, April 6, 2003.

— Joel Benin, "Tel Aviv's Influence on American Institutions," *Le Monde Diplomatique*, July 2003.

— John F. Sugg, "Stealth Spin Doctor," *The Weekly Planet*, January 28, 1999.

— John F. Sugg, "Steven Emerson's Crusade," *Extra!* January/February 1999.

— John F. Sugg, "Was CBS Suckered by 'Anonymous'?" *Creative Loafing*, June 12, 2003.

— John F. Sugg, "Steven Emerson's Crusade," *Extra!* January/February 1999.

— John F. Sugg, "Stealth Spin Doctor," *The Weekly Planet*, January 28, 1999.

— Joseph Bodansky, "The New Islamist International," *Task Force on Terrorism & Unconventional Warfare, House Republican Research Committee*, February 1, 1993.

— Joseph Bodansky, *TARGET AMERICA: Terror in the U.S.* Shapolsky Publishers, 1993.

— Joseph Bodansky, *Terror: The Inside Story of the Terrorist Conspiracy in America* Shapolsky Publishers, 1994.

— Judith Miller, *God Has Ninety-Nine Names: Reporting from a Militant Middle East*, Simon & Schuster, 1996.

— Kathryn Lopez, "The Terrorist Hunter Speaks," *National Review*, June 26, 2003.

— Marc Perelman, "No Longer Obscure, Memri Translates the Arab World," *Forward*, December 7, 2001.

— Martin Dyckman, "USF should read and heed former governor's speech," *St. Petersburg Times*, August 25, 2002.

— Marium Mohiudidn, "Fountain of Youth Renews," *Islamic Horizons*, May/June 2003.

— Martin Davis, "Jews and Palestinians Begin to Talk, in America," *National Journal*, January 19, 2002.

— Martin Kramer, editor. *The Islamism Debate*, Moshe Dayan Center for Middle Eastern and African Studies, Tel Aviv University, 1997.

— Martin Kramer, "Arab Panic," *Middle East Quarterly*, vol. IX no. 3, Summer 2002.

— Martin Kramer, "Terrorism? What Terrorism?" *Wall Street Journal*, November 15, 2001.

— Mary Beth Sheridan and Douglas Farah. "Jailed Muslim Had Made a Name in Washington," *Washington Post*, December 1, 2003.

— Mary Jo Melone, "Genshaft's inaction is louder than words," *St. Petersburg Times*, August 22 2002.

— Mary Jo Melone, "As tempest roars, she fights for her family," *St. Petersburg Times*, June 30, 2002.

— *Media Relations Handbook for Muslim Activists* (Washington: CAIR, 1996). See also CAIR Newsletters.

— Melissa Radler, "Journalist Blew the Whistle, But No One Listened," *Jerusalem Post*, March 27, 2002.

— Michael Dobbs, "Back in the Political Forefront," *The Washington Post*, May 27, 2003.

— Michael Fechter, "Ties to Terrorists," *Tampa Tribune*, May 28, 1995.

— Michael Scherer, "Daniel Pipes, Peacemaker?" *Mother Jones*. May 26, 2003.

— MSA National. *Eighteenth Annual Report*, May 1981.

— M. Shahid Alam, "Scholarship or Sophistry: Bernard Lewis and the New Orientalism," *CounterPunch*, June 28, 2003.

— Muhammad Tawfiq, "Terrorism and Islam in the West," *Al-Majalla*, September 1, 1996.

— Omer Bin Abdullah, "MSA Story: Building a Community," *Islamic Horizons*, July/August 2003.

— Paul Findley, *Silent No More: Confronting America's False Images of Islam*, Amana Publications, 2001.

— Paul Findley, "Political Activism by U.S. Muslims," *The American Muslim*, April 2000.

— PNAC, "Letter to President Clinton on Iraq," January 26, 1998.

— Project for the New American Century, "Statement of Principles," June 3, 1997.

— *Prospectus and Publications, Catalogue 2000*, Annandale, Virginia: The United Association for Studies and Research, 2000.

— "Protecting Speech on Campus," *New York Times*, Jan 27 2002.

— "Putting Us to the Test," *New York Times*, March 1, 2002.

— "Radical Islamic Terrorism: How Serious is the Threat? What Should Be Done to Counter It?" An American Jewish Committee Luncheon Forum, The Washington Vista Hotel, Washington, D.C., December 6, 1994.

— Reuven Paz, Biography and CV. The Global Research in International Affairs (GLORIA), The Interdisciplinary Center.

— Reuven Paz, "Islamists Abroad," *The Review*, Australia/Israel & Jewish Affairs Council. September 2002.

— Reuvan Paz, "Islamists and Anti-Americanism," *Middle East Review of International Affairs*, vol. 7, no. 4, December 2003.

— Richard Bulliet, "Gulf 2000 no. 23: Islam/Gulf & The West"

— Richard Curtiss, "Book Review: The Agent," *Washington Report on Middle East Affairs*, September 1999.

— Richard H. Curtiss, "Elliott Abrams, Militant Zionist Chosen for NSC Post," *Washington Report on Middle East Affairs*, January/February 2003.

— Richard Lacayo, "A Campus War over Israel," *Time*, October 7, 2002.

— Richard Leiby, "Talking Out of School," *Washington Post*, July 28, 2002.

— Richard Wormser, *American Islam: Growing Up Muslim in America*, Walker Publishing Company, 1994.

— Rita Katz, *Terrorist Hunter*, HarperCollins, New York, NY, 2003.

— Rita Katz and Josh Devon, "A Global Network," *National Review*, June 30, 2003.

— Robert Satloff, "On Democracy," *The Middle East Quarterly*, September 1994.

— Robyn Blumner, "USF president's decisions have stained the school's reputation.

— Rochelle Renford, "No Man's Land," *Weekly Planet*, January 24–31, 2002.

— Rochelle Renford, "Smoke and Mirrors," *Weekly Planet*, June 18, 2002.

— Roger Kaplan, "Behind the Mullah's Angry Message," *Wall Street Journal*, May 3, 1996.

— Roger Owen, "Towering Misrepresentation," *Al-Ahram Weekly*. March 28, 2002.

— Saba Ali, "Birthing a Movement," *Islamic Horizons*, May/June 2003.

— Sabrina Enayatulla, "MSA Story: The New MSA," *Islamic Horizons*, November/December 2003.

— Salim Muwakkil, "The Devil and Daniel Pipes," *In These Times* September 15, 2003.

— Sam Tanenhaus, "Bush's Brain trust," *Vanity Fair*, July 2003.

— Samir Al-Yousef, "Bernard Lewis: Between Writing History and Promoting Hawks," *Al-Hayat*, Issue no. 14318, June 2, 2002.

— Scott Thompson and Jeffrey Steinberg, "Profile: Bernard Lewis, British Svengali Behind Clash of Civilizations," *Executive Intelligence Review*, November 30, 2001.

— Sharon Walsh, "Blaming the Victim," *Chronicle of Higher Education*, April 4, 2002.

— "Speak Freely, But Don't Offend," The Lakeland Ledger, Dec 21, 2001.

— Stephen Buckley, "The Al-Arian Argument," *St. Petersburg Times*, March 3, 2002.

— Steve Chapman, "Some really offensive ideas on campus," *Chicago Tribune*, Feb 3, 2002.

— Steven Emerson, "Visa for Terrorism Supporter: State Department Bows to Political Pressure," *Washington Times*, May 19, 2000.

— Steven Emerson, *American Jihad: The Terrorists Living Among Us*, Simon & Schuster, 2002.

— Steven Emerson, Prepared Testimony, *House Committee on the Judiciary Subcommittee on Immigration and Claims*, January 25, 2000.

— Steven Emerson. "Hillary and Hamas," *Wall Street Journal*. November 3, 2000.

— Steven Emerson, *The Jewish Monthly*, March 1995.

— Steven Emerson and Daniel Pipes, "Terrorism on Trial," *Wall Street Journal*, May 31, 2001.

— Sulayman Nyang, *Islam in the United States of America*, ABC International Group, 1999.

— Susan Schmidt and Caryle Murphy, "US Revokes Visa of Cleric at Saudi Embassy," *Washington Post*, December 7, 2003.

— Susan Taylor Martin, "Israel Shows its Muscle Dealing with Congress," *St. Petersburg Times*, May 12, 2002.

— "Sweden Distrusts Allegations by Israeli-American," *Sidsifnika* (Sweden) February 2, 2002.

— "Take censure most seriously," *The Oracle*, November 19, 2002.

— "The Israeli Lobby," *Prospect*, April 2002.

— *The Jerusalem Post*, September 17, 1994.

— "The Politics of Intimidation," *The Minaret*, Editorial, September 2000.

— "The Rediff Interview: Dr. Reuven Paz," December 6, 2001.

— Tom Davis, Letter to Judge Hilton, January 2004.

— Tom Jackman and Spencer Hsu. "Moran to Break with Muslim Activist," *Washington Post*, February 2, 2002.

— "USF's judicial rebuff," *St. Petersburg Times*, December 18, 2002.

— Waseem Shehzad, "Zionist Agent Steve Emerson Shows Real Chutzpah Trying to Defend His Unenviable Record and Reputation," *Crescent International*, June 16-30, 1999.

— "What is PRISM?" www.e-prism.org

— "We Are Not the Enemy: Hate Crimes Against Arabs and Muslims After September 11," *Human Rights Watch*, vol. 14, no. 6, November 2002.

— *Why Justice Matters*, vol. 1, no. 1, January 2004.

— William Rivers Pitt, "Blood Money," *Truthout*, February 27, 2003.

— www.cair-net.org "Who is Daniel Pipes?" January 18, 2001.

— www.meforum.org

— www.memri.org

— Yigal Schleifer, "Ready for the Challenge," *The Jerusalem Report*, September 9, 2002.

— Yvonne Haddad, *Muslims in the West: From Sojourners to Citizens*, Oxford University Press, 2002.

— Yvonne Haddad, *The Muslims of America*, Oxford Press: New York, 1991.

— Zachary Block, "One Man's War on Terror," *Brown Alumni Magazine*, November/December 2002.

Appendix A

THE MOSQUE IN AMERICA

• Islamic Center of Dar Al Hijra, Falls Church Virginia

T he *masjid,* or mosque, is an integral aspect of every
Muslim community across the world. It has been
the historic site of important occasions of celebration and
mourning, as well as spiritual, social, and even intellectual
and political development. In countries where Islam is in a
minority status, the mosque is of even greater importance,
as it represents the central physical space for believers to

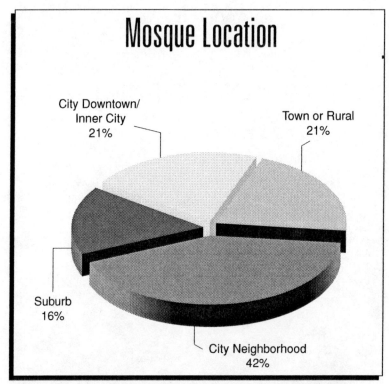

Mosque Location

City Downtown/
Inner City
21%

Town or Rural
21%

Suburb
16%

City Neighborhood
42%

• Source: The American Mosque: A National Portrait, CAIR, April 26, 2001

congregate and form the bonds of brotherhood and provide social and religious services. The United States has been an important setting for the development of Islamic communities through the building and establishment of mosques. Most of these buildings have historically been originally constructed for other purposes. Some were homes. Others were churches, lodges, fire stations, funeral homes, theaters, warehouses, and shops.[1] Mosques have been in America for many decades predating the massive influx of Muslim immigrants in the latter half of the twentieth century. Some of the earliest mosques date back to 1919, in Michigan, Indiana, and Iowa. Hundreds more appeared during the 1960s and 1970s, ranging from New York to California.

The significance of the mosque in American Muslim life stems from its centrality as not only a place of worship, but as a center for all community life. Children attend weekend and sometimes fulltime schooling at these locations. Weekly discussion meetings, potluck dinners, and recreational activities are commonplace at most Islamic centers. Therefore mosque leaders have always had a desire to expand their space to accommodate the many services offered by the mosque. With the exception of the Islamic Cultural Center in Washington DC, built in 1957, most

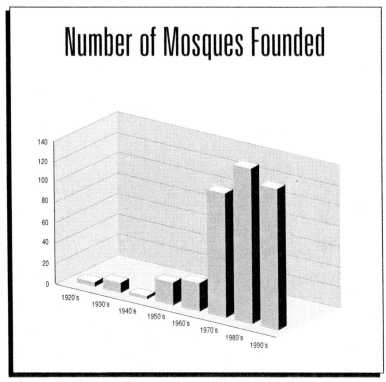

Number of Mosques Founded

• Source: The American Mosque: A National Portrait, CAIR, April 26, 2001

• Islamic Center of Greater Toledo, Ohio

mosques were previously existing buildings with other functions. Architecturally, the original construction of traditional-looking mosques began in later years, as the

• Islamic Center of Central Missouri

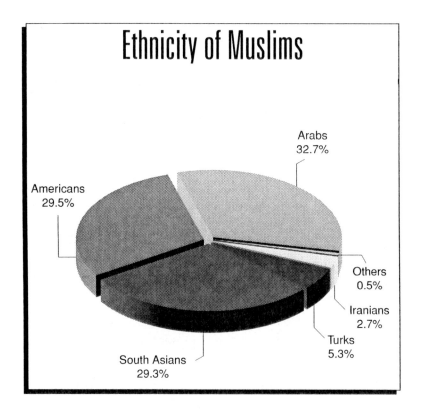

Ethnicity of Muslims

Arabs
32.7%

Americans
29.5%

Others
0.5%

Iranians
2.7%

Turks
5.3%

South Asians
29.3%

community grew in numbers as well as financial means. Islamic architecture is a feature of many current mosques, especially in some of the larger cities in America, which attract thousands of worshippers on a regular basis. Many of the architectural designs are from traditional mosques in the Arab world, while some derive their model from Turkish, South Asian, and even Andalusian traditional architecture.

There are currently over two thousand mosques and Islamic centers in America, with some cities having several dozen such buildings ranging from small, modest, unmarked designs to grand multi-million dollar mosques based on traditional architecture, and built to house

• Taqwa Masjid, Florida

thousands of worshippers and hold a diverse array of activities. And while some mosques in earlier periods were heavily funded by foreign Muslim governments such as

• Omar Ibn Al-Khattab Mosque, California

• Islamic Community Center of Tempe, Arizona

Egypt and Saudi Arabia, domestic Muslim communities in the US have shifted away from such projects and began a process of funding the mosques entirely on their own. One organization that has played an immense role in this process is the North American Islamic Trust (NAIT), which originated under the Islamic Society of North America (ISNA). Over the past two decades, NAIT has had a hand in the construction and maintenance of hundreds of Islamic centers across the country, leading to the successful establishment of Muslim communities throughout the United States. ■

---

[1] Yvonne Haddad, John Esposito. *Muslims on the Americanization Path?* Oxford University Press: New York, 2000.

NATIONAL MUSLIM ORGANIZATIONS

Islamic Society of North America (ISNA)

P. O. Box 38
Plainfield, IN 46168
Tel: (317) 839-8157
Fax: (317) 839-1840
Website: www.isna.net

Muslim American Society (MAS)

P.O. Box 1896
Falls Church, VA 22041
Tel: (703) 998-6525
Fax: (703) 998-6526
Website: www.masnet.org
Email: mas@masnet.org

Islamic Circle of North America (ICNA)

166-26, 89th Avenue
Jamaica, NY 11432
Tel: (718) 658-1199
Fax: (718) 658-1255
Website: www.icna.org
Email: info@icna.org

Council on American-Islamic Relations (CAIR)

453 New Jersey Avenue, S.E.
Washington, DC 20003
Tel: (202) 488-8787
Fax: (202) 488-0833
Website: www.cair-net.org
Email: cair@cair-net.org

MSA of the US and Canada

P.O. Box 18612
Washington, DC 20036
Tel: (703) 820-7900
Fax: (703) 820-7888
Website: www.msa-national.org
Email: office@msa-national.org

Muslim Public Affairs Council (MPAC)

3010 Wilshire Boulevard, # 217
Los Angeles, California 90010
Tel: (213) 383-3443
Fax: (213) 383-9674
Website: www.mpac.org
Email: salam@mpac.org

American Muslim Alliance (AMA)

39675 Cedar Blvd. Suite 220 E
Newark, CA 94560
Tel: (510) 252-9858
Fax: (510) 252-9863
Website: www.amaweb.org
Email: ama@amaweb.org

Islamic Assembly of North America (IANA)

PMB # 270
3588 Plymouth Rd.
Ann Arbor, Michigan 48105
Tel: (734) 528-0006
Fax : (734) 528-0066
Website: www.iananet.org
Email: iana@iananet.org

American Muslims for Jerusalem (AMJ)

208 G Street, NE
Washington, DC 20002
Tel: (202) 548-4200
Fax: (202) 548-4201
Website: www.amjerusalem.org
Email: amj@amjerusalem.org

Muslim Think Tanks

International Institute of Islamic Thought (IIIT)

500 Grove Street
Herndon, VA 20170
Tel: (703) 471-1133
Fax: (703) 471-3922
Website: www.iiit.org
Email: iiit@iiit.org

United Association for Studies & Research (UASR)

P.O. Box 1210
Annandale, VA 22003-1210
Tel: (703) 750-9011
Fax: (703) 750-9010
Email: uasr@aol.com

Islamic Institute

1920 L Street NW
Suite 200
Washington, DC 20036
Tel: (202) 955-7174
Fax: (202) 785-0261
Website: www.islamicinstitute.org
Email: general@islamicinstitute.org

Council on Islamic Education (CIE)

P.O. Box 20186,
Fountain Valley, CA 92728-0186
Tel: (714) 839-2929
Fax: (714) 839-2714
Website: www.cie.org
Email: info@cie.org

Center for the Study of Islam & Democracy (CSID)

1050 Connecticut Avenue, Suite 1000
Washington, DC 20036
Tel/Fax: (202) 772-2022
Website: www.islam-democracy.org
Email: feedback@islam-democracy.org

Publishers of Islamic Books

Amana Publications

10710 Tucker Street
Beltsville, MD 20705-2223
Tel: (301) 595-5777
Fax (301) 595-5888
Website: www.amana-publications.com
Email: amana@igprinting.com

Islamic Book Service (IBS)

2040-F Lord Baltimore Dr.
Baltimore, MD 21244-2501
Tel: (410) 265-0020
Fax: (410) 265-1233
Website: www.islamicbookstore.com

Case Study Information

Sami al-Arian

National Liberty Fund
P.O. Box 3568
Washington, D.C. 20007
Website: www.freesamialarian.com
Email: tampabayjustice@yahoo.com

Abdulhaleem Ashqar

www.free-ashqar.org
Free Dr. Ashqar Committee (FDAC)
P.O. Box 151264
Alexandria, Virginia
22315-1264

Elashi Brothers

www.muslimlegalfund.org
Muslim Legal Fund of America (MLFA)
2701 W. 15th St. Suite 640
Plano, TX 75075
Tel 1-866-MLFA-USA
Fax 1-866-MLFA-USA

Rafil Dhafir

www.jubileeinitiative.org/FreeDhafir.htm

Jamil al-Amin

www.mindspring.com/~altafb/ImamAlAmin.html
Imam Jamil al-Amin Legal Defense Fund
547 West End Place, SW
Atlanta, GA   30310
Tel. (770) 521-5386
ImamJamil@hotmail.com

INDEX